PUEBLA AND BEYOND

PUEBLA AND BEYOND

DOCUMENTATION
AND COMMENTARY

Edited by
John Eagleson and Philip Scharper

Translated by John Drury

ORBIS BOOKS
Maryknoll, New York 10545

Second Printing, August 1980

The Catholic Foreign Mission Society of America (Maryknoll) recruits and trains people for overseas missionary service. Through Orbis Books Maryknoll aims to foster the international dialogue that is essential to mission. The books published, however, reflect the opinions of their authors and are not meant to represent the official position of the society.

Library of Congress Cataloging in Publication Data
Main entry under title:
Puebla and beyond.

   Includes translation of Puebla: la evangelización en el presente y en el futuro de América Latina, documents from the third General Conference of the Latin American Episcopate, held in Puebla, Mexico, 1979.
   Includes bibliographical references and index.
   1. Catholic Church in Latin America—Congresses.
2. Evangelistic work—Latin America—Congresses.
I. Eagleson, John.   II. Scharper, Philip J.   III. Conferencia General del Episcopado Latinoamericano, 3d, Puebla, Mexico, 1979.
BX1425.A1P83   282'.8   79-24098
ISBN 0-88344-399-6

This translation, officially authorized by the U.S. National Conference of Catholic Bishops' Committee for the Church in Latin America, is based on the final typescript used in the preparation of the edition published by the Consejo Episcopal Latinoamericano (CELAM): *Puebla: La evangelización en el presente y en el futuro de América Latina* (III Conferencia General del Episcopado Latino-americano). This English version also incorporates corrections made in CELAM's second edition of the Puebla documents (30 June 1979).

The documentation in the English edition corresponds to that included in the CELAM edition, except that Pope John Paul II's address to the Indians of Oaxaca and Chiapas is not included in the CELAM edition. Paragraph numbers in the Final Document are identical in the CELAM and the English editions.

Biblical citations are taken from the *New American Bible*, sponsored by the Bishops' Committee of the Confraternity of Christian Doctrine.

Citations of conciliar documents are taken from Walter M. Abbott, S.J. (ed.), *The Documents of Vatican II* (New York: Guild-American-Association, 1966).

CONTENTS

THE FINAL DOCUMENT

Part One
Pastoral Overview of the Reality That Is Latin America

Part Two
God's Saving Plan for Latin America

Part Four
A Missionary Church Serving Evangelization
in Latin America

Part Five
Under the Dynamism of the Spirit:
Pastoral Options

IV. BEYOND PUEBLA

I
PUEBLA 1979

THE LONG PATH TO PUEBLA

Penny Lernoux

"I am a voice crying in the wilderness," Fray Antonio de Montesinos told his wealthy congregation. "You are in mortal sin . . . for the cruelty and tyranny you use in dealing with innocent people." "Tell me," he demanded of the estate owners, "by what right or justice do you keep these Indians in such cruel and horrible servitude? . . . Are these not men? . . . Have they not rational souls, are you not bound to love them as you love yourselves?"[1]

Spoken in 1511 from a pulpit in Hispaniola, the Dominican friar's plea for social justice has a familiar ring. Similarly strong-worded denunciations of the mistreatment of Indian and *mestizo* peasants can be heard in many Catholic churches in Latin America today, rural conditions having changed only marginally since Montesinos' time. As with the friar, who was recalled to Spain for his presumptuous censure of Indian slave labor, today's critical church leaders risk government and para-police persecution: in the decade since 1968, when the Latin American Church officially took up the cause of social justice at Medellín, over 850 religious, clergy, and bishops have been arrested, tortured, expelled, or murdered.[2]

Such men as Montesinos and Fray Bartolomé de las Casas, Spain's sixteenth century "Protector of the Indians," are often cited as the spiritual fathers of today's increasingly outspoken Catholic Church, though in fact they were very few. The vast majority of the missionaries who came to the New World shared the conquerors' contempt for the "heathen." For these missionaries the Indians "for years without number had been under the domination of Satan, immersed in vice and blinded with idolatry."[3] The fusion of cross and sword was officially sanctioned by Rome, almost from the first discoveries by Columbus, through a system called the *"real patronato de Indias."* Under this system the papacy conceded most of its power to the Spanish crown, including the exclusive right to license ecclesiastics to work in Latin America.[4] Thus from the very beginning, the region's Church was a dependent partner of the State, a condition that has survived to modern times and is a root cause of the growing divisions between a Church of accommodation and a Church of liberation.

In return for political servitude, the Church was given the right to arbitrate the social mores of colonial society and to inculcate the "heathen" with a Spanish Catholicism still rigidly bound to the Middle Ages. "When the Church of the apostolic age went forth, it learned to adjust to different cultures," said Robert L. Conway, a Precious Blood priest and professor of Hispanic studies.

3

"St. Paul was a Greek to the Greeks and a Jew to the Jews. But this willingness of responsible church members to transmit Christ's message through indigenous cultures came to a halt with the coming of the Middle Ages. Europe, apparently, was now Christian; there was no further need for accommodation."

Just when "new worlds opened up both in the East and in the West, . . . when great innovative missionary ideas were needed, the Council of Trent fearfully closed off all possible experimentation. Church teachings were to be couched in the phraseology of scholastic philosophy; the liturgy, the sacraments, all were to be dispensed in Latin. The post-Tridentine church was to be transported to the Indians of the New World."[5]

The men who transplanted this church were rarely of calibre, according to Dom Pedro Casaldáliga, bishop of the Brazilian Amazon and himself a Spaniard:

> The failures, those who could not make it in Europe, were sent to baptize the Indians and blacks. They came because of a "blind obedience" that, more often than not, castrated minds and wills, condemning the poor Churches that received them to support dead weights, twisted spirits, or men who rebelled against themselves, against their own institutions. These men brought their anger with them and vented it on Latin America.
>
> All who migrate to a "lesser" country . . . consider it a duty, a necessity, almost a question of hygiene, to avoid contamination from the lower level. They believe they have a right to impose, to dictate. I think this has been particularly true of the Church in Latin America, as, for example, in the attitudes toward theology, liturgy, and pastoral work.[6]

Handicapped by a superiority complex, by laws and customs fashioned for European Catholicism, and ignorant of the cultural heritage and values of the New World's indigenous peoples, most missionaries soon became "vending machines of the sacraments." Because of the distances and the difficulties of travel, they tended to baptize and marry the natives *en masse,* even as late as the 1960s. Mass was held perhaps once a year; no thought was given to religious instruction, the prevailing attitude being that the natives were second-class Christians. Yet with rare exceptions, the white Europeans fared no better. As church historian J. Lloyd Mecham pointed out:

> All were treated like children; their emotions were aroused by the use of lavish ceremonials, display, and imagery. What wonder, then, that the colonials, white and colored, came to believe that the essence of the faith was its trappings? There was much profane pomp with little piety. Theirs was a superficial faith, blind belief with little understanding. And there was no disposition on the part of the clergy to make them understand so long as they believed. Unreasoning obedience to church and king was inculcated by the clergy, who studiously avoided analysis of the foundations of this dual obedience.[7]

It is not surprising, then, that few Latin Americans understand the teachings of Christ, even though 90 percent of the region's 320 million people are baptized Catholics. On the contrary, the religions of the pre-Columbian civilizations and African tribes frequently survive under a veneer of Catholicism, a syncretic religion with a message of fatalism. Thus children do not die of malnutrition; it is God's will that they should die. Similarly, poverty is a condition of birth, not something that can be changed by individual or collective endeavor. Like the estate owner or distant dictator, God must be appeased through the intercession of the saints, who are bribed by offerings and prayers to help average Latin Americans get through their lives of misery in the vague hope of some better hereafter. On earth at least, all is preordained: born poor, die poor.

A tool of conquest, Catholicism, and its message of fatalism, formed part of the ideology of power of the Spanish Empire (and the Inquisition was the forerunner of the twentieth century's secret military and police, ferreting out political dissidents and foreign spies as well as religious heretics). Catholicism was used to found and sustain the social pyramid in Latin America, with a few white Europeans living in outrageous luxury while the mass of the people subsisted in misery. It is much the same today. As Brazil's Archbishop Helder Camara relates:

> Yes, African slavery has been ended, but we still have today, without admitting it, a national slavery. Workers are allowed to live on their employer's land, they receive a small hut to live in with their wife and children, they work for the boss, and almost always are given a patch of ground to till for their own needs.
>
> The boss feels downright noble for being such a generous, kindly father. The hut most likely has no water or light or toilet, but the boss salves his conscience by reflecting that God takes care of everyone's needs. (When will we stop making Him responsible for what our selfishness has done?)
>
> The boss thinks, then, that he has a right to pay whatever he pleases, and when he likes, because he has provided a house and the land it stands on, plus a job, and ground for a family garden. Tomorrow, though, if the worker were to feel that he was a citizen, got ideas into his head, went to school, joined a peasant league, or talked about his rights, the boss would feel he had grounds for alarm, because here is a whiff of subversion, if not communism. Without hesitating a second, he would evict the worker—and tear down his hut, just to make sure.[8]

Catholicism also helped perpetuate a spiral of violence that is one of the chief characteristics of Latin American life to this day. (Montesinos and de las Casas notwithstanding, very few of the early missionaries suggested that violence was unchristian.) As Malcolm Lowry noted in *Under the Volcano,* the sickness that engulfs Latin America came to the New World with the conquistadors. The killings and torture—the total disregard for human rights in a majority of the Latin American countries—can be understood only when seen through the prism of colonial Spain and Portugal. Thugs and adventurers for the most part, these colonists built a society based on exploitation, a society that has survived wars of independence and industrialization. Today the principal values of the ruling class in Latin America are still those of the white conquerors—brute force, or *machismo;* a contempt for the law (businessmen are expected to pay bribes but not taxes); disdain for manual labor (only the poor work with their hands); and racial discrimination (the level of education, income, and social standing is directly related to the color of a Latin American's skin, avowals to the contrary by white government officials notwithstanding).

It is a land, Lowry said, without compassion overrun by predators. "First Spaniard exploits Indian, then, when he had children he exploited the halfbreed, then the pure-blooded . . . *criollo,* then the *mestizo* exploits everybody, foreigners, Indians, and all. Then the Germans and Americans exploited him; now the final chapter, the exploitation of everybody by everybody else."[9]

Colonialism, said Rubem Alves, one of Latin America's first Protestant liberation theologians, distorted both oppressed and oppressor through a "form of violence that robbed man of any free relationship with his world and his future. The violence which this man suffered became part of his own being. It created him in its own image."[10]

"Every Latin American who is not blind is dissatisfied with this society," admitted a Venezuelan bishop. "Yet it is we [the Church] who more than anyone else have created and shaped it. Even today, nearly every influential person in Latin America, in or out of government, is an alumnus of our schools."[11]

"New Christendom"

The first historic act of disobedience against the will of the Iberian Church, the Wars of Independence in the early nineteenth century did not really change the basis of religion's relation to power: patronage was simply transferred from the Spanish crown to the fledgling republics. Catholicism was declared the state religion, and articles of strict intolerance of other faiths were incorporated into the constitutions. The Church continued its virtual monopoly over education and retained its vast, tax-free landholdings.

Increasingly rich and self-complacent, the Church came under attack in the latter part of the century by free-thinking politicians, or "liberals," who wanted to reduce its power. The Church therefore formed an alliance with ultra-reactionary parties, euphemistically called "conservative," which ran tyrannical governments. In the ensuing, often bloody conflicts between "liberals" and "conservatives" that lasted through the 1930s, and are still alive in some countries such as Colombia, the Church lost its monopoly over education and the birth and death registries; in several nations Church and State were officially separated and civil marriage and divorce were legalized.

Despite Leo XIII's 1891 encyclical *Rerum Novarum,* which recognized the need for change in church attitudes to such social challenges as labor unions, the Latin American Church lagged behind, castigating incipient labor movements as socialist and immoral. The people should be grateful for their poverty, the bishops told their flocks, because such a condition merited Christ's special love. Even the relatively progressive Chilean hierarchy of the early 1930s withheld publication of Pius XI's *Quadragesimo Anno* for two years because the encyclical dealt with social matters.[12] Although the winds of change had begun to penetrate a number of Latin American Churches by the mid-thirties, others clung to the reactionary ways of old. When, for example, Colonel Carlos Castillo Armas, the CIA puppet used in the overthrow of Guatemala's populist President Jacobo Arbenz, was murdered in 1957, the bishop of Guatemala City flew home from Washington in an American Air Force plane and declared the dead tyrant "as good as Christ." In Argentina the first speech of the pro-Axis military junta in 1943 was written by a priest.[13]

Thanks to the impact of the Reformation, the French Revolution, positivist liberalism, and laicism, Catholic influence had steadily declined in Europe and, to a lesser extent, in Latin America. Pius XI's fervent dream of rebuilding a Christendom of yore found its most successful expression in the Catholic Action movement, which spread to Latin America in the thirties at a time when a number of hierarchies had begun to distance themselves from their erstwhile allies in the landowning oligarchy (primarily in response to the new political classes created by industrialization). Though based on such traditional structures as schools and seminaries, as well as the Church's social doctrine, the Catholic Action movements offered the novel appeal of encouraging lay people to take co-responsibility for establishing a "New Christendom" in Latin America through labor, politics, and cultural activities. Obsessed with the threat of communism and inclined to dabble with fascism, the Catholic Action movements also were inspired by the martyrs of Mexico's "Cristeros War," which took place in the late twenties when the anti-clerical government deported priests, closed schools and convents, and accused the hierarchy of treason.

For all the organizations Catholic Action spawned, and its undoubted influence on the region's future political leaders, it failed to ignite a religious revival. Like most European imports, the movement was directed primarily at the small core of upper-class Latin American whites, ignoring the majority of the people, who were poor. The masses continued to baptize their children, to honor the priest on his annual visits to their village, and to pray to the saints, while remaining in almost total ignorance of the teachings of Christ.

In the end, Catholic Action's principal legacy was a revival of the Church's traditional alliance with a political power, this time a centrist movement influenced by the social teachings of the Church. Conceived as a "third way" between capitalism and communism, Christian Democracy quickly gained adherents throughout the hemisphere, capturing the presidencies of Chile and Venezuela. The Christian Democratic parties' appeal was based on a regional and international sense of urgency, reflected in the White House, the Vatican, and the United Nations, all of which recognized the need for rapid development in the impoverished Third World. The sudden concern for Latin America could be attributed in large part to Fidel Castro's successful 1959 revolution in Cuba, and the subsequent spread of guerrilla movements throughout the hemisphere, threatening the hegemony of Rome and Washington. By promising a "revolution in freedom," a phrase coined by Chile's Christian Democratic President Eduardo Frei, the Christian Democrats appeared to offer a popular and rapid solution to the continent's colonial inheritance of social injustice—without recourse to Marxism. In the political context of Latin America, the very promise of reform was itself sufficiently radical to attract dissident members of the upper and middle classes, as well as sizeable segments of the working class. The Christian Democrats also were exceptionally skilled in social diagnosis and statistical analysis, preparing functional and seemingly fail-proof plans for the development of their countries. (For years the Chilean Christian Democrats' development programs were held up as models of good planning by the World Bank and the United Nations.)

Thus "development" was on everyone's lips at the start of the sixties. UN Secretary General U Thant inaugurated the "First Development Decade." John XXIII spoke of his concern for the development of the poorer countries in his encyclicals *Mater et Magistra* and *Pacem in Terris*. And the Latin American bishops, meeting in an extraordinary assembly in Mar del Plata, Argentina, announced that their pastoral program would emphasize cooperation in the integral development of the continent. In 1961 the Alliance for Progress was born; in 1962 the Second Vatican Council opened; and in 1964 Frei was elected president of Chile, the first Christian Democrat to govern a Latin American country. (During this period populist governments also were elected in Argentina, Brazil, and Peru, though without a specifically Catholic hue.)

Agreement within the Latin American Church on development priorities was largely a reflection of external events—Vatican II's groundbreaking premise that the Church is of and with this world, the election of populist governments in Latin America, and Washington's new-found social concern for the continent. The bishops of Northeastern Brazil, for example, helped organize a government development agency, SUDENE, to eradicate poverty from the region. SUDENE cooperated with a church-sponsored literacy program for peasants, in which the education pioneer Paulo Freire played an important role. Peasant leagues were another spin-off.

Belgian theologian Joseph Comblin, who lived in the Northeast at the time as adviser to Recife's Archbishop Camara, described the alliance of Church and State as symbolic of the period. It was possible, he said, only because of "the populist nature of the government and popular support as expressed in democratic elections. Thanks to this populism, the Latin American Churches were able to convince themselves that the European and North American political systems could provide the political instruments for development."[14]

Cracks began to appear in this harmonious façade as early as 1963, when university students and pastoral agents working with the people questioned the premise of capitalist development. A few bishops in Brazil, notably Dom Helder, also began to doubt earlier assumptions as a result of the 1964 military coup in their country, which was to spell the beginning of the end for populism in Latin America and establish a model for a system of neo-Nazism. Meanwhile, the goals of the Alliance for Progress had been altered under duress from U.S. corporations, and by 1964 David Rockefeller was sufficiently satisfied with the "marked change in the attitudes of those responsible for the Alliance" to praise the State Department for recognizing that the Alliance "had had too much emphasis on social reform."[15] Thus the Agency for International Development (AID) was converted into a "grotesque money tree" for U.S. corporate interests, in the words of Senator Frank Church[16]: by the end of the decade of development some $2 billion per year in U.S. exports were being financed by the Foreign Aid Program.[17] An incredible 99 percent of the loans made by AID to the Latin American countries were spent in the United States for products costing 30 to 40 percent more than the going world price![18]

The 1960s also marked the beginning of U.S. counterinsurgency training for the Latin American military and a corresponding increase in loans for arms purchases. Intended to wipe out the nascent guerrilla movements—which they did—the training and arms were then used against the civilian population, as country after country succumbed to military dictatorship.

Contrary to predictions, the development programs of the sixties did not produce a redistribution in wealth or noticeably improve the region's economic performance. The growth in the gross national product was actually lower than that of the previous decade, and the gap between rich and poor continued to widen.

The frustrations caused by blighted hopes were evident everywhere. The Frei government in Chile was in trouble, unable to deliver on its promises and confronted with the challenge of an increasingly popular Marxist-Socialist coalition. In Argentina a corporative (fascist) military regime had risen on the ashes of a populist government; in Brazil the moderate military regime underwent a right-wing transformation, arresting thousands and decreeing an Orwellian state in which the people would think and do as the government dictated. The polarization between right and left also affected the Church, with the simultaneous rise of such reactionary Catholic groups as Tradition, Family, and Property and the desertion of a Colombian priest, Camilo Torres, to the guerrillas.[19] By 1968 many of the Church-sponsored development programs that once seemed so promising had stagnated or been discarded, some voluntarily, others under government coercion, as in Brazil.

These events, in addition to the reforms begun by Vatican II and Pope Paul's audacious encyclical *Populorum Progressio* (which was directed specifically at Latin America), had the effect of spring cleaning the Latin American Church, the first such cleaning in history. Musty ideas and traditions were swept aside in an effort to understand reality. One result was a growing conviction that to fulfill its gospel mission the Church could no longer serve as a handmaiden of the State, or any political power. It was also evident, said Brazil's Bishop Cándido Padim, that the prevailing conditions of misery and injustice in Latin America were in total disaccord with Christ's teachings.

A Theology of Liberation

The intellectual support for the Church's housecleaning came from many sources—the theological, philosophical, and economic studies of U.S. and European Catholics and Protestants and the Latin Americans' own experience with the repeated failure of such populist experiments as Christian Democracy. While Latin American critics, including Brazil's Celso Furtado, had early expressed scepticism about the advantages of "development," a widely published study by Paul Baran and Paul Sweezy in 1966 provided hard data confirming the Latin Americans' worst suspicions. They offered convincing evidence of the growing monopolization of the Latin American economies by U.S. corporations and "the new character of dependence": by the mid-sixties the former Spanish colonies had become economic vassals of the United

States. The "development of underdevelopment" was further elaborated by Andre Gunder Frank, who has written extensively on the problems of developing countries. His study of U.S.-Brazilian economic relations questioned the popular thesis that underdevelopment in Latin America was the result of the people's laziness and of economic backwardness. On the contrary, he said, underdevelopment is the dark side of capitalist development. In other words, said José Míguez Bonino, a leading Protestant liberation theologian, capitalism has been "able to 'buy off' its proletariat in the developed world through the use of the 'external proletariat' of the Third World."[20]

In order to understand capitalist development, critical church leaders, particularly theologians, had recourse to Hegel and Marx, the former because of his emphasis on liberation. As Hegel insisted:

> Man is the agent of history, and history is nothing more than the process of the liberation of man. True history is the history of human emancipation, and it is man liberating himself who makes history.[21]

Marx helped the Latin Americans clarify their situation of neocolonial dependence on capitalism. The Latin Americans also agreed with his theory that knowledge of reality is the first step in the transformation of society. The Church had served as an obstacle to such transformation in Latin America, they acknowledged, by providing the ruling classes with an ideology that opposed any change in social structures. Latin American theologians did not accept Marx uncritically, however—any more than the enlightened psychiatrist believes Freud infallible—objecting particularly to Marx's commitment to historical materialism and his denial of religion. But both Marx and Hegel helped explain why the "means of understanding and changing the history of Latin America cannot be thought of in terms of development because the problem is not underdevelopment," as Baptist theologian Alan Neely said. "The problem is domination and dependence. Liberation, not economic integration, is what must be achieved."[22]

What gave a specific Latin American content to this theology of liberation, as it was soon known, was a methodology based on the reality of Latin America—the reality of poverty and oppression—an insistence on the *integral liberation* of human beings, both temporal and spiritual, and an approach to God through humanity. As Gustavo Gutiérrez, liberation theology's best-known exponent, put it, humanity is the temple of God, *who became human.* Thus to love God is to love human beings. Because most Latin Americans are poor and oppressed, just as most Galileans were in the time of Christ, the Church must make Christ's option for the poor its own. And it must do so by announcing Christ's Good News of liberation:

> The spirit of the Lord is upon me; therefore he has anointed me. He has sent me to bring glad tidings to the poor, to proclaim liberty to captives, recovery of sight to the blind, and release to prisoners, to announce a year of favor from the Lord (Luke 4:18–19).

The intellectual ferment within the Church was supported by a hemispheric infrastructure created in 1955, the Latin American Episcopal Conference

(CELAM), linking communications among the national episcopacies. Although little of importance was discussed at the founding meeting in Rio de Janeiro, <u>CELAM's birth represented the first, timid step away from Rome's tutelage—a wholly Latin American organization</u>.

A second hemispheric conference was scheduled in 1968 in the Colombian city of Medellín to coincide with Pope Paul's visit to the capital, Bogotá, to attend the International Eucharistic Congress. The aim of the Medellín conference was to examine the situation in Latin America in light of the conclusions of Vatican II, a situation greatly worsened since the start of the decade and the subject of intense theological and sociological debate.

Although Paul spoke eloquently of the needs of the poor during his visit to Bogotá, it fell to the bishops meeting in Medellín to change history. Most of the 130 prelates present had some inkling of the problems facing Latin America, but as Brazil's Bishop Padim recalled,

> Only when we had assembled at Medellín and spent a week in discussions, with slide presentations illustrating the statistics of poverty, did we begin to have a global vision. For many of those attending, such as Cardinal Antonio Samoré [then president of the Pontifical Commission for Latin America], it was an eye-opening experience as well as cause for fright, because the situation was much worse than they had suspected. So the delegates were prepared to make a commitment.[23]

<u>Medellín's commitment to the poor and oppressed was indeed prophetic. For the first time in history, the Latin American hierarchy recognized that the continent was living in a "situation of sin."</u> The poverty of the masses, and their repression, was particularly scandalous on a Catholic continent, the bishops said. The upper classes and "foreign monopolies" representing an "international imperialism of money" were responsible for "institutionalized violence" against the people, who yearned for "liberation from all servitudes." Calling for a theology of the "signs of the times," the bishops proposed to help transform Latin American society through radical changes in liturgy and evangelization, including such priorities as education for the poor to raise the level of community awareness and promotion of popular organizations, particularly Christian grassroots communities (*comunidades de base*).[24]

In espousing the cause of the poor, Medellín made three major breakthroughs. Of foremost importance was the Church's rupture with existing social and political structures in order to promote a transfer of power to the impoverished masses. As Helder Camara, one of the architects of Medellín, described it, "The Spirit of God was with us pushing us to discover, in our continent, the most painful of colonialisms: privileged internal groups who maintain personal wealth at the expense of the misery of their countrymen."[25] This rupture, in turn, meant the renunciation of centuries of state patronage and the transformation of the Church into a servant of the poor, with neither privileges nor riches. "<u>Medellín was a fundamental commitment to work for the construction of a community Church instead of the vertical Church we inherited with its pyramid of power</u>," explained Leonidas Proaño, Ecuador's "Bishop of the Indians."[26] While the Medellín Conclusions condemned Marxism, the bishops' frontal attack on neocolonialism and capitalism represented a significant change, depriving capitalism of one of its traditional supports in Latin America.

The document's strong social criticism and prophetic commitment sent shock waves through the continent and beyond, to Europe and North America. Rich or poor, radical or reactionary, the Latin Americans were dumbfounded: how could traditionally conservative bishops have written such a document!

The answer of course was that they hadn't. For one thing, only three sections of the sixteen-part document—those dealing with justice, peace, and poverty—made an impact. The remainder of the document offered little novelty or inspiration. Even in the most critical sections the bishops failed to analyze the causes of "institutionalized violence" or offer an alternative, still holding out for a "third way" between communism and capitalism, though Christian Democracy had proved a failure. But once committed to official paper, with stamps and signatures, words take on a life of their own, and so it was with the Medellín Conclusions, certain phrases of which, such as "institutionalized violence," were written into the Magna Carta of a socially activist Church.

Nor were the 130 bishops who signed the document unanimously satisfied with the results. Despite the "eye-opening experience" described by Padim, a number of bishops objected to the document, including the conservative Colombian delegation. Thanks to the liberating influence of Vatican II and the predominance of prophetic bishops in the CELAM hierarchy, the momentum for change carried the meeting. As Padim admitted, those who did not participate in the conference reacted with shock and fright. But even among the participants were bishops who would later claim they did not realize the significance of what they had signed, just as other prelates earlier had disclaimed Vatican II on the same grounds. Thus while the commitment made at Medellín was irreversible, only a minority of bishops would heed its call.

A "Redeeming Crusade"

In the arduous, decade-long journey from Medellín to Puebla, where the bishops would next meet in a hemispheric conference, there was no road to follow, for the Church had embarked on a wholly unchartered course. Internal divisions and external persecution would be the landmarks of this march, as well as a gradual awakening of the masses.

Nelson Rockefeller was the first to alert western power centers to the new realities of the Latin American situation, following his tour of Latin America in 1969. Subsequently used as the basis for Nixon's Latin American policy, the Rockefeller Report made two important observations. First, it noted the upsurge in nationalism and the determination of the people to seek social change, a challenge that could endanger "national security" and U.S. investments in the region. Second, the report predicted, correctly, that the military and the Church would be the principal actors in Latin America's coming political drama. While welcoming the emergence of the military, the report was frankly distrustful of the changes occurring in the Church.[27]

As in the sixties, when Frei's Christian Democratic government had symbolized the hopes of both a reformist Church and the Alliance for Progress,

Chile attracted international attention in the early seventies with the election of a Marxist-Socialist coalition led by Salvador Allende. His victory confirmed the worst fears of the Rockefeller Report; it also brought into the open the divisions within the Church that had been simmering since Medellín, with the split of two intensely antagonistic factions. One was led by Belgian Jesuit Roger Vekemans, who had worked closely with the Christian Democrats and whose various development institutes in Chile were used as a conduit for CIA funds for Frei's successful presidential bid in 1964.[28] (According to a U.S. Senate investigation, the CIA contributed $2.6 million to Frei's election, or more than half his total campaign budget and twice as much per voter as Johnson and Goldwater together spent in their presidential campaigns that year.[29]) The other included such left-wing priests as Gonzalo Arroyo, who openly identified with the goals of the Allende government. The confrontation had many ramifications. On one, much publicized level, it questioned Christian-Marxist dialogue. On another, of more lasting significance, it raised the issue of church participation in politics and its mission in society.

Vekemans' followers took a partisan position with the Christian Democrats, openly politicking for the famous "third way," really a façade for capitalism with a thin veneer of populist reforms. Arroyo's group, which evolved into Christians for Socialism, was equally partisan, publicly supporting Marxist class struggle and a "praxis of revolution."[30] Vekemans left Chile for Colombia before Allende's inauguration; the Christians for Socialism movement in Chile was destroyed by the 1973 military coup. The antagonisms born in Chile would have lasting repercussions for the Church, however, colliding with and often obscuring the goals of Medellín.

While the Medellín Conclusions could in no way be described as a platform for revolution, such minority groups as Christians for Socialism seized on the document as support for partisan political positions. In Argentina, for example, the Third World Movement of priests cited Medellín to rationalize their close identification with the left wing of the Peronist party. Some of their concern for the impoverished masses rubbed off on the bishops, but for the most part these movements suffered from what liberation theologian Comblin described as "an excessive enthusiasm with little critical analysis" and an "absence of serious political reflection."[31] Thanks to their often vociferous defiance of the hierarchy and their radical positions, these groups attracted considerable press coverage, confirming the fears of those bishops who had earlier viewed Medellín as a Pandora's Box for Marxist revolution. Yet the critics ignored both the Church's history of involvement with partisan politics as well as reality itself: very few Latin American clergy or religious ever accepted Christians for Socialism's revolutionary interpretation of Medellín, or a partisan commitment to political movements.

Not ever having approved of Medellín or its "community" Church, the Roman Curia put its own interpretation on events. For example, Cardinal Gabriel María Garrone, prefect for the Sacred Congregation of Education, wrote a widely publicized letter chastizing the CELAM leadership and the Latin American Confederation of Religious for placing too much stress on "liberating education" which, he warned, could lead to politicization.[32] Conservative bishops who had privately decried the Medellín documents also began to speak out against the emphasis on liberation, particularly the theology of liberation, which Medellín had officially recognized. In Bogotá, Vekemans seized on the work of the most radical theologians, such as Brazil's Hugo Assmann, and the ferment in Chile, to equate liberation theology with Christians for Socialism and a "theology of violence." In a request for funds from the West German bishops' agency Misereor to underwrite a "redeeming crusade" against liberation theology, Vekemans claimed that the "seditious" theology was a Latin American variation of European Marxism that was "contesting" hierarchical authority and producing "agitators" who took advantage of existing ecclesiastical structures, with the open consent of weak authorities. "In other words," wrote Vekemans in the inquisitorial style that has become his hallmark, "guerrilla warfare is the only tactic [of liberation theology], ranging from armed groups in the mountains to the most merciless kind of urban terrorism."[33]

Nothing was further from the truth, but as Mexican theologian Luis del Valle pointed out, "There is no better way of obtaining money than fear: fear that the system producing the money will be subverted, fear that the current system of power and status will be lost, and fear that people may open their eyes to reality."[34]

Vekemans' claim that Jesuit Superior General Pedro Arrupe supported his project was denied by Arrupe, whose prophetic leadership had helped place the Jesuits on the side of the poor. But the authenticity of the second sponsor was never in doubt—Colombia's right-wing Cardinal Aníbal Muñoz Duque, the leader of the dissenting conservatives at Medellín. A close associate of the cardinal, Vekemans gave a series of lectures at Bogotá's Catholic Javeriana University and organized a hemispheric seminar on "Marxist penetration" in the Church, with Muñoz Duque's sponsorship. The cardinal also supported the founding of Vekemans' Research Center for the Development and Integration of Latin America (CEDIAL) in Bogotá and the magazine *Tierra Nueva,* aimed almost exclusively at smearing liberation theology.

Riding on the backlash from Medellín, with not a little help from Vekemans and the Roman Curia, Bogotá's conservative Auxiliary Bishop Alfonso López Trujillo was elected secretary general of CELAM in 1972. A staunch opponent of liberalization, with a tongue as sharp as Vekemans', López Trujillo immediately set about dismantling the CELAM departments associated with Medellín, claiming such cuts were necessary for budgetary reasons. Those that survived were restaffed by conservative European theologians such as Pierre Bigo, who shared Vekemans' disdain for the Latin Americans' upstart liberation theology.

Not all the bishops agreed with this trend. Brazil's Bishop Casaldáliga said he was "indignant that certain European theologians denigrate the liberation theologians. When finally there emerge among us some theologians with the capacity and desire to think for themselves, other theologians from Europe arrive to cut them short. Frankly, it seems to me a-scientific, unjust, and anti-evangelical."

Europe's attempts to monopolize theology smacked of colonialism, said Casaldáliga. "It seems to me that these European theologians spend a lot of time thinking but perhaps not so much living. They want to think for others but not live with others, specifically the poor."[35]

But perhaps the most graphic description of the differences between theologians in the Old and New Worlds was given by Argentine theologian Enrique Dussel:

> Our thinking is so different . . . that theologians from other parts of the world do not understand when we try to explain it to them; sometimes they do not feel it is any concern of theirs at all. In Quito I had a conversation with a German theologian. I was telling him that we were now reflecting on the whole matter of liberation. He expressed surprise and interest, and he asked me to tell him more about it. But do you know what was really uppermost in his mind at that moment? Hans Küng's book on papal infallibility. Europeans are down to splitting hairs, whereas the problem that occupies us right now is liberation.[36]

"National Security" DOCTRINE

Just as Castro's revolution marked the beginning of one chapter in Latin American history, the rise of a right-wing military dictatorship in Chile opened another. Unlike Brazil, where the process of militarization had been gradual, the bloody 1973 coup in Chile brought home to many bishops the truth of Dom Helder Camara's warning that fascism was as much a threat to the Church in Latin America as communism. Chile was but one example, albeit the most publicized, of a new, institutionalized militarism with an arsenal of sophisticated weaponry and a neo-Nazi ideology called the "doctrine of national security." Behind this system stood the economic and political might of a post-capitalist phenomenon—the empire of the multinational corporations, with the world's third largest economy, after the United States and Russia. Thanks to the work of such pioneers as Brazil's Bishop Padim and theologian Comblin, who studied the new militarism in a systematic way, church leaders began to perceive the connection between U.S. counterinsurgency training and aid, the Rockefeller Report's advocacy of militarism, the sudden growth in multinational subsidiaries in Latin America, and the simultaneous rise of dictatorships. There was ample evidence to document this connection, in Brazil, Uruguay, Chile, Bolivia, and Central America.[37]

A decade after the event, it could be seen that 1964 was the turning point, only the signals were mixed. Attention was focused on Frei's Christian Democratic experience in Chile in the belief that this was the Alliance for Progress's "showcase" alternative to the Cuban experience. In fact, the "showcase" merely obscured the necessary consequence of U.S. aid and counterinsurgency training: the real model was the regime installed by the Brazilian military that year.[38]

"As Brazil goes," President Nixon predicted, "so will go the rest of that Latin American continent." And so it went. The "Brazilian model," constructed with billions of dollars in U.S. foreign aid and $625.9 million in U.S. armaments, set the example for the rest of the region's regimes, with a geopolitical doctrine justifying the establishment of the military as a one-party state in order to protect "national security" and "profit and stability" in the global war between communism and the West. Individual, social, and economic rights, which characterized Latin America's evolving societies under the populist governments of the fifties and sixties, were destroyed by a military apparatus that legalized repression in the name of a Cold War without end. All organizations not directly controlled by this apparatus, all those who questioned repression, were judged subversive, "communist," the enemies of "internal security." Political parties, labor unions, the press, universities, Churches, and associations of any type whatsoever were persecuted or destroyed as agents of the internal enemy.

Thus it was that such moderate churchmen as Chile's Cardinal Raúl Silva, a critic of Christians for Socialism, came under military attack for denouncing human rights violations, including the torture and assassination of political prisoners. Nor was Chile the only case. Military coups in Bolivia, Argentina, and Uruguay unleashed a wave of terror unprecedented in the continent's history—up to 20 thousand people arrested or kidnapped in Argentina alone, according to the Nobel Prize-winning human rights organization Amnesty International.[39] Persecution of the Church also escalated in Brazil, the more traditional dictatorships of Central America and Paraguay, and even in "democratic" Mexico.

In addition to cultural, political, and religious repression, the principal characteristics of the doctrine of national security include an upward income redistribution favoring the wealthiest classes and the military;[40] heavy dependence on the multinational corporations and banks; an enormous foreign debt (as of 1979, Brazil had a $41 billion foreign debt, the highest in the developing world); state capitalism; inflation; the forced exodus of peasants to urban slums to free land for agribusiness exports; and high rates of unemployment and underemployment (30 million Latin Americans as of 1978, by CELAM's estimate). Fifty percent of the region's people receive a mere 14 percent of its income, according to a survey by the Organization of American States. Some 207 million people in the six most populous countries earn less than $75 a year.[41]

As a report by the theological-pastoral commission of the bishops of Northeastern Brazil pointed out, these extreme inequalities can be imposed only through a military state:

> Such a development model was possible because it could count on the inflexible power of the State, which suppressed all the voices of opposition or rendered them completely ineffective. . . . To impose a development model which favored a small minority was precisely to maintain or create a repressive State, which in turn provokes a situation of civil war.[42]

Christian in name only, these regimes are in many ways a throwback to the lawless societies of colonial days. Among their better known apologists, for example, is Tradition, Family, and Property (TFP), a reactionary—some say medieval—Catholic organization founded in Brazil, with branches throughout the hemisphere, including the United States.[43] Fanatic defenders of the divine right of property and privilege who long for the return of a seventeenth-century Church, TFP members have been used as stormtroopers in Brazil, Argentina, and Chile. (Contrasting with Hitler's Brownshirts, TFP militants do battle in flowing red capes and carry banners emblazoned with a medieval lion.) Religious vigilante squads for the military regimes, these groups have been active in the persecution of bishops in Brazil, Argentina, Uruguay, and Chile; they have used smear campaigns, para-police harassment, and the attempted expulsion of foreign clergy and bishops.[44]

The CIA also played a role in the persecution, in 1975 helping the Bolivian Interior Ministry to hatch a plot, known as the "Banzer Plan" after the local dictator, to harass progressive bishops and arrest and expel foreign priests and nuns. The CIA was reported to be particularly helpful in supplying the Bolivian ministry with data on U.S. and other foreign missionaries.[45]

A year later, forty-eight bishops and priests, including four U.S. bishops,[46] were arrested by Ecuador's military regime while attending a pastoral conference sponsored by Riobamba's Bishop Leonidas Proaño. Both the methods used in the bishops' interrogation and the subsequent smear campaign indicated that the arrests were part of a regional conspiracy. Chile's bishops denounced the arrests, and the subsequent manhandling of the Chilean delegates by the secret police on their arrival at the Santiago airport, as "part of a system that threatens to engulf Latin America unresisted. Always on the grounds of national security, a justification from which there is no appeal, a model of society is gradually being fashioned that eliminates all basic liberties, tramples on the most elementary rights and subjects its citizens to a fearful and powerful police state."[47]

At a meeting the following year in Asunción, Paraguay, the Latin American Anti-Communist Confederation, supported by most of the region's dictators, heard a verbatim repeat of the "Banzer Plan" by the Bolivian delegation, which listed many of the bishops arrested in Riobamba as subversive and "communist." The delegation also proposed that the "Banzer Plan" be adopted on a hemispheric basis.[48]

Himself a victim of military repression, Dom Pedro Casaldáliga believes that one of the major causes of the change in attitudes since Medellín has been the martyrdom of the Church.[49] In any number of cases, bishops who started out by mildly scolding the regime for failing to respect human rights ended up at war with the military. Such was the experience of the Churches in Chile, Paraguay, and Brazil. The more the Church protested, the harsher the repression against the Church; and the fiercer the repression, the more the Church protested. It was a vicious circle but a purifying experience: out of adversity was emerging a socially conscious Church with a new sense of mission—to defend human rights, to be the "voice of the voiceless."

The Medellín Conclusions had said as much, but it was only by taking up the cross that the bishops were able to find their way through the ideological labyrinth created by those in the Church who feared change and preached accommodation, condemning a community Church and the people's liberation.

Unlike Latin America's political parties and labor unions, the Church cannot be silenced through persecution. Cross and sword colonized Latin America; now they stand in opposition. If the Church cannot end repression, neither can the military cow the bishops into submission. For all its defects and desertions, the Catholic Church is still a power to be reckoned with in Latin America, as much a part of society's fabric as Islam in the Middle East. As the only institution capable of withstanding the military, the Church has become a surrogate for democracy, providing a protective umbrella for popular organizations, such as labor unions and peasant federations, which otherwise would succumb to repression.

By any historical measure the cost of this commitment has been high. Hundreds of priests have suffered harassment, arrest, torture, expulsion, even death. Unlike Camilo Torres, very few died fighting with the guerrillas—or in any political cause. The vast majority were martyred because of their work on behalf of the poor, such as Father Héctor Gallego in Panama and Jesuit Rutilio Grande in El Salvador, who were murdered by para-police forces because of their defense of the peasants' right to organize cooperatives and unions.[50] Or Father Rodolfo Aguilar, who was killed in Chihuahua, Mexico, because he defended the slum inhabitants' right to build a sewer.[51] And the five Irish priests and seminarians who were slaughtered by the Buenos Aires Federal Police after one of them preached a sermon against the death penalty.[52]

Nor were bishops immune. San Salvador's Archbishop Oscar Romero and Managua's Archbishop Miguel Obando y Bravo repeatedly have been threatened with death because of their opposition to the military regimes in their countries. In Brazil Dom Adriano Hypólito, the crusading bishop of Nova Iguaçu, on the slum periphery of Rio, was kidnapped, stripped, beaten, and painted red by a para-police squad for having questioned the dictatorship's lawless society in the diocesan newspaper.[53] In Argentina Bishop Enrique Angelelli, the outspoken defender of the Indian peasants of La Rioja, was killed in a fake automobile accident.[54]

Thousands of laypeople were similarly tortured and murdered. In Nicaragua, for example, the bishops reported that Christian communities could not hold religious services without permission from the local military commander; that troops had occupied the chapels; and that Christian lay leaders had been arrested and tortured while others had "disappeared."[55] In El Salvador peasants were hung by their thumbs in military interrogation centers to force them to report on the activities of local priests; in Chile laypeople were submerged in barrels containing urine and excrement to make them talk about priests working with the Vicariate of Solidarity sponsored by Cardinal Silva.[56] In Guatemala *240 laypeople were assassinated in the first month of 1979 alone*, most of them rural and urban poor.[57]

Symbol and sustenance of the Christian grassroots communities, the Church's martyrs reflect a new pastoral policy of solidarity with the suffering people. Institutional weight has been added to this policy by the body of pastoral letters produced by the bishops' conferences of twelve Latin American countries. These letters spell out the how and why of injustice, citing statistics and documented facts. As specific denunciations of "institutionalized violence," they form an important epilogue to Medellín and illustrate the close connection between repression and poverty in Latin America.

By far the most advanced and largest in number, the Brazilian Church's pastoral letters are considered by many to represent "the most remarkable set of official [church] statements in this decade," in the words of Thomas E. Quigley, adviser on Latin American affairs to the U.S. Catholic Conference. "They are a record of a Church doing theology out in the open and on the run, of a Church preaching and teaching and prophesying in the most authentic and effective way possible. The words don't substitute for actions; they derive from action, reflect on action, and stimulate further action."[58]

The Brazilian bishops also have the longest experience of the doctrine of national security. Thanks to the courage and prophetic commitment of such men as Camara, Casaldáliga, and Padim, and Cardinals Aloisio Lorscheider and Paulo Evaristo Arns, the Brazilian Church has taken the hemispheric lead in a three-pronged attack on religious and social alienation and economic and political marginalization.

The heart and soul of this pastoral activity—the first prong of the attack—is the Christian grassroots community (comunidad eclesial de base: CEB). In 1979 there were some 80,000 communities in Brazil, or twice as many as in 1976. Composed of small groups of neighbors (no more than twenty adults) in impoverished rural villages and urban slums, the communities usually start as a spin-off from the parish Church by relieving the hard-pressed priest of such duties as catechism classes. In sharing the responsibilities of the Church, community members often begin to share in other neighborhood concerns, such as a health center or a school. Because religious instruction emphasizes Medellín's concern with "liberating education," the Bible is read as a story of liberation. By applying biblical stories to their own situation, community members perceive an essential parallel: if the God of the Bible was on the side of the poor and oppressed back then, God must be on their side, too. This knowledge is the beginning of the end of the colonial inheritance of fatalism. Children do not die because it is God's will; they die because of lack of food and medicine and unhygienic living conditions. In understanding reality, community members want to change their situation, through cooperatives, a shanty-town association, or similar intermediate organizations that enable them to have some voice in their own destiny. In effect, the communities are practicing their own theology of liberation.

Grassroots Christian communities are unlike anything previously attempted ✳ in Latin America in three important respects: they are born at the bottom, not imposed by some government agency at the top; their principal characteristic is solidarity (in the communities it is more important to be a brother or sister than a boss); and they have the institutional support of the Church, both locally and regionally. (The government's knowledge that the Brazilian bishops are prepared to put all their influence on the line to protect the communities, and to call on international opinion if need be, has been a major factor in their survival.)

The second prong of the attack on alienation and marginalization is closely related to the Christian communities—a re-evaluation and redirection of popular piety to incorporate the symbols of the people in religious practice and to help them understand their faith, particularly the significance of the Resurrection, with its promise of liberation. The cross, which is the most widely used symbol of religiosity in Latin America, therefore takes on a new meaning: it no longer signifies death and defeat but is a sign of victory over both; it is a message of redemption. This is a different kind of religion in Latin America, consciously indigenous but at the same time more mature, encouraging the people to become "co-creators with God."

The third prong in the attack combines witness with prophecy. This means a continuing denunciation of human rights violations, in addition to support for the "constructors" of society—the people's intermediate organizations, the universities, even dissident members of the military—in their search for alternatives to the capitalist development model imposed by totalitarianism. "The upshot," said Ralph Della Cava, one of the United States' foremost authorities on Brazilian Catholicism, "has been the recent mushrooming of voluntary associations of all stripes and hues in a country and among workers not ordinarily thought capable of forging their own destiny:

> Yet in church halls and Roman Catholic school courtyards working-class mothers organize into clubs and skilled laborers into a state-wide movement to protest the high cost of living. Meanwhile, the bishops of São Paulo's industrial periphery, comprising the largest Roman Catholic diocese in the world, turn over the churches to their flocks to debate government wage policies, high prices, and political representation of workers, free of government agents and control. If the French Roman Catholic Church "invented" the "worker-priest," it is the Brazilian Roman Catholic Church that has transformed him into the rule rather than the exception.
>
> From the workers' side, there is also something different. There now exists an embryonic set of new structures—call them voluntary associations, not unlike those De Tocqueville perceived on his visit to the United States of America early in the last century—and by means of which men take their destiny into their own hands. That may be the single most salutary new development in the transition of Brazilian society into a modern industrial order.[59]

It has often been observed that Latin America is underdeveloped not only because it does not produce enough but because its people do not participate in national life. Participation, say Brazil's bishops, is the real meaning of development.

A German-Financed Smear Campaign

Of all the obstacles on the road to Puebla, none was harder to overcome than colonialism. Not only did Rome now want to relinquish control over Latin America; there was considerable concern in European chanceries and Washington that the natives might go off on their own, rejecting the customary western political mold for a new, indigenous model. Yet "if there is a place where the old culture must die," said Father Ernesto Balducci, Florence's prominent religious writer, "this is precisely Latin America, where culture has lost all semblance of dignity and appears as it has always been: a function of the exploitation and domination of consciences. And if there is a place where the relationship between faith and culture can no longer be thought of in the traditional intellectual way we know in Europe, but sought in the direct experience of the Gospel lived by a people in search of liberation, this place is Latin America."[60]

By 1977, when preparations for Puebla began, military repression had persuaded many church leaders to Balducci's view. Unlike the early post-Medellín period of ideological conflict, the issue no longer was the nonbeliever, but the "nonperson"—the poor and oppressed. In Chile, for example, the fierce confrontation over Christian-Marxist dialogue was forgotten in the common defense of human rights, and in caring for the needs of some 800,000 people without food or jobs. There was no doubt where the Chilean Church stood—with the people.

Many of those in the Church who had not suffered persecution or poverty, on the other hand, still clung to the sterile ideological debates of the early seventies, if anything, more frightened of a "people's Church." Not only were their progressive fellows questioning the continent's power structures; some were even challenging the economic and spiritual dominance of the First World.

As Mexican theologian del Valle had remarked during Roger Vekemans' early attacks on liberation theology, fear is an excellent means of obtaining money. The Belgian Jesuit had only to cry wolf once to panic the already nervous West German bishops into providing millions of dollars for his cause.[61] Equally worried, the Roman Curia joined forces with the Germans, through the office of Cardinal Sebastiano Baggio, prefect of the Sacred Congregation of Bishops and president of the Pontifical Commission for Latin America. The principal Latin American bishop in this intricate chess game was CELAM Secretary General López Trujillo, who had proved his ability to outmaneuver any lingering progressive leadership in CELAM.

The campaign against liberation theology and the increasing liberalization of the Latin American Church was formalized in Rome at a March 1976 meeting of the so-called "Church and Liberation Circle of Studies," which was co-sponsored by the Roman Curia and Adveniat, the German bishops' aid agency for the Latin American Church.[62] Led by López Trujillo and Vekemans, the list of participants read like a Who's Who of anti-liberationists. Although nothing new was said, Vekemans used the forum to pound home his now familiar theme that Christians for Socialism was another name for liberation theology, which, in turn, was a front for the Christian grassroots communities. Since these communities were multiplying by the thousands in Latin America, this proved that Marxism was spreading like a "contagion with a multiplication of the carriers of the bacillus."[63]

Vekemans' emphasis on Christians for Socialism was designed to frighten his audience. Although the movement had ceased to be important in Latin America because of military repression, it had reappeared in Italy, where it took on a new, and different, vitality through contact with Euro-Communism, spreading to such countries as Spain, Germany, and France. Fearful of a Marxist election victory in their own countries, the Europeans assumed that the Latin American reality was the same, when in fact it was just the opposite: only one communist country, Cuba, existed in the hemisphere, in contrast to eleven nations with right-wing totalitarian regimes. Thus the theology of liberation was misconstrued in Europe as a Trojan horse for Marxism. The Peruvian and Brazilian bishops' criticisms of capitalism were similarly misunderstood: the Europeans simply could not comprehend how a system that had proved so beneficial to them could be so iniquitous in Latin America.

As the largest foreign source of money for the Latin American Church,

Adveniat's public sponsorship of Vekemans' smear campaign raised some serious questions. In a scathing denunciation of Adveniat published in late 1977, over one hundred renowned German theologians demanded to know why the agency was financing a "not very brotherly attack . . . which endangers autonomous church evolution in Latin America . . . and is causing divisions between theologians and bishops in the national Churches." The Germans also called attention to Adveniat's "regrettable alliance" with Vekemans, who "has not only distinguished himself by his untiring action in Latin America and Europe against the theology of liberation, but has also become an ambiguous figure after the press accused him of having received millions of dollars in subsidies from the CIA to support imperialist policies in Latin America." They further questioned the actions of Bishop Franz Hengsbach, Adveniat's director and military bishop of the German armed forces, noting that he had received the Condor of the Andes decoration from the Bolivian military regime, the highest honor in Bolivia. The decoration was "grotesque," said the theologians, in view of the Bolivian government's persecution of the Church and the famous CIA "Banzer Plan."

Asked the theologians:

How is it that reasonable confrontation between different theologies in the Church can lead to such defamation of the adversary? What happened to the understanding of the highly-praised pluralism in the Church and the observance of the criterion of equilibrium so often demanded in church circles? . . . Are those in the German Church who approve of the campaign against the theology of liberation aware of whose interests they serve and how much damage they cause the Latin American Church? Do they realize how much fresh suffering their behavior will inflict on many Christians and priests who already have suffered enough under the yoke of military dictatorships?

We cannot accept that once again the German Church is under suspicion of making agreements with the powerful and of not seeing—whether in good or bad faith—the inhuman behavior of dictatorships which call themselves Christian.[64]

Among the signatories were Karl Rahner, Herbert Vorgrimler, and Johannes B. Metz, in addition to such Protestant leaders as Martin Niemoller, Helmut Gollwitzer, and Ernst Kasemann. Kasemann's inclusion was particularly significant: in 1977 his daughter was arrested, tortured, and killed by the government in Argentina for her activities on behalf of liberation.

Despite such denunciations, the smear campaign continued, Adveniat now sharing the costs with a Catholic organization in Milwaukee called the De Rance Foundation.[65] There was a sense of urgency in the attack because, contrary to expectations, a long-awaited study of liberation theology by the Vatican's International Theological Commission did not issue a condemnation when the results were released in September 1977. On the contrary, the commission acknowledged that the theme of liberation runs throughout the Bible and that the Church cannot avoid politics. The Church should not "surrender" to sheer neutrality or unsympathetic detachment to retire to a purely nonpolitical role, said the commission. Nor can it "remain silent when human dignity and elementary human rights are crushed."[66]

The Puebla meeting therefore represented a last chance to deal the theology of liberation a death blow and to stop the liberalization process begun by Medellín.

The centerpiece of the campaign was the preliminary consultative document for Puebla on "Present and Future Evangelization in Latin America," a 214-page tome released in December 1977 and promptly dubbed the "green book." Written by López Trujillo's conservative staff of sociologists and theologians with the intellectual support of Vekemans, the green book offered the classic argument for "developmentalism" with an overlay of western colonialism.

The text's basic assumption reflected the time-worn theory of development, i.e., that Latin America's social problems are the natural outgrowth of the transition from an agrarian to an urban-industrial society. Because civilian governments had proved unable to cope with the pressures created in this transition, military states necessarily had risen in the power vacuum. The Church's principal challenge in this changing world, according to the document, is to maintain a traditionally Catholic society in the face of growing secularism (among the upper and middle classes). The solution: a "New [Old] Christendom" representing a "third way" between capitalism and Marxism and inspired by the Church's social doctrine, i.e., Christian Democracy. Medellín's commitment to the poor was replaced by colonial fatalism: whatever their sufferings on earth, the poor would always have the consolation of a better hereafter. No mention was made of the Church's persecution or the reasons for it.

Triumphalist in tone, authoritarian in its view of a top-bottom Church, the document renounced Medellín's commitment to the poor and oppressed in favor of doctrinal orthodoxy and political accommodation, albeit critical, with existing power structures. Threaded throughout the green book were strands of colonialism, in the emphasis on European theology and the implicit assumption that, despite Latin America's rich cultural diversity, only western culture pertains, since this is the culture of science and technology, of urban industrialization, in sum, the culture of the dominant white civilization. As to the document's option for a "third way," said Father Balducci, it does not exist. "With the exception of Cuba, Marxism is far from being a real alternative [in Latin America] and, at any rate, has a minimal cultural impact, while capitalism is an almighty reality. Since the third way is impossible, or, at least, remains a purely theoretical postulate, what really comes out of the attractive ideogram is nothing other than conservation of the existing system, . . . with some democratic corrections which even President Carter desires."[67]

Despite López Trujillo's claim that criticism of the document was due entirely to "Marxist readings," the majority of the bishops conferences rejected it as "weak," "confusing," and "superficial." Even conservative churchmen objected to the document, including López Trujillo's fellow Colombian bishops.[68] Yet the document had one redeeming feature: because it so patently denied Medellín and all that had happened in the Church since, the green book set off a continent-wide debate unprecedented in scope and depth. In contrast to Medellín, when very few laypeople were involved in or even knew of the preparations, thousands of Christian grassroots communities discussed the Puebla consultative document with their priests and bishops. In clarifying and describing what it means to be a Christian in the continent today, both pastors and flocks achieved a new level of awareness. As one of the communities' documents explained: "We have discovered the limits of this system. . . . We have experienced a new power which liberates us from the fear of dying."[69] Thus even before the bishops met in formal conference, Puebla had served to evangelize Latin America, the very subject of the gathering.

In response to widespread criticism of the document, a small team of moderate bishops met in Bogotá in mid-1978 under the leadership of Brazil's Cardinal Aloisio Lorscheider, then CELAM president, in order to rewrite the green book. Shorter and more concise, the rewrite incorporated the language of Medellín, re-emphasizing the Church's commitment to the poor and oppressed. Although the Lorscheider document still contained certain ambiguities, including the famous "third way," it was hailed by moderate and progressive churchleaders as a relief column against López Trujillo's unremitting siege of Puebla.

Immune to the growing chorus of dissent, the CELAM secretary general remained on the offensive. The Latin American bishops were bombarded with publications produced by CELAM and Vekemans' CEDIAL Institute, underwritten by the De Rance Foundation, claiming that the Red Menace was about to engulf the continent. Latin America's liberation theologians and the progressive Latin American Confederation of Religious (CLAR) were singled out for abuse by Uruguayan lawyer Alberto Methol Ferré, a member of the CELAM Lay Department, a close associate of López Trujillo, and the conservatives' spokesman for an accommodation with the military regimes. (In one CELAM study sent to the bishops, Ferré stated that "if a society is in profound crisis, it is always the 'hour' of the army. The army is salvation."[70]) In an act of particular vindictiveness, López Trujillo barred CLAR's directors from attending Puebla, although they had had both voice and vote at Medellín. This caused such an outcry, including a threat by Lorscheider to resign the CELAM presidency, that Cardinal Baggio's office had to send the religious a belated invitation.

Most of the other openings to the progressives were blocked by López Trujillo in concert with Baggio, whose office was in charge of selecting 181 delegates, in addition to the 175 elected by the Latin American bishops conferences. All but one of the theologians chosen were opponents of the theology of liberation. The twelve additional bishops invited were unanimously right-wing, including Vekemans' sponsor, Cardinal Muñoz Duque, a brigadier general in the Colombian army. Indicative of the choice of lay delegates was Jorge Skinner Klee, a Helena Rubenstein executive in Guatemala. Shortly before his assassination in early 1979, Guatemala opposition leader Manuel Colóm Argueta described Skinner Klee as "the great de-nationalizer of our natural resources. He is the lawyer who has drafted every single unpatriotic law in this country. He was a lawyer for the United Fruit Company. . . . He is the author of the laws destroying the agrarian reform and of those handing petroleum over to foreign interests. He is also a teacher at the school of military studies."[71] Thus López Trujillo's delegates to Puebla.

For all the careful planning to ensure Puebla's rejection of Medellín, neither Vekemans, López Trujillo, nor Baggio could control one crucial factor— reality. The picture in Latin America at the beginning of 1979, when the bishops met at Puebla, was much darker than it had been at Medellín. Every yardstick of social progress showed a worsening in the plight of the masses, and with the poverty had come increasing repression. As the Theological Commission of the bishops of Northeastern Brazil succinctly put it: "If the Church were to summarize the past decade of 'development' in Latin America, it would have to state that the result is more hunger."[72]

All across the continent came the cry of a suffering people, a cry that could not be stifled by any amount of antiliberation propaganda. Observed Chilean theologian Segundo Galilea: "Much more than in 1968, the Catholic church appears as the only hope in many situations and countries. The hour of the gospel is more crucial than ever. A church is wanted with a leadership to meet history."[73]

NOTES

1. Hubert Herring, *A History of Latin America* (New York: Alfred A. Knopf, 1956), p. 173.

2. "Amérique Latine: Dix ans de répression contre l'Église," *DIAL* (Diffusion de l'Information sur l'Amérique Latine; Paris), Bulletin no. 497, 11 January 1979.

3. Herring, *History of Latin America*, p. 169.

4. J. Lloyd Mecham, *Church and State in Latin America* (Chapel Hill: The University of North Carolina Press, 1966), p. 23.

5. Robert L. Conway, "Latin America's Pattern: How the Church Changed," *National Catholic Reporter*, 2 February 1979.

6. "Pérdidas y ganancias de la Iglesia en América Latina," *Christus* (Mexico City), August 1978, pp. 23–27.

7. Mecham, *Church and State*, p. 42.

8. "Modern-Day Slavery," LADOC Keyhold Series No. 12, Latin America Documentation, U.S. Catholic Conference, 1975.

9. Malcolm Lowry, *Under the Volcano* (Philadelphia: J. B. Lippincott Co., 1965), pp. 299–300.

10. Quoted in Alan Neely, "Liberation Theology in Latin America: Antecedents and Autochthony," *Missiology: An International Review*, July 1978, pp. 343–70.

11. Quoted in Carlos Rangel, "Sound Theology, Timely Politics," *Newsweek*, 12 February 1979, p. 10.

12. Conway, "Latin America's Pattern."

13. Rangel, "Sound Theology, Timely Politics."

14. Joseph Comblin, "La Iglesia latinoamericana desde el Vaticano II," *Contacto* (Mexico City), magazine of the Mexican Social Secretariat, February 1978, pp. 9–21.

15. Quoted in Simon Hanson, *Five Years of the Alliance for Progress* (Washington, D.C.: Inter-American Affairs Press, 1967), p. 188.

16. Quoted in "Yanqui Dollar," North American Congress on Latin America (New York), 1971, p. 41.

17. *Washington Post*, 2 November 1971.

18. "Yanqui Dollar," p. 51.

19. Camilo Torres died in the Colombian Andes in early 1966 in his first confrontation with the army.

20. José Míguez Bonino, *Christians and Marxists* (Grand Rapids: Eerdmans, 1976), p. 93; see Neely, "Liberation Theology," pp. 347–49.

21. Quoted by Gustavo Gutiérrez in "Hacia una teología de la liberación" (Montevideo: Centro de Documentación MIEC-JECI, 1969); see Neely, "Liberation Theology," pp. 345–46.

22. Neely, ibid., p. 349.

23. Author's interview, February 1979, Puebla, Mexico.

24. Medellín *Conclusiones* (Bogotá: Secretariado General del CELAM, 1976); English translation published by U.S. Catholic Conference.

25. Helder Camara, "CELAM: History Is Implacable," *Cross Currents*, Spring 1978, pp. 55–58.

26. *Christus* (August 1978), p. 49.

27. "Quality of Life in the Americas—Report of a Presidential Mission for the Western Hemisphere," *Department of State Bulletin*, 8 December 1969, p. 18.

28. Richard Rashke, "Chile Connection: White House, Church, CIA," *National Catholic Reporter*, 29 July 1977. Also Norman Kempster, " 'I Got $5 Million Covert,' Jesuit Priest Reported," *Washington Star*, 23 July 1975.

29. Rashke, "Chile Connection"; also "Covert Action in Chile, 1963–1973," Staff Report of the Select Committee to Study Governmental Operations with Respect to Intelligence Activities, U.S. Senate, 18 December 1975, 62 pages.

30. Rafael Avila, "Chronology of the Theology of Liberation (II)," Latinamerica Press (Lima), 20 December 1973.

31. Comblin, "Iglesia latinoamericana," p. 18.

32. Alfonso Murphy, "CLAR, CELAM and CIEC Scolded by Curia Cardinal," Latinamerica Press, 17 May 1973.

33. Quoted in Miguel Colonnese, "Liberation Priests Called 'Agitators' Using Church," Latinamerica Press, 21 April 1972.

34. Ibid.

35. "Pérdidas y ganancias."

36. Quoted in Neely, "Liberation Theology," p. 366.

37. See, for example, "Covert Action in Chile, 1963–1973," of the U.S. Senate's Select Committee on Intelligence Activities (1975); "Guatemala and the Dominican Republic," the Subcommittee on Western Hemisphere Affairs of the Senate Foreign Relations Committee (1971); "Human Rights in Nicaragua, Guatemala, and El Salvador: Implications for U.S. Policy," the House of Representatives Committee on International Relations (1976); and such RAND Corporation studies as Einaudi and Ronfeldt's "Internal Security and Military Assistance to Latin America in the 1970s" (1971).

38. Alain Touraine and Sergio Spoerer, "Ten Years of Latin American History," *The Church at the Crossroads* (Rome: International Documentation and Communication Centre [*IDOC*], 1978), p. 2.

39. "Amnesty International Newsletter" (London), July 1976.

40. In 1960 the richest 1 percent of Brazil's population received 11.7 percent of the country's total wealth. Ten years later that same 1 percent received 17.8 percent of the total. In contrast, the income of the poorest 50 percent of the population fell from 17.7 to 13.7 percent in the same period.

41. *Documento de consulta* (Bogotá: III Conferencia General del Episcopado Latinoamericano [CELAM], released December 1977), p. 36.

42. "Reflexión de teólogos y pastores de la Región Nord-este II de la CNBB," reported by Marcelo Pinto Carvalheira, published in "The Church and the Doctrine of National Security," by José Antonio Viera-Gallo, *The Church at the Crossroads*, p. 37.

43. A TFP front called the Foundation for a Christian Civilization purchased a 296-acre estate in Bedford, New York, in 1978 for its headquarters. Texas cattle and oil baron John F. Tatton, the foundation's chief U.S. benefactor, put up the $2.45 million for the property. In 1979 Bedford residents contested the foundation's proposal to open a school for boys on the estate, charging that the foundation posed a threat to the community. See "Cape Wearers Stir up Fears in Bedford" and "Banners, Capes and Crossbows," 12 March 1979, and "TFP's Story in Westchester" and "Millionaire Backer: A Texas Connection," 14 March 1979, *The Citizen Register* (Ossining, New York); Patricia Ploss, "Bedford Ponders Foundation Request," *Patent Trader* (Mount Kisco, New York), 28 February 1979.

44. Author's interviews with Uruguayan church officials, 1976, Montevideo; Leonardo Guerra, "Uruguayan 'TFP' Finding Communism in the Church," Latinamerica Press, 21 April 1977; Robinson Rojas Sandford, *The Murder of Allende* (New York: Harper & Row, 1975), pp. 101–02; Marlise Simon, "Whose Coup?" *Brazilian Information Bulletin*, No. 12 (American Friends of Brazil, Berkeley), Winter 1974, pp. 7–9; Ramón Marsano, "Blast by Conservative Group Draws Return Fire of Chilean Hierarchy and Nuncio," Latinamerica Press, 25 March 1976; "Sigaud versus Casaldáliga and Balduino," *LADOC*, January–February 1978, U.S. Catholic Conference, pp. 15–28; "Origins: Tradition, Family and Property," *The Citizen Register* (Ossining, New York), 13 March 1979.

45. "The Bolivian Government Plan against the Church," *LADOC*, June 1975, U.S. Catholic Conference, pp. 1–4; Luis del Río, "Escalating Campaign against Progressive Foreign Clergy in Bolivia," Latinamerica Press, 19 June 1975; and "CIA's Involvement Suspected in Repression of Mission Work in Bolivia," National Catholic News Service, 6 June 1975.

46. Roberto Sánchez, archbishop, Santa Fe; Juan Arzube, auxiliary bishop, Los Angeles; Gilberto Chaves, auxiliary bishop, San Diego; Patricio Flores, auxiliary bishop, San Antonio.

47. Press Conference, Chilean Bishops Conference, 17 August 1976, Santiago.

48. "Acuerdo presentado por la Comisión de Lucha contra la infiltración comunista en los medios religiosos," Bolivian Delegation, Third Congress of the Latin American Anti-Communist Confederation, Asunción, 28/30-III-77 of Documentation RRC-AMM, signed by Rvdo. Wilfredo López S., secretary, and Dr. Salvador Rubem Paredes, president (photocopy). Also "Ponencia—Delegación Boliviana," signed by Lic. Wilfredo López Suárez. Third Congress, etc. (photocopy). And "Principios tácticos de enfrentamiento a la infiltración marxista en la Iglesia Católica," Bolivian Delegation, signed by Dr. Julio Vera and Miss Margarita González, Third Congress, etc. (photocopy).

49. Numerous studies support this contention, including "Churches and Human Rights in Latin America" by Jesuit Brian H. Smith of the Woodstock Theological Center.

50. For a summary of Gallego's work and a description of his death, see the special commemorative issue of *Diálogo Social* magazine (Panama City), nos. 34–35, May–June 1972. "Violence and Fraud in El Salvador," published by the Latin American Bureau (London), July 1977, documents the persecution of the Salvadoran Church, including Grande's death.

51. "Bulletin No. 6," IDOC (Rome), June 1977.

52. "Death and Violence in Argentina," compiled by a group of priests in Argentina, Catholic Institute for International Relations (London), 18 October 1976, p. 4. Also author's interviews, July 1976, Buenos Aires.

53. "Comunicado pastoral ao Povo de Deus," National Conference of Brazilian Bishops (Rio de Janeiro), 25 October 1976, mimeograph in Portuguese. Also "Entrevista com D. Adriano," Serviço de Documentação, Editora Vozes (Rio de Janeiro), May 1977 (official documentation service of the Brazilian Bishops Conference).

54. "Death and Violence in Argentina," pp. 7–8.

55. Pastoral Letter, National Bishops Conference of Nicaragua, 8 January 1977, quoted in "La Iglesia denuncia" by José Marins, *El Espectador* (Bogotá), 28 January 1979.

56. Author's interviews, January 1979, Puebla, Mexico, and August 1976, Santiago, Chile.

57. Milton H. Jamail, "Guatemalan Christians Ask for End to Government Repression," Latinamerica Press, 29 March 1979.

58. Thomas E. Quigley, "Latin America's Church: No Turning Back," *Cross Currents,* Spring 1978, p. 81. Among the Brazilian bishops' best known pastoral letters are: "The Marginalization of a People" (1973), "I Have Heard the Cry of My People" (1973), "You Shall Not Oppress Your Brother" (1975), "Communication to the People of God" (1976), and "Christian Requirements of a Political Order" (1977).

59. Ralph Della Cava, "The Roman Catholic Church in Brazil in April 1978: A Vision of Short-Term Politics and Long-Term Religion," paper presented at the workshop on Religion and Politics in Latin America, 22–23 May 1978, organized by the Latin American Program of the Woodrow Wilson International Center for Scholars (the Smithsonian Institution).

60. Ernesto Balducci, "The Relationship between Faith and Culture and the Proposal for a 'Christian Civilization,'" *The Church at the Crossroads,* p. 77.

61. According to the *New York Times,* Adveniat funneled over $100 million into CELAM, sizeable sums of which were used to finance Vekemans' campaign. Robert McAfee Brown, "From Medellín to Puebla: A Crucial Journey," unpublished paper, p. 24.

62. The German Church underwrites two aid agencies—Adveniat, which is specifically concerned with church projects in Latin America, such as the construction of a chapel or a seminary for priests, and Misereor, which supports social development programs in the Third World, including health centers and schools.

63. Penny Lernoux, "Christians for Socialism Challenge Catholicism and Communism," *Alicia Patterson Foundation Newsletter* (New York), 12 July 1976.

64. "Protesting a Campaign against Liberation Theology," a memorandum from theologians in West Germany, 26 December 1977 (mimeograph).

65. Headed by Harry John, the foundation is identified with such traditional U.S. Catholic movements as the Family Rosary Crusade. Vekemans received approximately $200,000 from De Rance for his anti-liberation campaign as Latin American director of the foundation's Institute of the Sacred Heart. The De Rance Foundation also contributed $140,000 to the Puebla Conference; Adveniat, $100,000; and the U.S. Bishops Conference, $70,000. "'Rightwingers' Added to CELAM List," *National Catholic Reporter,* 15 December 1978. Also Gary MacEoin and Nivita Riley, "Velvet Curtain Shields Bishops at Puebla," Latinamerica Press, 15 February 1979.

66. Brown, "From Medellín to Puebla," p. 15.

67. Balducci, "Relationship between Faith and Cultures," p. 75.

68. *Aportes de las Conferencias Episcopales,* III Conferencia General del Episcopado Latinoamericano, Libro Auxiliar 3 (Bogotá: CELAM, 1978), pp. 79–348.

69. *The Church at the Crossroads,* p. iii.

70. "The Manipulation of CELAM," *Cross Currents,* Spring 1978, p. 64.

71. "Colóm Argueta's Last Interview," *Latin America Political Report* (London), 6 April 1979.

72. Penny Lernoux, "CELAM III: To Build or Tear Down?" *National Catholic Reporter,* 14 July 1978.

73. Penny Lernoux, "Dilemma of Change vs. Status Quo," *National Catholic Reporter,* 11 August 1978.

REPORT FROM THE CONFERENCE

Moises Sandoval

As the press, participants, the curious, and interested observers converged on Puebla for the opening of the Third General Conference of the Latin American Episcopate, no one seemed in a more advantageous position than Archbishop Alfonso López Trujillo. Everything he had done since becoming CELAM secretary general in 1972 had pointed to the end-game strategy that now threatened his opponents. As if somehow flaunting his position, the granite-faced secretary general, eyes hidden behind sunglasses, appeared fleetingly on the TV screen wherever the pope went during his tumultuous first days in Mexico City.

Everything said and done seemed to favor the secretary general's side: the run-away adulation of the Mexican people for the pope; vague warnings by John Paul II about "interpretations that are sometimes contradictory, not always correct, and not always beneficial for the Church" (HG:4); the demonstration of a popular religiosity that portrayed Our Lady of Guadalupe as a consoling mother wiping away the tears of her humble children rather than leading them in a struggle for freedom from oppression; and the inaccurate reporting by some reporters who seemed anxious to put in the pope's mouth words condemning the progressives in the Latin American Church. The certainty and assurance of the López Trujillo camp seemed to be growing by the minute as the conference approached.

In contrast, the uncertainties seemed to be multiplying for other protagonists coming down the winding highway from the mountain pass between Mexico City and Puebla. The progressive bishops appeared to have no clear plan to avoid repudiation of the commitments made at Medellín. The journalists were puzzled by the ambiguities of John Paul II's statements and unable to assess the meaning of the unprecedented adulation of millions of Mexicans who lined the roads. The excluded progressive theologians didn't know whether to attempt to hold an alternate Puebla Conference or try to infiltrate the CELAM III process. The lobbyists—representatives of "disappeared" persons in Argentina and El Salvador playing out their last shred of hope in a desperate gamble that somehow their pilgrimage would bring their loved ones back, the advocates of women's rights, spokespersons of an estimated 20 million Hispanics in the U.S., and others—had no assurance that they would get a hearing. As for the hundreds of thousands of campesinos who lined the 130 kilometers of superhighway from Puebla to Mexico, they could not possibly have had an inkling that they would influence the conference simply by

28

seeking to catch a glimpse of the pope so that generations hence they could tell their children and grandchildren what they had seen and felt on that historic day.

Puebla de los Angeles and the Palafoxiano

Entering Puebla, the visitor could not escape the feeling of returning to a bygone age. The visible ecclesiastical presence was not the Church of the poor, pursued and persecuted by Latin America's dictators, symbolized by human relationships rather than by buildings and held together by love rather then by mortar and hierarchical power. The Church the arriving delegates and visitors saw was the Church of history. Indeed, history was almost palpable in the narrow streets lined with colonial buildings. On the heights above the city, Mexico had scored one of its greatest military victories, crushing a French imperial army in 1862—an event observed as a national holiday on 5 May each year. Puebla was also the site of the opening skirmish of the Mexican Revolution in 1910.

The arriving delegates saw massive churches towering all over the downtown area. Puebla and its environs are said to have more churches than days of the year. The ornate cathedral casts its shadow over the Zócalo—the beautifully landscaped main square—seemingly blessing the idyll of couples strolling hand in hand and the transactions of the businesses around the square. The colonial reliquary of the region, Puebla seemed the essence of tradition and well-ordered priorities—the wistful dream of bishops yearning for a less troubled time. Puebla had the look of a tranquil island spared the disrupting tides of a troubled civilization. Even chaotic Mexico City, where a thousand new residents arrive daily on a desperate odyssey for jobs and food, seemed light years away.

But it was not just Puebla's visual images that had caught the eye of López Trujillo and the other CELAM III planners. Many areas had bid for the meeting, most notably Brazil, Mexico, Puerto Rico, and Rome. But Rome was too vulnerable to claims of manipulation by the Curia and Puerto Rico too open to uninvited tampering by the U.S. Central Intelligence Agency. Brazil had hosted CELAM I and Colombia CELAM II for the Bolivarian countries. Further, Mexico was perhaps the only major nation that would welcome visitors of any political persuasion.

However, that openness did not characterize Puebla, Mexico's most conservative city. Even before the bishops arrived, there had been street demonstrations against liberation theologians. But the CELAM plan demanded even more security than that offered by a militantly conservative city. Puebla was to be principally a meeting of bishops isolated from troublesome elements and unwanted participants. The meeting site, on the northeast outskirts of Puebla, was perfect from Lopez Trujillo's point of view: a huge seminary, named for a seventeenth-century viceroy-archbishop of Mexico, Don Juan de Palafox y Mendoza, set within an eighty-acre campus surrounded by a stone wall over ten feet high.[1]

Only delegates, press, and staff could gain entry to the grounds. The press had access to only two areas of the seminary, one where typewriters and transmitting facilities were set up, and another furnished for the single daily news conference in which a few delegates responded only to questions submitted and pondered in advance. A high counter barred a passageway to the other wings where the bishops roomed, ate, and met. Security guards were always there to insure that the barrier was respected. With rooms provided at the seminary, there was no need for the delegates to leave the compound. There would be only a single opportunity for the delegates to meet with the "People of God": Masses at many of the local churches and visits to surrounding neighborhoods on the first Sunday following the opening of the conference. But the conditions then would be less than ideal for a free and open exchange. A special bulletin on Puebla from the Diocese of Quetzaltenango, Guatemala, said: "Meetings between the bishops and the people have been planned but without spontaneity, very regulated, with tight security, and meticulous programming about what the bishops should be given to eat, the gifts that should be given, what ought to be discussed. What most attracts attention are the security measures for accompanying the bishops to the churches."[2]

The Participants

If nothing had been left to chance in selecting Puebla and the Palafoxiano seminary, the delegates were chosen with equal care. Controlling the process were López Trujillo and his powerful ally in the Vatican—Cardinal Sebastiano Baggio, prefect of the Sacred Congregation for the Bishops and president of the Pontifical Commission for Latin America. They made sure that the delegate-selecting processes they controlled brought in mainly conservatives. During his seven years at CELAM, López Trujillo had replaced all the liberals of the Medellín era with conservatives. And even though the other classes of voting delegates—presidents of episcopal conferences and elected representatives from each nation's bishops—tended to be either conservative or moderate, Baggio and López Trujillo wanted even better odds. So they prevailed upon John Paul I to name 12 additional delegates with voice and vote, most of them conservatives. That made 187 delegates with voice and vote, of whom only 20 or 25 were progressives as opposed to 35 to 40 conservatives, with the remainder in the middle but tending toward the right.

There were reports that John Paul I was asked by the Curia to name a total of 117 delegates. Though only the previously mentioned 12 had a vote, the others would be able to influence the debate. According to unconfirmed reports in Puebla, the pope argued bitterly with a curial cardinal about those appointments on the day before he died. The speculation was that the quarrel may have been a factor leading to his heart attack. After some study, John Paul II approved the Curia's request.

At first, CELAM president Cardinal Aloisio Lorscheider was designated as the presiding officer of CELAM III. But barely a month after Cardinal Baggio announced, on 12 December 1977, who could participate in the conference, the presidency was expanded to a triumvirate of Lorscheider, Baggio, and the conservative Archbishop (now Cardinal) Ernesto Corripio Ahumada of Mexico City. Thus, any advantage that the progressives may have had originally with the progressive Lorscheider at the helm was erased.

The conservatives avoided another potential problem by having the pope appoint the *periti*, or experts, from nominees suggested by the Curia or by episcopal conferences. For CELAM II, the bishops had been free to bring their own experts. Rome's choices for Puebla turned out to be overwhelmingly conservative.

These maneuvers gave a tremendous edge to the conservatives. As the delegates arrived in Puebla, some of Latin America's leading progressive bishops were conspicuously absent, among them Pedro Casaldáliga of São Felix, Brazil; the embattled archbishop of Managua, Miguel Obando y Bravo; José María Pires of Paraiba, Brazil; Arturo Rivera y Damos of Santiago de María, El Salvador; Luis Fernández of Vitoria, Brazil; Jaime Francisco de Nevares of Neuquen, Argentina; Samuel Ruiz García of San Cristóbal de Las Casas, Mexico; José Parra León of Cumaná, Venezuela; Alberto Devoto of Goya, Argentina; Sergio Méndez Arceo of Cuernavaca, Mexico; Tomás Balduino of Goias, Brazil; Antonio Batista Fragoso of Crateus,Brazil; and Marcelo Pinto Carvalheira of Paraiba, Brazil.[3]

These bishops are in the vanguard of an evangelization that is truly liberating, living a life of poverty, defending human rights, encouraging formation of the Christian base communities and enduring—in the cases of Obando y Bravo, Rivera Damos, Parra León, Balduino, and Casaldáliga—persecution because of their identification with the poor and oppressed. Casaldáliga has survived two attempts on his life; Parra León has been marginated by his own brother bishops in the Venezuelan episcopacy because of his commitment to the poor.

Though excluded from the Puebla proceedings, Parra León warned the bishops to be courageous: "Latin America will never forgive the participants of Puebla if they let themselves be overcome by fear and fail to denounce precisely the situations of injustice, oppression, falsehood, and lies to which the powers of the continent, the military enthroned in civil power and the rich and powerful, have submitted the Latin American people."[4]

Missing among the experts were all of Latin America's best known theologians: Gustavo Gutiérrez, Juan Luis Segundo, Leonardo Boff, Hugo Assmann, Jon Sobrino, Ignacio Ellacuría, Raúl Vidales, Enrique Dussel, Segundo Galilea, Pablo Richard, and José Comblin.

In addition to the 187 voting delegates, there were 79 priests, deacons, religious, and lay persons, 5 officers of the Confederation of Latin American Religious (CLAR), 11 representatives from the Pontifical Commission for Latin America, 9 Italian dignitaries from the Vatican, 5 nuncios, 7 superiors general, 9 representatives from episcopal conferences in the U.S., Canada, Europe, Africa, Madagascar, and Asia, 17 representatives of foreign aid agencies or foundations, 5 observers from other Churches, and 16 experts—for a total of 350. Another six were added after the list was published. Geographically, 287 of the delegates were from Latin America and 63 from outside, including 23 from the Vatican.

John Paul II

But the most important Vatican presence was John Paul II himself, the first non-Italian pope in five centuries, elevated to the throne of Peter only three months before, and now given the first opportunity to reveal the style, content, and focus of his pontificate. The response to the pope in Mexico was beyond the wildest dream of any political leader. An estimated 20 million turned out in wild adulation to see him during his five-day visit. It was as if the legendary divinity Quetzalcóatl had returned. Jesuit writer Enrique Masa wrote in Mexico's respected newsweekly *El Proceso*:

> They [the adoring people] do not care whether what he says is from the left or from the right. They know he does not lie (like all their political leaders do). They know that they can trust him, that he represents the truth, and justice, and love of the people. That is something no Mexican politician can give. . . . People can't give what they don't have. And the pope has it. From the left or from the right. But he has it. And he gives it. And the people surrender as they surrender to no Mexican politician. It was a message from the people. And if that is not the significance of the demonstration, it will be just one more sign that the people, as always, do not count.[5]

Such adulation had a tremendous effect on the delegates to CELAM III. As Juan José Hinajosa said in *El Proceso*: "The numbers, good behavior, and the enthusiasm of that presence cannot be attributed to curiosity alone. It was an undeniable plebiscite of popularity, of adherence to the person and the truth he represents."[6] Thus the delegates could hardly do anything but endorse his words. This seemed to represent yet another gain for the conservatives as the participants assembled to hear the pope's address officially opening the conference.

Moreover, in his talks during the first days of his journey, John Paul appeared to be echoing what López Trujillo himself had been saying. In the CELAM bulletin for January 1979, López Trujillo had stated that Puebla would advance beyond Medellín but would not accept "the false interpretations of Medellín."[7] In his opening address at CELAM III, the pope said: "This third conference . . . will have to take Medellín's conclusions as its point of departure, with all the positive elements contained therein, but without disregarding the incorrect interpretations that have sometimes resulted and that call for calm discernment, opportune criticism, and clear-cut stances" (OAP).

Speaking to priests and men religious in Mexico City, the pope seemed to be attempting to withdraw the clergy and religious from the arena of struggle in Latin America. "You are priests and religious," he said. "You are not social directors, political leaders, or functionaries of a temporal power." He urged the priests and religious to a life of prayer, cultivating a union with God through a profound interior life. "This should be your first interest. Do not fear that the time consecrated to the Lord will take something away from your apostolate" (AP).

To many, such statements signaled retreat. Father Ricardo Ramírez, vice-president of the Mexican American Cultural Center in San Antonio, Texas, and one of those present in the basilica during the pope's talk to the clergy, found the Holy Father's words "extremely disappointing." Conservatives, though, found them very encouraging.

However, the press, by its inaccurate reporting, did even more to create a widespread impression that John Paul II wanted the Latin American Church to turn away from the direction it had taken since Medellín. Chatting with reporters on the Alitalia plane taking him from Santo Domingo to Mexico, the pope made a statement that was quoted by Alan Riding of *The New York Times* as follows: "You know that liberation theology is a true theology. But perhaps it is also a false theology because if it starts to politicize theology, apply doctrines of political systems, ways of analysis which are not Christian, then this is no longer theology. That is the problem. Theology of liberation, yes, but which one?"[8]

Hours after the pope's plane landed, headlines in Mexican dailies proclaimed that the Holy Father had rejected the theology of liberation. That story, first transmitted by a European news agency, was then picked up by others. Some reporters had apparently heard the opposite of what Riding reported. Jorge Sandoval of *El Sol de Puebla* reported that John Paul said: "The theology of liberation is a false theory. If it starts to politicize, theology is no longer theology. It is social doctrine, a type of sociology, not religious doctrine."[9] Such misinterpretations contributed to the despondency of progressives, even though the full context of the pope's talks did not present such a one-sided picture.

It seemed clear that the "theology of conspiracy," which José Comblin diagnosed as being in a virulent stage, infected even the pope. The major elements of such a "theology" were that there existed in Latin America a conspiracy against the Church, "a broad movement penetrating clandestinely all the structures of the Church, financed from outside Latin America, and able to achieve a radical division of the Church."[10] Furthermore, according to this "theology of conspiracy," these forces of darkness were infiltrating the CEBs, CLAR, theology, catechetics, and much more, and if the Church did not wake up, one day it would find itself completely destroyed.

Indeed, this "theology of conspiracy" seemed to be on John Paul's mind as he gave his opening address. Progressive theologians outside the Palafoxian complex, noting a number of statements out of character with the main thrust of his talk, speculated that conservatives had asked him to address certain dangers: for example, that some christologists were portraying Jesus as a revolutionary or guerrilla, that some held that the popular Church came from the people (rather than from Jesus), and that some were reducing liberation to its political and economic aspects.[11]

The pope also warned of the dangers of a "parallel magisterium," which, according to José Comblin, exists only in the fantasies of the conservatives. "There is no conspiracy in the Latin American Church," Comblin said, "not even the threat of a schism. There is no open or occult rebellion against the authority of the pope." As to complicity of priests and religious in partisan politics, Comblin said he could not point to a single priest so involved in Brazil or Chile and added that there were more priests involved in politics in Belgium than in all Latin America. "In Spain there must be ten or twenty times more. Nevertheless, there is no talk of schism in Belgium, or in Spain," Comblin declared.[12]

However, the pope's opening address had another current, which gave encouragement to the progressives. He spoke about the necessity of serving "the poor, the needy, the marginalized: i.e., all those whose lives reflect the suffering countenance of the Lord" (I,4). He spoke about proclaiming the complete truth about human beings: "human beings are not the pawns of economic or political processes, . . . instead these processes are geared toward human beings and subject to them" (I, 9). He called for the advancement of human liberation, asking that the Church's voice be heard "when the growing affluence of a few people parallels the growing poverty of the masses" (III, 4). He emphasized that "there is a *social mortgage* on all private property" (III, 4). He spoke of the "sometimes massive increase in violations of human rights in many parts of the world, . . . the right to be born; the right to life; the right to responsible procreation; the right to work; the right to peace, freedom, and social justice; and the right to participate in making decisions that affect people and nations" (III,5).

Such statements lightened the hearts of the progressives. These, after all, were the issues that the theology of liberation was addressing, the causes for which Latin America's martyrs were dying. Even more important, however, the pope set the delegates free from the daze that the explosion of adulation had produced. The bishops came to see that the pope had not come to dictate what they should do in Puebla. By implication rather than directly, he gave the bishops the responsibility for setting the course of the Church in Latin America.

Using that as his cue, Cardinal Lorscheider further brought the bishops down to earth by pointing out the challenges of transforming a society characterized by "a profound imbalance," growing inequalities, and increased domination by an expanding technocracy. He told the delegates that their most urgent duty was "the defense or the proclamation of the dignity of the human person, the proclamation of fundamental human rights in Latin America in the light of Jesus Christ."[13]

The Conference Process: Inside and Outside the Walls

Over the next seventeen days the bishops addressed themselves to the task embodied in the theme "Evangelization in Latin America's Present and Future," selected by CELAM and the Vatican with the design of bringing the Church back to what López Trujillo and other Latin American conservatives saw as its primary concern: the "spiritual" dimension, as distinguished from the socioeconomic and political preoccupations of the liberation movement.

López Trujillo and his conservative colleagues had learned well the lessons of Medellín. During that historic session, the delegates did not begin writing the documents until they had mingled freely during a week of dialogue, getting to know one another, exchanging ideas, and permitting dynamic personalities such as Dom Helder Camara to convince others of their insights and build support. The CELAM bureaucracy decided there would be no such opportunity in Puebla. Instead, delegates were broken into small groups at the very beginning and kept isolated as work began on the Final Document immediately. During the plenary sessions there was no opportunity for frank expression of views. Not until the waning days of the conference did that opportunity arrive, too late to change the ideological balance of the assembly.

Thus it seemed that López Trujillo and Baggio had left nothing to chance. But the unforeseen began to influence the proceedings and the pope himself played a role in a chain of events that changed the outcome of the conference.

Something significant happened to John Paul II on the way to Puebla—or at least that was the speculation by delegates and observers. Some said that seeing the poor lined shoulder-to-shoulder the entire length of the seventy-eight-mile route from Mexico City to Puebla deeply influenced the pontiff. At any rate, it was reported that the pope rewrote his speech to the Indians at Oaxaca upon returning from Puebla on 28 January. Delivered the following day, the Oaxaca talk had none of the ambiguities of the previous talks the pope gave in Mexico, hitting hard on such topics as the rights of the poor, the "social mortgage" on property, and the urgency of reforms, even by expropriation if the common good demanded it.

Curiously, it was a member of the López Trujillo team, theologian Pierre Bigo, who walked unsolicited into the press room in Puebla to volunteer that the pope had changed his talk. That stirred speculation that the pope had undergone a conversion or that perhaps he thought that too much attention had been given to those elements in his earlier talks that seemed (to the press anyway) to suggest an attempt to withdraw the Church from the arena of human struggle in Latin America.

Another important development that aided the progressives occurred outside the walled compound of the Palafoxiano. Denied the opportunity to bring their own experts, the progressive bishops in many instances asked their theologians and social scientists to come anyway, although at the time the bishops did not have a clear vision of how they could make an input. At first there was talk of an alternate Puebla. In fact, the Associated Press prematurely seized on that story. However, after an intense discussion by some forty progressive theologians and social scientists outside the seminary, they decided instead to try to support their bishops inside. Breaching the "wall of freedom," as López Trujillo called it, proved simple. Though the outsiders could not go into the compound, the bishops could not be denied exit and entry by the ever-present security guards. So as soon as a document became available it was quickly taken by one of the progressive bishops to a convent three blocks away from the Palafoxiano, where it was analyzed by the liberation group; their position papers were soon circulating in the assembly. So efficient and dedicated were the outside experts that four hours after the pope gave his opening talk to the bishops on 28 January, forty bishops had a twenty-page analysis written and duplicated by the outsiders. Within two or three days after the meeting opened, the input of the progressives was being openly acknowledged by the CELAM people. However, no move was made to invite them into the Palafoxiano.

By working day and night (at one point Gustavo Gutiérrez went twenty-four hours with only one hour of sleep) the outside theologians and social scientists were able to prepare eighty-four position papers for the twenty-one commissions as the document went through four drafts. As a result, according to several delegates, at least 25 percent of the final document was written directly by these uninvited assistants.

The Press

The press was another variable that backfired on the well-organized López Trujillo. His failure to cooperate with reporters proved detrimental to him in unexpected ways. As mentioned earlier, the press difficulties began with the in-flight papal press conference. López Trujillo and the Roman Curia had so convinced the press of an impending victory over the progressives that the press began making interpretations that could not be substantiated.

In twenty-seven talks the pope gave during his visit to Mexico, he did not mention liberation theology even once. Yet from 26 January onward many of the most prestigious media in the U.S. saw in the pope's words a rejection of liberation theology. Only a few of the reporters from the largest U.S. dailies— Roy Larson of the *Chicago Sun Times*, Russell Chandler of the *Los Angeles Times*, and Tom Carney of the *Des Moines Tribune*—avoided being ensnared with the *New York Times, Time* and *Newsweek* magazines, the wire services, and many others who seemed compelled to follow the pack.

Perhaps the organizers of the conference were to blame for not making experts available to analyze the pope's talks, or for sealing the delegates away from the press, or for not releasing the texts, particularly the Puebla speech, in time to permit reporters to digest the content before their deadlines. But reporters were also poorly prepared to meet the challenge. Some did not even know that there was a working document for the meeting, itself a revision of a document of consultation. Others knew but had not read either one. Some, including reporters from most of the big U.S. dailies, could not speak Spanish.

To back up their interpretations of the pope's talks, the reporters cited unnamed sources—"observers" (*Washington Post*), "Church officials" (*Chicago Tribune*)—or simply said that it seemed that the pope was discouraging liberation theology (*New York Times*).

But the news magazines and editorial writers threw all caution to the winds. *Time* (12 February) said of the pope's opening address: "The Pope emphatically rejected liberation theology without ever using that phrase." *Newsweek* (12 February) tried to have it both ways. While saying that the pope "pleaded for the liberation of the people from poverty" and, "in Puebla, ignored the controversial theology of liberation, . . ." a cutline under a page-wide photo of John Paul II motorcading through Puebla said: "John Paul II in Puebla: a rejection of liberation theology but a plea for liberation from poverty." The *New York Times* (30 January) said he "flatly rejected liberation theology."

The unseemly deference that editors have for the *New York Times* led other reporters into difficulties with their editors. Carney of the *Des Moines Tribune* said: "The executive editor told me what the *Times* had. I had to convince him that the *Times* was wrong. . . . But the editorial board had already written an editorial along the lines of what the *Times* said, and it had the effect of debunking my story."

Jim Toedtman, news editor of *Newsday*'s Washington bureau and that paper's expert on Latin America, had the sad experience of seeing what he considered his best story in a month in Mexico eroded to a mere sidebar by a flood of negative wire-service reporting of the pope's talk in Puebla. Toedtman had juxtaposed the main thrust of the pope's talk with the views of Dom Helder Camara, revealing a remarkable degree of correlation.

One might have guessed that such poor coverage would have filled the conservatives with glee, especially since they would have welcomed a rejection of liberation theology. Instead, however, it united progressives, moderates, and conservatives in declaring that the pope had not condemned it. It was not clear whether the conservatives responded out of a sense of fairness or in response to orders from above or because they saw that such inaccuracies were beginning to cause unforeseen difficulties. General Augusto Pinochet, Chile's strongman, had called a press conference to say, among other things, that the pope had set the Church on the right course. In Brazil, *Newsweek* reported, conservative clerics began to cite the pope's words to justify their opposition to Christian base-level communities.

But the most significant press report was the publication on 1 February by Mexico's respected daily *Uno Mas Uno* of a tape-recorded letter that López Trujillo had dictated to Archbishop Luciano J. Cabral Duarte of Aracaju, Brazil, president of CELAM's Department of Social Action. In it López Trujillo belittled Cardinals Lorscheider, Evaristo Arns of São Paulo, Eduardo F. Pironio, former president of CELAM and now prefect of the Sacred Congregation for Religious and Secular Institutes, and Father Pedro Arrupe, head of the 26,000-strong Jesuit order. Contained on a cassette tape that López Trujillo gave to a reporter who came to interview him and ran out of his own, the recording revealed the secretary general's plans to manipulate the conference. The publication so damaged López Trujillo's prestige that there were some insiders who said he was "fried"; one delegate said the letter had been his Watergate. As it turned out, such assessments contained more hope than reality, but for the duration of the conference at least this event was a plus for the progressives.

Harassment from the Right

Puebla lived up to its reputation as a place unfriendly to the progressives. Human rights groups and other lobbyists complained of an atmosphere of intimidation by right-wing Catholics, government officials, and "auxiliaries" hired by CELAM to provide security for the bishops. Representatives of 13,000 Argentines who have disappeared in recent years said that during a press conference in Puebla an unknown person attempted to photograph them and obtain their names. Spokeswomen for the Women for Dialogue, a feminist lobby from Latin America, Europe, and the U.S., said the group was told by local religious and civil leaders that it was not welcome in Puebla. Families hosting the women received anonymous telephone threats, including that of excommunication. Conferences being held by the women at a Puebla museum had to be moved to a hotel because the museum's director was told she would lose her job if she didn't cancel the meetings.

CENCOS reported that a group of progressive priests who planned a daily prayer service for the people of each country represented at the bishops' conference, featuring testimony of visitors from those nations, were told they could not meet by the local bishop and counter-intelligence agents of the State. However, the authorities allowed aggressive street demonstrations by rightist groups condemning liberation theologians.

Liberation theologians and social scientists also reported harassment. When Gustavo Gutiérrez, the Peruvian priest who pioneered liberation theology in Latin America, gave a press conference sponsored by CENCOS at a downtown hotel, the local rightist press attributed to him inflammatory statements he never made.

Priests at Sacred Heart of Mary parish reported ecclesiastical and police threats because the parish house was used for meetings by the liberation group. One member of the group said he had been followed by a blue sedan for three hours as he chauffeured delegates to and from meetings. Another person complained of being photographed repeatedly in the seminary press room by a CELAM auxiliary.

Relations with the press were further soured by denying credentials to U.S. writer and author Gary MacEoin; Father Enrique Masa of Mexico; Father Teófilo Cabestrero, a Spanish Claretian who writes for the Spanish magazine *Vida Nueva*; Alfonso Castillo, editor of the Mexican Jesuit monthly *Christus*; Saturnino Rodríguez of the Spanish bishops' weekly *Ecclesia* and Spanish radio and television; and Colombian Jorge Laureano Gómez of Radio Serpal of Bogotá. The denial of credentials led to protests from their colleagues during one of the official press conferences and a walkout by some sixty journalists.

Even the delegates were not immune from harassment. Mexico's Union of Fathers of Families, which claims more than a million members, demanded in a letter that the bishops "renounce liberating education." The union also listed sixteen bishops and priests as communists, including Panama's Archbishop Marcos McGrath and Brazil's Cardinal Arns. Eduardo García, president of the Puebla Chamber of Commerce, blamed "Marxists in priests' dress" for independent unions, economic instability, crazy strikes, and inflationary salaries. He called Cardinal Juan Landázuri Ricketts, vice president of CELAM, and Bishop Leonidas Proaño of Ecuador "Marxist manipulators."

Such statements angered the presidency of the bishops' conference; they issued a bulletin on 11 February protesting "the unjust and unobjective treatment given to the bishops of the Coordinating Commission. . . . To taint them as being partial to Marxism or of any posture against the pope or CELAM cannot be more absurd, . . ." the presidency declared.

Another target of the rightists was CENCOS and its president, José Alvarez Ycaza. CENCOS provided documents and sponsored press conferences that were a refreshing contrast to the farcical official ones in the Palafoxiano. Theologians, social scientists, lobbyists, and delegates to the bishops' meeting engaged in wide-open exchanges with the press. In one such meeting, the announcement was made that the authorities could not guarantee the safety of anyone present, but nothing happened. CENCOS provided the forum where the lobbyists could meet conference delegates and express their views in the hopes that the bishops would consider them in their deliberations.

López Trujillo's plan to isolate the delegates prevented face-to-face contact between them and most of the lobbyists. Only a few were able to get audiences with delegates, and some were totally frustrated. A spokesperson for the women's lobby said her group was not able to get a hearing from any of the nineteen women delegates. The women as well as other lobbyists—both progressive and conservative—relied on other means to get their message into the Palafoxiano. Puebla's high school Youth for Christ Movement, for example, held a demonstration outside the main seminary gate protesting Fidel Castro's regime, Christians for Socialism, and "Marxist priests." The Bank of Mexico (Bancomer), an affiliate of the U.S. Bank of America, made its pitch by providing watermarked stationery, pens, and handsome black attaché cases for the delegates. The National Bank of Mexico paid for the press room in the Alameda Hotel in downtown Mexico City.

Drafting the Document

Inside the Palafoxiano, delegates were assigned to twenty-one different permanent commissions by 31 January; the previous two days had been spent in opening formalities and an explanation of the procedures of the meeting. Each commission was assigned to develop one theme of the document. These would be grouped into four chapters, or nuclei: (1) pastoral overview of the reality that is Latin America; (2) God's saving plan for Latin America; (3) evangelization in the Latin American Church; and (4) the missionary Church at the service of evangelization.

Three other commissions were named later, one to identify pastoral options (the fifth chapter of the document), another to work on a face-saving shorter version of the final document in case the bishops could not reach agreement on the more ambitious effort, and one to prepare the introductory message to the peoples of the Americas.

Making sure the process worked was a powerful steering commission. The way it was chosen and the personnel selected to serve on it gave the first hint on 29 January that conservatives would not dominate the proceedings. The plan had been to have the conservative-dominated presidency name the members, but the assembly decided that they should be elected. Surprisingly, only one of the bishops chosen, Justo Oscar Laguna, was a conservative. Three were progressives—Luis Bambarén of Peru, Juan Flores of the Dominican Republic, and Luciano Méndez de Almeida of Brazil—and the chairman was Archbishop Marcos McGrath of Panama, a moderate.

The process called for each commission to write its section of the document and circulate it to the other delegates. After time for study there was a vote— "yes," "no," or "yes, with amendments." Then the commissions went back to work to incorporate the new input. This process was repeated four times. The first draft of the Puebla document was completed on 3 February, the second on 5 February, the third on 9 February, and the fourth on 11 February, when all but a section of the first chapter passed by the required two-thirds vote. Titled

"Pastoral Overview of the Sociocultural Context" (Part One, Chapter II), the vote fell eight short of approval, leaving the outside theologians wondering out loud what might have happened if Pope John Paul I had not named the twelve additional delegates. The paragraph that conservatives could not accept read: "Countries such as ours, which in their systems do not respect fundamental human rights—life, health, education, housing, and work—are in the position of permanently violating the dignity of the person."

That section was re-written to exclude the reference to systems (cf. FD:41) and then passed by the required two-thirds vote. Minor adjustments were made to the other parts of the 240-page typewritten document. Then on 13 February, the doors of the Palafoxiano were opened and the people were finally invited in for the closing Mass.

From the beginning two of the most difficult issues were the perspective on Latin American reality and the option for the poor (Chapter One and Commission XVIII). López Trujillo and his CELAM team had attempted to change the perspective from that of oppressors and oppressed, as in the Medellín documents, to one of culture, industrialization, and secularization. While Medellín saw its theological challenge as evangelization of the poor, CELAM in 1977 saw it as evangelization of culture. This was clearly evident in the consultative document and in the working document. The vote in Puebla revealed that the desired consensus was not achieved despite all the refining that the document underwent.

The pastoral overview of Latin American reality (Part One) registered more "no" votes than any of the others. Besides the chapter that had to be rewritten, there were two others that did not receive an unqualified "yes" from the majority. The vote on "Pastoral Reality Today in Latin America" (Part One, Chapter III) was 57 "no," 47 "yes, with amendments," with only 74 voting "yes." On "Evangelization in the Future" (Part One, Chapter IV), the count was 53 "no," 44 "yes, with amendments," and only 76 "yes."

Though the option for the poor was approved by the necessary two-thirds vote, 43 delegates voted "no," and 56 could accept that section only with amendments. The other sections came closer to achieving a consensus.

The Final Result

When the bishops finally released their document seventeen days after the ordeal began, there were no specific condemnations—of liberation theology, of the Christology of Leonardo Boff and Jon Sobrino, of the parallel magisterium conjured up by conservatives, of the CEBs, or even of Marxist analysis. "There is one ambiguous statement that might be taken as a rejection of Marxist analysis," said Chilean theologian Sergio Torres, "but it is not a condemnation." At the same time, however, there was no condemnation of specific military regimes.

While there had been fears that Puebla would turn the Church away from the prophetic options of Medellín, CELAM III reinforced them and in some cases restated them in stronger language. Jesuit Father Alfonso B. Deza, a delegate from the Philippines, said Puebla went further than Medellín in clarifying the means to carry out the directives of Medellín.

Taking their cue from the pope, the bishops rejected a partisan role in politics—but only for the sake of unity, according to Father Deza. There was never any claim or even suggestion that engaging in partisan politics was sinful for clergy or religious.

The Puebla document is ambiguous, with elements to please both conservatives and progressives. The conservatives seem to have prevailed in the doctrinal sections, the progressives in the description of reality and in committing the Church firmly on the side of the poor. Jesuit writer James R. Brockman declared that if a camel is an animal put together by a committee, the Puebla document represents twenty-five camels kicking and jostling each other.

A liberation theologian who asked not to be identified but was one of the outside consultants in Puebla said that part of the Puebla document could be used by dictators against their people. On the other hand, "The group that had hoped to have the conference condemn the popular Christian movements, the basic Christian communities, and the theology of liberation did not achieve its goal," he said. "The document, although in many points frankly mediocre, has a positive climate and will permit (though without much encouragement) the Church to continue to work alongside the poor and the oppressed."

The bishops at Puebla acknowledged the existence of a permanent violence of structures and institutions against the poor and powerless, but they spoke out against counterviolence, calling instead for a "civilization of love" (MPLA:8). They condemned capitalist liberalism as the "idolatrous worship of wealth in individualistic terms" and Marxist collectivism as the "idolatrous worship of wealth—but in collectivist terms" (FD:542–43).

Similarly, the bishops, while emphasizing Christianity's mission to work for the liberation of human beings from all the evils that ensnare them, cautioned against letting ideologies modify the Gospel. A liberation that utilizes "evangelical means," emphasized the Latin American bishops in their document, "does not resort to violence of any sort, or to the dialectics of class struggle. Instead it relies on the vigorous energy and activity of Christians, who are moved by the Spirit to respond to the cries of countless millions of their brothers and sisters" (FD:486).

The bishops had enough difficulty keeping the unreachable stars of Medellín in sight without having to look for new ones, but in at least one respect they did break new ground: in calling attention to the Church's challenge in serving 30 million indigenous peoples in Latin America. This is one area where the theology of liberation has been weak.

Puebla and Beyond

Despite the millions of words that flowed out of Puebla describing the proceedings before, during, and after, the oft-asked question still remains: "What happened in Puebla?" Faith Annette Sand and Harvey Cox answered that question in *Christianity and Crisis*: "Not very much, really." Yet to progressives who had to return to their dioceses to take up once again a struggle to which they have committed their lives, much indeed had happened. As Dom Helder Camara said: "As bishops we have not betrayed our people, but on the contrary, with divine grace, have been able to carry forward the strength of Medellín."

What happened? Well, for one thing it was evident that López Trujillo had attempted to turn the Church and history back to a hierarchical age. His efforts to assemble an overwhelming conservative majority at Puebla, his exclusion of Latin America's best-known theologians, his selection of a process that denied leadership the chance to surface and coalitions the opportunity to form— these, along with the regressive consultative document that CELAM prepared, reveal the design of an attempt to manipulate the conference.

The unity that John Paul II so obviously desired proved elusive, despite a process that sought to hammer out a consensus through writing and rewriting the document. True, the Puebla document had more of a consensus than those of Medellín, as Dom Cándido Padim, bishop of Baurú, Brazil, observed. But the unity was always tenuous, despite the efforts of López Trujillo and Cardinal Baggio to pass off the impression of one happy family in the Palafoxiano. At one point Cardinal Evaristo Arns of São Paulo, Brazil, entered the press area to announce that progressives had won an important vote. López Trujillo, hard on the heels of the cardinal, rushed in to interject that there were no winners or losers in Puebla. Progressives were dismayed when Bishop Arnoldo Aparacio, president of the Salvadorian Episcopal Conference, blamed the Jesuits for the violence being suffered by the Church in El Salvador. So when Bishop Aparacio got up to give the homily on the last day of the meeting, four bishops walked out.

When CELAM held its elections late in March, conservatives elected López Trujillo president to replace the progressive Cardinal Aloisio Lorscheider, who did not seek re-election for health reasons. The moderate Archbishop McGrath, who would have had the confidence of both sides, was defeated. Progressives saw the election of López Trujillo as a backlash against the achievements of progressives in Puebla.

Ultimately, the final measure of the Third General Conference of Latin American bishops will be what happens now in the twenty-two nations represented at Puebla. From the very beginning, the progressives emphasized that Medellín was not just a document but a ten-year history of commitment that would not be halted by a lukewarm or even adversary document from Puebla. The 100,000 basic Christian communities are not going to disappear. The theologians are not going to stop looking to the Gospel and Scriptures for answers to the harsh reality of oppression. The victims of military regimes will not give up the fight for freedom. All of these Christians will not stop being loyal to their Church or to cease demanding its presence alongside them in their struggle. Neither will bishops like Camara, Oscar Romero of El Salvador, Obando y Bravo of Nicaragua, and Pedro Casaldáliga of Brazil—and many others who have committed themselves fully to the poor—desert their flock because of what was said or not said in Puebla.

NOTES

1. *Puebla '79, Boletín de Información y Documentación sobre la Conferencia General del Episcopado Latinoamericano*, nos. 9 and 10, Diocesis de Quetzaltenango, September–October 1978, p. 8.
2. Ibid., p. 19.
3. "Puebla '78: Presencias y ausencias," *Christus*, no. 515, October 1978, p. 25

4. Ibid.

5. Enrique Masa, "El Papa, la religíon y el mensaje del pueblo," *El Proceso,* no. 119, 12 February 1979, p. 17.

6. Ibid., p. 39.

7. Alfonso López Trujillo, "El Secretariado General del Celam responde a cuestiones sobre Puebla," *CELAM,* Año XII, no. 135, p. 6.

8. "A Voice against Liberation Theology," *New York Times,* 30 January 1979.

9. "Rechazo papal al 'Socialismo Humano,' Negó validez a la teología de liberación," *El Sol de Puebla,* 26 January 1979.

10. José Comblin, "Es hora de decir ¡Basta! Las maniobras de una teología de la conspiración," Centro Nacional de Comunicación Social, Servicios especiales de prensa, Informativo no. 11, 6 November 1978, pp. 1–7.

11. Special briefing by Father Sergio Torres on behalf of the "outside" group of theologians and social scientists to a select group of journalists in Puebla.

12. Comblin, "Es hora de decir ¡Basta!" p. 2.

13. Cardinal Lorscheider's opening talk at the Third General Conference of Latin American Bishops, 29 January 1979.

II

THE POPE AT PUEBLA

THE POPE'S OPENING ADDRESS: INTRODUCTION AND COMMENTARY

Virgilio Elizondo

Listening to John Paul in Mexico was like watching an artist add strokes to the emerging image of an icon; only when the work is completed is the message clearly discerned. It was fascinating as the entire image gradually appeared, but it was painful as the U.S. press consistently missed or confused the point. They wanted one-liners, while the pope was slowly constructing an icon that clearly reveals the divine image in the human and the human image of the divine.

During the Holy Father's visit, he repeatedly told his audiences that he was giving them only part of his message and that they would have to listen to the rest of his talks—what he had said before and what he would say afterwards—to get his complete message. Hence, even though his Opening Address to the bishops assembled in Puebla was certainly the major presentation of his Latin American journey, it can be properly understood only when studied in the light of all his actions and words as they were lived and spoken during his entire pilgrimage.

The Whole Gospel

As the pope's message started to emerge, several major lines became eminently clear: fidelity, wholeness, truth, and a preferential loving identification with those in greatest need.

Throughout his stay in Mexico, he spoke about fidelity to the whole and integral truth about God, Jesus Christ, the Church, tradition, and human beings in the fullness of their concrete needs and aspirations. The pope was not speaking about abstract or philosophical truth, but about the very real saving truth as it liberates humanity from any and every form of enslavement and oppression. Fidelity to God is fidelity to the dignity of every human person. "Respect the human being, who is the image of God" (III,5).

It is important to note that for the pope fidelity to tradition means neither a holding on to the secondary things of the past (Address at the Cathedral of Mexico, 26 January) nor a mere defense of the status quo. In fact, this very fidelity to the tradition of the Church demands that we continue to work for the ongoing transformation of persons and society through bold, creative, heroic, and innovative action (cf. PP:32; Addresses at the Cathedral of Mexico, 26

47

January, and Oaxaca, 29 January). The tradition of the Church is the progressive liberation of humanity as sinful hearts and structures are transformed
into hearts and structures of grace.

In fidelity to the whole truth of the Gospel, the pope clearly expressed in both
his prepared texts and his spontaneous activity his preferential love and
concern for the most needy of society: the sick, the dying, the afflicted, the
aged, the silenced, the marginated, the exploited, and the victims of the
manipulations of society.

> With him [Paul VI] I would like to reiterate —with an even stronger
> emphasis in my voice, if that were possible—that the present pope
> wishes to be "in solidarity with your cause, which is the cause of the
> humble people, the poor people" (Address to Peasants, 23 August 1968).
> I wish to reiterate that the pope is with these masses of people who are
> "almost always left behind in an ignoble standard of living and some-
> times harshly treated and exploited" (ibid.). . . .
>
> The pope chooses to be your voice, the voice of those who cannot
> speak or who have been silenced. He wishes to be the conscience of
> consciences, an invitation to action. . . . The cry of the destitute and
> above all the voice of God and the Church join me in reiterating to you
> that it is not just, it is not human, it is not Christian to continue certain
> situations that are clearly unjust (AO).

It is from this perspective of the poor in their struggles for integral Christian
liberation, in their struggles to transform society, and in their persecution and
oppression by the forces of evil hidden in the mechanisms of society that the
addresses of John Paul are to be studied, reflected upon, and understood.

The radicalness of John Paul is neither of the left nor of the right nor even
one of the middle of the road. It is the radicalness of the whole and integral
message of the Gospel in which the disinherited of the world play a pivotal role
in the salvation of everyone. It should be noted that Matthew 25:31–46 appears
to be one of the key texts frequently used by the pope. His fears and warnings
stem from his dedication to the whole message: do not reduce, empty, exag-
gerate, partialize, for only the whole message can truly serve human beings
and liberate humanity.

Introduction to the Opening Address

In the introduction to his Opening Address, John Paul immediately makes
clear that he is speaking specifically to his brother bishops, who are to let
themselves be guided by the Spirit to "study more deeply as a group the
meaning of your mission in the face of the new exigencies of your peoples."
The meeting is thus to be collegial in nature and the bishops are called to truly
listen to the demands of the people. Like a deaf-mute who cannot speak
because he cannot hear, a bishop will not be able to speak if he has not listened
to the needs of all his people.

Taking Medellín as the point of departure, the bishops were to be guided in
their debates by two documents that themselves were the fruit of a long and

intensive listening process: (1) the *documento de trabajo,* which was produced after the *documento de consulta* had been widely studied, reflected upon, and debated by the masses of the faithful throughout Latin America, and (2) *Evangelii Nuntiandi,* which was prepared by Paul VI "from the wealth of the Synod [of 1974]" (EN: 5) and thus represented the pope speaking as a pastor who had truly listened to his people.

The pope closes the introduction by reminding the bishops that the entire Church will be the beneficiary of their work and, it is hoped, will follow their example. Out of the poor and suffering Church of Latin America will emerge leadership for the universal Church. The very poverty of Latin America can become the evangelical poverty that will invite the rich, proud, and powerful of the world to convert to the way of the Lord who freely chose not only to be poor and lowly (cf. Matt. 5:3), but to make of these very rejected ones the salt and light of the world. It is the poor of the world who have the greatest potential for being the bearers of the Good News of the Gospel to the rest of humanity.

Teachers of the Truth

The main body of the Puebla address is like a triptych, an image-message in which each one of the panels enriches and completes the other two.

In the first panel John Paul tells the bishops that, as pastors, their principal duty is to be teachers of truth—not a human or rational truth but God's truth, which is the principle of authentic liberation. This emphasis on truth as it serves and liberates humanity is one of the outstanding characteristics of John Paul II; it is interesting how often he speaks of the Gospel of John and the epistles of Paul as they refer to truth as the basis for freedom and authentic love. Without the truth, freedom and love are easily reduced to license and mere sense pleasure, both of which enslave rather then fulfill the human person.

The pope subdivides this liberating truth into three aspects: the truth about Christ, about the mission of the Church, and about human beings. From a solid Christology will emerge a well-founded ecclesiology and the anthropology that the Church has to offer to humanity.

In I,2–5, he develops the theme of the living knowledge of the whole mystery of Jesus of Nazareth, the Son of God, as the basis for everything: our identity, mission, existence, and life. Since it is only the full and entire *truth about Jesus Christ* that liberates humanity, any reduction, silence, disregard, mutilation, or inadequate emphasis regarding the entire mystery will cause confusion and cannot be the valid content of evangelization. The pope mentions in particular certain "re-readings" of the Gospel, the result of theoretical speculations, that pass over the divinity of Christ in silence or try to present him as a revolutionary fighting against Roman oppression. These comments should be read in the context of the rest of the pope's remarks, for example, in III,4, where he speaks of the need for a just socioeconomic order and adds that "Christ did not remain indifferent in the face of this vast and demanding imperative of social morality."

Otherworldly "re-readings," which tend to pass over or minimize the humanity of Christ and its function in relation to the society of his time, would likewise destroy the integrity of the Gospel. To reduce the Gospel in any way is to fail both God and humanity. Therefore the bishops are reminded: "Even if we, or an angel from heaven, should preach to you a gospel not in accord with the one we delivered to you, let a curse be upon him" (Gal. 1:8, in I,3). This integral proclamation of the Gospel will never be easy: "All this imposes exacting demands on the attitude of any Christians who truly wish to serve the least of their brothers and sisters, the poor, the needy, the marginalized: i.e., all those whose lives reflect the suffering countenance of the Lord" (I,4, citing LG:8).

Against "re-readings" of the Gospel that distort the full liberating message of Jesus, John Paul clearly states where to find the authentic "faith of the Church," which alone guarantees the necessary authenticity to every re-reading of the Gospel: Jesus Christ as he permeates the history of Latin America and the best values of the Latin American people; as he reveals the vocation to harmony and unity that drives away war; as he is expressed in the religious practices and popular piety of the faithful of Latin America (I,5).

Both Paul VI and John Paul II give positive importance to popular expressions of faith. They recognize that the piety of the people is a privileged expression of the true spirit of God present in the community—an evangelical instinct of discernment (cf. III,6). This *sensus fidelium* not only expresses the unity and universality of the local church (FD: 444–49) but is the very wisdom of God incarnated in the collective soul of his people and celebrated in their spontaneous and traditional feasts (Luke 10:21; FD: 448; OAP: III,6). For those who belong, it is a living appreciation of God present in our midst, yet it remains incomprehensible to outsiders.

In I,6–8, the pope develops the second aspect of truth entrusted to the bishops: that regarding *the mission of the Church.* There are four important points in this section.

a. The Church is born of our response in faith to Christ: "It is by sincere acceptance of the Good News that we believers gather together 'in Jesus' name to seek the Kingdom together, build it up, and live it' " (I,6, citing EN:13). Thus we become Church, and, as a living faithful witness to the way of Christ, the Church in turn gives birth to new disciples. Hence the Church is our mother, and it is only through that love composed of fidelity and trust that we will be able to truly know the Church. It is not a question of loving some ideal, abstract mother, but the real mother-church—frail, weak, and sinful yet the mysterious instrument for the liberation of humanity.

b. In this loving fidelity, the bishops must study carefully the ecclesiology of *Lumen Gentium,* for only a well-founded ecclesiology can ensure authentic evangelization: "for no one is evangelizing an isolated, individual act; rather, it is a profoundly ecclesial action" (EN:60, in I,7). In order to evangelize, the Church must grow in its own understanding of the uniqueness of its mission and function.

c. As for those who would identify the Kingdom of God with human structures, the pope, quoting his predecessor, reminds them that it is wrong to identify the *regnum Dei* with the *regnum hominis* (I,8). We must work for the transformation of human structures, but human structures can never be identified with the Kingdom of God. The mission of the Church cannot be reduced to social or political structures, but, as is evident from the pope's other presentations, neither can it be carried out in isolation from them or without affecting them profoundly. Human structures are the mediations through which sin and grace operate. To ignore them is to ignore the full reality of the Incarnation.

d. The fourth point that the pope makes refers to the "institutional" or "official" Church and its relationship to the Church of the people. The pope rejects any type of opposition or parallelism. It is most interesting to note that it is precisely in the areas of Latin America where the hierarchy is in intimate communion with the masses of the people, where it has taken on the struggles of the suffering, and where it has gone out to the people to foster the birth and development of Christian ecclesial communities, that the greatest unity and collaboration between all segments of the Church is in evidence. Whenever church leadership goes out to the people to form true assemblies of believers, the unity and dynamism of the Church flourishes. And it is precisely in these areas where "the humble and the poor are evangelized, become his disciples and gather together 'in his name' in the great community of those who believe in him" (EN:12), that the Church, without resorting to any ideology, is challenging the abuses of present-day situations with no other power than the living truth of the Gospel. On the other hand, it is in those areas where the officials of the Church have failed to go out among the people, to identify with them, to evangelize in the manner of Christ, and to bring about a response of faith, that the Church appears to be reduced to the visible "institution" or "official" elements and splits appear between the Church (officials) and the people.

In my own experience in working with the poor and needy of the U.S., I find that the people want to be with the Church, if only the Church will be with them. It is not the people who split from the Church, but the officialdom of the Church that sometimes splits from the people, especially the most needy. One of the sad sins of church leaders is that when those most silenced by society ask them to unite with their cries for help, they sometimes respond that they cannot do so because it might disrupt the "unity" of the Church, which of course means not the fundamental unity of faith, but unity with those in power who are easily scandalized when the suffering of society cry out for justice. When the Church is united to the poor, the poor will be united to the Church, for they will experience in the Church the loving mother who will not allow her children to be stepped on or destroyed.

In I,9, the pope speaks of the *truth concerning human beings*. This section should be studied in conjunction with Part III of his address, where he elaborates at greater length on human dignity. In this section he affirms that the truth of the Gospel and of the Church is the truth about human beings—an anthropology that affirms that the human being "is the image of God and cannot be reduced to a mere fragment of nature or to an anonymous element in the human city." True promotion of the identity, dignity, and mission of every human person is the major contribution—and often the most controversial one—that the Church has to offer to human society (cf. RH:16).

Any structure or ideology that diminishes or ignores the divine dimension of the human person is an inadequate view that weakens civilization and eventually destroys it (I,9). The reduction of the human person is one of the most obvious weaknesses of modern-day ideologies: Marxism because it reduces persons to wards of the State; capitalism because it reduces persons to profit-objects; militarism because it denies the fundamental liberty of the human spirit; secularism because it imprisons persons within the sphere of our own people-made worlds; individualism because it blinds persons to the fundamental need for belonging and community; and otherworldly religions because they reduce the human person by dividing that which cannot be divided in the authentically human—the terrestrial and the celestial.

The pope pleads to God that the Church may not be prevented from proclaiming the full truth about human beings, or, worse yet, afraid to do so (I,9). This plea echoes his prayers at the Basilica of Guadalupe: "Mother! Grant that we may learn how to serve [the Church] in truth and in justice. Grant that we ourselves will follow that road and lead others, never straying into tortuous byways and dragging others along with us" (HG:5). Indeed, the Church is sometimes too involved with the powerful of the world to be free to really champion the full dignity and rights of the indigenous peoples, the campesinos, and the marginated (FD:623,1140); this prayer of John Paul seems to bring out that only divine power can shake the bishops loose from their earthly ties to their own blood families and the economic-political allies that compromise them as pastors of all the people, especially the most disinherited (III,2). It is as if the pope sensed and wanted to point out clearly—without offending publicly—what has been one of the main sins of the institutional Church of Latin America: the alliance of the Church with the powerful against the powerless.

Signs and Builders of Unity

The second panel of the triptych presents the bishops as signs and builders of unity. It is precisely in times of turbulence and rapid change that the bishops must live out that fraternity that is "a sign and fruit of the unity that already exists" (II,1) and that is a gift from God. This unity comes not from human calculations and strategy, but from that which truly makes them one: the confession of faith. This deep unity of faith allows them to argue and debate with each other, not because they are against each other, but because together they are seeking to grow in the understanding and appreciation of the full implications in today's world of the infinite riches of God's saving mystery (Eph. 3).

The pope states: "Unity among the bishops finds its extension in unity with priests, religious, and the faithful laity" (II,2). It is the unity of a priestly people wherein everyone shares intelligently and responsibly in the mission of Christ (John Paul II, Inaugural homily of his pontificate, 22 October 1978). This unity of the Church is one of fellowship in service that springs forth from the growing awareness of collegiality at every level of the Church—from the *comunidad de base* to the Universal Church (RH:5). He goes on to challenge the religious in a special way to "the task of blazing the trail for evangelization." They are to make new breakthroughs and not be content with following the routine and ordinary ways.

Unity is essential if the Church's mission of making its own the causes and struggles of the oppressed for justice is to succeed. Bishops cannot allow the unjust mechanisms of society and their protagonists to play them off one against the other. The unjust powers of the world will hesitate to go against a truly united Church.

Defenders and Promoters of Human Dignity

In the final panel of the triptych, John Paul passes on to the role of bishops as defenders and promoters of human dignity. He points out "admirable bishops" and the familiar criterion for such a designation is the valiant defense of human dignity: "They regarded human dignity as a gospel value that cannot be despised without greatly offending the Creator" (III,1; cf. HSD). He tells the bishops: "You cannot fail to concern yourselves" (III,1). One cannot proclaim the truth of the Gospel without concerning oneself with the concrete problems of society: identifying ourselves with the struggles of the disinherited, the sick, the imprisoned, the hungry, the landless, and the lonely (III, 2, 3, 5).

The Church has learned from the Gospel that action for justice and the tasks of human advancement are an essential part of its evangelizing mission. Yet its motives for involvement can never be opportunism or the thirst for novelty. "It is prompted by an authentically evangelical commitment which, like that of Christ, is primarily a commitment to those most in need" (III,3).

He explores the two main areas that disregard and destroy human dignity: economic structures and violence of various types. In the midst of a continent plagued with wealthy landowners, often absentee, who exploit the land and the people without any regard for the common good, the pope does not hesitate to speak about "the delicate question of property ownership." He cites the constant tradition of the Church that clearly teaches that "private property does not constitute for anyone an absolute and unconditional right. No one is justified in keeping for his exclusive use what he does not need, when others lack necessities" (PP:23). Furthermore, those who legitimately own property continue to have a social obligation for the good of all the people: the more the property the greater the obligation.

When we consider the massive gap that exists between the rich who daily become wealthier and the growing misery of the masses, the words of the pope appear as a strong and clear indication of one of the priorities of mission: "Christ did not remain indifferent in the face of this vast and demanding imperative of social morality. Neither could the Church. . . . Let us get back to work in this field" (III,4). If we have to go back to work, it is clear that at this moment we are not working!

Without the conversion and transformation of the existing structures of society, wars and revolutions are sure to come. The only way to peace will be through the construction of economic and social systems based upon liberty, equality, justice, and fraternity. If we want peace, we must work to overcome injustice, especially the injustice that permeates the mechanisms of our unjust world.

Not only individual persons and civil powers violate the most basic human rights; there are also various forms of collective violence like discrimination against individuals and groups and physical and psychological torture. The evil is not only personal and social, but cultural, that is to say, it has impregnated the mental and symbolic structures of groups to such a degree that even well-intentioned persons are guilty of this violence without even being aware that they are doing wrong. This collective sin of social blindness to the violence inflicted upon the "lesser" groups is one of the great sins of our contemporary society.

In order that human beings might be respected, the Church must evangelize, "so that the Lord may transform hearts and humanize political and economic systems, with the responsible commitment of human beings as the starting point" (III,5). In order to bring this about, pastoral commitments in this field must be encouraged "through a correct Christian conception of liberation." This liberation begins when we recognize that God is our Father and hence all men and women are our brothers and sisters. This experience of love urges us toward fellowship that overcomes "the forms of bondage and idols fashioned by human beings" and allows the growth of the new human being to take place (III,6). This liberation will free men and women so that they may participate freely and without coercion in the structures that govern their lives (III,1). It is liberation from everything that oppresses people. This correct idea of Christian liberation will be developed very carefully in the Final Document of Puebla in nos. 321–29.

To safeguard the originality of Christian liberation, we must be, on the level of content, faithful to the word of God, to the Church's living tradition, and to its magisterium. On the level of attitudes, we must be in communion with the bishops and with the other sectors of the People of God, contributing to the build-up of the community; we must lovingly care for the poor, the sick, the dispossessed, the neglected, and the oppressed, seeing in them the image of the poor and suffering Jesus and striving to serve Christ in them (III,6; LG:8). This multiple unity is presented by the pope as a visible sign of orthodoxy that helps us to distinguish true Christian liberation from one based on ideologies. Just as those who struggle for justice must stay in communion with the Church, so the Church, and especially the officials, must be in loving communion with the victims of injustice. It is easy to see what happens when people separate themselves from the Church, but what happens when the Church, especially the officials, separates itself from the struggles of the dispossessed? Can one remain in visible communion with those on the top but not with those at the bottom? Does separation from the dispossessed who are struggling to build more human communities constitute a type of schism?

To carry out this all-important task, the Church must be involved in the formation of the social consciousness of the people, basing this formation upon the Church's social teachings. The ministry of the laity should not be limited simply to helping in specifically church work, but rather should include the entire work of building up the new civilization. The actual transformation of the various structures of society is the proper and privileged ministry of the laity.

Priority Tasks and Conclusion

Finally, in Part IV of the address, the pope concludes with some specific priority tasks that are of immediate concern—the family, priestly and religious vocations, and youth. These must not be treated as isolated topics, but in the context of the total reality of Latin America.

He concludes with the challenge of Christian faith: "The future is in God's hands. But somehow God is also placing the future of a new evangelization impetus in your hands." Faith in God demands a faith in humanity and in ourselves who are the image and children of God—especially when we are bringing order out of chaos, freedom out of enslavement, and life out of death.

POPE JOHN PAUL II:
OPENING ADDRESS
AT THE PUEBLA CONFERENCE

Delivered in the Seminario Palafoxiano,
Puebla de los Angeles, Mexico,
on 28 January 1979

Beloved brothers in the episcopate:

This hour that I have the happiness to experience with you is certainly a historic one for the Church in Latin America. World opinion is aware of this; so are the faithful members of your local Churches; and you yourselves, in particular, are aware of it because you will be the protagonists and responsible leaders of this hour.

It is also an hour of grace marked by the passing by of the Lord, by a very special presence and activity of God's Spirit. For this reason we have confidently invoked this Spirit as we begin our labors. For this reason also I now want to make the following plea, speaking to you as a brother to his very beloved brothers: all the days of this conference and in every one of its proceedings, let yourselves be led by the Spirit; open up to the Spirit's inspiration and impulse; let it be that Spirit and none other that guides and strengthens you.

Under the guidance of this Spirit, for the third time in the last twenty-five years you are coming together as bishops. You have come here from every country of Latin America, as representatives of the whole Latin American episcopate, to study more deeply as a group the meaning of your mission in the face of the new exigencies of your peoples.

The conference now opening was convoked by our revered Paul VI, confirmed by my unforgettable predecessor, John Paul I, and reconfirmed by me as one of the first acts of my pontificate. It is linked with the already distant conference held in Rio de Janeiro, whose most noteworthy result was the foundation of CELAM. And it is even more closely linked with your second conference in Medellín, marking its tenth anniversary.

How far humanity has travelled in those ten years! How far the Church has travelled in those ten years in the company and service of humanity! This third conference cannot disregard that fact. So it will have to take Medellín's conclusions as its point of departure, with all the positive elements contained therein, but without disregarding the incorrect interpretations that have sometimes resulted and that call for calm discernment, opportune criticism, and clear-cut stances.

In your debates you will find guidance in the working draft, which was drawn up with great care so that it might serve as a constant point of reference.

But you will also have in your hands Paul VI's Apostolic Exhortation entitled *Evangelii Nuntiandi*. How pleased and delighted that great pontiff was to give his approval to the theme of your conference: "Evangelization in Latin America's Present and Future."

Those close to him during the months when this meeting was being prepared can tell you this. They can also tell you how grateful he was when he learned that the scenario for this whole conference would be that text, into whch he poured his whole pastoral soul as his life drew to a close. And now that he "has closed his eyes on this world's scene" (Testament of Paul VI), his document becomes a spiritual testament. Your conference will have to scrutinize it lovingly and diligently, making it one of your obligatory touchstones and trying to discover how you can put it into practice. The whole Church owes you a debt of gratitude for what you are doing, for the example you are giving. Perhaps other local Churches will take up that example.

The pope chooses to be with you at the start of your labors, grateful for the gift of being allowed to be with you at yesterday's solemn Mass under the maternal gaze of the Virgin of Guadalupe, and also at this morning's Mass; because "every worthwhile gift, every genuine benefit comes from above, descending from the Father of the heavenly luminaries" (James 1:17). I would very much like to stay with you in prayer, reflection, and work. Be assured that I shall stay with you in spirit while "my anxiety for all the churches" (2 Cor. 11:28) calls me elsewhere. But before I continue my pastoral visit through Mexico and then return to Rome, I want at least to leave you with a few words as a pledge of my spiritual presence. They are uttered with all the concern of a pastor and all the affection of a father. They echo my main preoccupations concerning the theme you are dealing with and the life of the Church in these beloved countries.

I. TEACHERS OF THE TRUTH

It is a great consolation for the universal Pastor to see that you come together here, not as a symposium of experts or a parliament of politicians or a congress of scientists or technologists (however important such meetings may be), but rather as a fraternal gathering of church pastors. As pastors, you keenly realize that your chief duty is to be teachers of the truth: not of a human, rational truth but of the truth that comes from God. That truth includes the principle of authentic human liberation: "You will know the truth, and the truth will set you free" (John 8:32). It is the one and only truth that offers a solid basis for an adequate "praxis."

I,1. Carefully watching over purity of doctrine, basic in building up the Christian community, is therefore the primary and irreplaceable duty of the pastor, of the teacher of faith—in conjunction with the proclamation of the Gospel. How often this was emphasized by St. Paul, who was convinced of the seriousness of carrying out this obligation (1 Tim. 1:3–7; 1:18–20; 1:11–16; 2 Tim. 1:4–14)! Besides oneness in charity, oneness in truth ever remains an urgent demand upon us. In his Apostolic Exhortation *Evangelii Nuntiandi*, our very beloved Paul VI put it this way: "The Gospel that has been entrusted to us is the word of truth. This truth sets us free, and it alone provides peace of heart. It is what people are looking for when we announce the Good News. The truth about God, the truth about human beings and their mysterious destiny, the truth about the world. . . . The preacher of the Gospel will be someone who, even at the cost of renunciation and sacrifice, is always seeking the truth to be transmitted to others. Such a person never betrays or misrepresents the truth out of a desire to please people, to astonish or shock people, to display originality, or to strike a pose. . . . We are pastors of the People of God; our pastoral service bids us to preserve, defend, and communicate the truth, whatever sacrifices may be entailed" (EN:78).

The Truth about Jesus Christ

I,2. From you, pastors, the faithful of your countries expect and demand first and foremost a careful and zealous transmission of the truth about Jesus Christ. This truth is at the core of evangelization and constitutes its essential content: "There is no authentic evangelization so long as one does not announce the name, the teaching, the life, the promises, the Kingdom, the mystery of Jesus of Nazareth, the Son of God" (EN:22).

The vigor of the faith of millions of people will depend on a lively knowledge of this truth. On such knowledge will also depend the strength of their adhesion to the Church and their active presence as Christians in the world. From it will flow options, values, attitudes, and behavior patterns that can give direction and definition to our Christian living, that can create new human beings and then a new humanity through the conversion of the individual and social conscience (EN:18).

It is from a solid Christology that light must be shed on so many of the doctrinal and pastoral themes and questions that you propose to examine in the coming days.

I,3. So we must profess Christ before history and the world, displaying the same deeply felt and deeply lived conviction that Peter did in his profession: "You are the Messiah, . . . the Son of the living God" (Matt. 16:16).

This is the Good News, unique in a real sense. The Church lives by it and for it, even as the Church draws from it all that it has to offer to all human beings, regardless of nation, culture, race, epoch, age, or condition. Hence "on the basis of that profession [Peter's], the history of sacred salvation and of the People of God should take on a new dimension" (John Paul II, Inaugural homily of his pontificate, 22 October 1978).

This is the one and only Gospel. And as the apostle wrote so pointedly, "Even if we, or an angel from heaven, should preach to you a gospel not in accord with the one we delivered to you, let a curse be upon him" (Gal. 1:8).

I,4. Now today we find in many places a phenomenon that is not new. We find "re-readings" of the Gospel that are the product of theoretical speculations rather than of authentic meditation on the word of God and a genuine evangelical commitment. They cause confusion insofar as they depart from the central criteria of the Church's faith, and people have the temerity to pass them on as catechesis to Christian communities.

In some cases people are silent about Christ's divinity, or else they indulge in types of interpretation that are at variance with the Church's faith. Christ is alleged to be only a "prophet," a proclaimer of God's Kingdom and love, but not the true Son of God. Hence he allegedly is not the center and object of the gospel message itself.

In other cases people purport to depict Jesus as a political activist, as a fighter against Roman domination and the authorities, and even as someone involved in the class struggle. This conception of Christ as a political figure, a revolutionary, as the subversive from Nazareth, does not tally with the Church's catechesis. Confusing the insidious pretext of Jesus' accusers with the attitude of Jesus himself—which was very different—people claim that the cause of his death was the result of a political conflict; they say nothing about the Lord's willing self-surrender or even his awareness of his redemptive mission. The Gospels show clearly that for Jesus anything that would alter his mission as the Servant of Yahweh was a temptation (Matt. 4:8; Luke 4:5). He does not accept the position of those who mixed the things of God with merely political attitudes (Matt. 22:21; Mark 12:17; John 18:36). He unequivocally rejects recourse to violence. He opens his message of conversion to all, and he does not exclude even the publicans. The perspective of his mission goes much deeper. It has to do with complete and integral salvation through a love that brings transformation, peace, pardon, and reconciliation. And there can be no doubt that all this imposes exacting demands on the attitude of any Christians who truly wish to serve the least of their brothers and sisters, the poor, the needy, the marginalized: i.e., all those whose lives reflect the suffering countenance of the Lord (LG:8).

I,5. Against such "re-readings," therefore, and against the perhaps brilliant but fragile and inconsistent hypotheses flowing from them, "evangelization in Latin America's present and future" cannot cease to affirm the Church's faith: Jesus Christ, the Word and Son of God, becomes human to draw close to human beings and to offer them, through the power of his mystery, the great gift of God that is salvation (EN:19,27).

This is the faith that has informed your history, that has shaped what is best in the values of your peoples, and that must continue to animate the dynamics of their future in the most energetic terms. This is the faith that reveals the vocation to concord and unity that must banish the danger of warfare from this continent of hope, a continent in which the Church has been such a potent force for integration. This, in short, is the faith that has found such lively and varied expression among the faithful of Latin America in their religiosity or popular piety.

Rooted in this faith in Christ and in the bosom of the Church, we are capable of serving human beings and our peoples, of penetrating their culture with the Gospel, of transforming hearts, and of humanizing systems and structures.

Any form of silence, disregard, mutilation, or inadequate emphasis on the whole of the mystery of Jesus Christ that diverges from the Church's faith cannot be the valid content of evangelization. "Today, under the pretext of a piety that is false, under the deceptive appearance of a preaching of the gospel message, some people are trying to deny the Lord Jesus," wrote a great bishop in the midst of the hard crises of the fourth century. And he added: "I speak the truth, so that the cause of the confusion that we are suffering may be known to all. I cannot keep silent" (St. Hilary of Poitiers, *Ad Auxentium*, 1–4). Nor can you, the bishops of today, keep silent when this confusion occurs.

This is what Pope Paul VI recommended in his opening address at the Medellín Conference: "Speak, speak, preach, write, take a position, as is said, united in plan and intention, for the defense and elucidation of the truths of the faith, on the relevance of the Gospel, on the questions that interest the life of the faithful and the defense of Christian conduct. . . ."

To fulfill my duty to evangelize all of humanity, I myself will never tire of repeating: "Do not be afraid. Open wide the doors for Christ. To his saving power open the boundaries of State, economic and political systems, the vast fields of culture, civilization, and development" (John Paul II, Inaugural homily of his pontificate, 22 October, 1978).

The Truth about the Church's Mission

I,6. As teachers of the truth, you are expected to proclaim unceasingly, but with special vigor at this moment, the truth about the mission of the Church, an object of the Creed we profess and a basic, indispensable area of our fidelity. The Lord instituted the Church "as a fellowship of life, charity, and truth" (LG:9); as the body, *pleroma*, and sacrament of Christ, in whom dwells the fullness of divinity (LG:7).

The Church is born of our response in faith to Christ. In fact it is by sincere acceptance of the Good News that we believers gather together "in Jesus' name to seek the Kingdom together, build it up, and live it" (EN:13). The Church is the gathering together of "all those who in faith look upon Jesus as the author of salvation and the source of unity and peace" (LG:9).

But on the other hand we are born of the Church. It communicates to us the riches of life and grace entrusted to it. The Church begets us by baptism, nourishes us with the sacraments and the Word of God, prepares us for our mission, and leads us to God's plan—the reason for our existence as Christians. We are the Church's children. With just pride we call the Church our Mother, repeating a title that has come down to us through the centuries from the earliest days (Henri de Lubac, *Méditation sur l'Eglise*, p. 211ff.).

So we must invoke the Church, respect it, and serve it because "one cannot have God for one's Father if one does not have the Church for one's Mother" (St. Cyprian, *De catholicae ecclesiae unitate*, 6, 8). After all, "how can one possibly love Christ without loving the Church, since the most beautiful testimony to Christ is the following statement of St. Paul: 'He loved the Church and gave himself up for it'?" (EN:16). Or, as St. Augustine puts it: "One possesses the Holy Spirit to the extent that one loves the Church of Christ" (*In Ioannis evangelium*, Tractatus, 32, 8).

Love for the Church must be composed of fidelity and trust. In the first address of my pontificate, I stressed my desire to be faithful to Vatican II, and my resolve to focus my greatest concern on the area of ecclesiology. I invited all to take up once again the Dogmatic Constitution *Lumen Gentium* and "to ponder with renewed earnestness the nature and mission of the Church, its way of existing and operating, . . . not only to achieve that communion of life in Christ among all those who believe and hope in him, but also to help broaden and tighten the oneness of the whole human family" (John Paul II, Message to the Church and the World, 17 October 1978).

Now, at this critical moment in the evangelization of Latin America, I repeat my invitation: "Adherence to this conciliar document, which reflects the light of tradition and contains the dogmatic formulas enunciated a century ago by Vatican I, will provide all of us, both pastors and faithful, a sure pathway and a constant incentive—to say it once again—to tread the byways of life and history" (ibid.).

I,7. Without a well-grounded ecclesiology, we have no guarantee of a serious and vigorous evangelizing activity.

This is so, first of all, because evangelizing is the essential mission, the specific vocation, the innermost identity of the Church, which has been evangelized in turn (EN:14–15; LG:5). Sent out by the Lord, the Church in turn sends out evangelizers to preach "not themselves or their personal ideas, but a Gospel that neither they nor the Church own as their own absolute property, to dispose of as they may see fit . . ." (EN:15). This is so, in the second place, because "for no one is evangelizing an isolated, individual act; rather, it is a profoundly ecclesial action, . . . an action of the Church" (EN:60). Far from being subject to the discretionary authority of individualistic criteria and perspectives, it stands "in communion with the Church and its pastors" (EN:60). Hence a correct vision of the Church is indispensable for a correct view of evangelization.

How could there be any authentic evangelization in the absence of prompt, sincere respect for the sacred magisterium, a respect based on the clear realization that in submitting to it, the People of God are not accepting the word of human beings but the authentic word of God? (1 Thess. 2:13; LG:12). "The 'objective' importance of this magisterium must be kept in mind and defended against the insidious attacks that now appear here and there against some of the solid truths of our Catholic faith" (John Paul II, Message to the Church and the World, 17 October 1978).

I am well aware of your attachment and availability to the See of Peter and of the love you have always shown it. In the Lord's name I express my heartfelt thanks for the deeply ecclesial outlook implied in that, and I wish you yourselves the consolation of counting on the loyal adherence of your faithful.

I,8. In the abundant documentation that went into the preparation of this conference, and particularly in the contributions of many Churches, one sometimes notices a certain uneasiness in interpreting the nature and mission of the Church. Allusion is made, for example, to the separation that some set up between the Church and the Kingdom of God. Emptied of its full content, the Kingdom of God is understood in a rather secularist sense: i.e., we do not arrive at the Kingdom through faith and membership in the Church but rather merely by structural change and sociopolitical involvement. Where there is a certain kind of commitment and praxis for justice, there the Kingdom is already present. This view forgets that "the Church . . . receives the mission to proclaim and to establish among all peoples the kingdom of Christ and of God. She becomes on earth the initial budding forth of that kingdom" (LG:5).

In one of his beautiful catechetical instructions, Pope John Paul I alludes to the virtue of hope. Then he says: "By contrast, it is a mistake to state that political, economic, and social liberation coincide with salvation in Jesus Christ; that the *regnum Dei* is identified with the *regnum hominis*" (John Paul I, Catechetical Lesson on the Theological Virtue of Hope, 20 September 1978).

In some instances an attitude of mistrust is fostered toward the "institutional" or "official" Church, which is described as alienating. Over against it is set another, people's Church, one which "is born of the people" and is fleshed out in the poor. These positions could contain varying and not always easily measurable degrees of familiar ideological forms of conditioning. The Council has called our attention to the exact nature and mission of the Church. It has reminded us of the contribution made to its deeper oneness and its ongoing construction by those whose task is to minister to the community and who must count on the collaboration of all the People of God. But let us face the fact: "If the Gospel proclaimed by us seems to be rent by doctrinal disputes, ideological polarizations, or mutual condemnations among Christians, if it is at the mercy of their differing views about Christ and the Church, and even of their differing conceptions of human society and its institutions, . . . how can those to whom we address our preaching fail to be disturbed, disoriented, and even scandalized?" (EN:77).

The Truth about Human Beings

I,9. The truth we owe to human beings is, first and foremost, a truth about themselves. As witnesses to Jesus Christ, we are heralds, spokesmen, and servants of this truth. We cannot reduce it to the principles of some philosophical system, or to mere political activity. We cannot forget it or betray it.

Perhaps one of the most glaring weaknesses of present-day civilization lies in an inadequate view of the human being. Undoubtedly our age is the age that has written and spoken the most about the human being; it is the age of various humanisms, the age of anthropocentrism. But paradoxically it is also the age of people's deepest anxieties about their identity and destiny; it is the age when human beings have been debased to previously unsuspected levels, when human values have been trodden underfoot as never before.

How do we explain this paradox? We can say that it is the inexorable paradox of atheistic humanism. It is the drama of people severed from an essential dimension of their being—the Absolute—and thus confronted with the worst possible diminution of their being. *Gaudium et Spes* goes to the heart of the problem when it says: "Only in the mystery of the incarnate Word does the mystery of man take on light" (GS:22).

Thanks to the Gospel, the Church possesses the truth about the human being. It is found in an anthropology that the Church never ceases to explore more deeply and to share. The primordial assertion of this anthropology is that the human being is the image of God and cannot be reduced to a mere fragment of nature or to an anonymous element in the human city (GS:12,14). This is the sense intended by St. Irenaeus when he wrote: "The glory of the human being is God; but the receptacle of all God's activity, wisdom, and power is the human being" (St. Irenaeus, *Adversus haereses*, III, 20, 2–3).

I made especially pointed reference to this irreplaceable foundation of the Christian conception of the human being in my Christmas Message: "Christmas is the feast of the human being. . . . Viewed in quantitative terms, the human being is an object of calculation. . . . But at the same time the human being is single, unique, and unrepeatable, someone thought of and chosen from eternity, someone called and identified by name" (John Paul II, Christmas Message, 25 December 1978).

Faced with many other forms of humanism, which frequently are locked into a strictly economic, biological, or psychological view of the human being, the Church has the right and the duty to proclaim the truth about the human being that it received from its teacher, Jesus Christ. God grant that no external coercion will prevent the Church from doing so. But above all, God grant that the Church itself will not fail to do so out of fear or doubt, or because it has let itself be contaminated by other brands of humanism, or for lack of confidence in its original message.

So when a pastor of the Church clearly and unambiguously announces the truth about the human being, which was revealed by him who knew "what was in man's heart" (John 2:25), he should be encouraged by the certainty that he is rendering the best service to human beings.

This complete truth about human beings is the basis of the Church's social teaching, even as it is the basis of authentic liberation. In the light of this truth we see that human beings are not the pawns of economic or political processes, that instead these processes are geared toward human beings and subject to them.

I have no doubt that this truth about human beings, as taught by the Church, will emerge strengthened from this pastoral meeting.

II. SIGNS AND BUILDERS OF UNITY

Your pastoral service to the truth is complemented by a like service to unity.

Unity among the Bishops

II,1. First of all, it will be a unity among you yourselves, the bishops. As one bishop, St. Cyprian, put it in an era when communion among the bishops of his country was greatly threatened: "We must guard and maintain this unity . . . we bishops, in particular, who preside over the Church, so that we may bear witness to the fact that the episcopate is one and indivisible. Let no one mislead the faithful or alter the truth. The episcopate is one . . ." (St. Cyprian, *De catholicae ecclesiae unitate*, 6, 8).

This episcopal unity does not come from human calculation or maneuvering, but from on high: from service to one single Lord, from the inspiration of one single Spirit, from love for one and the same unique Church. It is the unity resulting from the mission that Christ has entrusted to us. Here on the Latin American continent that mission has been going on for almost half a millennium. Today you are boldly carrying it on in an age of profound transformations, as we approach the close of the second millennium of redemption and ecclesial activity. It is unity centered around the Gospel of the body and blood of the Lamb, of Peter living in his successors; all of these are different but important signs of Jesus' presence in our midst.

What an obligation you have, dear brothers, to live this pastoral unity at this conference! The conference itself is a sign and fruit of the unity that already exists; but it is also a foretaste and anticipation of what should be an even more intimate and solid unity! So begin your labors in an atmosphere of fraternal unity. Even now let this unity be a component of evangelization.

Unity with Priests, Religious, and the Faithful

II,2. Unity among the bishops finds its extension in unity with priests, religious, and the faithful laity. Priests are the immediate collaborators of the bishops in their pastoral mission. This mission would be compromised if close unity did not exist between priests and their bishops.

Men and women religious are also particularly important subjects of that unity. I know well how important their contribution to evangelization has been, and continues to be, in Latin America. They arrived here in the dawning light of discovery, and they were here when almost all your countries were taking their first steps. They have labored here continually by the side of the diocesan clergy. In some countries more than half of your priests are religious; in others the vast majority are. This alone indicates how important it is here, even more than in other parts of the world, for religious to not only accept but loyally strive for an indissoluble unity of outlook and action with their bishops. To the bishops the Lord entrusted the mission of feeding the flock. To religious belongs the task of blazing the trail for evangelization. Bishops cannot and should not fail to have the collaboration of religious, whose charism makes them all the more available as agents in the service of the Gospel. And their collaboration must be not only active and responsible, but also docile and trusting. In this connection a heavy obligation weighs on everyone in the ecclesial community to avoid parallel magisteria, which are ecclesially unacceptable and pastorally sterile.

Lay people are also subjects of this unity, whether involved as individuals or joined in organs of the apostolate for the spread of God's Kingdom. It is they who must consecrate the world to Christ in the midst of their day-to-day tasks and in their varied family and professional functions, maintaining close union with, and obedience to, their legitimate pastors.

This precious gift of ecclesial unity must be safeguarded among all those who are part of the wayfaring People of God, in line with what *Lumen Gentium* said.

III. DEFENDERS AND PROMOTERS OF HUMAN DIGNITY

III,1. Those familiar with the history of the Church know that in every age there have been admirable bishops deeply involved in the valiant defense of the human dignity of those entrusted to them by the Lord. Their activity was always mandated by their episcopal mission, because they regarded human dignity as a gospel value that cannot be despised without greatly offending the Creator.

On the level of the individual, this dignity is crushed underfoot when due regard is not maintained for such values as freedom, the right to profess one's religion, physical and psychic integrity, the right to life's necessities, and the right to life itself. On the social and political level it is crushed when human beings cannot exercise their right to participate, when they are subjected to unjust and illegitimate forms of coercion, when they are subjected to physical and psychic torture, and so forth.

I am not unaware of the many problems in this area that are being faced in Latin America today. As bishops, you cannot fail to concern yourselves with them. I know that you propose to reflect seriously on the relationships and implications existing between evangelization and human promotion or liberation, focusing on the specific nature of the Church's presence in this broad and important area.

Here is where we come to the concrete, practical application of the themes we have touched upon in talking about the truth about Christ, about the Church, and about the human being.

III,2. If the Church gets involved in defending or promoting human dignity, it does so in accordance with its mission. For even though that mission is religious in character, and not social or political, it cannot help but consider human persons in terms of their whole being. In the parable of the Good Samaritan, the Lord outlined the model way of attending to all human needs (Luke 10:30ff.); and he said that in the last analysis he will identify himself with the disinherited—the imprisoned, the hungry, and the abandoned—to whom we have offered a helping hand (Matt. 25:31ff.). In these and other passages of the Gospel (Mark 6:35–44), the Church has learned that an indispensable part of its evangelizing mission is made up of works on behalf of justice and human promotion (see the Final Document of the Synod of Bishops, October 1971). It has learned that evangelization and human promotion are linked together by very strong ties of an anthropological, theological, and charitable nature (EN:31). Thus "evangelization would not be complete if it did not take into account the mutual interaction that takes hold in the course of time between the Gospel and the concrete personal and social life of the human being" (EN:29).

Let us also keep in mind that the Church's activity in such areas as human promotion, development, justice, and human rights is always intended to be in the service of the human being, the human being as seen by the Church in the Christian framework of the anthropology it adopts. The Church therefore does not need to have recourse to ideological systems in order to love, defend, and collaborate in the liberation of the human being. At the center of the message of which the Church is the trustee and herald, it finds inspiration for acting in favor of brotherhood, justice, and peace; and against all forms of domination, slavery, discrimination, violence, attacks on religious liberty, and aggression against human beings and whatever attacks life (GS:26,27,29).

III,3. It is therefore not out of opportunism or a thirst for novelty that the Church, the "expert in humanity" (Paul VI, Address to the United Nations, 5 October 1965) defends human rights. It is prompted by an authentically evangelical commitment which, like that of Christ, is primarily a commitment to those most in need.

In fidelity to this commitment, the Church wishes to maintain its freedom with regard to the opposing systems, in order to opt solely for the human being. Whatever the miseries or sufferings that afflict human beings, it is not through violence, power-plays, or political systems but through the truth about human beings that they will find their way to a better future.

III,4. From this arises the Church's constant preoccupation with the delicate question of property ownership. One proof of this is to be found in the writings of the Church Fathers during the first thousand years of Christianity's existence (St. Ambrose, *de Nabuthae*, c. 12, n. 53). It is demonstrated by the vigorous and oft reiterated teaching of St. Thomas Aquinas. In our day the Church has appealed to the same principles in such far-reaching documents as the social encyclicals of the recent popes. Pope Paul VI spoke out on this matter with particular force and profundity in his encyclical *Populorum Progressio* (PP:23–24; MM:104–15).

This voice of the Church, echoing the voice of the human conscience, did not cease to make itself heard down through the centuries, amid the most varied sociocultural systems and circumstances. It deserves and needs to be heard in our age as well, when the growing affluence of a few people parallels the growing poverty of the masses.

It is then that the Church's teaching, which says that there is a *social mortgage* on all private property, takes on an urgent character. Insofar as this teaching is concerned, the Church has a mission to fulfill. It must preach, educate persons and groups, shape public opinion, and give direction to national officials. In so doing, it will be working for the good of society. Eventually this Christian, evangelical principle will lead to a more just and equitable distribution of goods, not only within each nation but also in the wide world as a whole. And this will prevent the stronger countries from using their power to the detriment of the weaker ones.

Those in charge of the public life of States and nations will have to realize that internal and international peace will be assured only when a social and economic system based on justice takes effect.

Christ did not remain indifferent in the face of this vast and demanding imperative of social morality. Neither could the Church. In the spirit of the Church, which is the spirit of Christ, and supported by its ample, solid teaching, let us get back to work in this field.

Here I must once again emphasize that the Church's concern is for the whole human being.

Thus an indispensable condition for a just economic system is that it foster the growth and spread of public education and culture. The juster an economy is, the deeper will be its cultural awareness. This is very much in line with the view of Vatican II: i.e., that to achieve a life worthy of a human being, one cannot limit oneself to *having more;* one must strive to *be more* (GS:35).

So drink at these authentic fonts, Brothers. Speak in the idiom of Vatican II, John XXIII, and Paul VI. For that is the idiom that embodies the experience, the suffering, and the hope of contemporary humanity.

When Paul VI declared that development is the new name for peace (PP:76–79), he was thinking of all the ties of interdependence existing, not only within nations, but also between them on a worldwide scale. He took into consideration the mechanisms that are imbued with materialism rather than authentic humanism, and that therefore lead on the international level to the ever increasing wealth of the rich at the expense of the ever increasing poverty of the poor.

There is no economic norm that can change those mechanisms in and by itself. In international life, too, one must appeal to the principles of ethics, the exigencies of justice, and the primary commandment of love. Primacy must be given to that which is moral, to that which is spiritual, to that which flows from the full truth about the human being.

I wanted to voice these reflections to you, since I regard them as very important; but they should not distract you from the central theme of this conference. We will reach human beings, we will reach justice through evangelization.

III,5. In the light of what has been said above, the Church is profoundly grieved to see "the sometimes massive increase in violations of human rights in many parts of the world. . . . Who can deny that today there are individual persons and civil authorities who are violating fundamental rights of the human person with impunity? I refer to such rights as the right to be born; the right to life; the right to responsible procreation; the right to work; the right to peace, freedom, and social justice; and the right to participate in making decisions that affect peoples and nations. And what are we to say when we run up against various forms of collective violence, such as racial discrimination against individuals and groups and the physical and psychological torturing of prisoners and political dissidents? The list grows when we add examples of abduction and of kidnapping for the sake of material gain, which represent such a traumatic attack on family life and the social fabric" (John Paul II, Message to the United Nations, 2 December 1978). We cry out once more: Respect the human being, who is the image of God! Evangelize so that this may become a reality, so that the Lord may transform hearts and humanize political and economic systems, with the responsible commitment of human beings as the starting point!

III,6. Pastoral commitments in this field must be nurtured with a correct Christian conception of liberation. "The Church . . . has the duty of proclaiming the liberation of millions of human beings, . . . the duty of helping to bring about this liberation" (EN:30). But it also has the corresponding duty of proclaiming liberation in its deeper, fuller sense, the sense proclaimed and realized by Jesus (EN:31ff). That fuller liberation is "liberation from everything that oppresses human beings, but especially liberation from sin and the evil one, in the joy of knowing God and being known by him" (EN:9). It is liberation made up of reconciliation and forgiveness. It is liberation rooted in the fact of being the children of God, whom we are now able to call Abba, Father! (Rom. 8:15). It is liberation that enables us to recognize all human beings as our brothers or sisters, as people whose hearts can be transformed by God's mercifulness. It is liberation that pushes us, with all the force of love, toward communion; and we find the fullness and culmination of that communion in the Lord. It is liberation as the successful conquest of the forms of bondage and idols fashioned by human beings, as the growth and flowering of the new human being.

It is a liberation that, in the framework of the Church's specific mission, "cannot be reduced simply to the restricted domain of economics, politics, society, or culture, . . . can never be sacrificed to the requirements of some particular strategy, some short-term praxis or gain" (EN:33).

If we are to safeguard the originality of Christian liberation and the energies that it is capable of releasing, we must at all costs avoid reductionism and ambiguity. As Paul VI pointed out: "The Church would lose its innermost meaning. Its message of liberation would have nothing original, and it would lend itself to ready manipulation and expropriation by ideological systems and political parties" (EN:32). There are many signs that help us to distinguish when the liberation in question is Christian and when, on the other hand, it is based on ideologies that make it inconsistent with an evangelical view of humanity, of things, and of events (EN:35). These signs derive from the content that the evangelizers proclaim or from the concrete attitudes that they adopt. At the level of content one must consider how faithful they are to the Word of God, to the Church's living tradition, and to its magisterium. As for attitudes, one must consider what sense of communion they feel, with the bishops first of all, and then with the other sectors of God's People. Here one must also consider what contribution they make to the real building up of the community; how they channel their love into caring for the poor, the sick, the dispossessed, the neglected, and the oppressed; and how, discovering in these people the image of the poor and suffering Jesus, they strive to alleviate their needs and to serve Christ in them (LG:8). Let us make no mistake about it: as if by some evangelical instinct, the humble and simple faithful spontaneously sense when the Gospel is being served in the Church and when it is being eviscerated and asphyxiated by other interests.

As you see, the whole set of observations on the theme of liberation that were made by *Evangelii Nuntiandi* retain their full validity.

III,7. All that we have recalled above constitutes a rich and complex heritage, which *Evangelii Nuntiandi* calls the social doctrine, or social teaching, of the Church (EN:38). This teaching comes into being, in the light of God's Word and the authentic magisterium, from the presence of Christians in the midst of the world's changing situations and their contact with the resultant challenges. So this social doctrine entails not only principles for reflection but also norms for judgment and guidelines for action (OA:4).

To place responsible confidence in this social doctrine, even though some people try to sow doubts and lack of confidence in it; to study it seriously; to try to apply it; to teach it and to be loyal to it: in children of the Church, all this guarantees the authenticity of their involvement in delicate and demanding social tasks, and of their efforts on behalf of the liberation or advancement of their fellow human beings.

Permit me, then, to commend to your special pastoral attention the urgency of making your faithful aware of the Church's social doctrine.

Particular care must be devoted to forming a social conscience at all levels and in all sectors. When injustices increase and the gap between rich and poor widens distressingly, then the social doctrine of the Church—in a form that is creative and open to the broad areas of the Church's presence—should be a valuable tool for formation and action. This holds true for the laity in particular: "Secular duties and activities belong properly, although not exclusively, to laymen" (GS:43). It is necessary to avoid supplanting the laity, and to study seriously just when certain ways of substituting for them retain their *raison d'être*. Is it not the laity who are called, by virtue of their vocation in the Church, to make their contribution in the political and economic areas, and to be effectively present in the safeguarding and advancing of human rights?

IV. SOME PRIORITY TASKS

You are going to consider many pastoral topics of great importance. Time prevents me from mentioning them. I have referred to some, or will do so, in my meetings with priests, religious, seminarians, and lay people.

For various reasons, the topics I mention here are of great importance. You will not fail to consider them, among the many others your pastoral perspicacity will indicate to you.

a. The family: Make every effort to ensure that there is pastoral care for the family. Attend to this area of such priority importance, certain that evangelization in the future depends largely on the "domestic Church." The family is the school of love, of knowledge of God, of respect for life and human dignity. This pastoral field is all the more important because the family is the object of so many threats. Think of the campaigns advocating divorce, the use of contraceptives, and abortion, which destroy society.

b. Priestly and religious vocations: Despite an encouraging revival of vocations, the lack of vocations is a grave and chronic problem in most of your countries. There is an immense disproportion between the growing number of inhabitants and the number of workers engaged in evangelization. This is of immeasurable importance to the Christian community. Every community must acquire its vocations, just as a proof of its vitality and maturity. An intensive pastoral effort must be reactivated. Starting off from the Christian vocation in general and an enthusiastic pastoral effort among young people, such an effort will give the Church the servants it needs. Lay vocations, indispensable as they are, cannot be a satisfactory compensation. What is more, one of the proofs of the laity's commitment is the abundance of vocations to the consecrated life.

c. Young people: How much hope the Church places in them! How much energy needed by the Church circulates through young people in Latin America! How close we pastors must be to young people, so that Christ and the Church and brotherly love may penetrate deeply into their hearts!

V. CONCLUSION

Closing this message, I cannot fail to call down once again the protection of the Mother of God upon your persons and your work during these days. The fact that this meeting of ours is taking place in the spiritual presence of Our Lady of Guadalupe—who is venerated in Mexico and in all other countries as the mother of the Church in Latin America—is a cause of joy and a source of hope for me. May she, the "star of evangelization," be your guide in the reflections you make and the decisions you arrive at. From her divine Son may she obtain for you:

— the boldness of prophets and the evangelical prudence of pastors;
— the clearsightedness of teachers and the confident certainty of guides and directors;

— courage as witnesses, and the calmness, patience, and gentleness of fathers.

May the Lord bless your labors. You are accompanied by select representatives: priests, deacons, men and women religious, lay people, experts, and observers. Their collaboration will be very useful to you. The eyes of the whole Church are on you, in confidence and hope. You intend to measure up to their expectations, in full fidelity to Christ, the Church, and humanity. The future is in God's hands. But somehow God is also placing the future of a new evangelization impetus in your hands: "Go, therefore, and make disciples of all nations" (Matt. 28:19).

POPE JOHN PAUL II:
HOMILY AT THE BASILICA OF GUADALUPE

This homily was delivered in the Basilica of Our Lady of Guadalupe in Mexico City, on 27 January 1979, during a Mass concelebrated with participants in the Puebla Conference.

1. Hail, Mary!

Dear Brothers in the episcopate and well beloved children, how deep is my joy that the first steps of my pilgrimage, as the successor of Paul VI and John Paul I, bring me to this place precisely. They bring me to you, Mary, in this sanctuary of the people of Mexico and all Latin America, where you have already manifested your maternity for so many centuries.

Hail, Mary!

It is with great love and reverence that I utter those words, which are at once so simple and so marvelous. No one could ever offer you a more stupendous salutation than the one that the archangel offered you at the moment of the Annunciation. *Ave Maria, gratia plena, Dominus tecum*. I repeat those words that are cherished in so many hearts and pronounced by so many lips around the world. Those of us present here repeat it in unison, realizing that these are the very words with which God himself greeted you through his messenger. You are the woman promised in Eden, the woman chosen from eternity to be the Mother of the Word, the Mother of divine Wisdom, the Mother of the Son of God.

Hail, Mother of God!

2. Your son, Jesus Christ, is our Redeemer and Lord. He is our Teacher. All of us gathered here are his disciples. We are the successors of the apostles, of those to whom the Lord said: "Go, therefore, and make disciples of all the nations. Baptize them in the name 'of the Father, and of the Son, and of the Holy Spirit.' Teach them to carry out everything I have commanded you. And know that I am with you always, until the end of the world!" (Matt. 28:19–20).

Gathered here as the successor of Peter and the successors of the apostles, we note how marvellously these words have been fulfilled in this land.

In 1492 the work of evangelization began in the New World, and the fact is that the faith arrived in Mexico within the next twenty years or so. A little later the first archepiscopal see was established under Juan de Zumárraga. He would be aided by other great figures in the work of evangelization, who would carry Christianity to wide areas.

Other epic religious deeds, no less glorious, were performed in this hemisphere by St. Toribio de Mogrovejo and many others who deserve mention. The path of faith continued to expand. By the end of the first century of evangelization

72

there were more than seventy episcopal sees on this new continent and some four million Christians. This singular undertaking would continue over a long period of time so that today, after five centuries of evangelization, almost half of the whole Catholic Church is to be found here. And the Catholic Church has deep roots in the culture of the Latin American people, forming part of its very identity.

As the mandate of Christ took effect in these lands and the grace of baptism multiplied the children of divine adoption everywhere, there also appeared Christ's mother. Indeed it was to you, Mary, that the Son of God, who is also your Son, pointed out a man from his place on the cross and said: "Woman, there is your son" (John 19:26). In that man he entrusted each and every human being to you. At the moment of the Annunciation you concentrated your whole life's program in the simple words: "I am the servant of the Lord. Let it be done to me as you say" (Luke 1:38). And so you embrace all, draw near to all, and maternally look out for all, thus fulfilling what the last Council affirmed about your presence in the mystery of Christ and the Church. You persevere in a wondrous way in the mystery of Christ, your only begotten Son, because you are everywhere that human beings, his brothers and sisters, and the Church are to be found.

3. The first missionaries who came to America were from lands with an eminent Marian tradition. Along with the rudiments of the Christian faith they also taught love for you, the Mother of Jesus and of all human beings. Ever since the Indian Juan Diego spoke of the gentle Lady of Tepeyac, you, the Mother of Guadalupe, have entered the Christian life of the Mexican people in a decisive way. No less impressive has been your presence in other areas, where your children invoke you with tender names: e.g., Our Lady of Altagracia, of Aparecida, of Luján. Of course there are many other names for you, no less endearing, with which the people of Latin America in every nation and region express their deep devotion to you; and under these names you protect them in their journey of faith. But the list of these names could go on forever.

The pope comes from a country in which your images—particularly one, that of Jasna Góra—are also a sign of your presence in the nation's life and its unfortunate history. So he is particularly sensitive to this sign of your presence here in the life of God's People in Mexico and their history, which likewise has not been easy and at times even tragic. But you are equally present in the life of so many other peoples and nations of Latin America, presiding over and guiding not only their remote or recent past but also the present age with all its uncertainties and shadows. In the depths of his heart the pope glimpses the special bonds that link you with these people and them with you. This people, which affectionately calls you *La Morenita* ("the dark damsel"), and indirectly this whole vast continent, lives its spiritual unity thanks to the fact that you are the Mother—a mother whose love creates, conserves, and enlarges the atmosphere of neighborliness between her children.

Hail, Mother of Mexico!

Mother of Latin America!

4. We find ourselves here together at this unusual and stupendous moment in world history. We come here, aware that we are facing a crucial moment. Through this episcopal meeting we wish to link up with the preceding confer-

ence of the Latin American episcopate, which took place ten years ago in Medellín. That conference coincided with the Eucharistic Congress in Bogotá, and Pope Paul VI of unforgettable memory took part in it. We have come here, not so much to re-examine the same problem at the end of ten years, as to rework it in a new way, a new place, and a new historical moment.

We want to take as our point of departure the things that are contained in the documents and resolutions of that earlier conference. And at the same time, on the basis of the experiences of the last ten years, of further developments in thought, and of the experiences of the whole Church, we want to take a proper and necessary step forward.

The Medellín Conference took place shortly after the close of Vatican II, the Council of our century; its objective was to bring together the essential materials and formulations of Vatican II in order to apply them and to make them a guiding force in the concrete situation of the Latin American Church.

Without Vatican II, the Medellín Conference would have been impossible. For the Medellín Conference sought to be an impulse for pastoral renewal and a new "spirit" in the face of the future, while displaying fully ecclesial fidelity in its interpretation of the signs of the times in Latin America. Its evangelizing intent was quite clear. It is evident in the sixteen topics broached, which were brought together under three main areas that were mutually complementary: human promotion, evangelization and growth in the faith, and the visible Church and its structures.

With its option for the Latin American human being seen whole, its preferential but not exclusive love for the poor, and its encouragement of full, integral liberation for human beings and peoples, Medellín—the Church present there —was a hope-filled call to more Christian and more human goals.

But ten years have passed. And there have been interpretations that are sometimes contradictory, not always correct, and not always beneficial for the Church. So the Church is looking for ways to comprehend the mission it has received from Jesus Christ more fully and carry it out in more dedicated fashion.

Of great importance in this area have been the meetings of the Synod of Bishops that have taken place in these past ten years. This is particularly true of the 1974 Synod, which focused on evangelization. Its conclusions were then taken up and reiterated in a lively, inspiring way in Paul VI's Apostolic Exhortation entitled *Evangelii Nuntiandi*.

This is the topic that we place before us today in proposing to study "Evangelization in Latin America's Present and Future."

Meeting together in this holy place to begin our labors, we turn our eyes back to the Cenacle in Jerusalem, the place where the Eucharist was instituted. After the Lord's Ascension, the apostles returned to that same place so that they, remaining in prayer with Mary, the Mother of Christ, might prepare their hearts to receive the Holy Spirit at the moment of the Church's birth.

We, too, have come here for that reason. We, too, await the descent of the Holy Spirit to show us the pathways of evangelization through which the Church is to carry on and be reborn on our great continent. We, too, today and in the coming days, wish to persevere in prayer with Mary, the Mother of our Lord and Teacher; with you, Mary, Mother of Hope, Mother of Guadalupe.

5. At this solemn moment I, John Paul II, bishop of Rome and pope, join with my brothers in the episcopate who represent the Church of Mexico and of all Latin America. Mary, permit us to offer and entrust to you, the servant of the Lord, the whole patrimony of the Gospel, of the cross and resurrection, of which we all are witnesses, apostles, teachers, and bishops.

Oh, Mother! Help us to be faithful stewards of the great mysteries of God. Help us to teach the truth that your son announced, and to extend the love that is the chief commandment and the first fruit of the Holy Spirit. Help us to confirm our brothers and sisters in the faith. Help us to enkindle hope in eternal life. Help us to look after the great treasures stored in the souls of the People of God who have been entrusted to us.

We offer you this whole People of God. We offer you the Church of Mexico, the Church of this whole continent. We offer this Church to you as your own possession. You have entered so deeply into the hearts of the faithful through the beacon of your presence embodied in your image in the sanctuary of Guadalupe. May you therefore live in their hearts in the future too, as if it were your own home. Be one of the household in our families, our parishes, our missions, our dioceses, and all our nations.

Do this through the holy Church. Imitating you, Mary, the Church desires to be a good mother in turn and to look after souls in all their needs; proclaiming the Gospel; administering the sacraments; safeguarding family life through the sacrament of matrimony; gathering all together in the eucharistic community through the holy sacrament of the altar; and accompanying them lovingly from the cradle to their entry into eternity.

Oh, Mother! Awaken in young people an openness to serve God exclusively. Beseech God on our behalf for abundant local vocations to the priesthood and the consecrated life.

Oh, Mother! Confirm the faith of all our brothers and sisters in the laity. In every area of social, professional, cultural, and political life may they act in accordance with the truth and the law that your son brought to humanity in order to lead all to eternal salvation and, at the same time, to make life on earth more human, more worthy of human beings.

The Church that carries out its labors in the nations of the Americas, the Church in Mexico, wishes to serve this sublime cause with all its strength and with a revitalized missionary spirit. Oh, Mother! Grant that we may learn how to serve it in truth and in justice. Grant that we ourselves will follow that road and lead others, never straying into tortuous byways and dragging others along with us.

We offer and entrust to you all the people and all the things that are the object of our pastoral responsibility, trusting that you will be with us and that you will help us to carry out what your son has commanded us (John 2:5). We come to you with this unlimited confidence. With it all of us here—I, John Paul II, and all my brothers in the episcopate of Mexico and Latin America—wish to link you even more forcefully with our ministry, with the Church, and with the life of our nations. We wish to place in your hands our whole future, the future of the evangelization of Latin America.

Queen of the Apostles! Accept our readiness to serve unreservedly the cause of your son, the cause of the Gospel, and the cause of peace based on justice and love among human beings and nations.

Queen of Peace! Save the nations and peoples of this whole continent, who have such great trust in you, from war, hatred, and subversion.

Grant that all the people, rulers and ruled, may learn to live in peace, to be educated for peace, and to do what justice and respect for the rights of every human being require if peace is to be consolidated.

Accept our confident submission to you, Oh, Servant of the Lord. May your maternal presence in the mystery of Christ and of the Church become a wellspring of joy and freedom for each and all; a wellspring of the liberty for which "Christ freed us" (Gal. 5:1); and finally, a wellspring of the peace that the world cannot give, that only Christ can give (John 14:27).

Finally, Oh, Mother, recalling and confirming the act of my predecessors Benedict XIV and Pius X, who proclaimed you Patron of Mexico and of all Latin America, I present you with a diadem in the name of all your children in Mexico and Latin America. May you keep them under your protection. May you watch over their harmony in the faith and their fidelity to Christ, your son. Amen.

POPE JOHN PAUL II:
HOMILY IN PUEBLA

This homily was delivered in the Seminario Palafoxiano of Puebla on 28 January 1979, during a celebration of the Eucharist on the outdoor recreation grounds. It was attended by all the members of the Puebla Conference and a large crowd of the faithful.

Dearly beloved Sons and Daughters:

1. Puebla de los Angeles: today the resonant and expressive name of your city is on the lips of millions of people in Latin America and around the world. Your city has become a symbol and a beacon for the Latin American Church. For it is here, starting today, that bishops from all over your continent, convened by the successor of Peter, are meeting to reflect on the mission of pastors in this part of the world at this singular moment in history.

The pope has chosen to mount this hilltop, from which all of Latin America seems to open out before him. It is with the idea of contemplating the contours of each one of the nations that the pope, on this altar erected on the highlands, has chosen to celebrate the eucharistic sacrifice. He wishes to call down upon this conference, upon its participants and its labors, the light, the glowing warmth, and all the gifts of the Spirit of God, the Spirit of Jesus.

Nothing could be more natural or more necessary than to invoke that Spirit on such an occasion. The great conference now convening is, after all, an ecclesial meeting down to its very core. It is ecclesial by virtue of those who are meeting here: i.e., pastors of the Church of God in Latin America. It is ecclesial by virtue of the topic it is studying: i.e., the mission of the Church on this continent. It is ecclesial by virtue of its objectives: i.e., to make ever increasingly vital and effective the original contribution that the Church is obligated to make to the well-being, harmony, justice, and peace of these peoples. And the point is that there can be no ecclesial gathering unless the Spirit of God is present there in all the fullness of his mysterious activity.

The pope invokes that Spirit with all the fervor of his heart. May the place where the bishops meet each other be a new Cenacle, much larger than the one in Jerusalem where only eleven apostles were to be found that morning but, like that Cenacle in Jerusalem, open to the flames of the Paraclete and to the power of a Pentecost repeated. In you bishops gathered here may the Spirit fulfill the multiform mission that the Lord Jesus entrusted to him. *God's interpreter*, who is to make clear his plan and his message that are not accessible to human reason on its own (John 14:26), open up the understanding of these pastors and introduce

77

them to the Truth (John 16:13). *Witness to Jesus Christ*, bear witness in their minds and hearts, transforming them in turn into witnesses who will be consistent, credible, and effective in their labors (John 15:26). *Advocate or Consoler*, give them courage against the sin of the world (John 16:8) and give them the words they must utter, particularly at a time when their witness will cost suffering and fatigue.

Beloved sons and daughters, I ask you to join me in invoking the Spirit at this Eucharist. It is not for themselves or for their personal interests that bishops from all over the Latin American continent are meeting here. It is for you, the People of God in these lands, and for your good. So do participate in this Third Conference in the way I have suggested, i.e., by calling down an abundance of the Holy Spirit upon each and every one of the bishops.

2. There is a profound and beautiful saying that our God, in his innermost mystery, is not a loneness but a family, since God embodies paternity, filiation, and the essence of the family that is love. In the divine family that love is the Holy Spirit. So the theme of the family is not alien to the theme of the Holy Spirit. Please allow the pope to say a few words to you about this theme, the family, which certainly will occupy the attention of your bishops in the upcoming days.

You know how urgently and seriously the bishops of the Medellín Conference spoke about the family. In 1968 they saw in your great family feeling a primordial trait of your Latin America culture. They pointed out that the families of Latin America should always possess three dimensions, if your countries were to prosper: that your families should be educators in the faith, shapers of persons, and promoters of development. They also stressed the grave obstacles preventing families from carrying out this threefold commitment. And "therefore" they urged that pastoral attention be paid to families as a priority task for the Church on your continent.

Ten years having passed, the Church in Latin America feels happy about all it has managed to accomplish on behalf of the family. But it humbly recognizes how much remains to be done; and it sees that pastoral care of the family, far from having lost its priority character, appears even more urgent today as an important element of evangelization.

3. The fact is that the Church is aware that the family in Latin America is facing serious problems these days. In recent years some countries have passed legislation permitting divorce, which entails a new threat to the integrity of the family. In the majority of your countries people must lament the fact that an alarming number of children, who are the future of your nations and their hope, are being born into homes with no stability, that they are being born into what people call "incomplete families." Furthermore, this same hope is on the verge of disappearing in some areas of this "continent of hope." For many of the families cannot live a normal existence because the more negative results of development have a particularly heavy impact on them: truly depressing indications of unhealthiness, poverty and even misery, ignorance and illiteracy, inhuman housing conditions, chronic malnutrition, and countless other realities that are just as sad.

In defense of the family against these evils, the Church pledges its help; and it invites governments to adopt, as a key point of their action, a socio-family policy that is intelligent, bold, and persevering—recognizing that herein undoubtedly lies the future, the hope, of the continent. It must be added that such a family policy is not to be viewed as an indiscriminate effort to reduce the birth rate at any price—which my predecessor, Paul VI, referred to as "decreasing the number of people invited to the banquet of life." For it is well known that a well-balanced population index is indispensable for development. Rather, it is a matter of combining efforts to create the conditions that will favor the existence of sound, well-balanced families. To use the words of Paul VI again, it is a matter of "increasing the food on the table."

Besides the defense of the family, we must also talk about the advancement of the family. Here many organisms must make their contribution: governments and governmental organisms, schools, labor unions, the media of social communication, neighborhood organizations, and the many different voluntary or ad hoc organizations that are flourishing everywhere.

The Church must also offer its contribution, in line with its spiritual mission to proclaim the Gospel and lead human beings to salvation. For that mission also has enormous repercussions on the well-being of the family. What can the Church do by joining forces with others? I am sure that your bishops will make every effort to provide adequate, correct, and worthwhile answers to that question. I would simply point out to you how much benefit for the family there is in what the Church is already doing in Latin America: e.g., in preparing future spouses for marriage; in helping families when they go through normal crises, which can be fruitful and enriching when they are faced properly; in turning each Christian family into an authentic "domestic Church," with all the rich implications of that term; in preparing many families to carry out their evangelizing mission to other families; in stressing all the values of family life; in coming to the aid of incomplete families; and in encouraging rulers to elaborate in their countries the socio-family policy of which I spoke above. The Puebla Conference will certainly support these initiatives, and it may have others to suggest. It is pleasing to think that the history of Latin America will thus have reason to thank the Church for all that it has done, is doing, and will do for the family on this vast continent.

4. Very beloved Sons and Daughters: Today, at this altar, the successor of Peter feels singularly close to all the families of Latin America. It is almost as if each and every home were opening its doors and the pope could enter in: homes where food and well-being are not lacking, but harmony and joy perhaps are; homes where families live rather modestly, uncertain of the morrow, helping one another to live a difficult but dignified existence; poor habitations on the outskirts of your cities where there is much hidden suffering, though the simple joy of the poor dwells there; humble shanties of peasants, indigenous peoples, immigrants, etc. To each family the pope would like to say a particular word of encouragement and hope. You families that can enjoy well-being, do not close yourselves off in your own felicity; open up to others, sharing your surplus that others lack. Families oppressed by poverty, do not lose heart; without making luxury your ideal, or wealth the basis of your happiness, join with all in seeking to take the difficult steps and to hope for better days. Families visited by the anxieties of physical or moral suffering, or tested by illness or misery, do not add bitterness or despair to those sufferings; be wise enough to alleviate your suffer-

ings with hope. All families of Latin America, rest assured that the pope knows you and wants to know you even better, because he loves you with the tenderness of a father.

In the framework of the pope's visit to Mexico, this is Family Day. So I would ask all your families of Latin America to welcome the visit that the pope wishes to make to each one of you. Welcome it through your presence around this altar, through radio, and through television. Give the pope the joy of seeing you grow in the Christian values that are yours, so that in its millions of families Latin America will find reason to have confidence, to hope, to struggle, and to build.

POPE JOHN PAUL II:
ADDRESS TO THE INDIANS
OF OAXACA AND CHIAPAS

This address was delivered to thousands of Indian peasant farmers in the moun-tain village of Cuilapan in the state of Oaxaca on 29 January 1979.

I am glad to meet you, and I thank you for your enthusiastic presence and your words of welcome to me. I can find no better greeting, to express to you the sentiments that now fill my heart, than the words of St. Peter, the first pope of the Church: "Peace to you who are in Christ." Peace to you who make up this crowded throng.

You too, you the inhabitants of Oaxaca, Chiapas, Cuilapan, and other places represented here, heirs of the blood and culture of your noble ancestors—particularly the Mixtecs and the Zapotecs—have been "called to be a holy people, as . . . all those who, wherever they may be, call on the name of our Lord Jesus Christ" (1 Cor. 1:2).

The Son of God "dwelt among us" to make those who believe in his name the children of God (John 1:11ff.); and he entrusted the Church with the continuation of this saving mission wherever human beings might be. So it is not surprising that one day, in the now distant seventeenth century, intrepid missionaries arrived here out of fidelity to the Church. They were anxious to assimilate your lifestyle and customs so as to better reveal and give living expression to the image of Christ. We remember with gratitude the first bishop of Oaxaca, Juan José López de Zárate, and numerous other missionaries—Franciscans, Dominicans, Augustinians, and Jesuits. They were men to be admired for their faith and their humane generosity.

They knew very well how important culture is as a vehicle for transmitting the faith, so that human beings might progress in their knowledge of God. In this matter there can be no differences of race or culture: "There is no Greek or Jew, . . . slave or freeman. Rather, Christ is everything in all of you" (Col. 3:11). This constitutes a challenge and a stimulus for the Church. For, in being faithful to the Lord's genuine and complete message, the Church must be open and interpret all human reality in order to impregnate it with the power of the Gospel (EN:20,40).

Very beloved brothers and sisters: My presence in your midst is meant to be a living, authentic sign of this universal preoccupation on the part of the Church. The pope and the Church are with you and they love you. They love your

81

persons, your culture, your traditions. They admire your marvellous past, encourage you in the present, and have great expectations for the future.

But that is not all I want to talk about. Through you, peasants and indigenous peoples, there comes before my eyes the vast multitude of the agricultural world. It is still the prevalent sector on the Latin American continent, and it is still a very large sector today on our planet.

Before this imposing spectacle reflected in my eyes, I cannot help but think of the same scene that was contemplated ten years ago by my predecessor Paul VI in his memorable visit to Colombia, and more specifically in his meeting with the peasants.

With him I would like to reiterate—with an even stronger emphasis in my voice, if that were possible—that the present pope wishes to be "in solidarity with your cause, which is the cause of the humble people, the poor people" (Address to Peasants, 23 August 1968). I wish to reiterate that the pope is with these masses of people who are "almost always left behind in an ignoble standard of living and sometimes harshly treated and exploited" (ibid.).

I adopt the view of my predecessors, John XXIII and Paul VI, and of Vatican II (see MM; PP; GS:9,71; etc.). Seeing a situation that remains alarming, that is seldom better and sometimes even worse, the pope chooses to be your voice, the voice of those who cannot speak or who have been silenced. He wishes to be the conscience of consciences, an invitation to action, to make up for lost time, which has frequently been a time of prolonged sufferings and unsatisfied hopes.

The disheartened world of field work, the laborers whose sweat waters their disheartened state as well, cannot wait any longer for their dignity to be recognized really and fully—a dignity no whit inferior to that of any other social sector. They have a right to be respected. They have a right not to be deprived of the little they have by maneuvers that sometimes amount to real plunder. They have a right not to be blocked in their desire to take part in their own advancement. They have a right to have the barriers of exploitation removed. These barriers are frequently the product of intolerable forms of egotism, against which their best efforts at advancement are dashed. They have a right to effective help, which is neither a handout nor a few crumbs of justice, so that they may have access to the development that their dignity as human beings and as children of God merits.

For their sake we must act promptly and thoroughly. We must implement bold and thoroughly innovative transformations. Without further delay, we must undertake the urgently required reforms (PP:32).

It should not be forgotten that the measures taken have to be suitable. The Church defends the legitimate right to private property in itself; but it is no less clear in teaching that there is always a social mortgage on all private property, so that goods may serve the general assignment that God has given them. And if the common good demands it, there is no need to hesitate at expropriation itself, done in the right way (PP:24).

The realm of agriculture has great importance and great dignity. It is this realm that offers society the products it needs for its nourishment. It is a task that merits appreciation and grateful esteem from all, which are a recognition of the dignity of those who work at it.

This dignity can and should be enhanced by contemplating God. He encourages contact with nature, which mirrors his divine activity. God looks after the grass of the fields, nurtures its growth, and makes the earth fruitful. He sends the rain and the wind so that it may also feed the animals, who are the helpmates of human beings, as we read in the beginning of Genesis.

Work in the fields entails no small difficulties. There is the effort it takes, the scorn in which it is sometimes held, and the obstacles encountered. Sometimes only long-term effort can surmount the problems. Without that, the flight from countryside to the cities will continue. And that frequently creates problems: the extensive, anxiety-ridden proletarianization of human beings, their overcrowding in native dwellings, and so forth.

A fairly widespread evil is the tendency toward individualism among field workers. By contrast, a more coordinated and solidary effort could be a big help. Think about that, beloved children.

Despite everything, the peasant world possesses enviable human and religious riches: deeply rooted love for the family; a sense of friendship; helping those most in need; a deep humanism; love for peace and shared civic life; a vital religious life; trust in God and openness to him; a cultivation of love for the Virgin Mary; and many other things.

What the pope wishes to express to you is a well deserved tribute of thanks, which society owes you. Thank you, peasants, for your valuable contribution to the social welfare. Humanity owes you much. You can be proud of your contribution to the common good.

To you, responsible officials of the people, power-holding classes who sometimes keep your lands unproductive when they conceal the food that so many families are doing without, the human conscience, the conscience of the peoples, the cry of the destitute, and above all the voice of God and the Church join me in reiterating to you that it is not just, it is not human, it is not Christian to continue certain situations that are clearly unjust. You must implement real, effective measures on the local, national, and international levels, following the broad line marked out by the encyclical *Mater et Magistra* (Part III). And it is clear that those who can do most are the ones most obligated to collaborate in this effort.

Most beloved brothers and sisters and children: work for your advancement as human beings. But do not stop there. Improve yourself more and more in morality and religion. Do not harbor sentiments of hatred and violence, but look to the Lord and Master of all, who gives to all the recompense their acts deserve. The Church is on your side. It urges you to live out your status as children of God united in Christ, under the gaze of Mary, our most holy Mother.

The pope asks you for your prayers, and he offers you his. And as I bless you and your families, I bid you farewell with words of St. Paul the Apostle: "Give a greeting and a good kiss to all the brethren." May this be a call to hope. Amen.

III

THE FINAL DOCUMENT

THE PUEBLA FINAL DOCUMENT: INTRODUCTION AND COMMENTARY

Archbishop Marcos McGrath, C.S.C.

Many who are drawn to Puebla because of its obvious ecclesial and social significance will be put off by the document the conference published. Long, heavy, uneven, repetitious: it does not make easy reading. Much more than was the case for the documents of Medellín, it needs an introduction, both historical and textual.

In this essay, presuming the historical presentation, we will present the text. Before actually going through it, part by part and chapter by chapter, there are two very important points I would stress:

a. Puebla has given us only one document, not many, as did Medellín, and this one document must be viewed as a whole.

b. There is an inner dynamism to the text, which relates the parts and illumines the whole.

This done, we can:

c. Run through the text, looking for highlights and helping to explain, historically, some whys and wherefores of what is said and what is not said. Our effort is to help the text speak to its readers, or, more properly, help the readers grasp what the conference says to them, through the text.

d. Conclude with an effort to bind up all the parts of the text in the light of its dominant themes. This will be our final key to the understanding of Puebla.

The Document Is One ...

Medellín gave us sixteen documents—simply because the dynamics of that conference had not provided sufficient time for the various texts to be put together into one. This had its advantages. Each single text was easier to read, to handle, to apply. It had its own "see-judge-act" format that lent itself admirably to discussion groups. But, in the long run, disadvantages cropped up. Many read only one or another of the documents, the ones they were attracted to. The secular press focused on the social texts, especially the first two, "Justice" and "Peace." The result was, for many, an unbalanced or at least an incomplete vision of Medellín.

Puebla wanted to avoid that danger. That is why from the start of the conference the whole method pointed toward putting together *one final document.* The Coordinating Commission (*Comisión de Empalme y de Articulación*) was particularly charged with this task. It was not easy. Nor was it fully achieved. The close reader can still make out the twenty-one separate parts that were incorporated, with the help of connecting and introductory paragraphs, exactly as they came out of the commissions and were approved by the Assembly.

The constant comparing of the separate texts in their various stages of composition, in meetings of the Coordinating Commission with the moderators of the particular commissions, did make it possible to try for certain common norms as regards both *style* and *content.* The *style* was to be that of pastors directing themselves, in the first place, to all their collaborators in the pastoral action of the Church in our countries. This specific choice of audience set a tone of personal address and of confidence.

The *content* was indicated in the topic outline approved by the Assembly in its first vote, Wednesday, 31 January. This was the revised version of Cardinal Lorscheider's proposal, as corrected by the Coordinating Commission on the basis of the recommendations of the temporary commissions that functioned the first two days. It was important, thereafter, that each particular commission adhere to the specific subject or subjects assigned to it, that it pay attention to the criticism addressed it by the other commissions or by individual members of the conference and especially by the whole Assembly, and, finally, that it always keep in mind the whole view of the document and the central theme (in Spanish, *"el hilo conductor"*) running through it.

The Final Document still contains unnecessary repetitions, occasionally quite obvious differences in style, and some interesting contrasts in doctrinal and pastoral emphasis. Evidently more time would have been required to fuse the whole into one well-blended text. But the desired effect is essentially achieved: a whole view, in one articulated presentation.

These observations explain more than the mere mechanics of the text. They help in deciding how best to present it to the public. It can be studied piecemeal, theme by theme. There will undoubtedly be many separate publications of individual parts: on the family, on the religious life, the whole long chapter on evangelization, etc. This can be useful—but always provided that one has grasped and does not lose sight of the overall picture. Without this, as happened with Medellín, many will be left with parts and parcels of Puebla.

In short, reading Puebla will be simpler than reading Medellín, because the oneness of the text invites to a whole view. But it will be much more difficult for many because of the length, the seriousness, and the density of the text. Introductions are needed, written and oral, as precise and as faithful as they can be to its letter, its spirit, and its whole purpose.

. . . With the Method and Dynamism of a Conciliar Text

The *aggiornamento,* or renovation, to which the Council calls the Church in our times and to which we must be deeply committed, as Pope John Paul II frequently reminds us, involves a double, somewhat dialectical movement: a return to the sources of Christian Catholic faith, and a going out to our secular, pluralistic world. Rightly understood, both movements resolve themselves into one: the Word and the Spirit of the Lord, authentically lived in the Church and in the world today.

The Council carried out this double movement in all its texts, but most fundamentally in its four great constitutions: *Dei Verbum, Lumen Gentium,* and *Sacrosanctum Concilium*, on the one hand, and *Gaudium et Spes,* on the other. Puebla, in its document, follows the pattern of *Gaudium et Spes,* but reflects the movement and the content of all four. This is just another reminder of what the Holy Father told us in the Basilica of Guadalupe: without the Council, there would have been no Medellín. Nor Puebla, we may add.

It will help to recall the pattern of *Gaudium et Spes.* This great pastoral constitution begins with a "preliminary exposition" on the situation of man and society in today's world. The description is graphic and realistic. The facts are not subjected to any interpretation or analysis that would involve a conciliar option for a particular economic or political system or ideology. But the Church, in the Council, proposes to scrutinize these "signs of the times" in the light of the Gospel (GS:4), detecting those basic human and spiritual questions (cf. GS:10) that it is the Church's task to address. They become the object of an extraordinarily rich Christian reflection in the entire first part of the constitution. The second part goes on to apply these fundamental reflections to specific areas of human endeavor. The inner dynamic of the constitution is obvious. In historical fact, the whole second part was basically elaborated more than a year before the first, and therefore did not benefit adequately from the reflections and the dynamic that the Council finally worked out for *Gaudium et Spes,* and that are better detected in the Introduction, the First Part, and the Conclusion.

Puebla does set out to follow the final dynamic of *Gaudium et Spes,* and on the whole succeeds. It begins by describing the reality of Latin America as seen by the pastors of the Church, in the light of the Gospel. This is already, quite obviously, a first mediation or interpretation of that reality. Puebla avoids a superficial reading of the conciliar dynamic that would pretend to such an "objective" presentation of the "signs of the times" as to preclude even the vision or interpretation of faith. On the other hand, it also carefully avoids the further analyses, economic, social, or political, that would, by the mediation of particular interpretations, lead to options beyond the area that is the proper and original contribution of the Gospel and of the Church. These considerations, here too simply stated, have much to do with the social role of the Church as such—a point on which Pope John Paul II insisted strongly—and consequently with the "social teaching" of the Church, as later described in the Final Document (nos. 472–79).

Part Two is entitled "God's Saving Plan for Latin America." It is phrased as a response to the first part. The Gospel is not preached in a void. It must be directed in Latin America today to our people living in the situation that the pastors have just described.

The Gospel, like the Lord Jesus, is the same yesterday, today, and always (cf. Heb. 13:8). But human beings and society are in continuous flux and development, in recent times more than ever. The Gospel must be preached anew, in new contexts, in face of new problems, leading to new applications, to new understandings. The Council proclaims this, both on the level of growing doctrinal understanding (cf. DV:8), and of pastoral and practical guidance (cf. GS:91). Puebla accepts this fact, which is at once a task and a challenge. How to preach the unchanging Gospel to the changing world of Latin America? The whole second part of the document responds, with regard to content (Chap. I) and with regard to the actual communication of the Gospel (Chap. II).

This conciliar dynamic carries into and through the third and fourth parts of the text. Faith and Life become, under certain aspects, Church and World: Church as the visible communion of its members, the sacrament of Christ's presence in the world; Church, too, as its members in and through the world— the working out of that sacrament as a true leaven for the greater union of all people among themselves and with God (LG:1).

The fifth and final part of the text simply recalls its central thrust and points toward applications after Puebla.

With this sense of the inner relationships within the text, we can now take a closer look at the parts.

A Closer View of the Text

Part One: Pastoral Overview of the Reality That Is Latin America

We have already stressed the word "pastoral" as it is intended in the title of this opening part of the document. It is the bishops who are describing the situation of Latin America. To enter upon these descriptions of tough social, cultural, economic, and political realities, they must be well informed. In the case of Puebla, two years of increasingly serious consultation made this possible. This, in itself, is an encouragement and an example that local pastors and local Churches, indeed "church people" in general, can follow, for the occasions in which they should offer pastoral guidance in similar affairs. To take this kind of preparation seriously would seem to be a necessary condition for dialogue with the "builders of a pluralistic society," about which Puebla speaks later on (nos. 1206–53). But when bishops talk about economics, as in this case, or about politics—even supposing that they be well informed on the subject—they should not pretend to talk like economists nor political scientists; in fact, the bishops are careful not even to sound like them. Speaking as pastors, they can lay stress on the objective facts of the temporal order that are the most significant and telling, true signs, which others perhaps ignore or play down. It is to these signs—and all the moral and spiritual values they involve—that the Gospel, and they as pastors, should speak.

Part One is divided into four chapters. Of these, the second and third are central, the foundation stone for the whole document. They describe the social and religious reality of Latin America in a manner that poses the questions and sets the tone for all that follows. The first chapter is an all too brief historical sketch of evangelization in Latin America, roughly from the conquest to Medellín. Chapter IV, on future tendencies, oversteps itself. It becomes a series of recommendations on the matters, social and religious, treated in the previous chapters, anticipating somewhat prematurely the rest of the document.

The "working document," distributed by CELAM to the participants in the General Conference in August 1978, provides most of the material for this first part. But the focus is heightened in Puebla.

The historical sketch speaks of evangelization as an effort of the entire Church over the centuries, thus seeking to correct the overly episcopal accent that was criticized in the pre-conference documents. The approach is balanced and objective, recognizing both "lights and shadows" in these nearly five hundred years. Clearly on the positive side are the first marvelous tasks of constitutive evangelization (no. 6), lasting over a century, to which we owe the "radical Catholic substrate" (no. 7) that pervades our people today; untold religious, educational, and social efforts by the whole People of God over the long generations; the special contribution of our saints and those intrepid defenders of the Indians and the poor, whose example moves us even today (they anticipate Puebla's modern option for the poor). On the negative side there are many factors, most of them, such as the scandalous neglect regarding the persons and rights of the African slaves, due to unhealthy "complicity with the earthly powers" (no. 10). Despite the divisions and persecutions that weakened the Church in the last century, the work of evangelization continues to make Latin America a "continent of hope" (no. 10). The recent revival of the Church, especially with the movement of the Council and of Medellín, raises this hope and sets the stage for the descriptions to follow, which concentrate upon developments after Medellín.

The description given in Chapters II and III, to which must be added a good part of Chapter IV, are the basic "see" before the "judge" and "act" of the entire Puebla document. Even though new observations of our reality do crop up throughout the whole text, nonetheless Part Two of the document is more the "judge," Parts Three and Four more the "act." They depend on Part One.

How does Puebla's description of Latin America's reality, social and religious, compare with the descriptive parts of Medellín? There is much in common in what is seen and how it is seen, with notable progression in both aspects.

Medellín took up the area of "human promotion" before speaking of promotion in the faith and about the structures of the Church. Puebla, likewise, in this descriptive part, speaks first of the sociocultural reality, and then of the religious or church situation.

The text, in its earlier stages at Puebla, was criticized by some members of the conference for dedicating proportionately much more space to the temporal than to the religious reality of the continent, and for being too negative regarding the former. For these same reasons Chapter II (the sociocultural context) turned out to be the only section of the whole text that did not receive the necessary two-thirds majority in the formal vote on Sunday, 11 February (it failed by a few votes). A small ad hoc commission had to slightly revamp the text, stating some of the more positive aspects at the outset of the description, and then the section was quickly approved in a new vote.

A careful reading of the sociocultural description balances out this way: There are hopes and advances in Latin America—the qualities and the efforts of the people; a growing sense in them of human and social dignity; better health and educational services; a global economic expansion. The scandal is all the greater because these means are not converted to just social purposes, due to the lack of political and moral will. Contrasts between rich and poor, privileged and marginal, have not improved (no. 28). The description of these contrasts, of poverty, of economic, social, and political oppression, is strong. Its causes are signaled out. They are both structural and moral, national and international, and are backed by economic and political ideologies: economic liberalism, Marxism, "National Security." Puebla calls out against the scandal of Christian nations, rulers, and business leaders who do not demonstrate conscience nor action in favor of the poor, in favor of a social justice that is due and that is possible. Ten years of speaking and acting in this domain have matured the Church and confirmed it in this mission of speaking and acting for and with the poor.

Chapter III, the description of church reality, points out first of all factors that are making evangelization by the Church in Latin America more difficult. Secularization, along with population explosion and urbanization, has resulted in large, often rootless masses, poorly grounded in their faith, in little contact with the Church, subject to many and diverse nonreligious influences as well as the confusing propaganda of various sects. Frequently the result, says Puebla, is a certain hollow ritualism in lieu of genuine religious commitment, or simply indifference, a turning away from God and religion.

The Church has awakened to this situation, especially since the Vatican Council and Medellín, with a growing awareness that its fundamental task is to evangelize, and that this requires a constant effort to relate the Gospel to the real condition of the people. Despite its lack of personnel and resources, the Church has intensely promoted studies, plans, and action to this end, characterized by a growing defense of human rights and a proximity to the poor, even though this has caused it at times to be rejected by other social groups.

Numbers 88 and 89 of the Final Document will long and often be quoted. Medellín, the text recalls, spoke of the muted cry of millions, begging liberation of their pastors. Today, the text affirms, that cry is "loud and clear, increasing in volume and intensity, and at times full of menace."

The situations of injustice challenge our evangelization. "Our mission to bring God to human beings, and human beings to God, also entails the task of fashioning a more fraternal society here" (no. 90). Some would set this aside in favor of a purely spiritual approach; others would reduce the Church's task to merely social development. The Church must continue its strong stand for social justice, but in its own proper role, not committing its priests nor its social position to party politics.

There should be a subtitle before no. 94. It takes up (through no. 126) a long description of evangelization in Latin America since Medellín: the growing awareness, the ministries, the structures—illuminating and encouraging. Much that Medellín hoped and called for has become widespread reality in the Church. A prime example is the multiplication and the central role of the CEBs (*comunidades eclesiales de base*); and there are many others.

A careful reading of these chapters (II, III, and IV) of Part One, sets the stage for the rest of the document. The Church of Latin America is largely committed to the renovation called for by the Council and Medellín. The facts of its life, culled from all over the continent, show this to be so. The pastors in Puebla recount these developments. Heartened by them, but deeply aware of the serious religious and social challenge facing the Church, these same pastors now ask themselves what the task of evangelization must be, and how it must be carried out.

Part Two: God's Saving Plan for Latin America

God's response to the pastoral reality of our continent is presented, first in its content, and then in the manner of its communication (the process of evangelization).

Chapter I: Content. The presentation of content follows the triple form (the "tripod," as it came to be called) proposed by Pope John Paul II in his Opening Address: the truth about Christ, about the Church, and about human beings.

a. On Christ and the Church. The two chapters on Christ and the Church, with the "epilogue" on the Blessed Virgin, were demanded by the bishops from the earliest consultations in 1977. At first the stress was mostly upon the need to state clear doctrine and dispel ambiguities that existed in Christology and in ecclesiology, and that were causing some confusion both in theory and in pastoral practice. Some suggested that the doctrine be presented in a trinitarian and "salvation history" context. These preoccupations and suggestions were reflected in the preliminary consultative document of 1977. In its section on the Church it included, as well, a long *excursus* giving norms or criteria with which to clarify points in the suggested areas, such as the relation of magisterium and theology, the meaning of the "Church of the poor," etc.

The 1978 reports, given by the episcopal conferences, shifted the emphasis. It fell more on the whole effort and process of evangelization, with the experiences, the discoveries, and the needs of an evangelizing Church: e.g., the crying need for the Gospel in the face of massive and growing religious ignorance and/or indifference, and the necessity of a strong identification with the poor, primary object of Christ's preaching and of the Church's preoccupation in Latin America today. Many more clarifications of terms and concepts were requested, even a kind of glossary or index lexicon to accompany the text. The document of 1978, in response, appended a series of clarificatory notes, some a bit polemical, but incorporated the key notions into the preceding text.

The bishops' reports of 1978 called again for a trinitarian context and content of evangelization, within a historical presentation of salvation and liberation. A few offered outlines and texts: from the Father to the Son, in the Spirit; and from Jesus, the first Evangelizer, to the Church, at one and the same time evangelized and evangelizing. *Evangelii Nuntiandi* was to be the model. Several asked for more explicit reference to the historical Christ and to the call of the Church to *follow him,* in his sufferings for the poor and for the sins of humankind (cf. LG:8). There was frequent mention of reconciliation, communion, and participation as the goal of evangelization in the Church and among human beings generally. In short, the bishops had given considerable reflection to these topics before Puebla.

The first draft of the texts on Christ and the Church, especially the former, were criticized by conference members as too stiff and "essentialistic," too much in the style of a dogmatic profession of faith. Others defended the necessity of stating these points of doctrine. It gradually became clear that they would be stated, but in the context of the Father's response, through the Church, to the situation of Latin America.

Thus there developed a text on Christ that is very doctrinal, without being polemical. It speaks clearly of the historical Christ within the history of salvation: his "words and deeds," the radical following he demands, our incorporation into his paschal death and resurrection, the Kingdom he preaches and implants in the world. It speaks, as well, of the sending of the Spirit and the final destiny of human beings to participate in the communion of the Trinity.

"The Truth about the Church," with its beautiful pages on the Virgin, constitutes a long passage somewhat *sui generis* in the Puebla document. It is unusual more for its style than for its content. Less formal, less concise than the other sections, it develops the underlying themes in the relaxed, discursive manner of a confident and friendly professor who brings in familiar examples to make a point. The examples are taken from the Latin American background. Yet it is more the slant given some of the doctrinal themes that points the text toward our Churches.

The themes are conciliar, but developed in the context of Puebla. The considerations center on the notion of Church as *sacrament,* deliberately instituted by Christ as "trustee and transmitter" of his Gospel (no. 224); solely possessing "the fullness of the means of salvation" (no. 225); sign and first beginnings of the Reign of God, which the Lord charges the Church to announce. This Church realizes the communion of the holy, pilgrim people and family of God, which, as the sacrament of universal salvation, is at the service of all human unity and the unity of all people with God (no. 270, cf. LG:1).

The exposition of these themes here provides a basis for later pastoral texts. Occasional clarifications are useful—e.g., the Church as family in Latin America, the sense of "pilgrim Church," "popular Church,"—especially because the explanations draw both from theory and from experience.

The well-developed Marian texts reflect the doctrine of the Council and of Pope Paul VI, as well as the recent, vivid example of Marian devotion given us in Mexico by Pope John Paul II. Mary is the "sacramental presence of the maternal features of God" (no. 291), and she belongs, in the words of John Paul II, to "the innermost identity of the Latin American peoples" (no. 283). She is Mother and Model of the Church, especially in bringing new children to life in the Gospel, and in incarnating that Gospel in our people.

Pope John Paul II called for a "solid Christology" and a "well-grounded ecclesiology." To this purpose he urged the bishops to present the truth about Christ and the Church clearly and unambiguously. He recognized some contributions in recent theological reflection in this area, but also pointed out some defects, or at least some undue silences. Puebla follows this same pattern. It incorporates new reflection, especially the historical and incarnational aspects of Christ and the Church in the unfolding of the People of God as the sacrament of universal salvation. It also pins down some important points of doctrine that are sometimes passed over or left too much in the air.

But these texts have been criticized. It is said, for example, that the theology of Christ and the Church implicit in the later pastoral passages is better than the theology explicitly set forth in this section, which, while thoroughly orthodox, lacks important elements of present-day reflection. There is some truth to this remark. For example, despite passing references, one does not have the same sense of urgency and crisis in these texts that one definitely feels in the description of reality and the later pastoral applications that Puebla provides us. The Marian texts are also somewhat too far removed from the real blessings and dangers of popular devotion, such as later brought out by Puebla (cf. nos. 454ff. and 910ff.).

One could answer, certainly, that the earlier and later texts complement one another. More to the point, perhaps, one must recognize that some theological reflection in this area is very recent, especially in Latin America. Not a few points lack sufficient maturity and acceptance, even among theologians, and more so among bishops, such as to be included or assumed in an ecclesial text of the importance of Puebla. This point becomes a bit more evident when one reads some of the critics. What they would like to see in this part of the document is not always merely an "explicitation" of what is latent in the pastoral sections. Sometimes it amounts to an interpretation: for example, a theologico-social thesis on *conflict* in the mission of Christ and the realization of the Kingdom, a thesis with obviously strong pastoral impact in the life of the Church; or, to the contrary, the denial of this thesis. These interpretations weigh heavily upon the understanding of such notions as the "Popular Church," or upon the sense (religious, economic, political) that one gives to the "option for the poor."

In many places the document assumes that the Church will encounter conflict and even persecution if its members are faithful to the task of evangelization, with its full religious and social consequences. Yet this conflict is never willed by the Church, which rather seeks reconciliation, that is, communion and participation at all levels—but not, of course, at any cost. The practical discernment of the attitude the Church should adopt in these situations is not always easy. Puebla certainly provides us with the principles, whose serious and sincere application in these situations may spare us future divisions in the Church such as those that Puebla deplores (cf., e.g., nos. 89–92).

b. The Truth about Human Beings: Human Dignity. This section is in the text thanks to the insistence of the Holy Father. In his very first allocution as pope, in many later documents, and very clearly in his Opening Address at Puebla, he has made this theme central to evangelization today. The working document did not cover it as a specific heading, nor did the first outline proposed at Puebla by Cardenal Lorscheider. But two of the temporary commissions proposed it, in the sense suggested by the Holy Father, to supply in the text what was lacking for a sound basis of Christian anthropology, foundation stone of the Church's social teaching. This passage, as well as the section titled "Evangelization, Liberation, and Human Promotion" (nos. 470–506), develops the Gospel foundations of the Church's social teaching; together they constitute one of the most significant and illuminating contributions of Puebla, both theologically and pastorally.

Chapter II: What Does Evangelization Entail? A document as dense and complicated as that of Puebla can be better understood with the help of a few *"claves de lectura,"* or "reading helps." We have already seen the most important one. It can be simply stated: *from pastoral reality to theological reflection and then to pastoral guidance.* This is what we have called the *dynamic* of the text. It must be well understood. From start to finish it is a process of Faith and Life. It is perhaps the most important key to the understanding of the text, and of the post-conciliar renovation of church life in Latin America, which gives life, meaning, and validity to the text.

This *dynamic* governs the entire text, as we have pointed out.

But the *quid* of the whole conference is *evangelization*. And here, quite simply, we have another key to the reading of the text. The topic, the subject matter, the object of the whole discussion is *Evangelization in Latin America's Present and Future.*

Puebla is talking about evangelization. This leads Puebla to a look at all of society and the Church, but always from this particular angle. Though in some parts the text may forget itself, on the whole it is faithful to this principle and should be read in the light of it.

For example, what is said in Puebla about education, or communication media, or religious, or ministries, does not pretend to cover these areas completely, but rather just their part in and relationship to evangelization.

Part One, the pastoral overview, is looking specifically at the state of evangelization in Latin America, in the past, present, and future, to highlight the challenges and questions posed for the evangelizing Church.

Part Two takes up the response to this situation, specifically the Gospel, the evangelizing response. What does God, in the Gospel, say to this situation (Chap. I: Content), and what is this process of "Gospel-izing" or evangelizing (Chap. II). Parts Three and Four will be the application of the response and the process to the Church itself and to the world.

With the help of these two keys to the reading of Puebla we will be able to arrive at a clearer reading of the central, driving theme of the whole text.

Why evangelization? The use of this term by the Catholic Church of Latin America is in itself a sign of radical conciliar change. Twenty years ago it would have been suspect. We are not far removed from the times, in Europe and the entire Catholic world, when the laity were forbidden to read the Scriptures directly and alone. The prohibition, in face of the rising biblical movement, later was applied to all texts except those edited, with explanatory notes, by the Catholic Church. Now, of course, there are excellent "ecumenical" translations; and Catholics throughout Latin America make wide use of Protestant or non-sectarian translations, as for example, the popular versions of the Gospel and New Testament done by the World Bible Association and sometimes published with a laudatory preface by CELAM.

The terms *"evangélicos," "evangelísticos," "evangelismo,"* and others, with varying nuances in each country, are still rather restricted to Protestants, specifically to what might be called in the United States "fundamentalists," the "Bible-belt Protestants." The "Four-Square Gospel" groups have their name in Spanish: the Church of "El Evangelio Cuadrado." Bible Protestants are referred to often, especially among the country people, as *"los cuadrados."*

Of course there is a fundamental reason for Catholic reticence, however overdone. It lies in the difference between the Protestant concept of individual interpretation, and the Catholic notion, most adequately expressed in Vatican II:

Since Holy Scripture must be read and interpreted according to the same Spirit by whom it was written, no less serious attention must be given to the content and unity of the whole of Scripture, if the meaning of the sacred texts is to be correctly brought to light. The living tradition of the whole Church must be taken into account along with the harmony which exists between elements of the faith. It is the task of exegetes to work according to these rules toward a better understanding and explanation of the meaning of sacred Scripture, so that through preparatory study the judgment of the Church may mature. For all of what has been said about the way of interpreting Scripture is subject finally to the judgment of the Church, which carries out the divine commission and ministry of guarding and interpreting the word of God (DV:12).

Catholics in Latin America have always spoken of the Gospels (*evangelios*) and their authors *(evangelistas).* Now the term *evangelización*, and its companion terms *evangelizadores* or *agentes de evangelización* (evangelizers or agents of evangelization), are common parlance in Catholic Church circles.

This is, of course, principally due to the Council and post-conciliar renovation and, more fundamentally, to the biblical movement at the heart of the Council.

As history broadens perspectives, the Vatican Council of 1962–65 stands out ever more clearly as a watershed of church history in modern times: the build-up to it through so many currents of church movement; the gradual unfolding of its rich principles of church reform. Its double accent or movement (back to the sources and out to the world) mark us all more and more.

The return to the sources is a mighty refreshment in the spirit and life of the apostolic Church, primarily manifested in the Scriptures. This accent has progressively impressed itself upon all aspects of Catholic teaching, worship, and life. The "Word of God" becomes once more the living and conscious foundation of Catholic living, a role from which for many it had been displaced by intermediate devotions and authorities—not in theory, perhaps, but certainly in practice.

In the closing days of the Council, Karl Rahner gave a conference in Rome on the Decree on Priestly Formation, just published by the Council Fathers. He stated that one of the most important decisions of the Council was the reordering of sacred studies, mandated with the simple statement: "Dogmatic theology should be so arranged that the biblical themes are presented first" (OT: 16).

This accent upon the primacy of the Gospel (or the Word of God generally) runs all through the Council texts, for every aspect of Church life. More and more it appears as the key to the entire conciliar renovation proposed by Vatican II.

As always, such a fundamental accent took time to work itself out and to be fully felt. Puebla, in 1979, for example, is far more Gospel-centered than was Medellín in 1968. The Church in Latin America over these years had also become much more consciously evangelizing, and evangelized.

The Vatican Synod of 1974 had brought the theme of evangelization to center stage. It was among the several subjects most proposed by episcopal conferences for that session of the Synod, along with youth and the family, and Pope Paul VI gave it his preference and approval. When the Council of the Permanent Secretariat of the Synod met in early 1973 to prepare an outline of topics for the Synod to be sent as preparatory material for the bishops conferences, both they and the few experts invited to assist them had to begin by trying to give an adequate description of the term "evangelization" itself. It could mean everything from the simple announcement of salvation (kerygma), to full personal and social conversion in Christ, the Church, and society.

The discussions of the 1974 Synod were rich in their manifestation of the Gospel at work in the Church and the world, and they provided the occasion for the simple, profound exhortation *Evangelii Nuntiandi* of Paul VI. These discussions, and above all the living of the Church, have helped and are helping to discover the full and precise meaning of evangelization. This has been the case, certainly, in Latin America, where the Gospel is renovating the missionary, catechetical, sacramental, and social attitudes and actions of Catholics more and more. Yet some of the terms, and the reality behind them, are not yet fully clear when we speak of evangelization.

All of this is evident in this chapter of Puebla, which is largely inspired by *Evangelii Nuntiandi*, and which constitutes in itself a significant Latin American Church statement on evangelization. It appears in the stream of worldwide conciliar renovation, in the aftermath of the Vatican Synod of 1974, but is still very deeply rooted in the Latin American situation. In the choice of this theme for their Third General Conference, approved then by the pope, the bishops of Latin America show their awareness that we live today the age of Vatican II.

The statement covers three principal questions: what is evangelization (nos. 342–84), how does it affect culture, especially the religious heart of culture (nos. 385–469), and how does it affect human promotion or liberation and relate to ideological and political determinations in this order (nos. 470–562).

We can point out a few important points, some historical, some regarding content, which may lend to a better understanding of the text.

The *Documento de consulta* (preliminary consultative document) of 1977 contains a very brief development on *evangelization* as such (DC: 626–29), borrowing a few notions from *Evangelii Nuntiandi*. The text affirms that evangelization is destined for all people, calling them to a new life. Then it takes up the gospel message itself and its consequences, particularly with regard to culture, personal and social liberation, and social doctrine.

The *Documento de trabajo* (working document) of 1978 develops these latter themes more adequately, under the headings Evangelization and Culture, Human Promotion, Social Teaching of the Church, and Liberating Evangelization. Among a series of notes, long and sometimes technical, appended to the document, it elaborates on Criteria of Evangelization, Evangelization of Culture, and Popular Religiosity. The effort to spell out what evangelization is in itself, as a goal, an act, a process, and a communication, is treated under the heading: "The Ministry of Evangelization" (DT: 394–415).

Cardinal Lorscheider's topic outline placed "Criteria of Evangelization" as the first chapter of the second part, in other words at the beginning of the doctrinal reflection. The subtitles of the chapter were those of the note, under the same title, in the working document (Faith of the People of God, Scripture, Magisterium, Theology, etc.). They did not include the references to evangelization itself.

The outline proposed by the Coordinating Committee kept the same chapter heading and placed it within the second, or doctrinal, part, but after the section on content, which we have just seen. This succeeded in relating this title (charged to the fifth commission) immediately to the aspects of evangelization to be treated by the sixth, seventh, and eighth commissions. By so doing it established a very necessary distinction in Part Two between the content (Chap. I) and the communication (Chap. II) of the Gospel.

All of this led to a greater unity in the treatment of evangelization as a communication and a process, in the five headings within Chapter II under the general title "What Does Evangelizing Entail?" The commissions involved (V, VI, VII, and VIII) compared their texts at the various stages of Puebla for a whole view. Thus "Evangelization, Culture, and Popular Religiosity," by common accord, was placed ahead of evangelization in reference to human promotion, ideologies, and politics, in order to proceed from the more basic to the more particular. Culture and Popular Religiosity were then divided into separate sub-chapters for more adequate treatment.

The first section is probably the most important, and the least successful: Evangelization in itself, its dimension, and its criteria—points that are basic to all the rest. The latter two (nos. 362–84) are treated less apologetically, more theologically and pastorally, than in the previous consultative and working documents. They are rich in content, but suffer from some lack of inner coherence. This derives, I believe, from the inadequacy of the first point, treated under the new subtitle: "The Mystery of Evangelization" (nos. 348–61).* The act and process of evangelization, human and divine, personal and social, in its various moments and stages, is not yet clearly nor maturely stated. Nor had it been in the preparatory documents. This does not surprise us, if we remember how new the whole terminology is and, even more important, how new are the present efforts and experiences of evangelization in our Churches. This is also a symptom and a warning. The ardent *kerygma* of Protestant *"evangélicos,"* on the one hand, and the messianic social appeal of Marxism, on the other, attract many of our people: often in opposite directions. A full, balanced Catholic evangelization, kerygmatic, sacramental, and social, is developing in Latin America in response to the situation of our Churches. But the Church at Puebla was not yet able to provide an adequate description of this rich and mysterious reality.

The key relations or consequences of evangelization come through all the preparatory stages of Puebla and emerge in the successive editions of the conference document with increasing clarity.

First among these, in the final disposition of the text, is culture. *Evangelii Nuntiandi* reminds us of this relation, which is always present. In its "Pastoral Overview" Puebla refers to the "radical Catholic substrate" found in our people (no. 7); but it also refers to the fact that the Church's presence and teaching are no longer so easily and generally accepted as in the past (no. 77). New cultural influences are at work, pluralistic, secularizing, in many instances, and intensified by modern communication media (nos. 51–62). What is culture, what is the spiritual heart of culture, and what is the significance of our option to evangelize the culture or cultures of Latin America? Puebla offers a timely, well reflected approach, valid both for intellectuals and for pastors at work at every level. The spiritual heart of our culture is what Paul VI calls the "religion of the people," developed in our context. It is being engulfed by an urban-industrial culture, scientific, technological, and highly secularizing, which tends to be or at least hopes to become a universal culture (no. 421). The motor of its civilization is the modern city.

The text singles out three principal conflicts: between the Church and that secularism that would separate or even oppose human beings to God; the

*Why was the subtitle "The *Ministry* of Evangelization" as found in the working document and Lorscheider changed in Puebla by Commission V in its first outline to "The *Mystery* of Evangelization"—even though the corresponding section and content it covers remain roughly the same? It is not simply a typographical error. "Ministry" was used first to stress the relationship between Christ the Evangelizer and the Evangelizing Church. Commission V no longer stresses this aspect. Hence, probably, the change.

② situations of injustice prevalent today, so at odds with the basic religious sentiments of the people (no. 437); and ③ a concept of "universality" that would not respect cultural differences in each nation and region and would even press for a uniformity that would signify an unjust supremacy and domination of some peoples and social sectors over others, particularly of the more powerful nations over Latin America (no. 427).

Section 3 of Chapter II (nos. 444ff.) moves on specifically to evangelization and popular religiosity. Medellín was very aware of this problem. It is the principal preoccupation of Medellín's sixth conclusion on "Pastoral Care of the Masses," which provides excellent insights, reflections, and recommendations. It calls for studies at all levels. What Medellín lacks and Puebla acquires is the fruit and study of these eleven intervening years, and, as a result, a much better theoretical and pastoral framework for the understanding and direction of the whole problem. The heart of this new realization is summed up by Puebla: "It is of the utmost importance that we pay heed to the religion of our peoples. Not only must we take it on as an object for evangelization. Insofar as it has already been evangelized, we must also accept it as an active, evangelizing force" (no. 396). Section 3 examines the various parts of this affirmation.

Puebla treats *piedad popular* (popular piety) in Part Three (Chap. III, nos. 895–963) as involving all the external manifestations and "devotions" (processions, patronal feasts, veneration of images, etc.) of the inner attitude of "popular religiosity." The latter is at the heart of the person, of those inner dispositions that constitute culture; the former is the world of practice and ritual, both personal and communal. The distinction is important, as is the relation between the two.

The treatment of popular piety relates it to other areas, especially private prayer and liturgy. No. 940 stresses the need to "celebrate our faith in the liturgy with cultural expressions that display a sound creativity," promoting adequate adaptations, etc. (cf. also no. 926). No. 465, in the treatment of popular religiosity, touches on the same point. One would have desired, however, a more serious and precise treatment of culture and liturgical signs in Latin America, since this lies so much at the heart of all liturgical-cultural adaptation.

Sections 4 and 5 of this chapter (nos. 470–562) represent one of Puebla's best and most significant moments. They catch the growth of Catholic thought and practice worldwide, especially as seen from the Vatican and the Vatican synods, and bring together the reality and the clarification of the Latin American Church.

They treat human promotion, ideology, and politics. They do so within the context of a theological reflection on the Gospel and its communication. This is a conscious step to break the dichotomy between theology and social action, between faith and life. The social teaching of the Church as presented by Puebla (nos. 472ff.) is the fruit of theologico-pastoral reflection on the social strivings of Christians. It involves the whole Church and its life situations. It expands, applies, and adapts according to the changing circumstances of time and place, in constant fidelity to the Gospel. The entire Christian community, guided by its pastors, is the subject and agent of this reflection.

This description of church social teaching overcomes many of the obstacles, and sometimes prejudices, to its acceptance and application. It also makes quite clear that this teaching is no more or less than one area of theologico-pastoral reflection, similar to many areas in what we commonly call doctrinal or moral teaching. In all these areas the experiences and the life of the whole Church must be fully assumed and interpreted.

Section 4 (nos. 470ff.), after the initial presentation of the validity of the Church's teaching and action in the area of human promotion, goes on to describe this more in depth. Pope John Paul II on occasions speaks of "liberation or human promotion," making the two somewhat synonymous. The term "human promotion" is a literal translation from the Spanish and might better be rendered in English by "human and social development," or "integral development," or some similar term. Puebla, in any case, takes up immediately the description of liberation, as we understand it in Christ. The notions are largely taken from *Evangelii Nuntiandi* and placed in our post-Medellín context, ending with a text of John Paul II that is implicitly the background for the discussion of "criteria" in Section 1 above (no. 489). The document then goes on to the very interesting reflections upon liberation *from* false gods and *for* our fruition in the one true God (nos. 491ff.).

This section will merit much attention. It was developed over the years of preparation, in both previous documents, and successfully and succinctly at Puebla. The Gospel rejects any absolute other than the true God. Wealth or comfort (the consumer society), power (the security state), sex, even the human person, if made absolutes, are idols, from which we must be liberated to reach our union with the true God in his Kingdom. Liberation, furthermore, is not primarily a freedom *from*, but rather a freedom *for*: at every intermediate level and in the final goal worthy of human desire, God himself. There is an obvious importance to this whole treatment of liberation. It is the Church of Latin America that has principally given impulse to the term and to reflection, theological and pastoral, on liberation. This was obvious in the Synod of 1974. That Synod's reflection, in turn, through *Evangelii Nuntiandi* and Paul VI, returns to guide Puebla.

Section 5 (nos. 507ff.) takes all this reflection into the area of the evangelization of ideologies and politics. No small part of the merit of the preparation and the criticism of the two preparatory documents for Puebla is the progressive clarification of many realities and their explanations. The experience and the reflection of the Church in Latin America in this process of clarification draws upon the conciliar renovation in the universal Church, guided, as it has been, by frequent and opportune documents of the popes and of the Vatican synods.

This is particularly true of the political area. Puebla begins (no. 507) by observing "a growing deterioration in the sociopolitical life of our countries" and the role of discernment the Church must fulfill in this regard, from the standpoint of the Gospel and its social teaching, even at the risk of its message being used as a "tool" (no. 511).

The Church in many of our countries, especially in the decade since Medellín, has acquired considerable experience with politics. The whole relation of Church to State in Latin America is in flux. In the wake of Vatican II, the Church generally tries to view the relation as less a question of the hierarchies on each side in confrontation or in collaboration, according to older Hispanic notions, and more a matter of the presence of the whole Church community in all its members and charisms in the whole of the secular community. Due respect is always to be given to the autonomy of each community in its own goals and structures, while Christians must make the distinction between their rights and duties as members of the Church and as members of the State (cf. LG:36).

This is more and more the vision proposed by the Church in Latin America, in its great documents of Medellín and Puebla, in the official statements of episcopal conferences, and in the thinking and acting of its most committed members and groups. But old ideas and attitudes do not die out easily. Many Catholics, especially among the more conservative, hold on to or hanker after some vestige of official relationship between Church and State; and they look to the heads of state and the bishops of the Church as those charged with making this work. This attitude is common, for instance, among the military who now rule most of the continent. They have little tolerance for "popular" expression, whether in secular or religious circles. Because of a nineteenth-century *forma mentis* that would reduce religion to the area of individual piety, they have little tolerance or sympathy for church statements or action, whether by the hierarchy or at other church levels, on matters of social and political consequence. This is a typical manifestation of a classical "liberal" mentality, which on this point, due to a common social matrix of the last century, is shared by the Marxists as well. Both would exclude any "political" influence of the Churches as entirely undue.

This great difference both in terminology and in basic attitudes toward the Church and its role in society complicates discussion and action. To existing conflict there is often added incommunication. To differences in values and moral judgment, there is added psychological and semantic incompatibility. This is particularly true regarding the conservative, military mentality, the "liberal" bent mentioned above; but is often the case with Marxist groups as well. It is, in both instances, the religious vs. the secular—in fact the modern, post-conciliar religious vs. the nineteenth-century secular. The lines are not that clearly drawn in every instance, but their existence helps to explain what Puebla sets out to clarify in this last section of its exposition on evangelization.

Puebla establishes at once its key distinction between politics "in the broad sense" and "party politics" (nos. 502–23). The Church must be very active in the former through the promotion of values that "should inspire politics," while leaving party politics to groups of citizens who set out to obtain political power to resolve social questions according to their criteria and ideology. Those who speak or act in the name of the Church, especially bishops, priests, and religious, but also lay persons who are active directors of pastoral action, should limit themselves to politics in the broad sense. Lay persons in the world should have the help of the Church in their moral and social formation, but are called to act under their own responsibility in fidelity to their Christian conscience in all that refers to "party politics" (nos. 524–25). Priests active in this area should not simultaneously exercise their priestly ministry (no. 527).

These principles are universally stated by the Church. Witness the Vatican Synod of 1971. Their application is more difficult in some areas than others. In some instances, for example, in our countries the Church may well be the only entity with sufficient moral authority to act or even to speak in the face of widespread political oppression. Yet here we may well say that the exception should not become the rule. Any exception must be clearly described as such, as in the case just stated of the priest who takes up political office or goes into party politics. To act or speak otherwise would be to diminish the credibility of the Church in its own properly religious message and mission, and in fact, as the pope warned at Puebla, to reduce that mission to a purely secular solution. This is clearly Puebla's stand.

There follows a brief passage (nos. 531–34) that rejects violence from any quarter and strongly recommends active Christian nonviolence. Much more should and eventually must be said by the Church on this whole subject. The text's clear-cut condemnation of state-practiced torture, kidnappings, and persecution leaves no doubt. The condemnation of terrorism is equally categorical. But as to the "guerrilla," whose violence is rejected in this text as "cruel and uncontrollable when it is unleashed," there remains the doubt about just insurrection, referred to in *Populorum Progressio* (PP: 31) and Medellín (Med-P:18). This whole matter is the object of grave moral dilemmas, as for instance in the recent situation of Nicaragua. The bishops there had not specifically condemned the armed rebellion. This was already significant. But later, in the final months, they made a statement that was widely interpreted as declaring the insurrection to be justifiable. To my memory, it is the first time this has happened since the Latin American Wars of Independence in the first quarter of the last century.

Medellín is far more complete in its treatment of violence (Med-P:15–19), though Puebla does give more explicit support to the movement of active nonviolence, typified by Mahatma Gandhi, Martin Luther King, Jr., and Helder Camara.

There follows a treatment of ideologies, in which the principles are stated with the clarity of theory proven in practice. These ideas were the subject of many debates, both in the preparatory period and in the conference itself. Ideologies offer "a view of the various aspects of life from the standpoint of a specific group in society" (no. 535). They are necessary for the inner cohesion, the projection, and the mystique of these groups, for instance, political parties; and they are valid insofar as they do not tend to absolutize themselves and exclude all other ideologies or points of view (no. 536; note strong dependence here upon Pope Paul VI's letter *Octagesima Adveniens* of 1971).

The Gospel is not an ideology, nor is the social teaching of the Church. They rather question all ideologies, from the ever-original vantage point of God's word (no. 540).

The text then briefly describes the most prevalent ideologies in Latin America today (cf. the similar passages in Part One, nos. 47–49, and the discussion of the different visions that lie at the heart of these ideologies in Part Two, nos. 308–15). All three ideologies presented here are severely criticized. Christians are called upon to project the contents of Christian anthropology into ideological frameworks and, even more, into working models of society (no. 553). The Church does not assume any one ideology, nor propose any alternative models for society (cf. no. 1211). There is therefore no talk of a "third way" that the Church would propose, between capitalism and Marxism. There are many possible ways. Christians in each nation should seek the best, and in fact can borrow from and dialogue with all (no. 554).

We may take brief note of paragraph 541. Several had requested the eighth commission, charged with this section, to state something positive about the right and the necessity of the State, reminiscent of Vatican II's chapter on the

"Political Community" (*Gaudium et Spes*, Part II, chap. 4, avoids the terms "State"). One proposition suggested that some of our political woes are due to the inadequacy of our States, organized on a nineteenth-century pattern while trying to face up to twentieth-century problems. The present text was included in the third writing of this chapter and emended in the fourth and final version with the addition of the final phrase, which stresses the prevailing caution of the Church vis-à-vis the State in today's Latin America.

The section closes with a warning and an exhortation. The warning: the manipulation of the Church by politics and ideologies normally comes about through the fault of the Christians themselves, pastors included, who either too passively accept the status quo or permit the Gospel to be reduced to and subordinated to ("re-read by") any given ideology or political or economic system. The exhortation: the mission of the Church for justice is enormous and is the task of all of us.

Parts Three, Four, and Five: Evangelizing the Church and the World

Within the dynamics of the Puebla document, we now move into the third and final phase of the text. Part One is the pastoral vision of our reality; Part Two is the gospel answer to that situation, and its communication; Parts Three and Four, with a conclusion in Part Five, will be the pastoral conclusions, recommendations, guidelines, or, a term more popular in Puebla, the pastoral options.

Puebla describes the term: "Pastoral options are a choosing process. This process enables us, after pondering and analyzing both positive and negative realities in the light of the Gospel, to find and adopt the pastoral response to the challenges posed to evangelization" (no. 1299). These "options" are found throughout the text, especially in the third phase, as we call it, that is, Parts Three, Four, and Five. But precisely because they are so many, Part Five, as a conclusion, endeavors to point out the unifying theme that holds them together, and also the need for pastoral planning in each local Church to establish concrete priorities and coordination in these options.

Puebla grew out of the entire Latin American Church, from its very root groups, into this General Conference. Similarly, its descriptions, its message and its recommendations are addressed to all of Latin America. They make up one essential and existential whole. Nonetheless, in the unity and variety that is Latin America, some descriptions, some aspects of the message, some of the options are more relevant to certain parts of Latin America, some to others. This variety in the details makes it all the more important that the main outlines of Puebla stand out very clearly.

The pastoral options in Medellín constituted the final part (in the see-judge-*act* method) in each of the sixteen Conclusions. They were variously titled: pastoral projections, recommendations, orientations, or conclusions. In Puebla, as we have seen, it was decided early that there would be one integrated document, rather than several smaller ones. The problem arose, then, as to the discussion in the pastoral area. In a dynamic of see-judge-act, how do you choose topics in "act" before going through "see" and "judge"? Ideally, perhaps, Puebla should have first worked exclusively on Parts One and Two, and only then proposed the divisions for the discussion of pastoral options.

But this would have been thoroughly impractical. The Church is alive and is constantly working out, at every level, pastoral options. Puebla was not meant to create or invent the Church of Latin America, but reflect it, and in that reflection to discern and guide its life and action. It was natural, then, that the consultations in preparation for Puebla, from the very beginning, came up with suggested pastoral options.

The first round of consultations, during 1977, was based largely upon the four regional meetings of bishops, attended by delegates of the episcopal conferences of the respective regions. There had been no time yet for a serious consultation on the part of the bishops within their local Churches. Not suprisingly, then, the "consultative document," distributed to the bishops by CELAM at the end of the year, though it contained some excellent elements, suffered from a lack of precision, concreteness, and inner coherence. Nor did it adequately reflect the rich vitality of church life in Latin America. This was particularly true of the Third Part, that of pastoral conclusions, dedicated to the "Pastoral Action of the Church."

The first two parts ("General Situation" and "Doctrinal Framework") had been worked out by one team of social experts and theologians, assisted at the end by four bishops, one from each of the four episcopal regions. The intention, evidently, was to set the document up withing the dynamic of *Gaudium et Spes* and Medellín, such as we have described it above. But, as a matter of fact, for practical reasons, the Third Part was worked out by an entirely different team, working separately. They were largely directors and consultors of most of the pastoral departments of CELAM. They put together some thirty pages under two headings: "Agents of Evangelization" and "Priorities in Evangelization." The former was a listing, from bishops to laity, with a brief commentary on the "situation" and a "reflection." The latter attempted to point from this to priority areas of evangelization: in "human promotion," within the Church, and in a missionary projection. Each point was treated, once more, in its situation and then in a reflection, but more pointed to pastoral action than under the first heading.

This presentation of pastoral conclusions was obviously quite unsatisfactory. Throughout the month of July 1978, Cardinal Lorscheider directed the complicated task of reading and putting together the mountain of suggestions that had come in as a result of the second round of consultations. This time the most voluminous and most important had come directly from the episcopal conferences and as a result, in many instances, of a wide and serious consultation in the local Churches. Along with the descriptions of reality and the suggestions for evangelization, both in content and communications, there were many pastoral recommendations. It was important that in the working document, which had to be drawn up, the dynamic connection between these three phases be real and also that it be evident. Over a week was spent in reading and classifying the reports, in search of the most common and the most basic preoccupations, judgments, and suggestions—in a word, the driving and central themes proposed by the bishops. As this began to work itself out, descriptions, judgments, and suggestions began to fall into an organic whole.

There were, however, several difficulties. This was to be only a working document, which could serve as a "guide" and "a point of reference" in

Puebla, as Pope John Paul II would remark in his Opening Address. But no more. It would not be discussed in Puebla; nor should it in any way pretend to predetermine Puebla, especially in the area of pastoral conclusions. The working document should reflect the consultations, particularly of the bishops' conferences, with the central theme or themes they proposed and an indication of orientations or conclusions they suggest. No more.

Another difficulty arose from the nature of the project, as one sole document. How did one best order the pastoral suggestions in Part One? After much deliberation it was decided to cast the suggestions within an outline that would assist toward a process of pastoral planning. Thus the text briefly sums up, in the light of Parts One and Two, the principal problems and challenges posed for evangelization in Latin America and proposes to answer the most central of them in the order and development of pastoral planning. The text then develops through the stages of that planning: 1. Options; 2. General Objective; 3. Criteria; 4. Specific Objectives (and, within these, Goals). These terms, used as chapter headings, are given their precise pastoral meaning in footnotes. This is where and how Puebla came to speak of "Pastoral Options" in the sense cited above.

The "Option" and the "General Objective" described in the working document reappear simply as "options" in the conclusion of the final Puebla document (nos. 1302–6). They point to a Church that is a "sacrament of communion," a "servant" and a "missionary" Church, which is constantly in process of evangelization itself, in the light of the Word, and of evangelizing through the witnessing, proclaiming, and celebration of that Word, toward a just society, renewed in the Spirit, transforming the world.

The criteria suggested in the working document, toward the General Objective, are: Witnessing, the Word of the Lord, Conversion, Evangelization, Unity, Service, Preferential Option for the Poor, and Fidelity.

These are applied under the heading of Specific Objectives, which are: Evangelize with primary insistence on the Word of God; Celebration of the Faith (Liturgy); Missionary Church; Ministerial and Charismatic Church; Evangelize Culture and Cultures; Construct Unity: in the Church, and toward the world. Under each of these "Specific Objectives" a list of concrete *"metas,"* or goals, was listed, with a marginal reference to the episcopal conferences that had suggested it. (These marginal references to the episcopal conferences are given throughout the entire working document.)

The bishops at Puebla did not follow the outline of the working document. Many of the concrete points (under "Goals") do appear in the final text, and other elements reappear, but in changed and sometimes unclear shape, like misplaced remnants taken out of their former context. Thus the incomplete references to pastoral planning in Part Five of Puebla, and the inconsistent use of "option" throughout the text, for matters of quite different importance.

One remarkable feature of the Third Part of the working document, titled "Evangelizing Action," is the almost entirely exclusive reference to directly religious evangelizing. The final specific objective ("Construct Unity") had been written up entirely within the perspective of religious unity, with some reference to consequences in the temporal order. Finally, at the insistence of some that this did not reflect the description of the reality of Latin America given in the First Part of the document, nor the insistence of the bishops' conferences on serious social action, especially for the poor, the items related to the temporal order were put under a separate subheading ("Toward the World"), and more points were added, especially in reference to problems of the future (e.g., ecology), and of the world order (armaments, new international economic order, etc.).

Cardinal Lorscheider, in the topic outline he presented to the Puebla Conference on the opening day, changed the title given this part by the working document from "Evangelizing Action" to "Pastoral Action." He included most of the elements found in the working document, but in a different order and with a new focus. He left aside the attempt to set forth the pastoral conclusions in the form of a pastoral plan, maintaining from that approach some of the terminology, specifically the word "option," but only in reference to the poor. He broke the pastoral elements into four headings: 1. Who are to be evangelized? (all, but especially the poor). 2. Places or areas of evangelization. 3. Agents of evangelizing. 4. Means of evangelization.

Despite these changes the cardinal maintained the inclusion of the whole of "Pastoral Action" under direct religious evangelizing, even more exclusively than the working document had done. The purpose of this approach, for the authors of that document, had been to avoid a dichotomy in pastoral action between the religious and the social. But the effect as carried out, and especially in Cardinal Lorscheider's outline, was that the outline did not envisage discussing the concrete applications of so much that was mentioned earlier in the document, both under the description of reality and the doctrinal reflection, about injustice, human rights, politics, etc. The only exception were two subtitles on the poor: which called for a more precise understanding of the terms "poor" and "option for the poor."

The coordinating committee, which was elected the second day, took up immediately the suggestions of the twenty transitory commissions on Cardinal Lorscheider's proposed outline in a session that went through to dawn of the next day. The most significant changes, based upon the commissions' suggestions and then approved by the Assembly, were in Part Three. It appeared necessary to maintain the unitive aspect of "Pastoral Action" from the point of view of evangelization, which is the theme of the whole conference; but at the same time, precisely in this unititive vision of evangelization, it was necessary to bring the document to bear more directly upon the whole area of justice.

It was decided to divide "Pastoral Action" into two parts, (or "nuclei" as they were called at that moment). Both had to do with evangelization. But the emphasis in the first would be on the effort of the Church to evangelize itself, and in the second on the effort of the Church to evangelize the world. This double emphasis, in a simultaneous process of evangelization, follows *Evangelii Nuntiandi* (EN: 15) and had been stressed in the preparatory documents.

Part Three came to bear the title: "Evangelization in the Latin American Church: Communion and Participation." Lorscheider's first point (those to be evangelized and option for the poor) was divided. The first half went to the newly created chapter on evangelization in Part Two of the text, in its opening considerations. The second half, option for the poor, went to Part Four of the text, as we will see.

This allowed the multiple aspects of the Church, in its own process of being evangelized, to be grouped into the three headings suggested by the cardinal: centers (instead of places) of evangelization, agents, and means.

Part Four came to be titled: "A Missionary Church Serving Evangelization in Latin America." The title is not altogether apt. It intends to suggest the effort to maintain in view the theme of the assembly, which is evangelization, and to link it directly, not merely by some extrinsic application, to the moral issues of the temporal order. But it hardly suggests the deep social impact of the subjects to be treated.

The basic theme had to be the promotion of the human person and the person's dignity and rights. The commissions called for it; the whole preceding text demanded it. It was divided into two chapters: the national and the international scenes, which were subsequently, under the same commission (XXI), merged into one (nos. 1254–93).

The *option for the poor* was singled out for special attention because it had become increasingly a dominant theme of Puebla. It was placed at the start of Part Four, rather than in Part Three, because the prime concern of Puebla is for poverty as a social ill, as a social sin and scandal.

The coordinating commission proposed to follow this with a chapter on *option for young people.* Thereby it transferred the context of the youth from the immediate considerations of evangelization, as seen in the subtitles proposed in Cardinal Lorscheider's topic outline, to the world contexts in which youth find themselves today and in which their evangelization takes place.

Another theme had been appearing persistently throughout the preparatory period of Puebla and, thanks to the transitory commissions, now found its way into this newly created Part Four. The idea behind it was simple, despite the heavy title given the chapter: "Church Collaboration with the Builders of a Pluralistic Society in Latin America." An older Catholic Action mentality would have spoken about "making the Gospel meaningful through Christian leaders in the specialized environments of today." It is the old insistence of Pius IX on the "apostolate of like by like," forgotten for a time, and come to the fore again in a new way.

There is an advantage for the readers when they know how Puebla historically came to include the various elements we find in the Final Document. The advantage is obvious. It becomes easier to understand what Puebla meant to say, what it emphasizes, in what order and why.

This is particularly true in Parts Three and Four which, together, constitute the area of "pastoral" or "evangelizing" action. As we have mentioned, we can understand the rather devious manner in which the term "option" came to find itself in the text and the ambiguity surrounding it. For instance, in Part Four the first two chapters are presented as "Options," the latter two as areas of evangelizing. We could say that the options are directed to groups of persons (the poor, the young), whereas the fourth chapter concentrates on the human person, which includes all men and women. But then we have the third chapter which deals with the "builders of the pluralistic society," certainly a group of persons, and the sense of the chapter is an "option" for them. What is more, in Part Three there are many "options" (e.g., the family, no. 590; *Comunidades Eclesiales de Base,* no. 650; the religious life, no. 758; etc.). Part Five, after describing what Puebla means by "pastoral options" (no. 1299), refers to the fact that each of the commissions at Puebla, in the part of the text it composed, set forth its options and goes on to list some general options in conclusion. As a matter of another historical fact, Part Five was composed at the end of the conference by a separate commission, with little reference to the other commissions, nor to the coordinating commission; thus its summation and its use of the term "options," as well as its phrasing of some general options, rather hearkens back to the working document, as we pointed out above. It uses parts of that document, remnants we called them earlier, without the precision they were given there and without sufficient connection to the earlier part of the final document.

What may we conclude? The term "option" does maintain, where it is used, the general sense given it in no. 1299. But it is not used in the precise sense of pastoral planning which the working document, by that very description, intended to give it. That sense would have been the large options for the attitude and action of the Church, reflected, as we have seen, in Part Five, nos. 1302 to 1305. As a result, many of the "options" proposed in the text of Puebla would come under the working document's sense of "criteria" (preferential option for the poor, for example), "special objectives," and, within each special objective, concrete "goals."

Conclusion

1. The "pastoral options" of Puebla are not to be found only in Part Four. Some are distributed throughout the whole text (for example, the fourth chapter of Part I, nos. 127–61, which under the title of "Present-Day Tendencies" anticipates a series of implicit recommendations). The options are directly envisaged in both Parts Three and Four, which must be viewed together as providing the pastoral direction of Puebla.

2. The pastoral options stress some common elements, and the options are presented as valid for the whole of Latin America—while the Churches in each nation and area are called upon to plan their own options (no. 1307).

3. Some "options" that stand out most clearly in Parts Three and Four are:

a. For the family and *"Comunidades Eclesiales de Base."*

b. For a ministry at once hierarchical and widely shared in by the laity, especially in evangelization.

c. For the religion of the people, as both an object and a vehicle of evangelization.

d. For the poor, as a preferential option that is immediately social, but occurs within a full context of evangelization. It is interesting to observe that the preoccupation for the poor is in *crescendo* during the preparatory period (1977–78) and reaches its strongest expression precisely during the Assembly at Puebla and in its Final Document. The ambiguous usage of the term "pastoral option," or simply "option," throughout the text, which we have already discussed, ends up, fortuitously and providentially, by re-enforcing a most telling effect, namely, that the "option for the poor" stands out as the strongest and most characteristic option of Puebla and of the Church of Latin America in its evangelizing mission.

e. For youth, an option not well spelled out, but insistent for every area of evangelization.

f. For dialogue with and evangelization of groups of leaders in each specialized area of today's life, who in turn may incarnate the Gospel and spread its meaning and life in their specific worlds and areas of influence. This is particularly significant for the effort to evangelize culture (and cultures), to change structures, and to build up a dynamic social teaching of the Church.

g. For human dignity and human rights at every level, especially the international level.

h. For the orientation of both the agents and the means of evangelization within this vision.

i. For the full scope of evangelization. Evangelization is not merely the first kerygma, nor even a further catechesis. It aims at the full transformation of human beings (prayers, sanctity) in Christ, and of society, in the communion and participation of the Church. The Church is thus at one and the same time the sign, instrument, and ferment for the unity of people among themselves and with God—a sign of the intimate union of the Blessed Trinity.

In Part Five, the central theme is replayed: Evangelization for Communion and Participation. But evangelization must be liberating: of self, through conversion from sin to life in Christ; of society, from the effects of sin to justice, peace, and genuine fraternity. Evangelization leads to communion in the Church: the fullness of being and life in Christ, and through him, in the Father and the Spirit, with all the saints; and it leads to participation, which is the constant acting out of that deeply lived communion. Evangelization also makes itself felt in the secular community through persons and structures: as communion of thought, of fundamental belonging; and as participation in the genuine communication of goods of all orders.

This high theology of Puebla, a spelling out of the Church as the sacrament of God's life through Christ in humankind (LG:1), is at the same time an expression of the very practical form of pastoral realization that we find today in thousands of Comunidades Eclesiales de Base. These spring up in and from the people, not spontaneously or alone, but in response to the Word of God, proclaimed by the apostles or apostolic teams among them. This is a transforming word, which builds toward the community of Church—in the Eucharist and in daily communication as brothers and sisters in the Lord. The CEBs are signs giving example and life to the broader secular community (village or district) in which they live and exercise their influence. This is true in small rural communities. It is equally true of the Church in the city, the nation, and the world. Linked together in growing communities, the parish, the zone, the diocese, the nation, and the world, the sacrament is the same, Christ, the true evangelizer of the world, whose witnesses and ministers we are.

Part Five ends with a call to realism. All that is said here must be worked out at home, on every level. This conclusion is reminiscent of the closing words of Gaudium et Spes (GS: 91). Puebla specifies this remark by stressing the need for pastoral planning, in which the whole community of the Church takes part under the guidance of its pastors. This is a good point on which to end. The Church of Latin America has felt its unity in Puebla, and its diversity. It has expressed its universality, in the one Catholic Church, and its particular qualities as local Church: the Church of Latin America ("la patria grande"), and the Church of each nation and diocese. Pastoral reflection and planning at each level will deepen and make more effective all these realities—but only if they are filled with the spirit of the Gospel and animated by the Spirit of the Lord.

POPE JOHN PAUL II:
LETTER TO THE LATIN AMERICAN BISHOPS

Dear Brothers in the Episcopate:

The intense labors of the Third General Conference of the Latin American Episcopate, which I was permitted to inaugurate in person and which I followed through its different stages with particular affection and interest for the Church on your continent, are summed up in these pages that you have placed in my hands.

I retain a vivid and most pleasant memory of my meeting with you. United in the same love and solicitude for your peoples, we met in the Basilica of Our Lady of Guadalupe and then in the Puebla seminary.

Your document is the fruit of assiduous prayer, deep reflection, and intense apostolic zeal. As you intended, it offers a thorough, compact synthesis of pastoral and doctrinal guidelines concerning matters of the utmost importance. With its valid criteria, it is meant to provide light and an ongoing stimulus to evangelization in Latin America's present and future.

You can feel satisfied and optimistic over the results of this conference, which was so carefully prepared by CELAM with the shared, responsible participation of all your episcopal conferences. The Latin American Church has been fortified in its vigorous unity, its own particular identity, and its will to respond to the needs and challenges that were given such close consideration during your meetings. Indeed the outcome represents a great step forward for the Church's essential mission, i.e., evangelization.

Your experiences, guidelines, preoccupations, and yearnings—framed in fidelity to the Lord, the Church, and the See of Peter—should be converted into a way of life for the communities you serve.

To this end, all your episcopal conferences and local Churches should put forward plans that have concrete goals, are on the appropriate levels, and are in harmony with CELAM on the continental level.

God grant that in a short time all your ecclesial communities will be informed and suffused with the spirit of Puebla and the guidelines of this historic conference.

May the Lord Jesus, the supreme evangelizer and the Evangel itself, grant you abundant blessings.

May the Most Holy Mary, Mother of the Church and the Star of Evangelization, guide your footsteps in a revitalized effort at evangelization that will affect the whole Latin American continent.

The Vatican, 23 March 1979,
commemoration of St. Toribio de Mogrovejo.
JOANNES PAULUS PP. II

PRESENTATION

This text is the fruit of the work carried out by the Third General Conference of the Latin American Episcopate. We, as pastors, the representatives of our communities, were summoned to this meeting by the Holy Father.

As is well known, the Puebla Conference was preceded by two years of preparation in which all the Churches of Latin America actively and generously shared responsibility.

There was a campaign of fervent prayer and an ongoing process of consultation and contributions, principally by the episcopal conferences; these were brought together and systematized in the working document for the conference. It served as our tool for study and orientation.

We have been graced by the personal presence of the successor of Peter, Pope John Paul II. His word on this historic visit to Latin America has been a precious touchstone, stimulus, and orientation for our deliberations. We refer especially to his message to the participants of the Third Conference in the homily during the concelebration at the Basilica of Guadalupe, in the homily in the seminary at Puebla, and especially in his Opening Address—all of which are included in this volume.

The broad scope of the theme of this Third Conference, with all its richness and dynamic impact, made it necessary to establish priorities and properly coordinate the different topics. This gave rise to the twenty-one working commissions, which focused on nuclei: i.e., major units and their corresponding topics or themes. This *modus operandi,* complemented by plenary and semi-plenary sessions, ensured fuller participation by all: bishops, priests, deacons, religious, lay people, invited participants, and experts. And so it was unanimously approved at the start of our meeting.

The content of the nuclei and the topics does not purport to be some kind of systematic theological or pastoral tract. That notion was expressly rejected. We have tried to consider those aspects that have the greatest direct bearing on evangelization, and we have adopted a clear-cut pastoral perspective.

So the Puebla Conference, with its wealth of contributions and its intense labors, culminates in this document. But the Conference itself is primarily a spirit. It is the spirit of a Church reaching out with renewed vigor to serve our peoples, whose realization must follow the living, transforming summons of him who set up his tabernacle in the very heart of our history (John 1:14).

Puebla is also the beginning of a new stage in the ongoing process of our ecclesial life in Latin America. The Holy Father considered it to be such when he called it "a great step forward" in his letter of 23 March 1979.

These pages have the force of a new commission, a new sending out by Christ:

"Go into the whole world and proclaim the good news to all creation" (Mark 16:15).

These guidelines are of profound interest for our pastoral activity. A process of assimilating and interiorizing their content must take place at every level, if they are to be implemented. They must be explored and deepened through prayer and spiritual discernment. Here the episcopal conferences have a clear responsibility. It is first and foremost the episcopal conferences that will be obliged to translate and flesh out these directives, in accordance with their circumstances, possibilities, and appropriate mechanisms. But it is also the task of the local Churches, parishes, apostolic movements, base-level ecclesial communities, and ultimately all our communities. They all must see to it that Puebla, all of Puebla, spills over into life with its evangelical message.

Puebla is, moreover, a spirit, the spirit of communion and participation that runs as a central theme through the preparatory documents and that inspired the conference meetings. In those documents we said:

"The theologico-pastoral thrust in the working document consists of two complementary poles: *Communion and participation* (co-participation).

"Through a full and complete evangelization, there is a restoration and a deepening of communion with God and, also as an essential element, communion among human beings. As they live out their filiation in fraternity, human beings, as active subjects of history, are thus the vital image of God within the Church and the world.

"We speak of *communion* with God, in faith, in prayer, in sacramental life; a communion with our brothers and sisters in the various dimensions of our existence; a communion in the Church, among the episcopates, and with the Holy Father; a communion in the Christian communities; a communion of reconciliation and service; a communion that is the root and driving force of evangelization; a communion with our peoples.

"We speak of *participation* in the Church, in all its levels and tasks; a participation in society and its different sectors; in the nations of Latin America; in its necessary process of integration, in an attitude of continuous dialogue. God is love, family, communion; God is the wellspring of participation in all his trinitarian mystery and in the manifestation of his new revelation to human beings through filiation, and of human beings among themselves through brotherhood" (Working Document, Presentation, 3,3).

Noteworthy about the Third Conference was the harmony of wills focused on the main theme and the consistency of the content of the Final Document. Indeed it was approved by a vote of 179 "Placet," with one abstention.

It must be admitted that there were sound reasons for working out the final draft more carefully and cohesively to eliminate repetitiousness. After all, repetitions were bound to be numerous in a document that was basically drawn up by a series of commissions. But for the sake of objectivity, we preferred not to take out those repetitions. Indeed the conference itself did not have an opportunity to carry out that delicate and arduous task.

We have made every possible effort to provide references to places where specific themes are given special treatment.

Revision of the text was limited almost exclusively to editorial matters. In this revision attention was paid to the many corrections and suggestions of the working commissions, as well as to the lists of *errata* they provided. There was also a careful and patient examination of the various citations, in which we went back to the respective sources.

With the approval of the Holy Father, we also made some minor changes.

What we have written constitutes our hope. To it we commit ourselves under the gaze of Mary, who believed and hastened out on the road to announce the great new joy that pulsated in her heart.

CO-PRESIDENTS

Cardinal Sebastiano Baggio
Prefect of the Sacred Congregation for Bishops
President of the Pontifical Commission for Latin America (CAL)

Cardinal Aloisio Lorscheider
Archbishop of Fortaleza, Brazil
President of the CNBB
President of CELAM

Archbishop Ernesto Corripio Ahumada
Archbishop of Mexico City

SECRETARY GENERAL

Archbishop Alfonso López Trujillo
Coadjutor Archbishop of Medellín, Colombia
Secretary General of CELAM

MESSAGE TO THE PEOPLES
OF LATIN AMERICA

Our Word: A Word of Faith, Hope, and Charity

1. Between Medellín and Puebla ten years have gone by. Truly, with the Second General Conference of the Latin American Episcopate, which was solemnly inaugurated by Pope Paul VI of happy memory, a new period was opened in the life of the Latin American Church (Med-OA).

On our continent, sealed with the sign of Christian hope and overburdened with problems, "God shed an immense light that shines on the rejuvenated face of his Church" (Med-Pres).

The Third Conference of the Latin American Episcopate has met in Puebla de los Ángeles to reconsider the topics discussed earlier and to take on new commitments, under the inspiration of the Gospel of Jesus Christ.

John Paul II, the Universal Pastor of our Church, was present at the opening of our labors, amid pastoral cares that touched us deeply. His luminous words traced broad lines and touched deep levels for our own reflections and deliberations, breathing the spirit of ecclesial communion.

Nourished by the power and wisdom of the Holy Spirit and sheltered under the maternal protection of Mary most holy, Our Lady of Guadalupe, we are coming to the end of our immense task in a spirit of humility, trust, and dedication. We cannot depart from Puebla for our home Churches without addressing a word of faith, hope, and charity to the People of God in Latin America and, by way of extension, to all the peoples of the world.

First of all, we want to identify ourselves: we are pastors of the Catholic and Apostolic Church that was born from the heart of Jesus Christ, the Son of the living God.

Our Question and Our Plea for Pardon

2. In this pastoral colloquy our first question in the face of the collective conscience is the following: Are we really living the Gospel of Christ on our continent?

This challenging question, which we address to Christians, can also be analyzed by all those who do not share our faith.

Christianity, which implies the originality of love, is not always practiced in its

116

fullness by us Christians. To be sure, there is great hidden heroism, much silent holiness, and many marvelous acts of sacrifice. But we also recognize that we are still far from living all that we preach. For all our faults and limitations we pastors, too, ask pardon of God, our brothers and sisters in the faith, and humanity.

We want not only to help others to self-conversion but also to be converted along with them, so that our dioceses, parishes, institutions, communities, and religious congregations will provide an incentive for living the Gospel rather than being an obstacle to it.

If we focus our gaze on our Latin American region, what do we see? No deep scrutiny is necessary. The truth is that there is an ever increasing distance between the many who have little and the few who have much. The values of our culture are threatened. Fundamental human rights are being violated.

The major efforts undertaken on behalf of humanity are not adequately or successfully solving the problems that confront us.

Our Contribution

3. But what do we have to offer you in the face of the grave and complicated questions of our epoch? How can we collaborate in fostering the well-being of our Latin American peoples when some persist in maintaining their privileges at any price, others feel downtrodden and beaten, and the rest are initiating actions to promote their survival and the clear affirmation of their rights?

Dear brothers and sisters: Once again we want to state that in treating the social, economic, and political problems we are not doing so as experts or scholars in those areas, but rather as pastoral interpreters of our peoples and confidants of their yearnings—particularly of the lowliest, who make up the vast majority of Latin American society.

What do we have to offer you? Like Peter, when he was approached at the gate of the temple by a cripple, we note the magnitude of the structural challenges in our real-life situation and say: We have neither silver nor gold, but what we have we give you! In the name of Jesus of Nazareth, rise and walk! (Acts 3:6). And the cripple rose up and praised the wondrous deeds of the Lord.

Here the poverty of Peter became wealth, and his wealth is called Jesus of Nazareth. Jesus was put to death and rose again, and through his divine Spirit he is ever present in the apostolic college and the nascent communities formed under his guidance. Jesus cures the sick person. The power of God requires the maximum effort from human beings if its work of love is to break forth and be fruitful. And in this effort human beings must use all the available means: spiritual forces and the achievements of science and technology on behalf of humanity.

What do we have to offer you? In the inaugural address of his pontificate John Paul II offers us an incisive and admirable response, presenting Christ as the answer of universal salvation. Speaking in St. Peter's Square, he said: "Do not be afraid. Open wide the doors to Jesus Christ. Open up to his saving power the doors of States, economic and political systems, the broad fields of culture, civilization, and development" (John Paul II, Inaugural homily of his pontificate, 22 October 1978).

As we see it, herein lies the seedling potential of liberation for the people of

Latin America. Herein lies our hope of constructing day by day the reality of our true destiny. Thus the human being on this continent, who is the object of our pastoral concerns, has essential significance for the Church because Jesus Christ assumed humanity and its real-life condition, except for sin. And in doing so, he himself assumed the immanent and transcendent vocation of all human beings.

Human beings who struggle, suffer, and sometimes despair never succumb to discouragement; above all, these human beings want to live the full import of their divine filiation. Hence it is important that their rights be recognized, that their lives not be a kind of abomination, and that their nature, the work of God, not be debased in opposition to their legitimate aspirations.

For the most obvious and self-evident arguments, human beings demand an end to acts of physical and moral violence, the abuses of power, the manipulation of money, and the abuse of sex. In short, they demand compliance with the Lord's precepts because all that infringes upon human dignity somehow wounds God too: "All things are yours . . . and you are Christ's, and Christ is God's" (1 Cor. 3:21–23).

What interests us as pastors is the full and complete proclamation of the truth about Jesus Christ, about the nature and mission of the Church, and about the dignity and destiny of the human being (OAP:I,1).

Thus we see our message lit up by hope. The difficulties we find and the imbalances we advert to here are not symptoms of pessimism. The sociocultural context in which we live right now is so contradictory in its conception and way of operating that it not only fosters a dearth of material goods in the homes of the poorest but also, and even more seriously, tends to deprive them of their greater treasure: i.e., God. Verification of this fact prompts us to exhort all the aware members of society to re-examine their projects; and at the same time it imposes on us the sacred obligation of fighting to preserve and deepen the sense of God in the conscience of the people. Like Abraham, we are fighting against all hope (Gen. 18:23ff.), and we will continue to do so. This means that we will never stop hoping in the grace and power of the Lord, who established an irrevocable covenant with his People despite our betrayals.

It is deeply moving to detect the overflowing spiritual riches of faith, hope, and love in the soul of the people. In this respect Latin America is an example for the other continents, and tomorrow it will be able to expand its sublime missionary vocation beyond its own borders.

And so, *Sursum corda!* Let us lift up our hearts, beloved brothers and sisters of Latin America, because the Gospel we preach is such splendid Good News that it converts and transforms people's mental and emotional schemes. For it communicates the grandeur of human destiny as prefigured in the risen Jesus Christ.

Our pastoral preoccupations on behalf of the most lowly, impregnated with human realism, do not propose to exclude the other representatives of the social corpus in which we live from our thoughts or our hearts. On the contrary, they are serious and timely warnings designed to make sure that the distances do not grow greater, that the sins do not multiply, and that the Spirit of God does not withdraw from the Latin American family.

And because we believe that the re-examination and revision of people's religious and moral behavior should be reflected in the political and economic processes of our countries, we invite all, regardless of class, to accept and take up the cause of the poor as if they were accepting and taking up their own cause, the cause of Christ himself: "I assure you, as often as you did it for one of my least brothers, you did it for me" (Matt. 25:40).

The Latin American Episcopate

4. Brothers and sisters, do not be impressed by reports that the episcopate is divided. There are differences of opinion and outlook, but the truth is that we live the principle of collegiality, complementing each other in accordance with our God-given capabilities. Only in this way will we be able to face up to the great challenge of evangelization in Latin America's present and future.

In his Opening Address to this Third Conference, Pope John Paul II noted three pastoral priorities: the family, young people, and pastoral efforts to promote vocations (OAP:IV).

The Family

5. And so with special affection we invite the Latin American family to take its place in the heart of Christ, transforming itself more and more each day into a privileged locale of evangelization, respect for life, and communitarian love.

Young People

6. We cordially invite young people to overcome the obstacles that threaten their right to participate consciously and responsibly in the construction of a better world. We do not want to see them sinfully staying away from the table of life or sadly submitting to the imperatives of pleasure, indifferentism, or voluntary and unproductive solitude. The time has already passed for protest in its exotic forms and its untimely, heady outbursts. "Your capacity is enormous." The time has come for reflection, and for complete acceptance of the challenge to fully live the essential values of authentic, integral humanism.

Pastoral Agents

7. With words of affection and trust we greet all the self-sacrificing pastoral agents in our local Churches, whatever function they may have. In exhorting you to carry on your labors on behalf of the Gospel, we urge you to increase your pastoral efforts for vocations, which include the ministries entrusted to lay people by virtue of their baptism and their confirmation. The Church needs more diocesan and religious priests, as wise and as holy as possible, to carry out the ministry of the Word and the Eucharist and to give greater efficacy to the religious and social apostolate. The Church needs lay people who are conscious of their mission within the Church and in the construction of the temporal city.

People of Good Will and the Civilization of Love

8. And now we want to address ourselves to all people of good will, to all those who exercise functions and carry out tasks in the wide and varied fields of culture, science, politics, education, labor, the media of social communication, and art.

We invite you to be self-sacrificing constructors of the "civilization of love," as described in the luminous vision of Paul VI. It finds its inspiration in the message, life, and full self-giving of Christ, and its basis in justice, truth, and freedom. In this way we can be sure to obtain your response to the imperatives of the present hour, to the interior and social peace that is so eagerly sought on the level of individual persons, families, nations, continents, and the entire universe.

We wish to spell out the organic import of the civilization of love at this moment, which is both difficult and full of hope for Latin America.

What obligation does the commandment of love impose upon us?

Christian love goes beyond the categories of all regimes and systems because it entails the insuperable power of the paschal mystery, the worth of the sufferings of the cross, and the signal pledges of victory and resurrection. Love begets the happiness of communion and inspires the criteria of participation.

As we know, justice is a sacred right of all human beings that has been conferred by God himself. It is imbedded in the very essence of the gospel message. Truth, illuminated by faith, is the perennial source of discernment for our ethical conduct. It expresses the authentic forms of a dignified life. Freedom is a precious gift from God, a consequence of our human condition, and an indispensable factor in the progress of peoples.

The civilization of love repudiates violence, egotism, wastefulness, exploitation, and moral follies. At first glance it seems to be an expression lacking the strength needed to confront the grave problems of our age. But we can assure you that no stronger word exists in the Christian lexicon. It is one with the very force of Christ. If we do not believe in love, then neither do we believe in HIM who says: "This is my commandment: love one another as I have loved you" (John 15:12).

The civilization of love proposes to all the evangelical treasure of national and international reconciliation. There is no gesture more sublime than pardon. The person who does not know how to pardon will not be pardoned (Matt. 6:12).

On the balance-scale of shared responsibilities, much weight must be given to renunciation and solidarity if we are to bring a correct equilibrium into human relationships. Meditation on this truth would lead our countries to revise their behavior toward expatriates and their attendant problems, in line with the common good, in charity, and without prejudice to justice. Countless families on our continent are living a traumatized life.

The civilization of love condemns the absolute divisions and the psychological barriers that violently separate people, institutions, and national communities. For that very reason it fervently defends the thesis favoring the integration of Latin America. In unity and in diversity there are elements of continental value that deserve to be appreciated and explored more deeply than merely national interests. It is fitting to remind our nations in Latin America that there is an urgent need to preserve and foster the heritage of continental peace. Indeed they would be assuming an enormous historical responsibility if they were to break the bonds of Latin American friendship when, in our opinion, there are juridical and moral means to which they can have recourse to solve problems of common interest.

The civilization of love rejects subjection and any dependence prejudicial to the dignity of Latin America. We do not accept the status of satellite to any country in the world, or to any country's ideology. We wish to live fraternally with all nations, because we repudiate any sort of narrow, irreducible nationalism. It is time that Latin America advised the developed nations not to immobilize us, not to put obstacles in the way of our progress, and not to exploit us. Instead they would do well to help us magnanimously to overcome the barriers of our underdevelopment while respecting our culture, our principles, our sovereignty, our identity, and our natural resources. It is in that spirit that we will grow together as fellow members of the same universal family.

Another thing that sends a shudder through our heart and marrow is the arms race, which continues to engender instruments of death. It involves the sad ambiguity of confusing the right of national defense with the ambitious pursuit of illicit profits. It will not serve to fashion peace.

As we come to the close of our message, we respectfully and confidently invite all responsible officials in the sociopolitical sphere to ponder these reflections, which are the fruit of our personal experiences and our pastoral sensibilities.

Believe us when we say that we do desire peace; that to attain it, it is necessary to eliminate those factors that create tensions between what we already have and what we might become, between what is and the justice to which we aspire. To work for justice, truth, love, and freedom within the bounds of communion and participation is to work for universal peace.

Final Word

9. At the Medellín Conference we ended our message with these words: "We have faith in God, in human beings, and in the values and future of Latin America." Here in Puebla, taking up again that profession of divine and human faith, we proclaim:

God is present and alive, in Jesus Christ the Liberator, in the heart of Latin America.

We believe in the power of the Gospel.

We believe in the effectiveness of the gospel values of communion and participation for generating creativity and fostering pastoral experiments and new pastoral projects.

We believe in the grace and power of the Lord Jesus that suffuses life and moves us toward conversion and solidarity.

We believe in hope, which nourishes and fortifies human beings on their way to God, our Father.

We believe in the civilization of love.

May Our Lady of Guadalupe, the patron of Latin America, accompany us with her ever-present solicitude in this pilgrimage of peace.

EVANGELIZATION IN LATIN AMERICA'S PRESENT AND FUTURE

Final Document
of the Third General Conference
of the Latin American Episcopate

Puebla de Los Angeles, Mexico
27 January–13 February 1979

PART ONE
PASTORAL OVERVIEW OF THE REALITY
THAT IS LATIN AMERICA

The aim of this historical overview is:

—To SITUATE our own evangelization in continuity with the evangelization carried   **1**
out over the past five centuries. The pillars of that past evangelization still perdure,
providing a radical Catholic substrate in Latin America. After Vatican II and the Second
General Conference of the Latin American Episcopate in Medellín, this substrate was
still further enlivened by the Church's increasingly clear and deepening awareness of
its fundamental mission, namely, evangelization.

—To EXAMINE with a pastoral eye some of the aspects of the present sociocultural   **2**
context in which the Church is carrying out its mission, and also the pastoral reality
that confronts evangelization as it is operative today and as it moves into the future.

It includes:

Chapter I:	Historical Overview: Major Milestones in the Evangelization of Latin America
Chapter II:	Pastoral Overview of the Sociocultural Context
Chapter III:	The Ecclesial Reality Today in Latin America
Chapter IV:	Present-Day Tendencies and Evangelization in the Future

CHAPTER I
HISTORICAL OVERVIEW: MAJOR MILESTONES
IN THE EVANGELIZATION OF LATIN AMERICA

The Church has been given the mission of bringing the Good News to human   **3**
beings. To carry out this mission effectively, the Church in Latin America feels
that it is necessary to know the Latin American people in their historical context
and their varied circumstances. The Latin American people must continue to be

evangelized as heirs to a past, protagonists of the present, fashioners of a future, and pilgrims journeying toward the definitive Kingdom.

4   Evangelization is the very mission of the Church. The history of the Church is fundamentally the history of the evangelization of a people that lives through an ongoing process of gestation, and that is born and integrated into the life of nations over the ages. In becoming incarnate, the Church makes a vital contribution to the birth of nationalities and deeply imprints a particular character on them. Evangelization lies at the origins of the New World that is Latin America. The Church makes its presence felt in the origins and in the present-day reality of the continent. And, within the framework of it own proper mission and its realization, the Church seeks to contribute its services to a better future for the peoples of Latin America, to their liberation and growth in all of life's dimensions. The Medellín Conference itself re-echoed the statement of Paul VI that the vocation of Latin America was to "fashion a new and genial synthesis of the ancient and the modern, the spiritual and the temporal, what others bequeathed to us and what is our own original creation" (Med-Intro.:7).

5   In the sometimes painful confluence of the most varied cultures and races, Latin America forged a new mixture of ethnic groups as well as modes of thinking and living that allowed for the gestation of a new race that overcame the hard and fast separations that had existed previously.

6   The generation of peoples and cultures is always dramatic, enveloped in a mixture of light and shadow. As a human task, evangelization is subject to the vicissitudes of history; but it always tries to transfigure them with the fire of the Spirit on the pathway of Christ, the center and meaning of universal history and of each and every person. Spurred on by all the contradictions and lacerations of those founding epochs, and immersed in a gigantic process of domination and cultural growth that has not yet come to an end, the evangelization that went into the making of Latin America is one of the relevant chapters in the history of the Church. In the face of difficulties that were both enormous and unprecedented, the creative response was such that its vigor keeps alive the popular religiosity of the majority of our peoples.

7   Our radical Catholic substrate, with its flourishing, vital forms of religiosity, was established and animated by a vast legion of missionaries: bishops, religious, and lay people. First and foremost, there is the labor of our saints: Toribio de Mogrovejo, Rosa de Lima, Martín de Porres, Pedro Claver, Luis Beltrán, and others. . . . They teach us that the weakness and cowardice of the people who surrounded and sometimes persecuted them were overcome; that the Gospel in all its plenitude of grace and love was lived, and can be lived, in Latin America as a sign of spiritual grandeur and divine truth.

8   And then there were the intrepid champions of justice and proponents of the gospel message of peace: e.g., Antonio de Montesinos, Bartolomé de las Casas, Juan de Zumárraga, Vasco de Quiroga, Juan del Valle, Julián Garcés, José de Ancheita, Manuel Nóbrega, and all the others who defended the Indians against *conquistadores* and *encomenderos*—even unto death, as in the case of Bishop Antonio Valdivieso.* They prove, with all the force of actual fact, in what way the

---

*Unfortunately, the problem of the African slaves did not attract sufficient evangelizing and liberation-oriented attention from the Church.

Church promotes the dignity and freedom of the Latin American person. And that is a reality thankfully acknowledged by John Paul II when he first stepped on the soil of the New World:". . . those religious who came to announce Christ the Savior, to defend the dignity of the native inhabitants, to proclaim their inviolable rights, to foster their integral betterment, to teach brotherhood as human beings and as children of the same Lord and Father God" (HSD).

The evangelizing work of the Church in Latin America is the result of a unanimous missionary effort on the part of the whole people of God. We have the countless initiatives of charity, social assistance, and education; and we have the exemplary original syntheses of evangelization and human promotion by the missions of the Franciscans, Augustinians, Dominicans, Jesuits, Mercedarians, and others. We have the evangelical sacrifice and generosity of numerous Christians. Here women, by their abnegation and prayer, played an essential role. Inventiveness in teaching the faith was evident, along with a vast array of resources that brought together all the arts, ranging from music, song, and dance to architecture, painting, and the theater. This whole pastoral display of ability was associated with a time of great theological reflection and dynamic intellectual thinking that gave rise to universities, schools, dictionaries, grammars, catechisms in a variety of native languages, and extremely interesting historical accounts of the origins of our peoples. And then there was the extraordinary proliferation of lay organizations and confraternities, which came to serve as the vital heart and soul of the religious life of believers. They are the remote but fruitful source of the present-day community movements in the Latin American Church.

It is true that in its work of evangelization the Church had to bear the weight of its lapses, its acts of complicity with the earthly powers, its incomplete pastoral vision, and the destructive force of sin. But we must also recognize that evangelization, which makes Latin America a "continent of hope," has been far more powerful than the dark shadows that unfortunately accompanied it in the historical context through which it had to live. For us Christians today, this challenges us to measure up to our history at its best and to be capable of responding with creative fidelity to the challenges of our Latin American epoch.

After that era of evangelization in our lands, which was so decisive in the formation of Latin America, there came a cycle of stabilization, weariness, and routinism. This was followed by the great crises in the nineteenth century and the early part of the twentieth century, which brought bitter experiences and persecutions to the Church. It was subjected to bouts of uncertainty and conflict that shook it to its very foundations. Overcoming this harsh test, the Church undertook a mighty effort and managed to rebuild and survive. Today, especially since Vatican II, the Church has been undergoing renewal and, with a vigorous evangelizing spirit, it has been paying heed to the needs and hopes of the peoples of Latin America. The energy that in past centuries brought its bishops together in Lima, Mexico City, São Salvador de Bahia, and Rome, has now manifested its vitality in the conferences of the Latin American Episcopate in Río de Janeiro and Medellín. Those conferences activated the Church's energies and prepared it for the challenges of the future.

Since Medellín in particular, the Church, clearly aware of its mission and loyally open to dialogue, has been scrutinizing the signs of the times and is generously disposed to evangelize in order to contribute to the construction of a new society that is more fraternal and just; such a society is a crying need of our peoples. Thus the mutual forces of tradition and progress, which once seemed to be antagonistic in Latin America, are now joining each other and seeking a new, distinctive synthesis that will bring together the possibilities of the future and the energies derived from our common roots. And so, within this vast process of renewal that is inaugurating a new epoch in Latin America, and amid the challenges of recent times, we pastors are taking up the age-old episcopal tradition of Latin America and preparing ourselves to carry the Gospel's message of salvation hopefully and bravely to all human beings, but to the poorest and most forgotten by way of preference.

13 Throughout the course of a rich historical experience, filled with bright moments and dark shadows, the great mission of the Church has been its committed involvement in faith with the human being of Latin America: with that person's eternal salvation, spiritual victory, and full human development.

14 Taking inspiration from that great mission of yesteryear, we want to draw closer to the reality of today's Latin Americans with a pastoral eye and a Christian heart in order to understand and interpret it. Starting off from that reality, we want to proceed to analyze our pastoral mission.

CHAPTER II
PASTORAL OVERVIEW OF THE SOCIOCULTURAL CONTEXT

2.1. Introduction

15 As pastors, we journey with the people of Latin America through our history. There are many basic elements that are shared in common, but there are also shadings and differences peculiar to each nation. Starting off from the Gospel, which presents Jesus Christ doing good and loving all without distinction (Acts 10:38), and from our vision based on faith, we place ourselves in the reality of the Latin American as it finds expression in that human being's hopes, achievements, and frustrations. Our faith prompts us to discern the summonses of God in the signs of the times; to bear witness to, announce, and promote the evangelical values of communion and participation; and to denounce everything in our society that runs counter to the filiation originating in God the Father and the brotherhood rooted in Jesus Christ.

16 As pastors, we single out the successes and failures of recent years. In presenting this reality, we are not trying to dishearten people but rather to stimulate all those who can do something to improve it. The Church in Latin America has tried to help human beings to move on "from less human situations to more human ones" (PP: 20). It has made every effort to summon people to ongoing individual and social conversion. It asks all Christians to work together to change unjust structures and to communicate Christian values to the general culture in which they are living. It asks them to take cognizance of the successes achieved, to take heart from them, and thus to continue contributing to more and better successes.

We are happy to spell out some of the realities that fill us with hope:

17 —Latin Americans have an innate tendency to accept and shelter people; to share what they have with others; to display fraternal charity and generosity,

particularly among the poor; and to share the distress of others in need. Latin Americans place high value on the special ties of friendship rooted in the family, the role of godparents, and the bonds thus created.

—Latin Americans have increasingly taken cognizance of their dignity as **18** human beings and of the desire for political and social participation, despite the fact that in many areas these rights are crushed underfoot. There has been a proliferation of community organizations, such as cooperative movements, especially among the common people.

—There is growing interest in autochthonous values and in respecting the **19** originality of indigenous cultures and their communities. There is also great love for the land.

—Ours is a young people; and where they have had opportunities to develop **20** their abilities and organize, they have proved that they can win out and regain possession of their just rights and claims.

—The significant economic progress that has been experienced by our conti- **21** nent proves that it would be possible to root out extreme poverty and improve our people's quality of life. If that is possible, it becomes an obligation (PP: 76).

—We can see a growth in the middle class, though it has suffered decline in **22** some areas.

—The forward strides in education are clear to be seen. **23**

But in our many pastoral encounters with our people we also note what Pope **24** John Paul II noted when he visited peasants, laborers, and students. It is the deeply felt plaint—fraught with anxieties, hopes, and aspirations—of those whose voice we wish to be: "The voice of those who cannot speak or who have been silenced" (AO).

So we place ourselves within the dynamic thrust of the Medellín Conference **25** (Med-PC:2), adopting its vision of reality that served as the inspiration for so many pastoral documents of ours in the past decade.

The real situation in our countries was lucidly reflected in the words of Paul VI: **26** "We all know in what terms many bishops spoke during the recent Synod of Bishops. Bishops from every continent, particularly those from the Third World, spoke in pastoral accents that echoed the voices of millions of the Church's children who make up those peoples. We know only too well that all the energy and effort of those peoples are invested in the struggle to overcome the things that condemn them to live on the margin of life: hunger, chronic diseases, illiteracy, impoverishment, injustice in international relations and particularly in commercial interchanges, situations of economic and cultural neocolonialism that are sometimes as cruel as political neocolonialism, etc. The Church, said the bishops once again, has the duty to proclaim the liberation of millions of human beings, among whom are many of the Church's own children; the duty to help bring this liberation forth in the world, to bear witness to it and make sure that it is total. None of this is alien to evangelization" (EN:30).

2.2. Sharing People's Anxieties

We are concerned about the anxieties of all those who make up the people, **27** whatever their social condition may be. We are concerned about their loneliness, their family problems, and the lack of meaning in the lives of many of them.

Today we wish in particular to share the anxieties that stem from their poverty.

28   Viewing it in the light of faith, we see the growing gap between rich and poor as a scandal and a contradiction to Christian existence (OAP:III, 2). The luxury of a few becomes an insult to the wretched poverty of the vast masses (PP:3). This is contrary to the plan of the Creator and to the honor that is due him. In this anxiety and sorrow the Church sees a situation of social sinfulness, all the more serious because it exists in countries that call themselves Catholic and are capable of changing the situation: "They have a right to have the barriers of exploitation removed, . . . against which their best efforts at advancement are dashed" (AO).

29   So we brand the situation of inhuman poverty in which millions of Latin Americans live as the most devastating and humiliating kind of scourge. And this situation finds expression in such things as a high rate of infant mortality, lack of adequate housing, health problems, starvation wages, unemployment and underemployment, malnutrition, job uncertainty, compulsory mass migrations, etc.

30   Analyzing this situation more deeply, we discover that this poverty is not a passing phase. Instead it is the product of economic, social, and political situations and structures, though there are also other causes for the state of misery. In many instances this state of poverty within our countries finds its origin and support in mechanisms which, because they are impregnated with materialism rather than any authentic humanism, create a situation on the international level where the rich get richer at the expense of the poor, who get ever poorer (OAP:III, 3). Hence this reality calls for personal conversion and profound structural changes that will meet the legitimate aspirations of the people for authentic social justice. Such changes either have not taken place, or else they have been too slow in coming in the concrete life of Latin America.

31   This situation of pervasive extreme poverty takes on very concrete faces in real life. In these faces we ought to recognize the suffering features of Christ the Lord, who questions and challenges us. They include:

32   —the faces of young children, struck down by poverty before they are born, their chance for self-development blocked by irreparable mental and physical deficiencies; and of the vagrant children in our cities who are so often exploited, products of poverty and the moral disorganization of the family;

33   —the faces of young people, who are disoriented because they cannot find their place in society, and who are frustrated, particularly in marginal rural and urban areas, by the lack of opportunity to obtain training and work;

34   —the faces of the indigenous peoples, and frequently of the Afro-Americans as well; living marginalized lives in inhuman situations, they can be considered the poorest of the poor;

35   —the faces of the peasants; as a social group, they live in exile almost everywhere on our continent, deprived of land, caught in a situation of internal and external dependence, and subjected to systems of commercialization that exploit them;

36   —the faces of laborers, who frequently are ill-paid and who have difficulty in organizing themselves and defending their rights;

37   —the faces of the underemployed and the unemployed, who are dismissed because of the harsh exigencies of economic crises, and often because of

development-models that subject workers and their families to cold economic calculations;

—the faces of marginalized and overcrowded urban dwellers, whose lack of material goods is matched by the ostentatious display of wealth by other segments of society; **38**

—the faces of old people, who are growing more numerous every day, and who are frequently marginalized in a progress-oriented society that totally disregards people not engaged in production. **39**

We share other anxieties of our people that stem from a lack of respect for their dignity as human beings, made in the image and likeness of God, and for their inalienable rights as children of God. **40**

Countries such as ours, where there is frequently no respect for such fundamental human rights as life, health, education, housing, and work, are in the position of permanently violating the dignity of the person. **41**

To this are added other anxieties that stem from abuses of power, which are typical of regimes based on force. There are the anxieties based on systematic or selective repression; it is accompanied by accusations, violations of privacy, improper pressures, tortures, and exiles. There are the anxieties produced in many families by the disappearance of their loved ones, about whom they cannot get any news. There is the total insecurity bound up with arrest and detention without judicial consent. There are the anxieties felt in the face of a system of justice that has been suborned or cowed. As the Supreme Pontiffs point out, the Church, by virtue of "an authentically evangelical commitment" (OAP:III, 3), must raise its voice to denounce and condemn these situations, particularly when the responsible officials or rulers call themselves Christians. **42**

Then there are the anxieties raised by guerrilla violence, by terrorism, and by the kidnappings carried out by various brands of extremists. They, too, pose a threat to life together in society. **43**

In many of our countries lack of respect for human dignity also finds expression in the lack of social participation on various levels. We want to allude, in particular, to labor unionization. In many places labor legislation is either applied arbitrarily or not taken into account at all. This is particularly true in countries where the government is based on the use of force. There they look askance at the organizing efforts of laborers, peasants, and the common people; and they adopt repressive measures to prevent such organizing. But this type of control over, or limitation on, activity is not applied to employer organizations, which can exercise their full power to protect their interests. **44**

In some cases the over-politicization of labor unions at the top level distorts the aim of these organizations. **45**

In recent years we have also seen deterioration in the political sphere. Much harm has been done to the participation of citizens in the conduct of their own affairs and destiny. We also frequently see a rise in what can be called institutionalized injustice (Med-P:16). And by employing violent means, extremist political groups provoke new waves of repression against segments of the common people. **46**

The free-market economy, in its most rigid expression, is still the prevailing system on our continent. Legitimated by liberal ideologies, it has increased the gap between the rich and the poor by giving priority to capital over labor, **47** economics over the social realm. Small groups in our nations, who are often tied in with foreign interests, have taken advantage of the opportunities provided by these older forms of the free market to profit for themselves while the interests of the vast majority of the people suffer.

48 Marxist ideologies have also spread among workers, students, teachers, and others, promising greater social justice. In practice their strategies have sacrificed many Christian, and hence human, values; or else they have fallen prey to utopian forms of unrealism. Finding their inspiration in policies that use force as a basic tool, they have only intensified the spiral of violence.

49 In many instances the ideologies of National Security have helped to intensify the totalitarian or authoritarian character of governments based on the use of force, leading to the abuse of power and the violation of human rights. In some instances they presume to justify their positions with a subjective profession of Christian faith.

50 Our countries are going through cycles of economic crisis, despite the trend toward modernization and strong economic growth accompanied by varying degrees of hardship. These cycles intensify the sufferings of our people when a cold-hearted technocracy applies developmental models that extort a truly inhuman price from those who are poorest. And this is all the more unjust insofar as the price is not shared by all.

2.3. Cultural Aspects

51 Latin America is made up of different races and cultural groups characterized by varied historical processes; it is not a uniform, continuous reality. But there are elements that make up what might be called a common cultural patrimony of historical traditions and the Christian faith.

52 Unfortunately, the development of certain cultures is very precarious. In practice, values that are part of the rich, age-old tradition of our people are disregarded, marginalized, and even destroyed. But fortunately we also see the beginnings of a new valuation of our native cultures.

53 Due to dominant influences from abroad or the alienating imitation of imported values and lifestyles, the traditional cultures of our countries have been distorted and attacked. Our identity and our own specific values are threatened.

54 Hence we share our people's anxieties over the subversion of values that is at the root of many of the ills mentioned above:

55 —Individualistic materialism, the supreme value in the eyes of many of our contemporaries, works against communion and participation, posing obstacles to solidarity; and collectivist materialism subordinates the person to the State.

56 —Consumptionism, with its unbridled ambition to "have more," is suffocating modern human beings in an immanentism that closes them off to the evangelical values of generosity and austerity. It is paralyzing them when it comes to solidary communication and fraternal sharing.

57 —The deterioration of basic family values is disintegrating family communion, eliminating shared and responsible participation by all the family members and making them an easy prey to divorce or abandonment. In some cultural groups the woman finds herself in a position of inferiority.

58 —The deterioration of public and private integrity is evident. We also find

frustration and hedonism leading people into such vices as gambling, drug addiction, alcoholism, and sexual licentiousness.

We must also consider education and social communication as transmitters of culture. **59**

—Education has made great strides forward in recent years. School attendance has increased, though the drop-out rate is still high. Illiteracy has also diminished, though not enough in areas inhabited by indigenous peoples and peasants. **60**

Despite these advances, however, there are also deformations that have depersonalized many people. This is due to manipulation by small power-groups who are trying to safeguard their own interests and inculcate their own ideologies. **61**

—The aforementioned cultural traits are being strongly influenced by the media of social communication. Political, ideological, and economic power-groups succeed, through these media, in subtly penetrating both the environment and the lifestyle of our people. Information is manipulated by various authorities and groups. This is done particularly through advertising, which raises false expectations, creates fictitious needs, and often contradicts the basic values of our Latin American culture and the Gospel. The improper exercise of freedom in these media leads to an invasion of the privacy of persons, who generally are defenseless. Operating twenty-four hours a day, these media penetrate every area of human life: the home, work sites, places of recreation, and the streets. They also effect a cultural change that gives rise to a new idiom (EN:42). **62**

2.4. The Underlying Roots of These Realities

We want to point out some of the underlying roots of these phenomena so that we can offer our help and cooperation in bringing about needed changes. Here we adopt a pastoral perspective that focuses more directly on the needs of the people. **63**

a. We see the continuing operation of economic systems that do not regard the human being as the center of society, and that are not carrying out the profound changes needed to move toward a just society. **64**

b. One of the serious consequences of the lack of integration among our nations is that we go before the world as small entities without any ability to push through negotiations in the concert of nations (MPLA:8). **65**

c. There is the fact of economic, technological, political, and cultural dependence; the presence of multinational conglomerates that often look after only their own interests at the expense of the welfare of the country that welcomes them in; and the drop in value of our raw materials as compared with the price of the finished products we buy. **66**

d. The arms race, the great crime of our era, is both the result and the cause of tensions between our fellow countries. Because of it, enormous resources are allotted for arms purchases instead of being employed to solve vital problems (MPLA:8). **67**

e. There is a lack of structural reforms in agriculture that adequately deal with specific realities and decisively attack the grave social and economic problems of the peasantry. Such problems include access to land and to resources that would enable them to improve their productivity and their marketing. **68**

69   *f.* We see a crisis in moral values: public and private corruption; greed for exorbitant profit; venality; lack of real effort; the absence of any social sense of practical justice and solidarity; and the flight of capital resources and brain power. All these things prevent or undermine communion with God and brotherhood.

70   *g.* Finally, speaking as pastors and without trying to determine the technical character of these underlying roots, we ourselves see that at bottom there lies a mystery of sinfulness. This is evident when the human person, called to have dominion over the world, impregnates the mechanisms of society with materialistic values (HSD:3).

2.5. The Basic Setting: A Continent with Serious Demographic Problems

71   We note that almost all of our countries have experienced an accelerating rate of population growth. The vast majority of our population is composed of young people. Internal and external migrations bring with them a sense of uprooting. The cities are growing in a disorganized fashion; they are in danger of becoming uncontrollable megalopolises. It becomes harder every day to provide such basic services as housing, hospitals, schools, and so forth; and this increases social, cultural, and economic marginalization. The increase in those seeking work has outstripped the capacity of the present economic system to provide employment. And there are governments and international institutions that implement or support birth-control policies that are opposed to family morality.

CHAPTER III
THE ECCLESIAL REALITY TODAY IN LATIN AMERICA

3.1. Introduction

72   The above overview of our real situation in its social context shows us that the people of Latin America are journeying amid anxieties and hopes, frustrations and expectations (GS:1).

73   If we view those anxieties and frustrations in the light of faith, we see that they have been caused by sin, which has very broad personal and social dimensions. The hopes and expectations of our people arise from their deeply religious sense and their richness as human beings.

74   How has the Church viewed this reality? How has the Church interpreted it? Has the Church been successful in finding some way to focus on it and clarify it in the light of the Gospel? Has the Church managed to discern which aspects of this reality threaten to destroy the human being, who is the object of God's infinite love, and which aspects have been developing in line with God's loving designs? How has the Church been developing itself in order to carry out the saving mission that was entrusted to it by Christ and that is supposed to be implemented in concrete situations and reach out toward concrete human beings? What has the Church done in the last ten years in the face of the changing reality around it?

These are the great questions that we, as pastors, ask ourselves. Now we will   75
try to answer them, keeping in mind that the fundamental mission of the Church
is to evangelize in the here and now with an eye on the future.

3.2. Recent Changes

Until recently our continent had not been touched or swallowed up by the   76
dizzying flood of cultural, social, economic, political, and technological changes
in the modern age. At that time the weight of tradition helped the communication of the Gospel. What was taught from the pulpit was zealously welcomed in
the home and the school; and it was safeguarded and sustained by the social
pressure of the surrounding milieu.

Today nothing like that happens. The faith proposed by the Church is accepted   77
or rejected with much more freedom and with a notably critical-minded sense.
Even the peasants, who previously were isolated from contact with civilization to
a large extent, are now acquiring this same critical sense. This is due to the ready
contact with the present-day world that is afforded them, chiefly by radio and
means of transportation; it is also due to the consciousness-raising efforts of
pastoral agents.

Population growth has exceeded the current capacity of the Church to bring the   78
Good News to all. Compounding the problem is the shortage of priests, the
dearth of priestly and religious vocations, the desertions, the failure to rely more
directly on committed lay people in ecclesial functions, and the crisis that has
overtaken traditional apostolic movements. Ministers of the Word, parishes, and
other ecclesiastical structures have proved insufficient to satisfy the hunger of the
Latin American people for the Gospel. The empty spaces have been filled by
others, and this has often led to indifferentism and religious ignorance. As yet we
do not have a catechesis that embraces the whole of life.

Even more than atheism, indifferentism has become the problem among large   79
numbers of intellectuals, professionals, young people, and even the working
class. The enormously positive activity of the Church in defense of human rights
and its dealings with the poor have led groups with economic power, who
thought they were the front ranks of Catholicism, to feel that they have been
abandoned by the Church. As they see it, the Church has forsaken its "spiritual"
mission. Many others claim that they are Catholics "in their own way," though
they do not adhere to basic postulates of the Church. Many value their own
"ideology" more than their faith and their membership in the Church.

Many sects have not just been openly and persistently anti-Catholic; they have   80
also made unfair judgments on the Church and have tried to undermine its less
enlightened members. We must humbly confess that to a great extent, even
within segments of the Church, a false interpretation of religious pluralism has
permitted the propagation or erroneous or debatable doctrines regarding faith
and morals; and this has created confusion among the People of God.

All these problems have been aggravated by religious ignorance at every level,   81
ranging from the ranks of intellectuals to that of illiterates. And this is true even
though it must be admitted that real positive advances have been made in
catechesis, particularly with respect to adults.

Religious ignorance and indifference prompt many to prescind from moral   82 principles, whether personal or social. These people confine themselves to no more than ritualism, or to the social practice of a few sacraments and attendance at funerals as a token of their membership in the Church.

83   Secularization reclaims a legitimate measure of autonomy for earthly activity and can purify false images of God and religion. But frequently it has degenerated into a loss of value for the religious realm, or a secularism that turns its back on God and denies God any impact on public life. The image of the Church as an ally of the powers of this world has changed in most of our countries. Its firm defense of human rights and its committed effort to real societal improvement have brought the Church closer to the people; but it is still misunderstood in some instances, and some social groups have moved away from it.

84   Spurred on by Christ's mandate to preach the Gospel to every creature, by the immensity of that task, and by the changes now in progress, the Church in Latin America has both sensed its own human inadequacy and also realized that the Spirit of Christ is its moving inspiration. The Church has come to realize that it would commit a sin of disloyalty to its mission if it were to hang back or fail to move forward in the face of the demands posed by a changing world.

85   Since the First General Conference of the Latin American Episcopate in Rio de Janeiro (1955), which gave rise to CELAM, and particularly since Vatican II and the Medellín Conference, the Church has been acquiring an increasingly clear and deep realization that evangelization is its fundamental mission; and that it cannot possibly carry out this mission without an ongoing effort to know the real situation and to adapt the gospel message to today's human beings in a dynamic, attractive, and convincing way.

86   In this searching approach it can truly be said that the Church in Latin America has been intensely involved in activities. At every level it has organized study meetings, courses, institutes, get-togethers, and seminars on the most varied themes. And all of them have been geared in one way or another to a deeper exploration of the gospel message and a fuller knowledge of human beings, their concrete situation, and their aspirations.

3.3. The Clamor for Justice

87   From the depths of the countries that make up Latin America a cry is rising to heaven, growing louder and more alarming all the time. It is the cry of a suffering people who demand justice, freedom, and respect for the basic rights of human beings and peoples.

88   A little more than ten years ago, the Medellín Conference noted this fact when it pointed out: "A muted cry wells up from millions of human beings, pleading with their pastors for a liberation that is nowhere to be found in their case" (Med-PC:2).

89   The cry might well have seemed muted back then. Today it is loud and clear, increasing in volume and intensity, and at times full of menace.

90   The situation of injustice described in the previous section forces us to reflect on the great challenge our pastoral work faces in trying to help human beings to move from less human to more human conditions. The deep-rooted social differences, the extreme poverty, and the violation of human rights found in many areas pose challenges to evangelization. Our mission to bring God to human beings, and human beings to God, also entails the task of fashioning a more

fraternal society here. And the unjust social situation has not failed to produce tensions within the Church itself. On the one hand they are provoked by groups that stress the "spiritual" side of the Church's mission and resent active efforts at societal improvement. On the other hand they are provoked by people who want to make the Church's mission nothing more than an effort at human betterment.

There are other novel and disturbing phenomena. We refer to the partisan political activity of priests—not as individuals, as some had acted in the past (Med-PR:19), but as organized pressure groups. And we also refer to the fact that some of them are applying social analyses with strong political connotations to pastoral work. **91**

The Church's awareness of its evangelizing mission has led it in the past ten years to publish numerous pastoral documents about social justice; to create organisms designed to express solidarity with the afflicted, to denounce outrages, and to defend human rights; to give encouragement to the option of priests and religious for the poor and the marginated; and to endure the persecution and at times death of its members in witness to its prophetic mission. Much remains to be done, of course, if the Church is to display greater oneness and solidarity. Fear of Marxism keeps many from facing up to the oppressive reality of liberal capitalism. One could say that some people, faced with the danger of one clearly sinful system, forget to denounce and combat the established reality of another equally sinful system (HZ). We must give full attention to the latter system, without overlooking the violent and atheistic historical forms of Marxism. **92**

3.4. The Church Itself

The Church has felt itself summoned by a people who ask for the bread of God's Word and demand justice. The Church has turned its ear to this people, who are profoundly religious and who, for that very reason, place all their confidence in God. So in the past ten years the Church has put much effort into offering them an adequate pastoral response. **93**

Despite the sad facts mentioned earlier (see nos. 41–43 above), happy initiatives and experiments have been surfacing and maturing. Though some families are being torn apart and destroyed by the ravages of egotism, isolation, anxiety over their well-being, and legal or de facto divorce, other families can truly be called "domestic Churches." These families are living the faith, educating their children in it, and providing the good example of love, mutual understanding, and the radiation of their love to their neighbors in the parish and the diocese. **94**

On the one hand we cannot deny that there are painful generation-gap conflicts between parents and children; and that some young people, imbued with the philosophy of "getting to the top" and dominating others, are out solely to satisfy their own pleasure or to win some lucrative and prestigious position. But thanks to the education being provided in families, in schools that have revised their educational system, and in youth groups, other young people are vibrantly discovering Christ and living their faith intensely through a commitment to their neighbor, to the poor in particular. **95**

In 1968 base-level ecclesial communities [CEBs: *comunidades eclesiales de base*] were just coming into being. Over the past ten years they have multiplied and matured, particularly in some countries, so that now they are one of the causes for joy and hope in the Church. In communion with their bishops, and in line with **96**

Medellín's request, they have become centers of evangelization and moving forces for liberation and development.

97 The vitality of these CEBs is now beginning to bear fruit. They have been one of the sources for the increase in lay ministers, who are now acting as leaders and organizers of their communities, as catechists, and as missionaries.

98 In some places insufficient attention has been paid to the work required to develop CEBs. It is regrettable that, in some areas, clearly political interests try to manipulate them and to sever them from authentic communion with their bishops.

99 Other Christian church groups composed of lay men and women are also flourishing. They are earnestly seeking to reflect on the reality around them in the light of faith, to find original ways of expressing their faith in the Word of God, and to put that faith into practice.

100 Relying on these groups, the Church is clearly in the process of implementing renewal in its parochial and diocesan life through a new catechetics. Catechetical renewal does not apply simply to methodology or to the use of modern media. It also means presenting content that is vigorously aimed at introducing evangelical motives into people's lives so that they might grow in Christ.

101 The liturgy has undergone considerable purification of merely ritualistic habits. Celebrated in revitalized parishes and small groups, it has attained a high degree of active, personal participation, as Vatican II called for in *Sacrosanctum Concilium*. Unfortunately some groups have been averse to renewal, while others have introduced abuses. Despite initial signs of resistance and some lingering opposition, the Church has also successfully implemented renewal in the celebration of the sacraments. It has established and won acceptance of presacramental catechetical courses. And in the actual celebration of the sacraments the Church has made a place for the proclamation of the Word, thus ensuring greater enlightenment and depth to the Christian life.

102 It is a fact that painful doctrinal, pastoral, and psychological tensions still persist within the Church between pastoral agents of differing views; but these tensions are gradually being overcome through the practice of open and constructive dialogue. In many places priests have organized themselves into teams in order to lend each other support in their spiritual life and their pastoral work. Pastoral co-workers on these teams sometimes include male and female religious as well as lay people.

103 Our Churches and CELAM have received generous aid in personnel and economic resources from our sister Churches in Europe and North America. This aid has made a significant contribution to our evangelizing efforts throughout the continent, and we wish to express our deep thanks for it. It is a sign of the universal charity of the Church. And the effort to channel all this support within the framework of our local Churches is a sign of respect and communion.

104 In concluding this summary description of the ecclesial reality in Latin America, we would like to point out that our Church is living out communion on various levels, though of course there are some defects and gaps:

105 —There is the local, grassroots communion in Christian families, in CEBs, and in parishes. And efforts are being made to foster communication between parishes.

106 —There is the intermediate communion of the local Church or diocese, which

serves as the connecting link between the smaller bases and the universal Church. There is also inter-diocesan communication on the national and regional level. It is embodied in the various episcopal conferences and, on the level of Latin America as a whole, in CELAM.

—There is the universal communion stemming from ties with the Holy See and all the Churches on other continents. The Church in Latin America is aware of its own specific vocation, of its own role and contribution within the universal Church as a whole. It is framed within the ecclesial communion that finds its culminating expression in our adhesion to the Holy Father, the Vicar of Christ and supreme pastor. **107**

—The practice of ecumenism, which finds expression in dialogue and joint efforts at human promotion, is part of the move toward the unity we long for. **108**

—The new valuation of popular religiosity, in spite of its distortions and ambiguities, expresses the religious identity of a people. Purified of deformities, it affords a privileged locale for evangelization. The great popular devotions and celebrations have been a distinguishing feature of Latin American Catholicism. They maintain evangelical values, and they are a sign of membership in the Church. **109**

3.5. Structures of Evangelization

The parishes. It has become clear that the pastoral organization of the parish, be it territorial or personal, depends substantially on those who make it up, on the union that exists between them as a human community. **110**

In general, the rural parish is identified with the existing community insofar as its structures and services are concerned. It has sought to create and coordinate CEBs that correspond to the human groups scattered throughout the parish area. On the other hand urban parishes, overwhelmed by the number of people they must attend to, have put more emphasis on the cultic services of the liturgy and the sacraments. The multiplication of small territorial or neighborhood communities is becoming more and more necessary if we are to provide the more personalized evangelization that is needed. **111**

The school. The school is a locale of evangelization and communion. On the one hand the number of Catholic schools and academies has decreased proportionately to the demands of the community. But on the other hand there is a growing awareness of the need for the presence of committed Christians in public or private educational structures that are not run by the Church. Catholic educational centers are opening up more and more to all segments of society. **112**

3.6. Ministers and Charisms

Bishops. The image and situation of the bishop may well have undergone a change in these past ten years. One notices a greater spirit of collegiality among them, and a greater sharing of responsibility with the clergy, religious, and the laity. This is particularly true on the level of the local Church, though unfortunately we do not always find due attention being paid to the coordination needed on the national or regional levels. **113**

Today the bishop is being asked especially to bear personal evangelical witness **114** and to get closer to his priests and people. At present we certainly do find greater simplicity and poverty in the bishop's lifestyle.

115 The increase in the number of dioceses has also fostered contact between the bishop and the diocesan community.

116 *Priests.* The shortage of priests is alarming, though there is a resurgence of vocations in some countries. Priests are overburdened with pastoral work, particularly in those places where there has not been more acceptance of ministries entrusted to the laity and of cooperation in their mission. It is cheering to see the spirit of sacrifice displayed by many priests, who valiantly accept loneliness and isolation, particularly in rural areas.

117 However, we still find pastoral approaches that are not in tune with present-day situations and with an organic pastoral effort.

118 As regards the training of priests, though there is an insufficient number of teachers, there has been no lack of worthwhile experimentation. In some instances, however, there have been exaggerations that are now in' the process of being corrected.

119 *Permanent deacons.* The permanent diaconate is something new in our Churches. Though permanent deacons have been well received in their communities, there are still too few of them. The CEBs are the proper environment for nurturing more deacons; but in most places pastoral tasks tend to be entrusted to lay people, who are delegated to preach the Word, catechize, and so forth.

120 *The consecrated life.* The consecrated life is a major force in the evangelization of Latin America. It has been caught up in a search to define its own identity and its own specific charism. In the process it is trying to reinterpret itself in terms of new needs and deeper involvement in the overall pastoral work of the diocese.

121 In general, religious have experienced a renewal in their way of life. More personal relationships have grown up within specific communities and between different religious families. They have increased their presence in difficult areas and among the poor. The vast majority of missions to the indigenous peoples are in their care.

122 In some instances conflicts have arisen over the nature of their integration into the overall pastoral effort, or over the lack of such integration. Conflicts have also arisen over the lack of community support, the lack of sufficient preparation for work in the social sphere, or their lack of maturity in dealing with such experiences.

123 The contemplative communities are a spiritual bulwark for the life of the diocese. They, too, have gone through a period of crisis, but now vocations are on the rise again in various countries.

124 Secular institutes have also begun to flourish on our continent.

125 *Lay people.* The lay people's sense of belonging to the Church has clearly grown everywhere. This is due, not only to a more permanent commitment to the Church, but also to a more active participation in liturgical gatherings and apostolic work. The CEBs in many countries are proof of this involvement and desire for participation. But the committed involvement of the laity in the temporal sphere, which is so necessary for structural change, has been very inadequate. In general, we can say that there has been a more positive valuation of the necessary participation of the laity in the Church.

126 *Women* deserve special mention. Nuns, female members of secular institutes, and other lay women are now enjoying more and more participation in pastoral

responsibilities, even though such participation is still viewed with a great deal of suspicion in many areas.

CHAPTER IV
PRESENT-DAY TENDENCIES AND
EVANGELIZATION IN THE FUTURE

4.1. In Society

Viewing the present-day world with a pastoral eye, we note certain tendencies that we cannot fail to take into account.

Latin America will continue to have an accelerated rate of population growth, and this population will be concentrated in the big cities. The problems connected with public services will grow more and more acute. The vast majority of this population will be young, and they will find it increasingly difficult to find jobs. 127

On the one hand the society of the future will be more open and pluralistic; on the other hand it will increasingly be subject to the dictates of the communications media and their ever-increasing programming of life on both the individual and the societal levels. 128

It would seem that the programming of societal life will correspond more and more with models envisioned by the technocracy, despite people's yearnings for a more just international order as opposed to the tendency of current inequities to harden. 129

On the international level we see a growing awareness of the limited nature of the planet's resources and the need to rationalize their use. Some want to reduce the population, especially among poor peoples. Others propose a "rationed prosperity," that is, a frugality shared by all rather than a growing wealth not shared by all. 130

In the light of these tendencies we feel ourselves to be in solidarity with the Latin American people, of whom we are a part, and their history. We want to consider carefully their aspirations, both those that are clearly expressed and those that they can scarcely name. As we see it, those aspirations are: 131

—A more human quality of life, especially in terms of its unrenounceable religious dimension and its search for God and the Kingdom brought to us by Christ. The poorest sometimes seem to intuit this Kingdom in a privileged and forceful way. 132

—A more just distribution of goods and opportunities; work that is fairly remunerated, that will support all the members of a family with dignity, and that will close the gap between extravagant luxury and indigence. 133

—A fraternal life together in society, where human rights are encouraged and safeguarded, where the goals to be reached are determined by consensus rather than by force or violence, and where no one feels threatened by repression, terrorism, kidnapping, and torture. 134

—Structural changes that will ensure a juster situation for the vast majority of the people.

—A desire to be truly taken into account as responsible people and subjects of 135 history, who can freely participate in political options, labor-union choices, and the election of rulers.

136 —Participation in the production process and a sharing in the advances of modern science and technology, and also access to cultural development and dignified recreation.

137 All this will lead to greater integration among our peoples, which coincides with the universal thrust toward a more global and planetary society that is made increasingly feasible by communications media of enormous scope.

138 But so long as huge segments of society cannot manage to satisfy these legitimate aspirations while others indulge themselves to excess, the tangible goods of the modern world will turn into a source of growing frustrations and tragic tensions. The blatant and striking contrast between those who possess nothing and those who show off their opulence is an insuperable obstacle to establishing the Reign of peace.

139 If there is no change in present tendencies, the relationship between humanity and nature will continue to deteriorate, due to irrational exploitation of nature's resources and environmental pollution. Increasingly grave damage will be done to humanity and to ecological balance.

140 Underlying all this is the culminating human aspiration to be free to live one's faith and express it.

141 In a word, our people yearn for a full and integral liberation, one not confined to the realm of temporal existence. It extends beyond that to full communion with God and with one's brothers and sisters in eternity. And that communion is already beginning to be realized, however imperfectly, in history.

4.2. In the Church

142 Through its activity and social doctrine, the Church makes these aspirations its own. We need only recall the vigorous summons of the Medellín Conference, which expressed the resolve to ensure that the Gospel message might succeed in displaying its full potency as a leaven of transformation.

143 Reiterating that summons, our present Puebla Conference wishes to make available the resources of a pastoral line of action adapted to present-day circumstances.

144 The Church must become more and more independent of the powers in this world. Only thus can it enjoy a broad area of freedom that will enable it to carry out its apostolic work without interference. That work includes the practice of cultic worship, education in the faith, and the fostering of those many and varied activities that lead the faithful to implement the moral imperatives deriving from the faith in their private, family, and social life. Thus, free of compromising and vested only with its witness and teaching, the Church will be more credible and better heard. This will enable it to evangelize the very exercise of power for the common good.

145 The Church accompanies the searching of human beings with deep sympathy and is in agreement with their yearnings and aspirations. The Church desires nothing else but to be of service to them. By nurturing their efforts and enlightening their steps, it hopes to enable them to see the transcendent value of their lives and activities.

The Church takes up the defense of human rights and joins in solidarity with those who champion them. Here we will cite only one of the innumerable statements of the magisterium on this matter, but one of particular importance, the address of Pope John Paul II to the Diplomatic Corps, 20 October 1978: "The Holy See acts in this area with the knowledge that freedom, respect for the life and dignity of persons (who are never mere instruments), equal treatment, professional conscientiousness in one's work and a mutual quest for the common good, the spirit of reconciliation, and an openness to spiritual values are fundamental requirements for a harmonious life in society and for the progress of citizens and their civilization."   **146**

The Church has intensified its commitment to the dispossessed segments of the population, advocating their integral development. This effort has given some the impression that the Church is disregarding the affluent classes.   **147**

The Church now does a better job of emphasizing the evangelical value of poverty, which makes us available for the construction of a more just and fraternal world. The Church keenly feels the painful situation of those who are deprived of the basic necessities for a dignified life. And it invites all to transform their minds and hearts in line with the Gospel's scale of values.   **148**

The Church has more trust in the power of truth and in education for freedom and responsibility than in prohibitions; for its law is love.   **149**

4.3. Evangelization in the Future

Evangelization will give priority to the proclamation of the Good News, to biblical catechesis, and to the celebration of the liturgy as a response to the growing thirst for the Word of God.   **150**

It will make a maximum effort to preserve unity, both because the Lord wants unity and also in order to take advantage of all the available sources of energy by concentrating them within an organic plan of overall pastoral effort. This will prevent the fruitless dispersion of efforts and services. Such a pastoral effort is taking shape at the various levels: diocesan, national, and continental.   **151**

Importance will be placed on the urban pastoral effort with the creation of new ecclesial structures. Without disregarding the validity of the parish that has undergone renewal, the new structures will enable us to face up to the complex of problems posed by the enormous concentrations of people today. There will also be increased efforts to deal better with the rural pastoral effort.   **152**

Efforts will be made to increase the number of pastoral agents: clergy, religious, and lay people. The training of these agents will be adapted to the varying needs of communities and milieus.   **153**

The importance of the laity will be emphasized, not only when they engage in ministries in and for the Church, but also when they carry out the mission that is specifically theirs, that is, when they are sent out into the very midst of life in the world as the Church's vanguard, in order to remodel social, economic, and political structures in accordance with God's plan.   **154**

In order to train lay people and to provide them with support in their lives and activities, an effort will be made to incorporate them into apostolic organizations and movements. An effort will also be made to give real vitality and power to all their instruments of formation, particularly those relating to cultural devel-   **155** opment. Only in this way will we get a mature laity capable of evangelizing.

156   The validity of the experiences embodied in CEBs will be recognized, and their further growth in communion with their pastors will be fostered.

157   The Church will have to take great pains to educate the Christian faith of simple folk, who are naturally religious; it will also have to do an adequate job of preparing them to receive the sacraments.

158   The Church will give greater importance to the social communications media and will employ them in evangelization.

159   CELAM and its service-organs, as well as the general episcopal conferences, already are an embodiment of the pastoral integration of the Latin American Church. This will have to be further accelerated for the benefit of all the local Churches.

160   The collective voice of the bishops has been awakening a growing interest in public opinion; but frequently it also runs up against reservations in certain sectors with little social sensitivity. This is a sign that the Church is carrying out its role as Mother and Teacher of all.

161   In any case the Church must be ready to shoulder the consequences of its mission, which will never be accepted by the world without some resistance.

PART TWO
GOD'S SAVING PLAN FOR LATIN AMERICA

The Church in Latin America feels bound by intimate and real ties of solidarity to all **162**
the people of the continent (GS:1). For almost five centuries it has been at their side and
in their midst. It can do no less at this critical turning point in their history (MDP).

Having considered the reality of our people with the eyes of faith and with pastoral **163**
hearts, we now ask ourselves what exactly is God's plan of salvation for Latin America.
What paths of liberation does God offer to us?

Pope John Paul II has given us the answer: the truth about Christ, the Church, and
human beings.

We shall now ponder that truth against the backdrop of the aspirations and sufferings
of our fellow Latin Americans.

Evangelized by the Lord in his Spirit, we are sent out to bring this Good News to all **164**
our brothers and sisters, especially to the poor and the forgotten. This evangelizing task
leads us to complete conversion and communion with Christ in the Church. It will
impregnate our culture. It will incite us to the authentic improvement of our communities. And it will make us a critical-minded, guiding presence in the face of the
ideologies and policies that condition the fate of our nations.

It includes:

Chapter I: **The Content of Evangelization**
Chapter II: **What Does Evangelizing Entail**

CHAPTER I
THE CONTENT OF EVANGELIZATION

We now wish to shed the light of the truth that makes us free (John 8:32) on our **165**
compelling pastoral concern. It is now a truth that we possess as something of our
own. It comes from God. In its resplendent light we experience our own poverty.

We now propose to proclaim the central truths of evangelization: Christ, our **166**
hope, is in our midst as the Father's envoy, animating the Church with his Spirit

and offering his word and his life to people today in order to lead them to full and complete liberation.

167   The Church, a mystery of communion, the People of God in the service of human beings, continues to be evangelized through the ages and to bring the Good News to all.

168   For the Church, Mary is a cause for joy and a source of inspiration because she is the star of evangelization and the Mother of the Latin American peoples (EN:82).

169   Human beings, by virtue of their dignity as the image of God, merit a commitment from us in favor of their liberation and their total fulfillment in Christ Jesus. Only in Christ is the true grandeur of human beings revealed. Only in Christ is their more intimate reality fully known. Hence we, being pastors, speak to human beings and proclaim to them the joyful news that humanity has been assumed and exalted by the very Son of God. For he chose to share with human beings the joys, labors, and sufferings of this life and the heritage of eternal life.

1. The Truth about Jesus Christ, the Savior We Proclaim

1.1. Introduction

170   The Lord's fundamental question, "Who do you say that I am?" (Matt. 16:15), is perduringly addressed to the human beings of Latin America. Today, as yesterday, varying answers could be registered. For those of us who are members of the Church there is only one answer, that of Peter: "You are the Messiah, . . . the Son of the living God" (Matt. 16:16).

171   The vast majority of our Latin American people, who are deeply religious even before being evangelized, believe in Jesus Christ, true God and true human being.

172   This belief finds expression in many forms: e.g., in the many attributes of power, salvation, or consolation applied to him; in the titles of judge and king given to him; in the appellations that associate him with various places and regions; in devotion to the long-suffering Christ, to his birth in a manger and his death on the cross; in devotion to the resurrected Christ; and even more in the devotions to the Sacred Heart of Jesus and to his real presence in the Eucharist, which find manifestation in First Communion, nocturnal adoration, Corpus Christi processions, and Eucharistic Congresses.

173   We are aware of our inadequate proclamation of the Gospel and of the deficiencies in our people's life of faith. However, as heirs to almost five hundred years of evangelizing history and to the efforts at renewal that have taken place mainly since the Medellín Conference, we also have cause for joy in the self-sacrificing labor of the clergy and religious congregations and in the growth of Catholic institutions, lay apostolic movements, youth groups, and CEBs. We see that this labor and growth has brought many segments of the People of God closer to the Gospel and has prompted their search for the ever new face of Christ, who is the answer to their legitimate yearning for integral liberation.

174   This is not accomplished without problems. Given the contrast between efforts to present Christ as the Lord of our history and the source of inspiration for authentic social change on the one hand, and efforts to restrict him to the realm of

the individual conscience on the other, we believe that it is necessary to offer the following clarifications.

It is our duty to proclaim clearly the mystery of the Incarnation, leaving no **175** room for doubt or equivocation. This mystery includes both the divinity of Jesus Christ, as it is professed by the faith of the Church, and the reality and force of his human and historical dimension.

We must present Jesus of Nazareth sharing the life, the hopes, and the an- **176** xieties of his people; and we must point out that he is the Christ who is believed, proclaimed, and celebrated by the Church.

We must present Jesus of Nazareth as someone conscious of his mission, as the **177** proclaimer and realizer of the Kingdom, and as the founder of his Church, whose visible foundation is Peter. And we must present Jesus Christ as alive, present, and at work in history and his Church.

We cannot distort, factionalize, or ideologize the person of Jesus Christ. That **178** could be done in one of two ways: either by turning him into a politician, a leader, a revolutionary, or a simple prophet on the one hand; or, on the other hand, by restricting him, the Lord of history, to the merely private realm.

Echoing the words of the Holy Father in his opening address to this confer- ence, we tell you: "Any form of silence, disregard, mutilation, or inadequate emphasis on the whole of the mystery of Jesus Christ that diverges from the Church's faith cannot be the valid content of evangelization." It is one thing when we are talking about "re-readings of the Gospel that are the product of theoretical speculations," and "the perhaps brilliant but fragile and inconsistent hypotheses flowing from them." It is something else again when we are dealing with the Church's affirmation of faith: "Jesus Christ, the Word and Son of God, becomes human to draw closer to human beings and to offer them, through the power of his mystery, the great gift of God that is salvation" (OAP:I,4; I,5).

We are going to talk about Jesus Christ. We are going to proclaim once again **180** the truth of faith about Jesus Christ. We ask all the faithful to accept this liberating teaching. Their own temporal and eternal destiny is bound up with knowing him in faith and following him in love. For he is the one who enables us to imitate him through the outpouring of his Spirit. He, the one whom we call Lord and Savior, is precisely that.

In solidarity with the sufferings and aspirations of our people, we feel urgently **181** compelled to give them what is properly ours: the mystery of Jesus of Nazareth, the Son of God. We feel that it is the "power of God" (Rom. 1:16), capable of transforming our personal and social reality and putting it on the right road to freedom, brotherhood, and the full manifestation of God's Kingdom.

1.2. Humanity "Wondrously Created" by God

Sacred Scripture teaches us that we human beings were not the first to show **182** love, that God first loved us. God planned and created the world in Jesus Christ, who is God's own uncreated image (Col. 1:15–17). In so doing, God created us human beings so that we might share in the divine community of love composed of the Father, the only begotten Son, and the Spirit (Eph. 1:3–6).

This divine design was conceived by the Father in his Son before the creation **183** of the world (Eph. 1:9). It was meant for the good of human beings and for the glory of his immense love. The Father then revealed this to us as part of the mysterious plan he had for bringing human history to its full realization in Jesus Christ, through whom all things in heaven and on earth were to be brought into oneness (Eph. 1:10).

184   Human beings, "thought of and chosen from eternity" (OAP: I,9) in Jesus Christ, were to find their fulfillment as the created image of God. The divine mystery of communion was to be reflected in human beings and their fraternal life together through their active transformation of the world. Their dwelling place on earth was to be a haven of happiness, not a battleground ruled by violence, hatred, exploitation, and servitude.

1.3. From the True God to False Idols: Sin

185   From the very start, however, human beings rejected the love of their God. They had no interest in communion with him. They wanted to fashion a kingdom in this world while prescinding from God. Instead of worshipping the true God, they adored idols. They worshipped themselves, their own handiwork, and the things of this world. Human beings became torn within. Evil, death, violence, hatred, and fear entered the world.

186   Thus, through sin was broken the basic axis that subjects human beings to the loving dominion of the Father, and all the forms of bondage arose. The reality of Latin American life forces us to experience this power of sin in all its bitterness and extremes as something in flagrant contradiction to the divine plan.

1.4. The Promise

187   God the Father, however, did not abandon human beings to the power of their sinfulness. He initiated dialogue with them over and over again. He invited concrete human beings to make a covenant with him, to construct the world on the basis of faith and communion with him, and thus to agree to be his collaborators in his saving design. The history of Abraham and the election of the people of Israel; the history of Moses, of the people's liberation from slavery in Egypt, and of the Sinai covenant; the history of David and his reign; the Babylonian exile and the return to the promised land: all these events show us the powerful hand of God the Father, who announces, promises, and begins to realize the liberation of all human beings from sin and its consequences.

1.5. "The Word was made flesh and dwelled among us" (John 1:14): The Incarnation

188   When "the fullness of time" (Gal. 4:4) came, God the Father sent his Son, Jesus Christ, into the world. Christ, our Lord, is true God, born of the Father before all ages; and he is true human being, born of the Virgin Mary through the power of the Holy Spirit. In and through Christ, God the Father becomes one with human beings. The Son of God assumes everything human and everything created, re-establishing communion between his Father and human beings. The human being acquires an unimaginable dignity, and God breaks through into human history. In other words, God enters the wayfaring journey of human beings

toward freedom and fraternity, which now appear as a pathway to full encounter with God.

Thus the Latin American Church wishes to proclaim the true visage of Christ 189 because it radiates the glory and goodness of the provident Father and the power of the Holy Spirit, which proclaims the true and integral liberation of each and all of the human beings who make up our people.

1.6. Words and Deeds: The Life of Jesus

Jesus of Nazareth was born poor and lived as such among his people in Israel, 190 showing compassion for the multitude and doing good to all (Mark 6:34; 7:37; Acts 10:38). His people, suffocating under the weight of sin and suffering, were hopefully waiting for the liberation that he promised them (Matt. 1:21). In their midst Jesus made this announcement: "This is the time of fulfillment. The reign of God is at hand! Reform your lives and believe in the Gospel!" (Mark 1:15). Jesus was anointed by the Holy Spirit to bring glad tidings to the poor; to proclaim liberty to the captives, recovery of sight to the blind, and liberation to the oppressed (Luke 4:18–19). In the Beatitudes and the Sermon on the Mount he gave us his great proclamation of the new law of God's Kingdom (Matt. 5:1–12).

To his words Jesus joined his actions. They were wondrous deeds and surpris- 191 ing attitudes that show that the announced Kingdom is already present; that he is the efficacious sign of God's new presence in history; that he is the bearer of God's transforming power; that his presence unmasks the evil one; that God's love is redeeming the world; and that a new human being in a new world is already dawning.

The forces of evil, however, rejected this service of love. There was the in- 192 credulity of the people and his own relatives, the political and religious authorities of his day, and the incomprehension of his own disciples. In Jesus there then begins to appear more forcefully the sorrowful features of the "Servant of Yahweh," who is spoken of in the Book of Isaiah (Isa. 53). With complete love and obedience to his Father, the human embodiment of his eternal character as the Son, Jesus sets out on the road of self-sacrifice and self-giving. He rejects the temptation of political power and all recourse to violence. He gathers around him a few human beings chosen from various social and political strata of the day. Though confused and often unfaithful, they are moved by the love and the power that radiates from him. They are the ones who constituted the foundation of his Church. Drawn by the Father (John 6:44), they start out on the path involving the following of Jesus. It is not a path of arrogant self-assertion of human wisdom or power, nor a path of hatred or violence; instead it involves disinterested self-giving and sacrificial love. This love embraces all human beings; gives a privileged place to the weak, the lowly, and the poor; and gathers all together, integrating them into a fraternity that is capable of opening up the way to a new history.

Thus, in his own original and incomparable way, Jesus calls for a radical 193 discipleship that embraces the whole human being, all human beings, the whole earth, and the cosmos. Its radicalness means that conversion ever remains an unfinished process on both the personal and societal levels. For even though the

Kingdom of God comes to pass through historical realizations, it is not identified with these realizations nor exhausted in them.

1.7. The Paschal Mystery: Death and Life

194   Fulfilling the mandate received from his Father, Jesus freely surrendered himself to death on the cross, the goal of his life's journey. The bearer of the freedom and joy of God's Kingdom chose to be the decisive victim of this world's injustice and evil. The sorrow of creation is assumed by the Crucified One, who offers his life as a sacrifice for all. He is the High Priest who can share our weaknesses; the Paschal Victim who redeems us from our sins; the obedient Son who, in the face of his Father's saving justice, incarnates the cry of all human beings for liberation and redemption.

195   That is why the Father resurrects his Son from among the dead and exalts him in glory at his right hand. He fills him with the vivifying power of his Spirit. He establishes him as the Head of his Body, which is the Church. He constitutes him Lord of the world and of history. His resurrection is the sign and pledge of the resurrection to which we all are called, and of the ultimate transformation of the universe. Through him and in him the Father chose to re-create what he had already created.

196   The exalted Jesus Christ has not forsaken us. He lives within his Church, chiefly in the Holy Eucharist and in the proclamation of his Word. He is present among those who gather together in his name (Matt. 18:20), and he is present in the person of the pastors he has sent out (Matt. 10:40; 28:19ff.). And with particular tenderness he chose to identify himself with those who are poorest and weakest (Matt. 25:40).

197   Thus the Kingdom of God, shining resplendently on the visage of the risen Jesus Christ, is already planted in the center of human history. The justice of God has triumphed over the injustice of human beings. The old history began with Adam; with Jesus Christ, the new Adam, there begins a new history driven by an unfailing impetus. It will lead all human beings, made children of God through the efficacy of the Spirit, to ever more perfect dominion over the world, daily increasing fraternal communion, and the fullness of communion and participation that constitutes the very life of God. So we proclaim the Good News of the person of Jesus Christ to the people of Latin America, who are called to be new human beings in the newness of baptism and life according to the Gospel (EN:18). This should sustain their efforts and nurture their hope.

1.8. Jesus Christ Sends His Spirit of Filiation

198   Resurrected and elevated to the Father's right hand, Christ pours out his Holy Spirit on the day of Pentecost. It descends first on the apostles, and then on all those who have been called (Acts 2:39).

199   The new covenant that Christ sealed with his Father becomes interiorized through the Holy Spirit, who gives us the law of grace and freedom that he himself has written on our hearts. Thus the renovation of human beings, and subsequently of society, will depend first of all on the action of the Holy Spirit.

Laws and structures will have to be animated by the Spirit, who gives life to human beings and enables the Gospel to be fleshed out in history.

Latin America, which sealed this covenant with the Lord from the very outset of the evangelization process, must now renew that covenant and live it with the grace of the Spirit, fulfilling all its demands for love, self-sacrifice, and justice. **200**

The Spirit, who filled the whole earth, was also present in all that was good in pre-Colombian cultures. That very Spirit helped them to accept the Gospel. And today the Spirit continues to arouse yearnings for liberative salvation in our peoples. Hence we must discover the Spirit's authentic presence in the history of Latin America. **201**

1.9. A Spirit of Truth and Life, Love and Liberty

The Holy Spirit is called the "Spirit of truth" by Jesus; the Spirit is to bring us to the full truth (John 16:13). Within us the Spirit bears witness that we are children of God, that Jesus has risen, and that Jesus is "the same yesterday, today, and forever" (Heb. 13:8). Thus the Spirit is the principal evangelizer. It is this Spirit who is to animate all evangelizers and help them transmit the full truth without error or restriction. **202**

This Holy Spirit is the "giver of life," the living water flowing from the source in Christ that raises up those who are dead through sin and prompts us to hate all sin, especially in a time of such disorientation and corruption as the present. **203**

It is the Spirit of love and freedom. In sending us the Spirit of his Son, the Father has "poured out" his love into our hearts (Rom. 5:5). He has thus turned us away from sin and given us the freedom of his children. Freedom is necessarily linked with filiation and fraternity. People who are free in the gospel sense pledge themselves solely to actions that are worthy of God, their Father, and of their fellow human beings. **204**

1.10. The Spirit Joins Us in Oneness and Enriches Us with Diversity

Jesus Christ, the Savior of human beings, pours out his Spirit on all, without regard to persons. Those who exclude a single person from their love in the process of evangelization do not possess the Spirit of Christ. Hence apostolic activity must embrace all human beings, who are destined to be children of God. **205**

"Throughout all ages, the Holy Spirit gives the entire Church 'unity in fellowship and in service; He furnishes her with various gifts, both hierarchical and charismatic.' He vivifies ecclesiastical institutions as a kind of soul . . ." (AG:4). Thus, far from being an obstacle to evangelization, the hierarchy and institutions are instruments of grace and the Spirit. **206**

Charisms have never been absent from the Church. Various episcopal conferences have echoed Paul VI's pleasure over the spiritual renewal that appears in the most varied places and through the most varied means, and that leads to joyous prayer, intimate union with God, fidelity to the Lord, and a profound communion of souls. But this renewal demands good sense, orientation, and discernment from pastors so that dangerous exaggerations and deviations may be avoided (LG:12). **207**

208   The activity of the Holy Spirit reaches even those who do not know Jesus Christ. For the Lord "wants all men to be saved and come to know the truth" (1 Tim. 2:4).

1.11. The Consummation of God's Plan

209   The trinitarian life, which Christ communicates to us, will attain its plenitude only in glory. Insofar as it is a human and earthly institution, the wayfaring Church humbly acknowledges its mistakes and sins, which obscure the visage of God in his children (UR:6,7); but it is determined to carry on its work of evangelization in order to be faithful to its mission, putting its trust in the fidelity of its founder and in the power of the Spirit.

210   Jesus Christ always sought his Father's glory, and his submission to the Father reached its culmination on the cross. He is "the first-born of many brothers" (Rom. 8:29). The earthly journey of Jesus Christ was a journey to the Father; henceforth going to the Father means travelling the earthly road of Christ's Church, a People made up of brothers and sisters. Only in fraternal encounter with the Father will we find the fulfillment for which it is utopian to look here in time. While the Church waits for the union consummated with the divine spouse, "the Spirit and the Bride say, 'Come, Lord Jesus'" (Rev. 22:17–20).

1.12. Communion and Participation

211   After Christ's proclamation, which "reveals" the Father to us and gives us his Spirit, we come to discover the ultimate roots of our communion and participation.

212   Christ reveals to us that the divine life is trinitarian communion. Father, Son, and Spirit live the supreme mystery of oneness in perfect, loving intercommunion. It is the source of all love and all other communion that gives dignity and grandeur to human existence.

213   Through Christ, the one and only mediator, humanity shares in the life of the Trinity. Today, chiefly through his paschal activity, Christ brings us to participate in the mystery of God. Through his solidarity with us, he enables us to vivify our activity with love and to transform our effort and our history into a liturgical action. In other words, he enables us to be active agents with him in constructing a life together and a human dynamics that will reflect the mystery of God and constitute his living glory.

214   Through Christ, with Christ, and in Christ we come to participate in the communion of God. There is no other road that leads to the Father. Living in Christ, we come to be his mystical body, his people—a people of brothers and sisters united by the love that the Spirit has poured into our hearts. This is the communion to which the Father calls us through Christ and his Spirit. The whole history of salvation is oriented toward this communion, which represents the consummation of the loving plan of our Father who created us.

215   The communion that is to be fashioned between human beings is one that embraces their whole being, right down to the roots of their love. It must also manifest itself in every aspect of life, including economic, social, and political

life. Produced by the Father, the Son, and the Holy Spirit, it is the communication of their own trinitarian communion.

This is the communion so anxiously sought by the many people on this **216** continent when they trust in the providence of the Father, when they proclaim Christ as God and Savior, when they seek the grace of the Spirit in the sacraments, and even when they make the Sign of the Cross "in the name of the Father, and of the Son, and of the Holy Spirit."

In this trinitarian communion of the People and Family of God, we also **217** venerate and invoke the intercession of the Virgin Mary and all the saints. For "by its very nature every genuine testimony of love which we show to those in heaven tends toward and terminates in Christ, who is the 'crown of all saints.' Through him it tends toward and terminates in God, who is wonderful in His saints and is magnified in them" (LG:50).

Evangelization is a summons to participate in the communion of the Trinity. **218** Although other kinds of communion are not the ultimate destiny of human beings, they are, animated by grace, the foretaste of that destiny.

Evangelization prompts us to share in the groanings of the Spirit, who wishes **219** to liberate all creation. Moving us toward this liberation, the Spirit shows us the path to the unity of all human beings among themselves and between them and God, until ultimately "God may be all in all" (1 Cor. 15:28).

2. The Truth about the Church: The People of God, Sign and Service of Communion

Christ, who ascended to the Father and was hidden from human eyes, continues **220** *his visible work of evangelization through the Church. The Church is the sacrament of communion between human beings as the unique People of God journeying through history. To this end Christ sends it his Spirit, "who prompts each one to proclaim the Gospel and who, buried in the depths of people's consciences, enables them to accept and comprehend the word of salvation"* (EN:75).

2.1. The Good News of Jesus Christ and the Church

Two inseparable presences. The living presence of Jesus Christ in the history, **221** culture, and real life of Latin America is plain to see. As our people experience it, this presence is inseparably bound up with that of the Church; for it is through the Church that Christ's Gospel has resounded in our lands. The experience of our people embodies a profound intuition of faith regarding the innermost nature of the Church.

The Church and Jesus the Evangelizer. The Church cannot be separated from **222** Christ because he himself was its founder (LG:5,8; GS:40; UR:1). By an express act of his will he founded the Church on the Twelve, with Peter as their head (Matt. 16:18), establishing it as the universal and necessary sacrament of salvation. The Church is not a later "result" nor a mere consequence "set in motion" by the evangelizing activity of Jesus. It was born of this activity, to be sure, but in a direct way. For it was the Lord himself who called his disciples together and shared with them the power of his Spirit. He endowed the nascent community with all its essential elements and means, which the Catholic people acknowledge in faith to be of divine institution.

223   Furthermore, Jesus points to his Church as the normative way. Accepting or rejecting it is not left to human discretion as an inconsequential matter: "He who hears you, hears me. He who rejects you, rejects me. And he who rejects me, rejects him who sent me" (Luke 10:16). That is what the Lord says to his apostles. Hence accepting Christ necessarily entails accepting his Church (PO:14). The Church is part of the Gospel, of Jesus' legacy; and it is the object of our faith, love, and loyalty. We manifest this when we say: "I believe in the one, holy, catholic, and apostolic Church."

224   But the Church is also a trustee and transmitter of the Gospel. Loyal to the law of visible incarnation, the Church prolongs on earth the presence and evangelizing activity of Christ. Like Christ, the Church lives to evangelize. Its good fortune and specific vocation (EN:14) is precisely this: to proclaim the person and message of Jesus to human beings.

225   This Church is one single Church: the one built upon Peter, the one that the Lord himself refers to as "my Church" (Matt. 16:18). Only in the Catholic Church do we find the fullness of the means of salvation (UR:3) that were bequeathed to human beings by Jesus through his apostles. Hence it is our duty to proclaim the excellence of our vocation to the Catholic Church (LG:14), a vocation that is simultaneously an immense grace and a serious responsibility.

226   *The Church and the Kingdom proclaimed by Jesus.* The core of Jesus' message is the proclamation of the Kingdom, which is coming and is rendered present in Jesus himself. Though it is not a reality detachable from the Church (LG:8), it transcends the Church's visible bounds (LG:5). For it is to be found in a certain way wherever God is ruling through his grace and love, wherever he is overcoming sin and helping human beings to grow toward the great communion offered them in Christ. This activity of God is also found in the hearts of human beings who live outside the perceptible sphere of the Church (LG:16; GS:22; UR:3). But that definitely does not mean that membership in the Church is a matter of indifference (OAP: I,8).

227   Thus the Church received the mission to announce and establish the Kingdom (LG:5) among all peoples. The Church is its sign. In the Church we find the visible manifestation of the project that God is silently carrying out throughout the world. The Church is the place where we find the maximum concentration of the Father's activity. Through the power of the Spirit of Love, the Father is solicitously seeking out human beings to share his own trinitarian life with them—a gesture of ineffable tenderness. The Church is also the instrument that ushers in the Kingdom among human beings in order to spur them on to their definitive goal.

228   The Church "becomes on earth the initial budding forth of that kingdom" (LG:5). Under the influence of the Spirit, that seed is to grow in history until the day when God may be "all in all"(1 Cor. 15:28). Until then the Church will remain open to further perfection in many respects and permanently in need of self-evangelization, greater conversion, and purification (LG:5).

229   But the Kingdom is already here in the Church. The Church's presence on our

continent is Good News because it fully satisfies our peoples' hopes and aspirations, even if only in a germinal way.

Herein lies the "mystery" of the Church: it is a human reality made up of limited and impoverished human beings; but it is also suffused with the unfathomable presence and power of the triune God, who in the Church shines forth, calls together, and saves (LG:4,8; SC:2). 230

Today's Church is not yet the Church that it is called upon to be. It is important to keep this in mind to avoid a false triumphalistic outlook. On the other hand, too much emphasis should not be placed on its failings, because in it the power that will bring about the definitive Kingdom is already effectively present and at work in the world. 231

2.2. The Church Lives Its Mystery of Communion as the People of God

Our people love pilgrimages. In them the simple Christian celebrates the joy of feeling immersed in a multitude of brothers and sisters journeying together toward the God who is waiting for them. This action is a splendid sign and sacramental of the great vision of the Church offered to us by Vatican II: i.e., the Family of God, pictured as the People of God on pilgrimage through history and journeying toward the Lord. 232

Vatican II took place at a time when our Latin American peoples were facing great difficulties. They were years fraught with problems and an anxious quest for self-identity. The rising awareness of the masses of the common people and efforts at Latin American integration were preceded by the foundation of CELAM in 1955. CELAM prepared the groundwork for the Catholic people to open up somewhat more easily to a Church that would also describe itself as a People. This universal People permeates other peoples to help them grow toward the greater communion and brotherhood that Latin America itself was beginning to envisage. The Medellín Conference spread the new vision, which is as old as biblical history itself.* 233

Ten years after the Medellín Conference, the Church of Latin America here in Puebla is in an even better position to joyously reaffirm its reality as God's People. Since the Medellín Conference, our peoples have been living through important moments of encounter with each other, rediscovering the value of their history, their indigenous cultures, and the religiosity of the common people. Amid this process they are discovering the presence of this other People that accompanies our natural peoples through their history. And they are beginning to appreciate the contribution of this other People as a force for unifying our culture, on which it has so generously lavished the life-giving waters of the Gospel. The enrichment was reciprocal, because the Church was enabled to 234

---

*"It has pleased God, however, to make men holy and save them not merely as individuals without any mutual bonds, but by making them into a single people, a people which acknowledges Him in truth and serves Him in holiness. He therefore chose the race of Israel as a people unto Himself. With it He set up a covenant. Step by step He taught this people by manifesting in its history both Himself and the decree of His will, and by making it holy unto Himself" (LG:9). This people was a figure of the Church, the unique and definitive People of God founded by Jesus Christ.

incarnate itself in our own original framework of values and thus give new forms of expression to the treasures of the Spirit.

235   Furthermore, the view of the Church as the People of God seems necessary if we are to complete the transition, initiated at the Medellín Conference, from an individualistic way of living the faith to the great communitarian awareness opened up to us by Vatican II.

236   For the People of God is a universal People; the Family of God on earth; a holy People; a People on pilgrimage through history; a People that is sent out.

237   The Church is a universal People, destined to be a "light to the nations" (Isa. 49:6; Luke 2:32). It is not constituted by race, language, or any peculiarly human quality. It is born of God, through faith in Jesus Christ. Hence the Church is not in conflict with any other people. It can take on flesh and blood in all peoples to introduce the Kingdom of God into their histories: "The Church . . . foster[s] and take[s] to herself, insofar as they are good, the ability, resources, and customs of each people. Taking them to herself, she purifies, strengthens, and ennobles them" (LG:13).

238   *A People that is the Family of God.* Our Latin American people spontaneously refer to a church edifice as the "house of God" because they sense that it is there that the Church gathers together as the "Family of God." That is the very expression used repeatedly by the Bible, and also by Vatican II, to express the deepest and innermost reality of the People of God (Deut. 32:8ff.; Eph. 2:19; Rom. 8:29).

239   It is a view of the Church that speaks to the hearts of Latin Americans, who highly esteem family values and who are anxiously looking for some way to salvage those values amid the growing cold-bloodedness of the modern world. The reaction can be noticed in many countries. It is evident in the resurgence of a family-oriented pastoral effort and in the increase of CEBs. These experiences on the ordinary human level enable people to live the reality of the Church as the Family of God in an intense way.

240   Many parishes and dioceses are also stressing family life. They know that Latin Americans need and are looking for a family, and that they will thus find responses to their needs in the Church. It is not a matter of psychological tactics, but rather of fidelity to the Church's own identity. For the Church is not a place where human beings merely "feel" that they are the Family of God; it is a place where they "become" that—truly, deeply, and ontologically. They truly become children of the Father in Jesus Christ (1 John 3:1), who shares his life with them by the power of the Spirit in and through baptism. This grace of divine filiation is the great treasure that the Church should offer to the people of our continent.

241   Christian brotherhood is born out of this filiation in Christ. Modern humanity has not succeeded in fashioning any universal fraternity on earth because it is looking for a fraternity without any center or common origin. It has forgotten that the only way to be brothers and sisters is to come from one and the same Father.

242   The Church, the Family of God, is the homeground where every child and sibling is also a lord destined to share in Christ's lordship over creation and history. And this lordship is to be learned and acquired through an ongoing process of conversion and assimilation to the Lord.

243   The hearth-fire that gives life to the Family of God is the Holy Spirit. It is the Spirit who inspires the communion of faith, hope, and charity that constitutes

what might be called its invisible soul, its deepest dimension, and the core of all Christian sharing on other levels. Since the Church is made up of human beings with bodies and souls, interior communion should find external, visible expression. The capacity to share will be the gauge of the depths of interior communion and of the Church's credibility in the eyes of the outside world (John 17:21). That is why any disunity in the Church is so serious and so scandalous. For in it the very mission entrusted to the Church by Christ is at stake: i.e., the Church's ability to be a sign and proof that through it God wishes to turn all human beings into his own family.

244 The problems affecting Church unity arise in the diversity of its members. This multitude of brothers and sisters (Rom. 8:29), brought together in the Church by Christ, do not form a monolithic reality. They live their unity amid the diversity of gifts that the Spirit has given to each (1 Cor. 12:4–6), and this diversity is meant to contribute to the richness of the whole.

245 This diversity may be grounded simply on each individual's way of existing. Or it may be grounded on their specific function within the Church, which clearly distinguishes the role of the hierarchy from that of the laity. Or it may be grounded on the more specific charisms that the Spirit stimulates—such as the religious life and others. Hence the Church is like a Body, which is constantly engendered, nourished, and renewed by the Spirit and which thus grows toward the fullness of Christ (Eph. 4:11–13).

The primary force ensuring cohesiveness to the Family of God amid tensions and conflicts is the very vitality of its communion in faith and love. This presupposes not only the will to unity but also agreement in the full truth of Jesus Christ. Equally useful in ensuring and fashioning the unity of the Church are the sacraments. The Eucharist signifies it at its deepest level. It gathers the People of God together as a family to share at one and the same table. There the life of Christ is surrendered sacrificially to become the unique life of all.

247 The Eucharist relates us directly to the hierarchy, without which it is impossible. For it was to the apostles that the Lord gave his mandate to perform it "as a remembrance of me" (Luke 22:19). Thus the pastors of the Church, the successors of the apostles, constitute the visible center where the unity of the Church is knitted together here on earth.

248 According to Vatican II, the role of pastors is eminently paternal (LG:28; CD:16; PO:9). Hence it is natural that what happens in every family should be true in the Church: the unity of the children is basically woven together in an upward direction. And when communication with the Church has been weakened or broken, it is also the pastors who are the sacramental ministers of reconciliation (UR:3).

249 This paternal character is no reason to forget that the pastors are within the Family of God and at its service. They are brothers called upon to serve the life that the Spirit freely sparks in their other brethren. Pastors must respect, accept, foster, and give direction to that life, even though it may have arisen independently of their own initiative. Hence they must be on guard not to "stifle the Spirit" or "despise prophecy" (1 Thess. 5:19–20). Pastors live for the sake of others, so that others might have life and "have it to the full" (John 10:10). The task of ensuring unity does not mean the exercise of an arbitrary kind of power. Authority is to serve life. This service of pastors includes the right and the duty of giving correction and making decisions with the clarity and firmness that may be necessary.

250   *A holy people.* Being inhabited by the Spirit, the People of God is also a holy People. Through baptism, the Spirit himself shared the divine life with this people. The Spirit thus anointed it as a messianic People, garbed with a substantial holiness that is grounded in the holiness of the divine life it received. This holiness reminds the People of God of the vertical dimension that is constitutive of its communion. The People is not only born of God; it is also oriented toward God as a consecrated People to render him worship and glory. Thus the People of God appears as his living temple, as the dwelling-place of his presence among human beings; and Christians are the living stones of this temple (1 Pet. 2:5).

251   The citizens who make up this People must journey by way of this earth; but they are to do so as citizens of heaven, with their heart rooted in God through prayer and contemplation. This attitude does not entail escapism vis-à-vis the earthly world; rather, it is the precondition for any fruitful commitment to human beings. For if people have not learned to worship the will of God in the silence of prayer, they will have a hard time doing it when brotherliness calls for renunciation, suffering, and humiliation.

252   The worship that God asks of us—and that is expressed in prayer and the liturgy—finds its extension in daily life through our efforts to turn everything into an offering (Rom. 12:1). As members of a People already sanctified by baptism, all of us Christians are called upon to manifest this holiness: "You must be made perfect as your heavenly Father is perfect" (Matt. 5:48). This holiness demands that we cultivate the social virtues as well as personal morals. Everything that violates the dignity of the human body, which is called to be the temple of God, entails profanation and sacrilege; and thus it saddens the Spirit (Eph. 4:30). This holds true, not only for homicide and torture, but also for prostitution, pornography, adultery, abortion, and every other abuse of sexuality.

253   On this earth the Church will never succeed in fully living its universal vocation to holiness. It will continue to be composed of just people and sinners (LG:8). What is more, the dividing line between just person and sinner is one that runs right through the heart of every single Christian.

254   *A pilgrim People.* In viewing itself as a People, the Church defines itself as a reality in the midst of history that is journeying toward a goal not yet reached.

255   Insofar as the Church is a historical People, its very nature requires that it be visible as a socially structured entity (LG:8). Regarded as a "family," the People of God already connotes a visible reality, but on an eminently vital plane. Emphasis on the historical aspect brings out the necessity of giving institutional expression to this reality.

256   The Church's social and institutional character finds expression in a clear and visible structure. This structure gives direction to the life of its members and spells out their functions, relations, rights, and duties.

257   As the People of God, the Church recognizes only one authority: Christ. He is the one and only pastor who guides the Church. But the bonds that link the Church to Christ go far deeper than any mere labor of guidance and direction. Christ is the authority of the Church in the deepest meaning of the word: because he is the author of the Church; because he is the source of its life and oneness; because he is its Head. This headship is the mysterious, living relationship that

links him to all the members of the Church. And thus any participation in his authority by the pastors of the Church throughout history is rooted in his same reality. It is something much more than merely juridical authority. It is a participation in Christ's own headship. And therefore it is a reality of a sacramental order.

The Twelve, presided over by Peter, were chosen by Jesus to share in this mysterious relationship between him and the Church. He constituted and consecrated them as living sacraments of his presence to make him visibly present as Head and Pastor, in the midst of his People. It is from this deep-rooted communion in the mystery that the power of "binding and loosing" flows as a consequence (Matt. 16:19). Viewed in its totality, the hierarchical ministry is a reality of the sacramental, juridical, and real-life order, even as the Church itself is. **258**

This ministry was entrusted to Peter and the other apostles. Today their successors are the Roman Pontiff and the bishops, to whom priests and deacons are joined as collaborators. The pastors of the Church do not just guide it in the name of the Lord. They also exercise the role of teachers of the truth and preside as priests over divine worship. The duty of the People of God to obey the pastors who guide them is not grounded primarily on juridical considerations, but rather in their respect as believers for the sacramental presence of the Lord in their pastors. This is the objective reality of faith, independent of all personal considerations. **259**

Since Vatican II and the Medellín Conference, a great change can be noted in Latin America in the way that authority is exercised within the Church. Greater emphasis has been put on its character as service and sacrament and on the dimension of collegial concern. The latter has found expression in diocesan priests' councils, episcopal conferences, and CELAM. **260**

This view of the Church as a historical, socially structured People must also serve as the point of reference for theological reflection on the CEBs existing on our continent. For it introduces elements that complement the stress of the CEBs on the dynamic vitality of the grassroots level and on the faith that is shared in a more spontaneous way in small communities. Insofar as the Church is a historical, institutional People, it represents the broader, more universal, and better defined structure in which the life of the CEBs must be inscribed if they are not to fall prey to the danger of organizational anarchy or narrow-minded, sectarian elitism (EN:58). **261**

Some aspects of the whole problem of the "people's Church" [Iglesia popular], or of "parallel magisteria," fit in here. A sect always tends toward self-sufficiency on both the juridical and doctrinal levels. Integrated into the whole People of God, the CEBs will undoubtedly avoid such dangers and will measure up to the hopes that the Latin American Church has placed in them. **262**

The problem of the "people's Church," the Church born of the People, has various aspects. The first obstacle is readily surmounted if it is interpreted as a Church that is trying to incarnate itself in the ranks of the common people on our continent, and that therefore arises out of their response in faith to the Lord. This rules out the seeming denial of a basic truth: i.e., that the Church always arises from a first initiative "from above," from the Spirit who raises it up and from the Lord who convokes it. Nevertheless the appellation seems to be quite unfortunate. The "people's Church" seems to be something distinct from some "other" **263**

Church—the latter being identified with the "official" or "institutional" Church and accused of being "alienating." This suggests a division within the bosom of the Church and seems to imply an unacceptable denial of the hierarchy's function. As John Paul II indicated, such views could well be inspired by "familiar ideological forms of conditioning" (OAP:I,8).

264 Another critical problem in Latin America, which is bound up with the historical condition of the People of God, is the whole matter of changes in the Church. As it moves through history, the Church must necessarily change, but only in external and accidental ways. Hence there can be no talk of a contrast or opposition between the "new Church" and the "old Church," as some might claim (HM). The matter of changes has caused much suffering for many Christians, for they have seen the collapse of an ecclesial way of life that they believed to be completely immutable. It is important that they be helped to make a distinction between the divine and human elements of the Church. As the Son of God, Christ always remained himself and retained his self-identity; but in his human aspect he was constantly changing in bearing, visage, and outlook. The same is true of the Church.

265 At the other extreme we find those who want nothing but continual change. That is not what being pilgrims or wayfarers means. We are not out searching for everything. We already securely possess something in hope, and we are obliged to bear witness to it. We are pilgrims, but we also are witnesses. Our attitude is one of tranquil joy over what we have already found, and of hope for what we still lack. Nor is it correct to say that the whole journey takes shape as we travel along. That is true in terms of individual persons and their concrete circumstances. But the broad common highway of the People of God has already been opened and traversed by Christ and the saints. For us, there are the saints of our own Latin America in particular: those who died defending the integrity of the Church's faith and freedom, and serving the poor people, the Indians, and the slaves; and also those who reached the utmost heights of contemplation. They journey along with us, helping us with their intercession.

266 Being a pilgrim always and inevitably entails a certain amount of insecurity and risk. That is heightened by our awareness of our frailty and our sinfulness. It is part of our daily dying in Christ. Faith enables us to shoulder all that in an attitude of paschal hopefulness. The last ten years on our continent have been violent ones. We journey on, certain that the Lord will know how to transform all the sorrow, bloodshed, and death that our peoples and our Church are leaving behind on the pathway of history. Our hope is that the Lord will transform them into seeds of resurrection for Latin America. We also derive strength and consolation from the Spirit and our faithful Mother, who are always present on the journey of God's People.

267 *A People sent by God.* By virtue of their messianic consecration in baptism, the People of God are sent out to serve the growth of the Kingdom among other peoples. They are sent out as a prophetic People to announce the Gospel or discern the Lord's calls in history. They are to announce where the presence of the Lord's Spirit is manifested; and they are to denounce where the mystery of iniquity is at work through deeds and structures that prevent more fraternal participation in the construction of society and in the enjoyment of the goods that God created for all.

In the last ten years we have seen a definite increase in the function of prophecy. It has been a heavy task for pastors to shoulder this function. We have tried to be the voice of those who have no voice, and to bear witness to the Lord's own predilection for the poor and the suffering. We believe that our peoples have felt us to be closer to them. We certainly have managed to offer enlightenment and help. But it is equally certain that we could have done more. Now, acting in a collegial manner, we are trying to interpret the Lord's passage through Latin America. 268

Another privileged form of evangelization is the celebration of the faith in the liturgy and the sacraments. There we find the People of God acting as a priestly People. They are invested with a universal priesthood that is shared by all the baptized, but that differs essentially from the hierarchical priesthood. 269

2.3. The People of God Are in the Service of Communion

A servant People. As a universal sacrament of salvation, the People of God are wholly in service to the cause of communion between human beings and God on the one hand and among the whole human race on the other (LG:1). Thus the Church is a People made up of servants, and its specific way of serving is to evangelize. This is a service that only the Church can contribute. It defines its identity and its own original contribution. The evangelizing service of the Church is addressed to all human beings without distinction, but it should also reflect Jesus' special predilection for those who are suffering and those who are poorest. 270

All those who make up the People of God—the hierarchy, lay people, religious—are servants of the Gospel. Each serves in accordance with his or her own proper role and charism. As the servant of the Gospel, the Church serves both God and human beings. But it does so in order to lead the latter to the Kingdom of the Lord. The Church, along with Mary, proclaims itself the servant of this Lord alone; and all its service to human beings is subordinated to him. 271

The Church, sign of communion. The Church evangelizes, first of all, through the overall testimony of its life. In fidelity to its status as a sacrament, it tries more and more to be a transparent sign or living model of the loving communion in Christ that it proclaims and is striving to realize. The pedagogy of the Incarnation tells us that human beings need outstanding models as guides.* Latin America needs models of that sort. 272

Every ecclesial community in Latin America should strive to serve our continent as an example of a way of living together in which freedom and solidarity are successfully combined; in which authority is exercised in the spirit of the Good Shepherd; in which a different attitude toward wealth is lived out; in which efforts are made to establish participatory forms of organization and structure that are capable of paving the way for a more humane type of society; and, most importantly of all, in which it is unmistakably clear that any merely human form 273

---

*It has been said that the major political fact of the Middle Ages was the establishment of the Benedictine monks, because their form of community life became the major model of social organization for nascent Europe.

of communion, devoid of radical communion with God in Jesus Christ, is incapable of sustaining itself and is fated to end up turning against humanity.

274   *The Church, a school for makers of history.* Insofar as Christians themselves are concerned, the Church should become a place where they learn how to live their faith by experiencing it personally and seeing it incarnated in others. It is urgently necessary for the Church to be the school that educates human beings who will be capable of making history, who will join Christ in effectively moving the history of our peoples toward the Kingdom.

275   In the face of the historical challenges confronting our peoples, we find two extreme reactions among Christians. The "passivists" believe that they cannot or should not intervene, hoping that God will act and bring liberation all by himself. The "activists" adopt a secularized perspective. They view God as remote, as if he had handed over complete responsibility for history to human beings; thus they anxiously and frantically try to move history forward.

276   Jesus' posture was different. In him we find the culmination of the wisdom that God taught Israel, who had found God in the midst of its history. He invited Israel to join him in a covenant and to make history with him. God pointed out the road and the goal, but he demanded freely proffered collaboration based on faith from his People. Jesus, too, appears acting within history hand in hand with his Father. His attitude is simultaneously one of total trust on the one hand and of the utmost commitment and co-responsibility on the other. Jesus knows that everything is in the hands of the Father, who watches over the birds of the air and the lilies of the field (Luke 12:22–33); but he also knows that the work of the Father is meant to come to pass through his own work.

277   Since the Father is the principal protagonist, Jesus tries to follow his pathways and rhythms. His constant concern is to stay in strict and loyal harmony with what the Father wants. Knowing the goal and pushing forward is not sufficient. One must try to know and wait for the hour (John 2:4; 13:1) that the Father has fixed for each step by scrutinizing the signs of his providence. On this filial docility will depend the entire fruitfulness of one's labors.

278   What is more, Jesus clearly realizes that it is not just a question of liberating human beings from sin and its lamentable consequences. He fully realizes something that is all too often buried in silence today in Latin America: that liberation from suffering must come by way of suffering, i.e., by taking up the cross and transforming it into a source of paschal life.

279   If Latin America is to be able to transform its sufferings into growth toward a truly participatory and fraternal society, then it must train human beings who are capable of forging history in accordance with Jesus' "praxis"—understood in the sense that we have spelled out in terms of the biblical theology of history. Latin America needs human beings who realize that God is calling them to act in alliance with him; human beings of docile heart who can make their own the pathways and rhythms designated by providence; and in particular, human beings who can take up their own sorrows and those of their peoples and then transform them paschally into a demand for personal conversion, a source of solidarity with all those who share those sufferings, and a challenge to display initiative and creative imagination.

280   *The Church, instrument of communion.* Through the activity of evangelically committed Christians, the Church can fulfill its mission as the sacrament of

salvation. It can become an instrument of the Lord, truly and effectively moving the history of human beings and peoples toward him.

The realization of this evangelizing service in history will always prove to be 281 difficult and dramatic. Sin, a force making for breakdown and rupture, will always pose obstacles to growth in love and communion. It will always be operative, both within the hearts of human beings, and within the various structures which they have created and on which they have left the destructive imprint of their sinfulness. In that sense the situation of misery, marginalization, injustice, and corruption that afflicts our continent requires the People of God and every Christian to display authentic heroism in their commitment to evangelizing, if they are to be able to overcome such imposing obstacles. Confronted with such a challenge, the Church knows that it is tiny and impotent. But it also feels inspired by the Spirit and protected by Mary, whose powerful intercession will enable the Church to overcome the "sinful structures" in people's personal and social life and will win for it the "authentic liberation" that comes from Jesus Christ (HZ:11).

2.4. Mary, Mother and Model of the Church

Among our peoples the Gospel has been proclaimed with the Virgin Mary 282 presented as its loftiest fulfillment. From the very beginning—with her appearance in Guadalupe and the dedication of a shrine to her there—Mary has constituted the great sign of the nearness of the Father and Christ, inviting us to enter into communion with them; and she has served as a sign endowed with a maternal, compassionate aspect. Mary has also been the voice urging us on to union as human beings and as peoples. And like the shrine in Guadalupe, the other shrines to Mary on our continent are signs of the encounter between the faith of the Church and the history of Latin America.

Pope Paul VI affirmed that devotion to Mary is an "intrinsic . . . qualifying 283 element" of "the Church's genuine piety" and of "Christian worship" (MC:Intr., 56). That fact is a vital, concrete experience in the history of Latin America; it is part of the innermost "identity" of the Latin American peoples, as John Paul II has pointed out (HZ:2).

The people know that they encounter Mary in the Catholic Church. Marian 284 piety has often been the enduring bond that has kept segments of the people faithful to the Church in the absence of adequate pastoral attention.

The believing people recognize the Church as the family whose mother is the 285 Mother of God. And it is in the Church that they find confirmation of their evangelical instinct, which tells them that Mary is the perfect model of the Christian, the ideal image of the Church.

Mary, Mother of the Church. Vatican II tells us: "Taught by the Holy Spirit, the 286 Catholic Church honors her with filial affection and piety as a most beloved mother" (LG:53). Prompted by that same faith, Pope Paul VI chose to proclaim Mary as the "Mother of the Church" (AAS, 1964:1007).

The admirable fecundity of Mary has been disclosed to us. She becomes the 287 Mother of God, of the historical Christ, with her *fiat* at the Annunciation, when the Holy Spirit overshadowed her. She is the Mother of the Church because she is the Mother of Christ, the Head of the mystical body. She is also our Mother because she "cooperated out of love" (LG:53) when the family of the redeemed was born from Christ's pierced side. That is why "she is a mother to us in the order of grace" (LG:61). And the life of Christ breaks through victoriously at Pentecost, when Mary imploringly sought the life-giving Holy Spirit for the Church.

288   Through evangelization the Church begets new children. This process, which is an "inner transformation" and a "renewal of humanity itself" (EN:18), is a real rebirth. In this coming to birth, which takes place over and over again, Mary is our Mother. Glorious in heaven, she is at work on this earth. Already sharing in the lordship of the resurrected Christ, "by her maternal charity Mary cares for the brethren of her Son who still journey on earth" (LG:62). And her great concern is that Christians enjoy abundant life and attain the fullness of adult maturity in Christ (John 10:10; Eph. 4:13).

289   Mary's intercession does not stop at protecting the Church. Her heart is as big as the world itself, and she prays to the Lord of history for all the world's peoples. This fact is registered well by the faith of the common people, who entrust the destiny of our nations to Mary as maternal Queen.

290   While we are on pilgrimage, Mary will be the Mother who educates us in the faith (LG:63). She sees to it that the Gospel penetrates us, shapes our daily lives, and produces fruits of holiness. More and more she must become the teacher of the Gospel in Latin America.

291   Mary is truly the Mother of the Church, leaving her mark on the People of God. Paul VI adopts as his own a concise formula of tradition when he writes: "There can be no talk of the Church if Mary is not present" (MC:28). Here we are dealing with a feminine presence that creates the family atmosphere, receptivity, love, and respect for life; a sacramental presence of the maternal features of God; and a reality so deeply human and holy that it evokes from believers supplications rooted in tenderness, suffering, and hope.

292   *Mary, model of the Church.* First, Mary is *a model in her relationship to Christ.* In Mary, as God's plan would have it, "everything is referred to Christ and depends on him" (MC:25). Her whole life is one of complete communion with her Son. Mary gave her yes to this plan of love. She freely accepted it at the Annunciation, and she was faithful to her word right up to the martyrdom on Golgotha. She faithfully accompanied the Lord on every road he took. Her divine maternity led her to total self-surrender. It was a clear-eyed, generous gift that was consistently maintained. It wove together a history of love for Christ that was intimate and holy, that was truly unique, and that culminated in glory.

293   Led to the maximum degree of sharing with Christ, Mary is the close collaborator in his work. She was "something very different from a passively remissive woman or one with an alienating type of religiosity" (MC:37). She is not just the admirable fruit of the redemption; she is also the active co-worker in it. Mary shows quite clearly that Christ does not annul the creativity of those who follow him. She is Christ's partner, who develops all her human capabilities and responsibilities to the point where she becomes the new Eve alongside the new Adam. By virtue of her freely proffered cooperation in Christ's new covenant, Mary is the protagonist of history alongside him. Through this communion and participation, the Immaculate Virgin now lives immersed in the mystery of the Trinity, praising the glory of God and interceding for human beings.

Second, Mary is *a model for the life of the Church and of human beings.* Today, **294** when our Latin American Church wishes to take a new step forward in its fidelity to its Lord, we focus our gaze on the living figure of Mary. She teaches us that virginity is a gift exclusively to Jesus Christ, in which faith, poverty, and obedience to the Lord are made fruitful by the action of the Spirit. The Church, too, wishes to be the mother of all human beings, but not at the expense of its love for Christ. Rather than moving away from him or setting him to one side, the Church wishes to be the mother of all human beings through its intimate and total communion with him. The maternal virginity of Mary brings together these two realities in the mystery of the Church: to be wholly Christ's and, with him, to be wholly the servant of human beings. Silence, contemplation, and adoration give rise to the most generous-hearted mission, to the most fruitful evangelization of peoples.

Mother Mary awakens the filial heart that lies sleeping in every human being. **295** In this way she prompts us to develop the life of baptism through which we were made children of God. And at the same time this maternal charisma helps fraternity to grow in us. Thus Mary is the one who ensures that the Church is concretely experienced as a family.

Mary is recognized as the extraordinary model of the Church in the order of **296** faith (Mark 3:31–34). She is the believer in whom faith shines forth as self-giving, openness, response, and fidelity. She is the perfect disciple, who opens up to the word and lets herself be imbued with its dynamism. She does not reject it or cast it aside when it is incomprehensible to her or takes her by suprise; instead she ponders it and stores it up in her heart (Luke 2:51). And when it sounds harshly in her ears, she confidently persists in her dialogue of faith with the God who speaks to her. That is what she did when she found the boy Jesus in the temple, and that is what she did at Cana when her son at first rejected her supplication (John 2:4). Her faith will drive her to undertake the journey to Calvary and to associate herself with the cross as the one and only tree of life. Thanks to her faith, Mary is the faithful Virgin in whom the greatest beatitude finds fulfillment: "Blest is she who trusted that the Lord's words to her would be fulfilled" (Luke 1:45; cf. HG).

The Magnificat mirrors the soul of Mary. In that canticle we find the culmina- **297** tion of the spirituality of Yahweh's poor and lowly, and of the prophetic strain in the Old Testament. It is the opening proclamation of Christ's new Gospel, the prelude to the Sermon on the Mount. There Mary reveals herself to us as one utterly empty of self, who has placed all her confidence in the Father's mercifulness. In the Magnificat she presents herself as the model for all those described by Pope John Paul II: "Those who do not passively accept the adverse circumstances of personal and social life and who are not victims of 'alienation,' as the expression goes today, but who instead join with her in proclaiming that God is the 'avenger of the lowly' and will, if need be, depose 'the mighty from their thrones' . . . "(HZ:4).

Third, *Mary is blest among women.* The Immaculate Conception offers us in **298** Mary the visage of the new human being redeemed by Christ, in whom we find an "even more wondrous" (Collect for the Nativity of Jesus) re-creation of the Paradise project. Mary's Assumption makes clear to us the import and destiny of the body that has been sanctified by grace. In the glorified body of Mary, material creation begins to share in the resurrected body of Christ. Mary assumed into heaven is the full integrity of humanity, body and soul, now reigning in glory and interceding for those human beings who are wayfaring through history. These truths and mysteries shed bright flashes of light on a continent where the profanation of the human being goes on constantly, and where many curl up in a passive fatalism.

299   Mary is a woman. She is "blest among women." In her, God dignified woman to unsuspected dimensions. In Mary, the Gospel penetrated femininity, redeemed it, and exalted it. This is of capital importance for our cultural horizon, where the woman should be much more highly valued and where her social roles are now being defined more clearly and fully. Mary is the guarantee of woman's grandeur; she is the example of what being a woman means specifically—of her vocation to be the soul, a self-surrender that spiritualizes the flesh and fleshes out the spirit.

300   Finally, *Mary is the model of ecclesial service in Latin America*. The Virgin Mary made herself into the servant of the Lord. When she went to help Elizabeth give birth, so Scripture tells us, she did her the much greater service of proclaiming the Gospel to her in the verses of the Magnificat. In Cana she was mindful of the needs of the celebration, and her intercession culminated in the faith of the disciples, who "believed in him" (John 2:11). Her whole service to human beings consists in opening them up to the Gospel and urging them to obey it: "Do whatever he tells you" (John 2:5).

301   Through Mary, God became flesh, entered a people, and became the center of human history. She is the bond of interconnection between heaven and earth. Without Mary the Gospel is stripped of flesh and blood and is distorted into an ideology, into a spiritualistic rationalism.

302   Paul VI spelled out the breadth of Mary's service in words that find a timely echo on our continent today. Mary is a "strong woman who knew poverty and suffering, flight and exile" (Matt. 2:13–23). Such situations can hardly escape the attention of those who wish to corroborate the liberating efforts of human beings and society with the spirit of the Gospel. And they will present Mary as a woman whose actions nurtured the faith of the apostolic community in Christ (John 2:1–12), and whose maternal function broadened to take on universal dimensions on Calvary" (MC:37).

303   The people of Latin America know this well. The Church realizes that the important thing is "not to evangelize as if it were merely a decorative veneer" (EN:20). Having firmly and lucidly decided to evangelize in depth, to go to the very roots of our people and their culture, the Church turns to Mary so that the Gospel may more and more become the heart and flesh of Latin America. This is Mary's hour, the hour of a new Pentecost. She presides over this hour with her prayer as the Church, under the influence of the Holy Spirit, initiates a new stage on its journey. On this journey we pray that Mary may be "the star of a continually renewed evangelization" (EN:82).

3. The Truth about Human Beings: Human Dignity

304   Here we consider the Christian vision of the human being in the light of both

faith and reason, in order to judge the human situation in Latin America and to help toward building a more Christian, and hence more human, society.

3.1. Inadequate Views of the Human Being Propagated in Latin America

3.1.1. Introduction. In the mystery of Christ, God comes down to the very abyss of human beings in order to restore their dignity from within. Hence faith in Christ gives us the fundamental criteria for acquiring an integral vision of the human being. That vision complements and sheds light on the image conceived by philosophy and the contributions of the other human sciences regarding the being of humanity and its historical realization.   305

For its part, the Church has the right and the duty to proclaim the Christian vision of the human person to all peoples. It knows they need it in order to shed light on their own identity and the meaning of life. It also professes the belief that every attack on human dignity is simultaneously an attack on God himself, whose image the human being is. Thus evangelization in Latin America's present and future demands that the Church voice a clear message about the dignity of the human being. The aim is to correct or complete the many inadequate views that are being propagated on our continent. Some of them are attacks on identity and genuine freedom; some are obstacles to communion; and some do not promote shared involvement with God and with human beings.   306

Latin America is the historic locale of an encounter between three culture-worlds: that of the indigenous peoples, that of the whites, and that of the Africans. These cultures were later enriched by various waves of immigrants. In Latin America we also find the convergence of different ways of viewing the world, the human being, and God, and of reacting to them. A distinctively Latin American kind of intermingling and interbreeding has been forged. Though in spirit it remains based on religious experiences imprinted with the Gospel, we also see the emergence and intermingling of worldviews that are alien to the Christian faith. In the course of time various theories and ideologies have introduced new outlooks on the human being into our continent. These outlooks offer only a partial vision of the human being, distort various aspects of the full vision of the human being, or even close themselves off from any such integral vision.   307

3.1.2. The view of determinism. Today in Latin America we see a strong re-emergence of the primitive religious soul. Associated with that is a view of the person as a prisoner of magical ways of seeing the world and acting on it. People are no longer their own masters but rather victims of occult forces. For this deterministic view of the human being, the only suitable attitude is to collaborate with these occult forces or to bow down before them.* To this is sometimes added belief in reincarnation among adherents of various brands of spiritualism and oriental religions. And more than a few Christians, being ignorant of the proper autonomy of nature and history, continue to believe that everything that happens is determined and imposed by God.   308

---

*Thus in some areas we find sorcery being practiced and a growing interest in horoscopes.

309   A variant form of this deterministic view, which is more social and fatalistic, is based on the erroneous idea that human beings are not fundamentally equal. This supposed difference gives rise to many forms of discrimination and marginalization that are incompatible with human dignity. This lack of respect for the human person, rather than finding expression in theory, is more likely to come out in the attitudes and expressions of people who judge themselves superior to others. And frequently this gives rise to the situation of inequality lived by laborers, peasants, native peoples, domestic workers, and many other segments of the population.

310   *3.1.3. The view of psychologism.* Until recently this view was confined to certain segments of Latin American society, but it is now becoming more and more significant. It is the idea that human persons are ultimately reducible to their psychic mechanisms. In its most radical form this view presents the human person as the victim of a fundamental, erotic instinct or as a mere response-mechanism to stimuli that is devoid of freedom. The human being is closed off from God and other human beings because religion, culture, and history itself are merely sublimations of the sex instinct. This negation of personal responsibility often leads to pansexualism and justifies Latin American *machismo*.

311   *3.1.4. Economicist views.* Under this heading we can point to three views of the human being prevalent in Latin America which, though distinct, have a common root. Of the three, perhaps the least conscious but most pervasive is the consumptionist view. The human being is more or less thrown into the gears and machinery of industrial production, being regarded as nothing more than an instrument of production and an object of consumption. All production and selling is done in the name of such values as ownership, power, and pleasure, which are regarded as synonymous with human happiness. Thus blocking off access to spiritual values, in the name of profit people promote an unreal and very burdensome "participation" in the common good.

312   Operating in the service of consumer society but projecting its vision beyond it, economic liberalism and its materialistic praxis offer us an individualistic view of the human being. According to it, the dignity of human persons lies in economic efficiency and in individual freedom. Thus, closed off in themselves and often locked into a religious notion of individual salvation, people of this view are blind to the demands of social justice and place themselves in the service of the international imperialism of money. Associated with them in this service are many rulers, who forget their obligations to the common good.

313   Classical Marxism is opposed to classical economic liberalism and is in a permanent struggle against its unjust consequences. It replaces the individualistic view of the human being with a collectivist and almost messianic view. The goal of human existence is fixed in the development of the material forces of production. Human beings are not viewed as originally constituted by their own awareness and conscience. Instead they are alleged to be constituted by their social existence. Stripped of any inner free will that might point the way to personal realization, human beings get their norms of behavior solely from those who are in charge of changing social, political, and economic structures. Thus this view disregards human rights, particularly the right to religious freedom that is at the root of all freedoms (OAP: III, 1).

    According to the Marxist view, the religious dimension has its origin in conflicts within the economic infrastructure; it is oriented toward a messianic form of brotherhood that has no connection with God. Materialistic and atheistic, in the last analysis, Marxist humanism reduces the human being to external structures.

3.1.5. *The view of statism.* Less well known but currently operative in the organization of quite a few Latin American governments is what we might call the statist view of the human being, which is grounded on the theory of National Security. It enrolls the individual in unlimited service to the alleged total war against cultural, social, political, and economic strife—and thereby against the threat of communism. In the face of this permanent danger, be it real or merely possible, individual freedoms are restricted as they are in any emergency situation; and the will of the State is confused with the will of the nation. Economic development and the potential to wage war are given priority over the dire needs of the neglected masses. Now National Security is certainly necessary for any political organization. But when framed in these terms, it presents itself as an Absolute holding sway over persons; in its name the insecurity of the individual becomes institutionalized.

3.1.6. *The view of scientism.* The scientific and technological organization of some countries is fostering a scientistic vision of the human being, whose vocation is seen to be the conquest of the universe. The only truth recognized by this view is that which can be demonstrated by science, and human beings themselves are reduced to their scientific definition. Everything is justified in the name of science, even that which is an affront to human dignity. At the same time national communities are made subject to the decisions of a new authority: the technocracy. Social engineering, in one form or another, can regulate the range of freedom granted to individuals and institutions; and the underlying danger is that individuals and institutions will be reduced to mere elements in a process of calculation.

3.2. Doctrinal Reflection

3.2.1. *A basic proclamation.* To our brothers and sisters in Latin America we have a serious obligation to proclaim the dignity that properly belongs to all without distinction (Gen. 1:26–28; 9:2–7; Sir. 17:2–4; Wisd. 9:2–3; Ps. 8:5–9), but that we see crushed underfoot so frequently and so viciously. We are moved to reclaim and defend this dignity by the revelation contained in the message and person of Jesus Christ. He "was well aware of what was in man's heart" (John 2:25). Yet he did not hesitate to take on "the form of a slave" (Phil. 2:7); nor did he refuse to live his whole life, right up to his death, alongside the most neglected people in order to make them sharers in the exaltation that he himself merited from God the Father.

And so we profess that every man and every woman (Gal. 5:13–24), however insignificant they may seem, possesses an inviolable nobility that they themselves and others must respect, and ensure respect for, without any conditions attached; that every human life deserves to be dignified in itself, in whatever circumstances; that all human life together must be grounded on the common good, which lies in the ever more fraternal realization of the common dignity of all. And this requires that none be used as instruments for the benefit of others, and that all be willing even to sacrifice private benefits.

We condemn any and all denigration and violation of human persons and their

314

315

316

317

318

inalienable rights; all attacks on human life, from that which lies hidden in the mother's womb to that which is judged useless as it declines in old age; and all violation or degradation of life together shared by individuals, social groups, and nations.

319   It is certain that the mystery of the human being is fully and perfectly illuminated only by faith in Jesus Christ (GS:22; OAP: I, 9). For Latin America that faith has been the historical source of the yearning for dignity that today grows louder and louder among our believing and long-suffering peoples. Only the acceptance and following of Jesus Christ open us up to the most comforting certitudes and most difficult demands of human dignity; for this dignity is rooted in the gratuitous call to life that the heavenly Father continually issues anew through the struggles and hopes of history. But we have no doubt that in the struggle for dignity we are also united with all other clear-sighted human beings who make a sincere effort to free themselves of falsehoods and passions and to follow the light of the Spirit given to them by the Creator; such people also manage to see in their own person and that of others a magnificent gift, an irrenounceable value, and a transcendent task.

320   And so we feel compelled to use every means available to comply with what may well be the original imperative of this divine hour on our continent: i.e., a bold Christian profession and an effective promotion of human dignity and its divine foundations. And this is to be done specifically among those who are most in need of it—either because they despise human dignity or, even more importantly, because they suffer from this scorn and are seeking, however gropingly, for the freedom of the children of God and the coming of the new human being in Jesus Christ.

321   *3.2.2. Dignity and freedom.* We must once again give full value to the Christian image of human beings. There must once again sound out that word which embodies a lofty ideal of our people that has been inherited from the distant past: FREEDOM. Freedom is simultaneously a gift and a task, which cannot be truly achieved without integral liberation (John 8:36). In a real sense it is the goal of human beings, according to our faith. "It was for liberty that Christ freed us" (Gal. 5:1), so that we might have life in abundance (John 10:10) as children of God and co-heirs with Christ (Rom. 8:17).

322   Freedom always implies the capacity we all possess in principle to be our own person and to act on our own initiative (GS:17), so that we can go on fashioning community and participation, to be embodied in definitive realities, on three inseparable planes: our relationship to the world as its master, to other persons as brothers or sisters, and to God as God's children.

323   Through freedom projected on the material world of nature and technology, human beings achieve the initial realization of their dignity—always in and through a community of joint efforts. This initial realization entails subduing the world through labor and wisdom, and then humanizing it, in accordance with the Creator's plan.

324   But the dignity of truly free human beings requires that they not let themselves get locked up in worldly values (Matt. 4:4; Luke 4:4; Deut. 8:3), and particularly in material goods. As spiritual beings, they must free themselves from every sort of servitude to these things. They must move on toward the higher plane of personal relations where they encounter themselves and other human beings. The

dignity of human beings becomes real here in fraternal love, understood in the full sense that the Gospel has given it; and that includes mutual service as well as the acceptance and practical promotion of others, especially of those most in need (GS:24).

However, authentic and permanent attainment of human dignity on this second level would not be possible unless we were at the same time authentically freed to find self-realization on the transcendent level. This is the plane of the Absolute Good, where our freedom is always at stake even when we seem to be unaware of it. It involves an inescapable confrontation with the divine mystery of Someone. As Father, this divine Someone calls human beings, enables them to be free, and guides them providentially. But since they can close themselves to him and even reject him, he also judges them and sentences them to eternal life or eternal death, depending on the freely chosen self-realization of human beings themselves. So it is an immense responsibility, which is a sign of both the grandeur and the risk entailed in human dignity. **325**

Through the indissoluble unity of these three planes, the exigencies of communion and participation flowing from human dignity appear more clearly. If our freedom is fully realized on the transcendent plane by our faithful and filial acceptance of God, then we enter into loving communion with the divine mystery and share its very life (GS:18). The opposite alternative is to break with filial love, to reject and despise the Father. These are the two extreme possibilities, which Christian revelation calls grace and sin respectively. But these two possibilities do not occur without simultaneously extending to the other two planes and having enormous consequences for human dignity: **326**

The love of God, which is the root of our dignity, necessarily becomes loving communion with other human beings and fraternal participation. For us today it must become first and foremost a labor of justice on behalf of the oppressed (Luke 4:18), an effort of liberation for those who are most in need of it. The fact is that "one who has no love for the brother he has seen cannot love the God he has not seen" (1 John 4:20). Authentic communion and participation can exist in this life only if they are projected on to the very concrete plane of temporal realities, so that mastery, use, and transformation of the goods of this earth and those of culture, science, and technology find embodiment in humanity's just and fraternal lordship over the world—which would include respect for ecology. Confronted with the realities that are part of our lives today, we must learn from the Gospel that in Latin America we cannot truly love our fellow human beings, and hence God, unless we commit ourselves on the personal level, and in many cases on the structural level as well, to serving and promoting the most dispossessed and downtrodden human groups and social classes, with all the consequences that will entail on the plane of temporal realities. **327**

Sinfulness on the personal level, the break with God that debases the human being, is always mirrored on the level of interpersonal relations in a corresponding egotism, haughtiness, ambition, and envy. These traits produce injustice, domination, violence at every level, and conflicts between individuals, groups, social classes, and peoples. They also produce corruption, hedonism, aggravated sexuality, and superficiality in mutual relations (Gal. 5:19–21). Thus they establish sinful situations which, at the worldwide level, enslave countless human beings and adversely affect the freedom of all. **328**

329   It is from this sin, sin as the destroyer of human dignity, that we all must be liberated. We are liberated by our participation in the new life brought to us by Jesus Christ, and by communion with him in the mystery of his death and resurrection. But this is true only on the condition that we live out this mystery on the three planes described above, without focusing exclusively on any one of them. Only in this way will we avoid reducing the mystery to the verticalism of a disembodied spiritual union with God, to the mere existential personalism of individual or small-group ties, or to one or another form of social, economic, or political horizontalism (OAP:III,6).

330   *3.2.3. The human being renewed in Jesus Christ.* It is sin that is undermining human dignity, and Jesus Christ is the one who redeemed that dignity. Through his message, death, and resurrection, he has given us his divine life: the unsuspected eternal dimension of our earthly existence (1 Cor. 15: 48–49). Jesus Christ, living in his Church and particularly among the poorest, wishes today to exalt this likeness of God in his people. Through our sharing of the Holy Spirit in Christ, we too can call God Father and become brothers and sisters down to our very roots. Jesus Christ makes us take cognizance of the sin against human dignity that abounds in Latin America. Insofar as this sinfulness destroys the divine life in human beings, it is the worst harm that a person can inflict on self or others. But Jesus Christ offers us his grace, which abounds even more than all our sinfulness (Rom. 5:20). From him we derive the strength to liberate ourselves and others from this mystery of iniquity.

331   Jesus Christ restored the original dignity that human beings had received when they were created by God in his image (Gen. 1:26), called to holiness, or total consecration to the Creator, and given the destiny of leading history toward the definitive manifestation of this God (Eph. 1; Col. 1:13–19). In the meantime this God is pouring out his goodness, for the eternal happiness of his children in a Kingdom that has already begun.

332   In Jesus Christ we come to be children of God, brothers and sisters of Christ, and sharers of his destiny. We become responsible agents who are moved by the Holy Spirit to build up the Church of the Lord (2 Cor. 5:17).

333   In Jesus Christ we discovered the image of the "new human being" (Col. 3:10). We were configured to this image in baptism, and this configuration was sealed by confirmation. It is the image that every human being is called to be, the ultimate foundation of their dignity. In presenting the Church, we showed how human dignity is to be expressed and realized in it in a communitarian way. In Mary we found the concrete figure who represents the culmination of all liberation and sanctification in the Church. Today these figures must bolster the efforts of Latin American believers in their fight for human dignity.

334   With Christ and Mary in mind, we in Latin America must give new value and appreciation to the major features of the authentic image of man and woman. We all are fundamentally equal, and members of the same race, though we live our lives amid the diversity of sexes, languages, cultures, and forms of religiosity. By virtue of our common vocation, we have one single destiny. And because it includes the joyous proclamation of our dignity, it turns us today into evangelized and evangelizing witnesses to Christ on this continent (Gen. 2:18–25).

335   Amid the plurality and equality of all, all human beings preserve their unique value and place. All human beings in Latin America should feel loved and chosen

eternally by God (1 John 3:1), however much they may be vilified or however low may be their self-esteem. As persons in dialogue, we cannot realize our dignity except as co-responsible masters of the common destiny for which God has given us the necessary capabilities. We are and must be intelligent beings: i.e., capable of discerning the truth and following it in the face of error and deceit. We are and must be free: i.e., not inexorably subject to economic and political processes, even though we humbly recognize that we are conditioned by them and have an obligation to humanize them. By the same token we are and must be subject to a moral law that comes from God. It makes itself heard in the conscience of individuals and peoples to teach us, to warn us, to reproach us, and to fill us with the true freedom of the children of God.

God also grants us existence in a body, through which we can communicate **336** with others and ennoble the world. Because we are human beings, we need the society in which we are immersed. We, in turn, are in the process of transforming and enriching it by our efforts at every level, ranging from the family and intermediate groups to the state, whose indispensable function must be exercised in the service of persons and the international community. The integration of this community is needed, particularly in Latin America.

So we rejoice over the fact that among our peoples as well we find legislation **337** being drafted in defense of human rights.

The Church has an obligation to highlight this integral aspect of evangeliza- **338** tion: first, by constantly re-examining and revising its own life; and second, by simultaneously engaging in faithful proclamation and prophetic denunciation. If this is to be done in the spirit of Christ, we all must try to discern the nature of situations and the concrete summonses of the Lord at any given point in time. This requires that we maintain an attitude of conversion and openness, and that we seriously commit ourselves to what we have discerned to be authentically evangelical.

Only thus will we succeed in living the distinctively Christian message about **339** human dignity, which consists in being more rather than in possessing more (GS:35). On the one hand this Christian message will be lived by human beings who, even though they are harrassed by suffering, poverty, persecution, and death, do not hesitate to accept life in the spirit of the Beatitudes. On the other hand it will also be lived by those who renounce a life of ready pleasure and dedicate themselves to serving others in a realistic way in today's world. For that is the criterion and gauge that Christ is going to use in passing judgment on human beings, even on those who had not known him (Matt. 25).

CHAPTER II
WHAT DOES EVANGELIZING ENTAIL?

Our people are clamoring for the salvation and communion that the Father has **340**
prepared for them. In the midst of their struggle to live their lives and to find the
deeper meaning of life, they expect the proclamation of the Good News from us.
What does evangelizing entail? Who awaits our proclamation? What is the

nature of the transformation of persons and cultures that the seed of the Gospel is supposed to bring forth? What does the Church teach us about authentic Christian liberation? How are we to evangelize the culture and religiosity of our people? What does the Gospel have to say to people who are yearning for their own betterment and who want to live out their social and political commitment?

341   We now offer our reflections on these questions.
This chapter contains:

1. Evangelization: Its Universal Dimension and Criteria
2. The Evangelization of Culture
3. Evangelization and the People's Religiosity
4. Evangelization, Liberation, and Human Promotion
5. Evangelization, Ideologies, and Politics

1. Evangelization: Its Universal Dimension and Criteria

1.1. The Situation

342   We have been evangelizing in Latin America for some five centuries. Today we are living through an important and difficult moment in that process. It is true enough that the faith of our peoples finds clear and unmistakable expression. But we also note that it has not always reached full maturity and that it is threatened: by secularist pressure, by the shocks accompanying cultural changes, by theological ambiguities in our milieu, and by the influence of proselytizing sects and foreign brands of syncretism.

Our evangelization is marked by certain particular preoccupations and emphases:

343   —the integral redemption of the old and new cultures on our continent, with due attention to the religiosity of our peoples (EN:18,20);

344   —the promotion of human dignity and liberation from all forms of servitude and idolatry (EN:29ff.).

345   —the need to make sure that the Gospel's impact penetrates decision-making centers, "the sources of inspiration and the models of social and political life" (EN:19).

346   In some instances our evangelizers are suffering from some confusion and disorientation about their own identity, the import of evangelization, its content, and its underlying motivations.

347   We want to offer a clear word of encouragement and hope to meet this situation and to give new impetus to present efforts at evangelization. We hope it will inspire people to preach the Gospel joyously and boldly to our peoples, in whom we perceive a profound yearning to receive that message. With this aim in mind, then, we here recall the meaning of evangelization, its universal dimension and destiny, and also the signs and criteria that prove its authenticity.

1.2. The Mystery of Evangelization

348   The mission to evangelize is the mission of the whole People of God. It is their primordial vocation, "their innermost identity" (EN:14), their joy. The People of

God—with all its members, institutions, and levels—exists to evangelize. The dynamism of the Spirit of Pentecost animates this People and sends it out to all nations. Our local Churches must listen with renewed enthusiasm to the Lord's command: "Go, therefore, and make disciples of all the nations" (Matt. 28:19).

Every day the Church turns back again to the Word of truth; follows the incarnate, crucified, and risen Christ through the pathways of history; and becomes the handmaid of the Gospel in order to transmit it to human beings with full fidelity. **349**

Starting off with the person, who is called to communion with God and other human beings, the Gospel should penetrate people's hearts and experiences as well as their living patterns, their culture, and their milieu. It should fashion a new humanity with new human beings, and should point all toward a new way of existing, judging, and living as individuals and as social beings. All this is a service that urgently summons us to action. **350**

We affirm that evangelization "must always entail a clear proclamation that in Jesus Christ—the Son of God who became a human being, died, and rose again—salvation is offered to all people as a gift of God's grace and mercy" (EN:27). This is the basis, center, and culmination of its dynamism, the essential content of evangelization. **351**

Evangelization introduces Jesus as the Lord who reveals the Father to us and shares his Spirit with us. It summons us to conversion, i.e., reconciliation and new life, and leads us to communion with the Father that makes us his children and brothers and sisters. Through the charity that is poured into our hearts, it brings forth the fruits of justice, pardon, respect, dignity, and world peace. **352**

The salvation offered to us by Christ gives meaning to all human aspirations and achievements; but it also continually calls them into question and goes infinitely beyond them. Although "it certainly begins in this life, it finds its fulfillment in eternity" (EN:27). Originating in Christ, in his Incarnation and his whole life, "it is definitively achieved in his death and resurrection." It is carried on in human history (EN:9) through the mystery of the Church, under the perduring influence of the Spirit who goes before it, accompanies it, and gives it apostolic fruitfulness. **353**

This salvation, the center of the Good News, "is liberation from everything that oppresses the human being. But above all it is liberation from sin and the evil one in the joy of knowing God and being known by him, of seeing God and surrendering oneself to him" (EN:9). **354**

But salvation has "very strong ties" with human promotion and its aspects of development and liberation (EN:31), which are an integral part of evangelization. These aspects arise from the very richness of salvation, from the activation of God's charity in us, to which they remain subordinate. The Church "does not need to have recourse to ideological systems in order to love, defend, and collaborate in the liberation of the human being. At the center of the message of which the Church is the trustee and herald, it finds inspiration for acting in favor of brotherhood, justice, and peace; and against all forms of domination, slavery, discrimination, violence, attacks on religious liberty, and aggression against human beings and whatever attacks life" (OAP:III,2). **355**

Through its evangelizing dynamism, the Church initiates the following process:

—It bears witness to God, the God revealed in Christ by the Spirit who cries **356**

"Father" within us (Gal. 4:6–7). In this way it shares the experience of its faith in God.

357 —It announces the Good News of Jesus Christ, through the word of life. This proclamation gives rise to faith, preaching, and a progressive catechesis that nourishes and educates it.

358 —It engenders faith, which is conversion of one's heart and life, surrender to Jesus Christ, and participation in his death so that his life may be manifested in every human being (2 Cor. 4:10). This faith also denounces everything that is opposed to the construction of the Kingdom. This entails necessary and sometimes painful breaks.

359 —It leads people toward entry into the community of the faithful, who persevere in prayer, fraternal life together, the celebration of their faith and the sacraments. The high point of the sacraments is the Eucharist (Acts 2:42).

360 —It sends out those who have accepted the Gospel as missionaries. Its burning desire is that all human beings be consecrated to God and that all peoples praise him (Rom. 15:16).

361 Thus the Church, in each of its members, is consecrated in Christ through the Spirit and sent out, both to preach the Good News to the poor (Luke 4:18) and to "search out and save what was lost" (Luke 19:10).

1.3. The Universal Dimension and Destiny of Evangelization

362 Evangelization should penetrate deeply into the hearts of human beings and peoples. Thus its dynamism aims at personal conversion and social transformation. Evangelization should be spread to all nations. Hence its dynamic thrust encompasses the whole of the human race. Both aspects are highly relevant for the work of evangelization in Latin America's present and future.

363 The first and foremost basis of this universality is the Lord's mandate, "Go, therefore, and make disciples of all the nations" (Matt. 28:19), and the oneness of the human family, created by the very same God who saves it and marks it with His grace. Christ died for all, and he draws all through his glorification in the Spirit. The more deeply we are converted to Christ, the more intensely we are drawn by his universal desire for salvation. Likewise, the more alive a local Church is, the more it will render the universal Church visibly present and the stronger will be its missionary approach to other peoples.

364 In trying to fashion a more truly alive ecclesial community, our first duty is to make our Christians more faithful, to fashion Christians who are mature in their faith and nourish them with an adequate catechesis and a revitalized liturgy. Such Christians will be a leaven in the world, giving vigor and further scope to the process of evangelization.

A second task entails giving due attention to situations that are most in need of evangelization:

365 —Perduring situations: our indigenous peoples who are habitually left on the margins of life, and who are evangelized inadequately, or sometimes not at all; also the Afro-Americans, who are so often forgotten.

366 —New situations (AG:6), which arise from sociocultural changes and call for a new evangelization: emigrants to foreign countries; human urban conglomera-

tions in our countries; the masses in every social stratum whose faith-situation is precarious; and those most exposed to the influence of sects and ideologies that do not respect their identity and that provoke confusion and divisiveness.

—Particularly difficult situations: groups urgently in need of evangelization 367 that is often postponed, such as university students, military people, laborers, young people, and those in the media of social communication.

Finally, the time has come for Latin America to intensify works of mutual 368 service between local Churches and to extend them beyond their own frontiers *"ad gentes."* True, we ourselves are in need of missionaries; but we must give from our own poverty. By the same token, our Churches have something original and important to offer all: their sense of salvation and liberation, the richness of their people's religiosity, the experiences of the CEBs, their flourishing diversity of ministries, and their hope and joy rooted in the faith. We have already undertaken missionary efforts; these can now be deepened and should be expanded.

We cannot fail to say thanks for the generous help of the universal Church and 369 our sister Churches. We ask them to stay with us, particularly in the work of training native pastoral agents. In this way we will find ourselves continually fortified for the task of assuming our more universal commitment. And we will also be more capable of an adequate response in serving our own local Church.

1.4. Criteria and Signs of Evangelization

Those who do the work of evangelization share in the faith and the mission of 370 the Church that sends them out. They need criteria and signs that will enable them to discern what really accords with the faith and the mission of the Church—which is to say, with the Lord's will: "Everyone, however, must be careful how he builds. No one can lay a foundation other than the one that has been laid, namely Jesus Christ" (1 Cor. 3:10–11); "Continue, therefore, to live in Christ Jesus the Lord, in the spirit in which you received him. Be rooted in him and built up in him, growing ever stronger in faith, as you were taught, and overflowing with gratitude" (Col. 2:6–7).

These criteria and signs serve as the inspiration for an authentic and truly vital 371 evangelization. On the other hand evangelization is paralyzed or obstructed by distortions and uncertainties.

We would now like to offer the following basic criteria:

—There is the Word of God contained in the Bible and in the living Tradition of 372 the Church, which is expressed particularly in the creeds or professions of faith and the dogmas of the Church. Scripture should be the soul of evangelization. But it does not achieve full clarity on its own. It must be read and interpreted in the framework of the Church's living faith. Our creeds or professions of faith sum up the Scriptures and spell out the substance of the message, highlighting the " 'hierarchy' of truths" (UR:11).

—There is the faith of the People of God. It is the faith of the universal Church 373 that is lived and concretely expressed in its local communities. A local community embodies in itself the faith of the universal Church, thereby ceasing to be a private, isolated community. It overcomes its own localness in the faith of the total Church.

374   —There is the magisterium of the Church. The meaning of Scripture, the creeds, and the dogmatic formulations of the past do not flow solely from the text itself but from the faith of the Church. It is in the bosom of the community that we find the court of decision, of authentic and faithful interpretation of the faith and the moral law. This is the service of the successor of Peter, who confirms his brothers and sisters in the faith, and of the bishops, "who have received through episcopal succession the sure gift of truth" (DV:8).

375   —Theologians offer an important service to the Church. They systematize the doctrine and guidelines of the magisterium in a synthesis with a more ample context, converting it into an idiom more suited to a given age. They subject the facts and the words revealed by God to new investigation in order to relate them to new sociocultural situations (AG:22), or to new findings and problems raised by the sciences, history, or philosophy (GS:62). In performing this service, theologians will take care not to harm the faith of believers, either by offering difficult explanations or by posing debated or debatable questions to the public.

376   Theological labor entails a certain pluralism, the result of using "different methods and approaches in understanding and proclaiming divine things" (UR:17). So there is a sound and necessary pluralism, which tries to express legitimate differences without affecting cohesiveness and concord. But there are also forms of pluralism that foment divisiveness.

377   —We all share in the prophetic mission of the Church. We know that the Spirit distributes his gifts and charisms to us for the good of the whole body, and we must accept them gratefully. But discernment, that is, the evaluation of their authenticity and the regulation of their exercise, properly belongs to the authorities in the Church. Their primary task is not to suffocate the Spirit, but to test everything and keep what is good (LG:12).

    Various attitudes tell us when evangelization is authentic:

378   —A life of profound ecclesial communion (Gal. 2:2).

379   —Fidelity to signs of the Spirit's presence and activity among peoples and cultures, these signs being embodiments of legitimate human aspirations. This presupposes respect, missionary dialogue, discernment, and an attitude of operative charity.

380   —Real concern that the Word of truth reach the hearts of human beings and become life for them.

381   —Positive efforts toward the building up of the community.

382   —Preferential love and concern for the poor and needy (Luke 4:18; EN: 12).

383   —Holiness in the evangelizer (EN:76). Its characteristics are compassion, firmness, and patience in trials and persecutions, and joy in realizing that one is a minister of the Gospel (EN:80).

384   In conclusion, what is demanded of servants of the Gospel is that they be found faithful (1 Cor. 4:2). Their fidelity creates communion, and from communion "results great apostolic influence" (PC:15) that enriches the Church with the Spirit's abundant fruits (Gal. 5:22; HG).

2. The Evangelization of Culture

2.1. Culture and Cultures

The new and important pastoral contribution of *Evangelii Nuntiandi* lies in Paul VI's summons to face up to the task of evangelizing culture and cultures (EN:20). **385**

The term "culture" means the specific way in which human beings belonging to a given people cultivate their relationship with nature, with each other, and with God in order to arrive at "an authentic and full humanity." It is the shared lifestyle that characterizes different peoples around the earth, and so we can speak about "a plurality of cultures" (GS:53; EN:20). **386**

So conceived, culture embraces the whole life of a people. It is the whole web of values that inspire them and of disvalues that debilitate them; insofar as they are shared in common by all the members, they bring them together on the basis of a "collective consciousness" (EN:18). Culture also embraces the forms in which these values or disvalues find configuration and expression—i.e., customs, language, societal institutions and structures—insofar as they are not impeded or suppressed by the intervention of other, dominant cultures. **387**

In the context of this totality, evangelization seeks to get to the very core of a culture, the realm of its basic values, and to bring about a conversion that will serve as the basis and guarantee of a transformation in structures and the social milieu (EN:18). **388**

The essential core of a culture lies in the way in which a people affirms or rejects a religious tie with God, that is, in its religious values or disvalues. These values or disvalues have to do with the ultimate meaning of life. Their roots lie in the deeper zone where human beings formulate answers to the basic, ultimate questions that vex them. The answer may be a positively religious orientation on the one hand, or an atheistic orientation on the other hand. Thus religion or irreligion is a source of inspiration for all the other areas of a culture— family life, economics, politics, art, etc. They are either freed to seek out some transcendent meaning, or else they are locked up in their own immanent meaning. **389**

Evangelization takes the whole human being into account, and so it seeks to reach the total human being through that being's religious dimension. **390**

Culture is a creative activity of human beings. Thus it is in line with the vocation given to them by God to perfect all creation (Genesis), and hence their own spiritual and corporeal qualities and capabilities (GS:53, 57). **391**

Culture is continually shaped and reshaped by the ongoing life and historical experience of peoples; and it is transmitted by tradition from generation to generation. Thus human beings are born and raised in the bosom of a given society, conditioned and enriched by a given culture. They receive a culture, creatively modify it, and then continue to pass it on. Culture is a historical and social reality (GS:53). **392**

Cultures are continually subjected to new developments and to mutual encounter and interpenetration. In the course of their history they go through periods in which they are challenged by new values or disvalues, and by the need **393** to effect new syntheses of their way of life. The Church feels particularly summoned to make its presence felt, to be there with the Gospel, when old ways of social life and value-organization are decaying or dying in order to make room for new syntheses (GS:5). It is better to evangelize new cultural forms when they are being born than when they are already full-grown and established. This is the global challenge that confronts the Church today because we truly can "speak of a new age in human history" (GS:54). Hence the Latin American Church seeks to give new impetus to the evangelization of our continent.

2.2. The Pastoral Option of the Latin American Church: To Evangelize Culture Today and for Tomorrow

394   *The aim of evangelization.* Christ sent his Church to announce the Gospel to all human beings, to all peoples (Matt. 28:19; Mark 16:15). Since every human being is born into a culture, the Church in its evangelizing activity seeks to touch, not only the individual, but also the culture of a people (EN:18). Using the power of the Gospel, it tries "to reach and transform the criteria of judgment, the determining values, the points of interest, the lines of thought, the sources of inspiration, and the models of human life that are opposed to the Word of God and the plan of salvation. Perhaps we could put it this way: the work of evangelization is not to be a decorative veneer; it is to be done in a vital, in-depth manner so that it touches the very roots of human culture and cultures" (EN:19–20).

395   *Pastoral option.* The evangelizing activity of our Latin American Church must have as its overall goal the ongoing evangelical renewal and transformation of our culture. In other words, the Gospel must penetrate the values and criteria that inspire our culture, convert the human beings who live by these values, and, insofar as it is necessary, change the structures in which they live and express themselves so that they may be more fully human.

396   If we are to do this, it is of the utmost importance that we pay heed to the religion of our peoples. Not only must we take it on as an object for evangelization. Insofar as it has already been evangelized, we must also accept it as an active, evangelizing force.

2.3. The Church, Faith, and Culture

397   *Love for peoples and knowledge of their culture.* To carry out and expand its evangelizing activity realistically, the Church must truly know the culture of Latin America. But even before that, it starts off with a profound attitude of love for peoples. Thus, basing its work not only on a scientific approach but also on the connatural effective understanding that comes with love, it will be able to learn and discern the specific modalities of our culture as well as its crises and historical challenges; and it will then be able to make common cause with our culture within the context of Latin America's history (OA:1).

398   Here is one important criterion that must guide the Church in its effort to know our culture: it must note the overall direction in which the culture is heading rather than its side-pockets bound up with the past, its expressions that are operative today rather than those that are merely part of folklore.

The task of evangelizing our continent's culture must be organized against the backdrop of an established cultural tradition, now being challenged by the process of cultural change that has been affecting Latin America and the world in modern times and is now reaching its moment of crisis.

Faith's encounter with cultures. When the Church, the People of God, announces the Gospel and peoples accept it in faith, it becomes incarnate among them and assumes their cultures. This gives rise, not to an identification between the two, but to a close bond between them. On the one hand the faith transmitted by the Church is lived out on the basis of a presupposed culture. In other words, it is lived by believers who are deeply attached to a culture, and hence "the construction of the kingdom cannot help but take over elements from human culture and cultures" (EN:20). On the other hand the principle of incarnation embodied in the old adage of St. Irenaeus remains valid in the pastoral realm: "what is not assumed is not redeemed."

The general principle of incarnation breaks down concretely into several specific criteria:

Cultures are not vacuums devoid of authentic values, and the evangelizing work of the Church is not a process of destruction; rather, it is a process of consolidating and fortifying those values, a contribution to the growth of the "seeds of the Word" present in cultures (GS:57).

The Church is even more interested in assuming the specifically Christian values that it encounters among peoples already evangelized, and that are lived out by those peoples in their own cultural forms.

In its evangelization, the Church begins with those seeds sown by Christ and with those values that are the fruit of its own evangelization.

All this implies that the Church—of course the local Church—makes every effort to adapt itself. It tries to translate the gospel message into the anthropological idiom and symbols of the culture in which it immerses itself (EN:53,62–63; GS:58; DT:420–23).

When the Church proclaims the Good News, it denounces and corrects the presence of sinfulness in cultures; it purifies and exorcises their disvalues, thus establishing a critique of cultures. In the announcing of the Kingdom of God, the opposite side of the coin is the critical denunciation of various forms of idolatry, that is, of values that have been set up as idols or values that a culture has taken to be absolute when in fact they are not. The Church's mission is to bear witness to "the true God and one Lord."

So there is nothing insulting in the fact that evangelization invites peoples to abandon false conceptions of God, anti-natural patterns of conduct, and aberrant manipulations of some people by others.

The specific task of evangelization is to "proclaim Christ" (EN:53). This does not mean that cultures are to be invited to remain under the grip of an ecclesiastical regime. Instead they are to be invited to accept in faith the spiritual lordship of Christ, for they will not be able to attain their full measure outside of his truth and grace. Thus through evangelization the Church tries to make sure that cultures will be renovated, elevated, and perfected by the active presence of the risen Christ, the center of history, and of his Spirit (EN:18,20,23; GS: 58,61).

2.4. Evangelization of Culture in Latin America

We have indicated above the fundamental criteria governing the work of the Church in evangelizing cultures.

408 Our Church, for its part, carries out this work in the particular human area known as Latin America, whose historical and cultural process has already been described (see Part One).

So let us briefly review some of the principal items already established in Part One of this document so that we may be able to single out the challenges and problems posed to evangelization by the present moment of history.

409 **Types of culture and stages in the cultural process.** The origin of present-day Latin America lies in the encounter of the Spanish and Portuguese peoples with the pre-Columbian and African cultures. Racial and cultural intermingling has profoundly marked this process, and there is every indication that it will continue to do so now and in the future.

410 This fact should not prompt us to disregard the persistence of indigenous cultures or Afro-American cultures in a pure state, nor the existence of groups who are integrated into the nation in varying degrees.

411 Subsequently, during the last two centuries, new waves of immigrants have flowed into Latin America, and particularly into the southern cone of our continent. These immigrants brought their own characteristics with them, which basically were integrated with the underlying cultural stratum.

412 In the first epoch, from the sixteenth to the eighteenth centuries, were laid the bases of Latin American culture and its solid Catholic substrate. In that period evangelization was deep enough for the faith to become a constitutive part of Latin America's life and identity. It provided Latin America with a spiritual unity that still persists, despite later splintering into separate nations and divisions on the economic, social, and political planes.

413 So our culture is impregnated with the faith, even though it frequently has lacked the support of a suitable catechesis. This is evident in the distinctive religious attitudes of our people, which are imbued with a deep sense of transcendence and the nearness of God. It finds expression in a wisdom of the common people that has contemplative features and that gives a distinctive direction to the way our people live out their relationship with nature and their fellow human beings. It is embodied in their sense of work and festiveness, of solidarity, friendship, and kinship; and in their feel for their own dignity, which they do not see diminished by their own lives as simple, poor people.

414 Preserved more vividly as an articulation of life as a whole among the poor, this culture bears in particular the seal of the heart and its intuitions. Rather than finding expression in scientific categories and ways of thinking, it is more likely to find expression in artistic forms, in piety as a lived reality, and in solidary forms of social life.

415 From the eighteenth century on, this culture began to feel the impact of the dawning urban-industrial civilization, with its physico-mathematical brand of knowledge and its stress on efficiency. The impact was first felt by the *mestizo* culture, and then gradually by various enclaves of indigenous peoples and Afro-Americans.

The new urban-industrial civilization is accompanied by strong tendencies toward personalization and socialization. It produces a sharpened acceleration of history, demanding great efforts at assimilation and creativity from all peoples if they do not want to see their cultures left behind or even eliminated. **416**

Urban-industrial culture, which has as a consequence the intense proletarianization of various social strata and even peoples, is controlled by the great powers in possession of science and technology. It is a historical process that tends to make the problem of dependence and poverty more and more acute. **417**

The advent of urban-industrial civilization also entails problems on the ideological level, threatening the very roots of our culture. For in terms of real-life history and its workings, this civilization comes to us imbued with rationalism and inspired by two dominant ideologies: liberalism and Marxist collectivism. In both we find a tendency, not just to a legitimate and desirable secularization, but also to "secularism." **418**

Within this basic historical process we see arising on our continent certain particular but important phenomena and problems: increased migration and displacement of the population from rural to urban areas; the rise of various religious phenomena, such as the invasion of sects, which should not be disregarded by evangelizers simply because they may seem to be marginal; the enormous influence of the media of social communication as vehicles of new cultural guidelines and models; the yearning of women to better their situation, in line with their dignity and distinctiveness, within the overall framework of society; and the emergence of a laborer's world that will be decisive in the new configuration of our culture. **419**

Evangelizing activity: challenges and problems. The data given above also point to the challenges that must be faced by the Church. The problems are manifestations of the signs of the times, pointing toward the future where culture is now heading. The Church must be able to discern these signs if it is to consolidate the values and overthrow the idols that are feeding this historical process. **420**

The coming world culture. This urban-industrial culture, which is inspired by the scientific-technological outlook, driven by the great powers, and characterized by the aforementioned ideologies, proposes to be a universal one. Various peoples, local cultures, and human groups are invited or even constrained to become an integral part of it. **421**

In Latin America this tendency again brings to the fore the whole problem of integrating indigenous ethnic groups and realities into the political and cultural fabric of our nations. For our nations find themselves challenged to move toward greater development, to win new hands and lands for more efficient production, so that they can become a more integral and dynamic part of the accelerating thrust of world civilization. **422**

This new universality has different levels. First, there is the level of scientific and technical elements, which are the instruments of development. Second, there is the level of certain values that are given new emphasis: e.g., labor and the increased possession of consumer goods. And then there is the whole matter of "lifestyle" as a whole, which entails a particular hierarchy of values and preferences. **423**

Finding themselves at this critical juncture in history, some ethnic and social **424** groups draw back into themselves, defending their own distinctive culture in and through a fruitless sort of isolationism. Other groups, on the other hand, allow themselves to be readily absorbed by lifestyles introduced by the new world culture.

425   In its work of evangelization, the Church itself moves ahead by a process of delicate and difficult discernment. By virtue of its own evangelical principles, the Church looks with satisfaction on the impulses of humanity leading toward integration and universal communion. By virtue of its specific mission it feels that it has been sent, not to destroy cultures, but to help them consolidate their being and identity. And it does this by summoning human beings of all races and peoples to unite in faith under Christ as one single People of the universal God.

426   The Church itself promotes and fosters things that go beyond this catholic union in the same faith, things that find embodiment in forms of communion between cultures and of just integration on the economic, social, and political levels.

427   But the Church, as one would expect, calls into question any "universality" that is synonymous with uniformity or levelling, that fails to respect different cultures by weakening them, absorbing them, or annihilating them. With even greater reason the Church refuses to accept universality when it is used as a tool to unify humanity by inculcating the unjust, offensive supremacy and domination of some peoples or social strata over other peoples and social strata.

428   The Church of Latin America has resolved to put fresh vigor into its work of evangelizing the culture of our peoples and the various ethnic groups. It wants to see the faith of the Gospel blossom or be restored to fresh life. And with this as the basis of communion, it wants to see it burgeon into forms of just integration on all levels—national, continental Latin American, and universal. This will enable our peoples to develop their own culture in such a way that they can assimilate the findings of science and technology in their own proper way.

429   *The city.* In the transition from an agrarian culture to an urban-industrial one, the city becomes the moving force behind the new world civilization. This fact calls for a new type of discernment on the part of the Church. In general, it should find its inspiration in the vision of the Bible. On the one hand the Bible has a positive view of the human tendency to create cities, where human beings can live together in a more corporate and humane way; on the other hand it is highly critical of the inhumanness and sinfulness that has its origin in urban life.

430   In the present situation, therefore, the Church does not favor as an ideal the creation of huge metropolises, which become inhuman beyond all repair. Nor does it favor an excessively accelerated pace of industrialization that will cost today's generations their own happiness and require inhuman sacrifices.

431   The Church also recognizes that urban life and industrial change pose unprecedented problems. They undermine traditional patterns of behavior and institutions: the family, the neighborhood, and work life. And hence they also undermine the living situation of the religious human being, the faithful, and the Christian community (OA:10).

    These characteristics are aspects of what is called "the process of secularization," which is evidently bound up with the emergence of science and technology and the increase in urbanization.

432   There is no reason to assume that the elemental forms of religious awareness

are exclusively bound up with agrarian culture. The transition to an urban-industrial civilization need not entail the abolition of religion. But it obviously poses a challenge because it entails new forms and structures of living that condition religious awareness and the Christian life.

So the Church is faced with a challenge. It must revitalize its work of evangelization so that it will be able to help the faithful live as Christians amid the new conditioning factors created by the urban-industrial society. And it must realize that these new factors do have an influence on the practice of holiness, on prayer and contemplation, on interhuman relationships (that have now become more functional and anonymous), on people's work life, production, and consumption. **433**

Secularism. The Church accepts the process of secularization insofar as it means the legitimate autonomy of the secular realm. Taking it in this sense (GS:36; EN:55), it regards it as just and desirable. But the fact is that the shift to an urban-industrial society, viewed in terms of the real-life process of western history rather than in the abstract, has been inspired by the ideology that we call "secularism." **434**

Secularism essentially separates human beings from God and sets up an opposition between them. It views the construction of history as purely and exclusively the responsibility of human beings, and it views them in merely immanent terms. The world "is explained solely on its own terms, without any necessary reference to God. God, then, is superfluous, if not a downright obstacle. So in order to recognize the power of human beings, this brand of secularism ends up bypassing God, or even denying God altogether. The result seems to be new forms of atheism—an anthropocentric atheism that is practical and militant rather than abstract and metaphysical. And bound up with this atheistic secularism we find a consumer civilization, a hedonism exalted as the supreme value, a will to power and domination, and discrimination of all sorts. These are some of the other inhuman tendencies of this 'humanism'" (EN:55). **435**

Committed to its task to evangelize people and to arouse faith in God, the provident Father, and in Jesus Christ, who is actively present in history, the Church finds itself in a radical confrontation with this secularistic movement. It sees it as a threat to the faith and the very culture of our Latin American peoples. Hence one of the fundamental commitments in the new drive toward evangelization must be to revivify and reorganize the proclamation of the content of evangelization, basing our efforts on the very faith of our peoples. Our aim is that they themselves will be able to incorporate the values of the new urban-industrial civilization into a new vital synthesis, which will continue to be grounded on faith in God rather than on the atheism that is the logical consequence of the movement toward secularism. **436**

Conversion and structures. We have alluded to the inconsistency that exists between the culture of our people, whose values are imbued with the Christian faith, and the impoverished condition in which they are often forced to live by injustice.

Undoubtedly situations of injustice and acute poverty are an indictment in themselves, indicating that the faith was not strong enough to affect the criteria and the decisions of those responsible for ideological leadership and the organization of our people's socio-economic life together. Our peoples, rooted in the **437**

Christian faith, have been subjected to structures that have proved to be well-springs of injustice. These structures are linked with the expansion of liberal capitalism, though in some areas they have been transformed under the inspiration of Marxist collectivism; but they arise out of the ideologies of the dominant cultures, and they are inconsistent with the faith that is part of our people's culture.

438 The Church thus calls for a new conversion on the level of cultural values, so that the structures of societal life may then be imbued with the spirit of the Gospel. And while it calls for a revitalization of evangelical values, it simultaneously urges a rapid and thoroughgoing transformation of structures. For by their very nature these structures are supposed to exert a restraining influence on the evil that arises in the human heart and manifests itself socially; and they are also meant to serve as conditioning pedagogical factors for an interior conversion on the plane of values (Med-P:16).

439 *Other problems.* Within this general situation and its overall challenges are inscribed certain specific problems of major importance that the Church must heed in its new effort at evangelization. They include the following:

—Starting off from a sound knowledge of the cultural conditions of our peoples and a solid penetration into their lifestyle, the Church must organize an adequate catechesis. And there must be enough native pastoral workers of varied sorts to satisfy the right of our peoples not to stay immersed in ignorance about the faith or at the most rudimentary levels of knowledge.

440 —There must be a critical yet constructive examination of the educational system established in Latin America.

441 —Using past experience and imagination, the Church must draw up criteria and approaches for a pastoral effort directed at city life, where the new cultural styles are arising. At the same time the Church must also work to evangelize and promote indigenous groups and Afro-Americans.

442 —The Church must establish a new evangelizing presence among workers as well as intellectual and artistic elites.

443 —Humanistically and evangelically the Church must contribute to the betterment of women, in line with their specific identity and femininity.

3. Evangelization and the People's Religiosity

3.1. Basic Statements about This Notion

444 By the religion of the people, popular religiosity, or popular piety (EN:48), we mean the whole complex of underlying beliefs rooted in God, the basic attitudes that flow from these beliefs, and the expressions that manifest them. It is the form of cultural life that religion takes on among a given people. In its most characteristic cultural form, the religion of the Latin American people is an expression of the Catholic faith. It is a people's Catholicism.

445 Despite the defects and the sins that are always present, the faith of the Church has set its seal on the soul of Latin America (HZ:2). It has left its mark on Latin America's essential historical identity, becoming the continent's cultural matrix out of which new peoples have arisen.

446 It is the Gospel, fleshed out in our peoples, that has brought them together to form the original cultural and historical entity known as Latin America. And this identity is glowingly reflected on the *mestizo* countenance of Mary of Guadalupe, who appeared at the start of the evangelization process.

This people's religion is lived out in a preferential way by the "poor and simple" (EN:48). But it takes in all social sectors; and sometimes it is one of the few bonds that really brings together the people living in our nations, which are so divided politically. But of course we must acknowledge that there is much diversity amid this unity, a diversity of social, ethnic, and even generation groups.

447

At its core the religiosity of the people is a storehouse of values that offers the answers of Christian wisdom to the great questions of life. The Catholic wisdom of the common people is capable of fashioning a vital synthesis. It creatively combines the divine and the human, Christ and Mary, spirit and body, communion and institution, person and community, faith and homeland, intelligence and emotion. This wisdom is a Christian humanism that radically affirms the dignity of every person as a child of God, establishes a basic fraternity, teaches people how to encounter nature and understand work, and provides reasons for joy and humor even in the midst of a very hard life. For the common people this wisdom is also a principle of discernment and an evangelical instinct through which they spontaneously sense when the Gospel is served in the Church and when it is emptied of its content and stifled by other interests (OAP:III,6).

448

Because this cultural reality takes in a very broad range of social strata, the common people's religion is capable of bringing together multitudes. Thus it is in the realm of popular piety that the Church fulfills its imperative of universality. Knowing that the message "is not reserved for a small group of initiates or a chosen, privileged few, but is meant for all" (EN:57), the Church accomplishes its task of convening the masses in its sanctuaries and religious feasts. There the gospel message has a chance, not always pastorally utilized, of reaching "the heart of the masses" (EN:57).

449

The people's religious life is not just an object of evangelization. Insofar as it is a concrete embodiment of the Word of God, it itself is an active way in which the people continually evangelize themselves.

450

In Latin America this Catholic piety of the common people has not adequately impregnated certain autochthonous cultural groups and ones of African origin. Indeed in some cases they have not even been evangelized at all. Yet these groups do possess a rich store of values and "seeds of the Word" as they await the living Word.

451

Though the popular religiosity has set its seal on Latin American culture, it has not been sufficiently expressed in the organization of our societies and states. It has left standing what John Paul II has once again called "sinful structures" (HZ:3). The gap between rich and poor, the menacing situation faced by the weakest, the injustices, and the humiliating disregard and subjection endured by them radically contradict the values of personal dignity and solidary brotherhood. Yet the people of Latin America carry these values in their hearts as imperatives received from the Gospel. That is why the religiosity of the Latin American people often is turned into a cry for true liberation. It is an exigency that is still unmet. Motivated by their religiosity, however, the people create or

452

utilize space for the practice of brotherhood in the more intimate areas of their lives together: e.g., the neighborhood, the village, their labor unions, and their recreational activities. Rather than giving way to despair, they confidently and shrewdly wait for the right opportunities to move forward toward the liberation they so ardently desire.

453   Due to lack of attention on the part of pastoral agents and to other complicated factors, the religion of the people shows signs of erosion and distortion. Aberrant substitutes and regressive forms of syncretism have already surfaced. In some areas we can discern serious and strange threats to the religion of the people, framed in terms that lay excessive stress on apocalyptic fantasies.

3.2. A Description of the People's Religiosity

454   We can point to the following items as positive elements of the people's piety: the trinitarian presence evident in devotions and iconography; a sense of God the Father's providence; Christ celebrated in the mystery of his Incarnation (the Nativity, the child Jesus), in his crucifixion, in the Eucharist, and in the devotion to the Sacred Heart. Love for Mary is shown in many ways. She and "her mysteries are part of the very identity of these peoples and characterize their popular piety" (HZ:2). She is venerated as the Immaculate Mother of God and of human beings, and as the Queen of our individual countries as well as of the whole continent. Other positive features are: veneration of the saints as protectors; remembrance of the dead; an awareness of personal dignity and of solidary brotherhood; awareness of sin and the need to expiate it; the ability to express the faith in a total idiom that goes beyond all sorts of rationalism (chant, images, gesture, color, and dance); faith situated in time (feasts) and in various places (sanctuaries and shrines); a feel for pilgrimage as a symbol of human and Christian existence; filial respect for their pastors as representatives of God; an ability to celebrate the faith in expressive and communitarian forms; the deep integration of the sacraments and sacramentals into their personal and social life; a warm affection for the person of the Holy Father; a capacity for suffering and heroism in withstanding trials and professing their faith; a sense of the value of prayer; and acceptance of other people.

455   For some time now the religion of the people has been suffering from a divorce between elites and the common people. This indicates that there has been a lack of education, catechesis, and dynamic activity, due to a lack of proper pastoral concern on the part of the Church.

456   The negative aspects that we can point to are varied in origin. Some are of an ancestral type: superstition, magic, fatalism, idolatrous worship of power, fetishism, and ritualism. Some are due to distortions of catechesis: static archaism, misinformation and ignorance, syncretistic reinterpretation, and reduction of the faith to a mere contract with God. Some negative aspects are threats to the faith today: secularism as broadcasted by the media of social communication; consumptionism; sects; oriental and agnostic religions; ideological, economic, social, and political types of manipulation; various secularized forms of political messianism; and uprooting and urban proletarianization as the result of cultural change. We can state that many of these phenomena are real obstacles to evangelization.

3.3. Evangelizing the People's Religiosity: The Process, Attitudes, and Criteria

Like the Church as a whole, the religion of the people must be constantly evangelized over again. In Latin America, where the Gospel has been preached and the general population baptized for almost five hundred years, the work of evangelization must appeal to the "Christian memory of our peoples." Evangelization will be a work of pastoral pedagogy in which the Catholicism of the common people is assumed, purified, completed, and made dynamic by the Gospel. In practice this means renewing a pedagogical dialogue based on the last links that the evangelizers of yesteryear had forged in the heart of our people. To do this, we must know the symbols, the silent nonverbal language of the people. Only then can we engage in a vital dialogue with them, communicating the Good News through a renewed process of informational catechesis. **457**

Guided by the light of the Holy Spirit and imbued with "pastoral charity," the agents of evangelization will know how to elaborate a "pedagogy of evangelization" (EN:48). Such a pedagogy demands that they love the people and be close to them; that they be prudent, firm, constant, and audacious. Only then can they educate this precious faith, which is sometimes in a very weakened state. **458**

Concrete forms and pastoral processes must be evaluated on the basis of the criteria that characterize the Gospel as lived in the Church. Everything should help to make the baptized more truly children of God in the Son, more truly brothers and sisters in the Church, and more responsible missionaries in spreading the Kingdom. That is the direction which the maturing of the people's religion should take. **459**

3.4. Tasks and Challenges

We face an urgent situation. The shift from an agrarian to an urbanized, industrial society is subjecting the people's religion to a decisive crisis. As this millennium draws to a close in Latin America, the great challenges posed by the people's piety entail the following pastoral tasks: **460**

a. We must offer adequate catechesis and evangelization to the vast majority of the people who have been baptized but whose popular Catholicism is in a weakened state. **461**

b. We must mobilize apostolic movements, parishes, base-level ecclesial communities, and church militants in general so that they may be a "leaven in the dough" in a more generous way. We must re-examine the spiritual practices, attitudes, and tactics of church elites vis-à-vis the common people's religiosity. As the Medellín Conference pointed out: "Given this type of religious sense among the masses, the Church is faced with the dilemma of either continuing to be a universal Church or, if it fails to attract and vitally incorporate such groups, of becoming a sect" (Med-PM:3). We must develop in our militants a mystique of service designed to evangelize the religion of their people. That task is even more to the point today, and it is up to elites to accept the spirit of their people, purify it, scrutinize it, and flesh it out in a prominent way. To this end elites must participate in the assemblies and public manifestations of the people so that they may offer their contribution. **462**

463   *c.* We must proceed to put more planned effort into transforming our sanctuaries so that they might be "privileged locales" of evangelization (HZ:5). This would entail purifying them of all forms of manipulation and commercialism. A special effort in this direction is demanded of our national sanctuaries, which stand as symbols of the interaction between the faith and the history of our peoples.

464   *d.* We must pay pastoral attention to the popular piety of the peasants and the indigenous peoples, so that they might enjoy growth and renewal in line with their own proper identity and development and in accordance with the emphases spelled out by Vatican II. This will ensure better preparation for more generalized cultural change.

465   *e.* We must see to it that the liturgy and the common people's piety cross-fertilize each other, giving lucid and prudent direction to the impulses of prayer and charismatic vitality that are evident today in our countries. In addition, the religion of the people, with its symbolic and expressive richness, can provide the liturgy with creative dynamism. When examined with proper discernment, this dynamism can help to incarnate the universal prayer of the Church in our culture in a greater and better way.

466   *f.* We must try to provide the religiosity of the common people with the necessary reformulations and shifts of emphasis that are required in an urban-industrial civilization. The process is already evident in the big cities of the continent, where the Catholicism of the people is spontaneously finding new forms of expression and enriching itself with new values that have matured within its own depths. In this respect we must see to it that the faith develops a growing personalization and a liberative solidarity. The faith must nurture a spirituality that is capable of ensuring the contemplative dimension, i.e., gratitude to God and a poetic, sapiential encounter with creation. The faith must be a wellspring of joy for the common people and a reason for festivity even in the midst of suffering. In this way we can fashion cultural forms that will rescue urban industrialization from oppressive tedium and cold, suffocating economicism.

467   *g.* We must support the religious expressions of the common people *en masse* for the evangelizing force that they possess.

468   *h.* We must assume the religious unrest and excitement that is arising as a form of historical anxiety over the coming end of the millennium. This unrest and excitement must be framed in terms of the lordship of Christ and the providence of the Father, so that the children of God may enjoy the peace they need while they struggle and labor in time.

469   If the Church does not reinterpret the religion of the Latin American people, the resultant vacuum will be occupied by sects, secularized political forms of messianism, consumptionism and its consequences of nausea and indifference, or pagan pansexualism. Once again the Church is faced with stark alternatives: what it does not assume in Christ is not redeemed, and it becomes a new idol replete with all the old malicious cunning.

4. Evangelization, Liberation, and Human Promotion

In this section we shall discuss evangelization in terms of its connection with human promotion, liberation, and the social doctrine of the Church.

4.1. A Word of Encouragement

We fully recognize the efforts undertaken by many Latin American Christians **470** to explore the particularly conflict-ridden situations of our peoples in terms of the faith and to shed the light of God's Word on them. We encourage all Christians to continue to provide this evangelizing service and to consider the criteria for reflection and investigation; and we urge them to put special care into preserving and promoting ecclesial communion on both the local and the universal levels.

We are also aware of the fact that since the Medellín Conference pastoral agents **471** have made significant advances and encountered quite a few difficulties. Rather than discouraging us, this should inspire us to seek out new paths and better forms of accomplishment.

4.2. The Social Teaching of the Church

The contribution of the Church to liberation and human promotion has gradu- **472** ally been taking shape in a series of doctrinal guidelines and criteria for action that we now are accustomed to call "the social teaching of the Church." These teachings have their source in Sacred Scripture, in the teaching of the Fathers and major theologians of the Church, and in the magisterium (particularly that of the most recent popes). As is evident from their origin, they contain permanently valid elements that are grounded in an anthropology that derives from the message of Christ and in the perennial values of Christian ethics. But they also contain changing elements that correspond to the particular conditions of each country and each epoch.*

Following Paul VI (OA:4), we can formulate the matter this way: attentive to **473** the signs of the time, which are interpreted in the light of the Gospel and the Church's magisterium, the whole Christian community is called upon to assume responsibility for concrete options and their effective implementation in order to respond to the summons presented by changing circumstances. Thus these social teachings possess a dynamic character. In their elaboration and application lay people are not to be passive executors but rather active collaborators with their pastors, contributing their experience as Christians, and their professional, scientific competence (GS:42).

Clearly, then, it is the whole Christian community, in communion with its **474** legitimate pastors and guided by them, that is the responsible subject of evangelization, liberation, and human promotion.

The primary object of this social teaching is the personal dignity of the human **475** being, who is the image of God, and the protection of all inalienable human rights (PP:14–21). As the need has arisen, the Church has proceeded to spell out its teaching with regard to other areas of life: social life, economics, politics, and cultural life. But the aim of this doctrine of the Church, which offers its own specific vision of the human being and humanity (PP:13), is always the promotion and integral liberation of human beings in terms of both their earthly and their transcendent dimensions. It is a contribution to the construction of the

---

*See the explanatory note at the start of *Gaudium et Spes*, which explains why that conciliar Constitution is called "pastoral."

ultimate and definitive Kingdom, although it does not equate earthly progress with Christ's Kingdom (GS:39).

476   If our social teachings are to be credible and to be accepted by all, they must effectively respond to the serious challenges and problems arising out of the reality of Latin America. Human beings who are diminished by all sorts of deficiencies and wants are calling for urgent efforts of promotion on our part, and this makes our works of social assistance necessary. Nor can we propose our teaching without being challenged by it in turn insofar as our personal and institutional behavior is concerned. It requires us to display consistency, creativity, boldness, and total commitment. Our social conduct is an integral part of our following of Christ. Our reflection on the Church's projection into the world as a sacrament of communion and salvation is a part of our theological reflection. For "evangelization would not be complete if it did not take into account the reciprocal appeal that arises in the course of time between the Gospel on the one hand and the concrete personal and social life of human beings on the other" (EN:29).

477   Human promotion entails activities that help to arouse human awareness in every dimension and to make human beings themselves the active protagonists of their own human and Christian development. It educates people in living together, it gives impetus to organization, it fosters Christian sharing of goods, and it is an effective aid to communion and participation.

478   If the Christian community is to bear consistent witness in its efforts for liberation and human betterment, each country and local Church will organize its social pastoral effort around ongoing and adequate organisms. These organisms will sustain and stimulate commitment to the community, ensuring the needed coordination of activities through a continuing dialogue with all the members of the Church. Caritas and other organisms, which have been doing effective work for many years, can offer valuable help to this end.

479   If they are to be faithful and complete, theology, preaching, and catechesis must keep in mind the whole human being and all human beings. In timely and adequate terms they must offer people today "an especially vigorous message concerning liberation" (EN:29), framing it in terms of the "overall plan of salvation" (EN:38). So it seems that we must offer some clarifying remarks about the concept of liberation itself at this present moment in the life of our continent.

4.3. Discerning the Nature of Liberation in Christ

480   At the Medellín Conference we saw the elucidation of a dynamic process of integral liberation. Its positive echoes were taken up by *Evangelii Nuntiandi* and by John Paul II in his message to this conference. This proclamation imposes an urgent task on the Church, and it belongs to the very core of an evangelization that seeks the authentic realization of the human being.

481   But there are different conceptions and applications of liberation. Though they share common traits, they contain points of view that can hardly be brought together satisfactorily. The best thing to do, therefore, is to offer criteria that derive from the magisterium and that provide us with the necessary discernment regarding the original conception of Christian liberation.

482   There are two complementary and inseparable elements. The first is liberation from all the forms of bondage, from personal and social sin, and from everything

that tears apart the human individual and society; all this finds its source to be in egotism, in the mystery of iniquity. The second element is liberation for progressive growth in being through communion with God and other human beings; this reaches its culmination in the perfect communion of heaven, where God is all in all and weeping forever ceases.

This liberation is gradually being realized in history, in our personal history and that of our peoples. It takes in all the different dimensions of life: the social, the political, the economic, the cultural, and all their interrelationships. Through all these dimensions must flow the transforming treasure of the Gospel. It has its own specific and distinctive contribution to make, which must be safeguarded. Otherwise we would be faced with the situation described by Paul VI in *Evangelii Nuntiandi:* "The Church would lose its innermost significance. Its message of liberation would have no originality of its own. It would be prone to takeover or manipulation by ideological systems and political parties" (EN:32).   **483**

It should be made clear that this liberation is erected on the three great pillars that John Paul II offered us as defining guidelines: i.e., the truth about Jesus Christ, the truth about the Church, and the truth about human beings.   **484**

Thus we mutilate liberation in an unpardonable way if we do not achieve liberation from sin and all its seductions and idolatry, and if we do not help to make concrete the liberation that Christ won on the cross. We do the very same thing if we forget the crux of liberative evangelization, which is to transform human beings into active subjects of their own individual and communitarian development. And we also do the very same thing if we overlook dependence and the forms of bondage that violate basic rights that come from God, the Creator and Father, rather than being bestowed by governments or institutions, however powerful they may be.   **485**

The sort of liberation we are talking about knows how to use evangelical means, which have their own distinctive efficacy. It does not resort to violence of any sort, or to the dialectics of class struggle. Instead it relies on the vigorous energy and activity of Christians, who are moved by the Spirit to respond to the cries of countless millions of their brothers and sisters.   **486**

We pastors in Latin America have the most serious reasons for pressing for liberative evangelization. It is not just that we feel obliged to remind people of individual and social sinfulness. The further reason lies in the fact that since the Medellín Conference the situation has grown worse and more acute for the vast majority of our population.   **487**

We are pleased to note many examples of efforts to live out liberative evangelization in all its fullness. One of the chief tasks involved in continuing to encourage Christian liberation is the creative search for approaches free of ambiguity and reductionism (EN:32) and fully faithful to the Word of God. Given to us in the Church, that Word stirs us to offer joyful proclamation to the poor as one of the messianic signs of Christ's Kingdom.   **488**

John Paul II has made this point well: "There are many signs that help us to distinguish when the liberation in question is Christian and when, on the other hand, it is based on ideologies that make it inconsistent with an evangelical view of humanity, of things, and of events (EN:35). These signs derive from the content that the evangelizers proclaim or from the concrete attitudes that they adopt. At the level of content one must consider how faithful they are to the Word   **489** of God, to the Church's living tradition, and to its magisterium. As for attitudes, one must consider what sense of communion they feel, with the bishops first of all, and then with the other sectors of God's People. Here one must also consider what contribution they make to the real building up of the community; how they channel their love into caring for the poor, the sick, the dispossessed, the neglected, and the oppressed; and how, discovering in these people the image of the poor and suffering Jesus, they strive to alleviate their needs and to serve Christ in them (LG:8). Let us make no mistake about it: as if by some evangelical instinct, the humble and simple faithful spontaneously sense when the Gospel is being served in the Church and when it is being eviscerated and asphyxiated by other interests" (OAP: III,6).

490   Those who hold to the vision of humanity offered by Christianity also take on the commitment not to measure the sacrifice it costs to ensure that all will enjoy the status of authentic children of God and brothers and sisters in Jesus Christ. Thus liberative evangelization finds its full realization in the communion of all in Christ, as the Father of all people wills.

4.4. Liberative Evangelization for a Human Societal Life Worthy of the Children of God

491   Other than God, nothing is divine or worthy of worship. Human beings fall into slavery when they divinize or absolutize wealth, power, the State, sex, pleasure, or anything created by God—including their own being or human reason. God himself is the source of radical liberation from all forms of idolatry, because the adoration of what is not adorable and the absolutization of the relative leads to violation of the innermost reality of human persons: i.e., their relationship with God and their personal fulfillment. Here is the liberative word par excellence: "You shall do homage to the Lord your God; him alone shall you adore" (Matt. 4:10; cf. Deut. 5:6ff.). The collapse of idols restores to human beings their essential realm of freedom. God, who is supremely free, wants to enter into dialogue with free beings who are capable of making their own choices and exercising their responsibilities on both the individual and communitarian levels. So we have a human history that, even though it possesses its own consistency and autonomy, is called upon to be consecrated to God by humanity. Authentic liberation frees us from oppression so that we may be able to say yes to a higher good.

492   *Humanity and earthly goods.* By virtue of their origin and nature, by the will of the Creator, worldly goods and riches are meant to serve the utility and progress of each and every human being and people. Thus each and every one enjoys a primary, fundamental, and absolutely inviolable right to share in the use of these goods, insofar as that is necessary for the worthy fulfillment of the human person. All other rights, including the right of property and free trade, are subordinate to that right. As John Paul II teaches: "There is a social mortage on all private property" (OAP:III,4). To be compatible with primordial human rights, the right of ownership must be primarily a right of use and administration; and though this does not rule out ownership and control, it does not make these absolute or unlimited. Ownership should be a source of freedom for all, but never a source of domination or special privilege. We have a grave and pressing duty to restore this right to its original and primary aim (PP:23).

Liberation from the idol of wealth. Earthly goods become an idol and a serious obstacle to the Kingdom of God (Matt. 19:23–26) when human beings devote all their attention to possessing them or even coveting them. Then earthly goods turn into an absolute, and "you cannot give yourself to God and money" (Luke 16:13).   **493**

Turned into an absolute, wealth is an obstacle to authentic freedom. The cruel contrast between luxurious wealth and extreme poverty, which is so visible throughout our continent and which is further aggravated by the corruption that often invades public and professional life, shows the great extent to which our nations are dominated by the idol of wealth.   **494**

These forms of idolatry are concretized in two opposed forms that have a common root. One is liberal capitalism. The other, a reaction against liberal capitalism, is Marxist collectivism. Both are forms of what can be called "institutionalized injustice."   **495**

Finally, as already noted, we must take cognizance of the devastating effects of an uncontrolled process of industrialization and a process of urbanization that is taking on alarming proportions. The depletion of our natural resources and the pollution of the environment will become a critical problem. Once again we affirm that the consumptionist tendencies of the more developed nations must undergo a thorough revision. They must take into account the elementary needs of the poor peoples who constitute the majority of the world's population.   **496**

The new humanism proclaimed by the Church, which rejects all forms of idolatry, "will enable our contemporaries to enjoy the higher values of love and friendship, of prayer and contemplation, and thus find themselves. This is what will guarantee humanity's authentic development—its transition from less than human conditions to truly human ones" (PP:20). In this way economic planning will be put in the service of human beings rather than human beings being put in the service of economics (PP:34). The latter is what happens in the two forms of idolatry mentioned above (liberal capitalism and Marxist collectivism). The former is the only way to make sure that what human beings "have" does not suffocate what they "are" (GS:35).   **497**

Human beings and power. The various forms of power in society are a basic part of the order of creation. Hence in themselves they are essentially good, insofar as they render service to the human community.   **498**

Authority, which is necessary in every society, comes from God (Rom. 13:1; John 19:11). It is the faculty of giving commands in accordance with right reason. Hence its obligatory force derives from the moral order (PT:47), and it should develop out of that ground in order to oblige people in conscience: "Authority is before all else a moral force" (PT:48; GS:74).   **499**

Sin corrupts humanity's use of power, leading people to abuse the rights of others, sometimes in more or less absolute ways. The most notorious example of this is the exercise of political power. For this is an area that involves decisions governing the overall organization of the community's temporal welfare, and it readily lends itself to abuses. Indeed it may lead not only to abuses by those in power but also to the absolutizing of power itself (GS:73) with the backing of public force. Political power is divinized when in practice it is regarded as absolute. Hence the totalitarian use of power is a form of idolatry; and as such, the Church completely rejects it (GS:75). We grieve to note the presence of many   **500** authoritarian and even oppressive regimes on our continent. They constitute one of the most serious obstacles to the full development of the rights of persons, groups, and even nations.

501   Unfortunately, in many instances this reaches the point where the political and economic authorities of our nations are themselves made subject to even more powerful centers that are operative on an international scale. This goes far beyond the normal range of mutual relationships. And the situation is further aggravated by the fact that these centers of power are ubiquitous, covertly organized, and easily capable of evading the control of governments and even international organisms.

502   There is an urgent need to liberate our peoples from the idol of absolutized power so that they may live together in a society based on justice and freedom. As a youthful people with a wealth of culture and tradition, Latin Americans must carry out the mission assigned to them by history. But if they are to do this, they need a political order that will respect human dignity and ensure harmony and peace to the community, both in its internal relations and its relations with other communities. Among all the aspirations of our peoples, we would like to stress the following:

503   —Equality for all citizens. All have the right and the duty to participate in the destiny of their society and to enjoy equality of opportunity, bearing their fair share of the burdens and obeying legitimately established laws.

504   —The exercise of their freedoms. These should be protected by basic institutions that will stand surety for the common good and respect the fundamental rights of persons and associations.

505   —Legitimate self-determination for our peoples. This will permit them to organize their lives in accordance with their own genius and history (GS:74) and to cooperate in a new international order.

506   —The urgent necessity of re-establishing justice. We are not talking only about theoretical justice recognized merely in the abstract. We are talking also about a justice that is effectively implemented in practice by institutions that are truly operative and adequate to the task.*

5. Evangelization, Ideologies, and Politics

5.1. Introduction

507   Recent years have seen a growing deterioration in the sociopolitical life of our countries.

508   They are experiencing the heavy burden of economic and institutional crises, and clear symptoms of corruption and violence.

509   The violence is generated and fostered by two factors: (1) what can be called institutionalized injustice in various social, political, and economic systems; and (2) ideologies that use violence as a means to win power.

510   The latter in turn causes the proliferation of governments based on force,

---

*Hedonism, too, has been set up as an absolute on our continent. Liberation from the idol of pleasure-seeking and consumptionism is an imperative demand of Christian social teaching. We shall consider this issue more fully in Part Three, Chapter I, when we deal with educating people for love and family life (see nos. 582–89 below).

which often derive their inspiration from the ideology of National Security.

As a mother and teacher whose expertise is humanity, the Church must 511
examine the conditions, systems, ideologies, and political life of our continent
—shedding light on them from the standpoint of the Gospel and its own social
teaching. And this must be done even though it knows that people will try to use
its message as their own tool.

So the Church projects the light of its message on politics and ideologies, as one 512
more form of service to its peoples and as a sure line of orientation for all those
who must assume social responsibilities in one form or another.

5.2. Evangelization and Politics

The political dimension is a constitutive dimension of human beings and a 513
relevant area of human societal life. It has an all-embracing aspect because its aim
is the common welfare of society. But that does not mean that it exhausts the
gamut of social relationships.

Far from despising political activity, the Christian faith values it and holds it in 514
high esteem.

Speaking in general, and without distinguishing between the roles that may be 515
proper to its various members, the Church feels it has a duty and a right to be
present in this area of reality. For Christianity is supposed to evangelize the
whole of human life, including the political dimension. So the Church criticizes
those who would restrict the scope of faith to personal or family life; who would
exclude the professional, economic, social, and political orders as if sin, love,
prayer, and pardon had no relevance in them.

The fact is that the need for the Church's presence in the political arena flows 516
from the very core of the Christian faith. That is to say, it flows from the lordship
of Christ over the whole of life. Christ sets the seal on the definitive brotherhood
of humanity, wherein every human being is of equal worth: "All are one in Christ
Jesus" (Gal. 3:28).

From the integral message of Christ there flows an original anthropology and 517
theology that takes in "the concrete personal and social life of the human being"
(EN:29). It is a liberating message because it saves us from the bondage of sin,
which is the root and source of all oppression, injustice, and discrimination.

These are some of the reasons why the Church is present in the political arena 518
to enlighten consciences and to proclaim a message that is capable of transforming society.

The Church recognizes the proper autonomy of the temporal order (GS:36). 519
This holds true for governments, parties, labor unions, and other groups in the
social and political arena. The purpose that the Lord assigned to his Church is a
religious one; so when it does intervene in the sociopolitical arena, it is not
prompted by any aim of a political, economic, or social nature. "But out of this
religious mission itself come a function, a light, and an energy which can serve to
structure and consolidate the human community according to the divine law"
(GS:42).

Insofar as the political arena is concerned, the Church is particularly interested 520
in distinguishing between the specific functions of the laity, religious, and those
who minister to the unity of the Church—i.e., the bishop and his priests.

5.3. Notions of Politics and Political Involvement

521   We must distinguish between two notions of politics and political involvement. First, in the broad sense politics seeks the common good on both the
national and international plane. Its task is to spell out the fundamental values of
every community—internal concord and external security—reconciling equality
with freedom, public authority with the legitimate autonomy and participation
of individual persons and groups, and national sovereignty with international
coexistence and solidarity. It also defines the ethics and means of social relationships. In this broad sense politics is of interest to the Church, and hence to its
pastors, who are ministers of unity. It is a way of paying worship to the one and
only God by simultaneously desacralizing and consecrating the world to him
(LG:34).

522   So the Church helps to foster the values that should inspire politics. In every
nation it interprets the aspirations of the people, especially the yearnings of those
that society tends to marginalize. And it does this with its testimony, its teaching, and its varied forms of pastoral activity.

523   Second, the concrete performance of this fundamental political task is normally
carried out by groups of citizens. They resolve to pursue and exercise political
power in order to solve economic, political, and social problems in accordance
with their own criteria or ideology. Here, then, we can talk about "party politics." Now even though the ideologies elaborated by such groups may be inspired by Christian doctrine, they can come to differing conclusions. No matter
how deeply inspired in church teaching, no political party can claim the right to
represent all the faithful because its concrete program can never have absolute
value for all (cf. Pius XI, *Catholic Action and Politics*, 1937).

524   Party politics is properly the realm of lay people (GS:43). Their lay status
entitles them to establish and organize political parties, using an ideology and
strategy that is suited to achieving their legitimate aims.

525   In the social teaching of the Church lay people find the proper criteria deriving
from the Christian view of the human being. For its part the hierarchy will
demonstrate its solidarity by contributing to their adequate formation and their
spiritual life, and also by nurturing their creativity so that they can explore
options that are increasingly in line with the common good and the needs of the
weakest.

526   Pastors, on the other hand, must be concerned with unity. So they will divest
themselves of every partisan political ideology that might condition their criteria
and attitudes. They then will be able to evangelize the political sphere as Christ
did, relying on the Gospel without any infusion of partisanship or ideologization. Christ's Gospel would not have had such an impact on history if he had not
proclaimed it as a religious message: "The Gospels show clearly that for Jesus
anything that would alter his mission as the Servant of Yahweh was a temptation
(Matt. 4:8; Luke 4:5). He does not accept the position of those who mixed the
things of God with merely political attitudes (Matt. 22:21; Mark 12:17; John
18:36)" (OAP:I,4).

527   Priests, also ministers of unity, and deacons must submit to the same sort of
personal renunciation. If they are active in party politics, they will run the risk of

absolutizing and radicalizing such activity; for their vocation is to be "men dedicated to the Absolute." As the Medellín Conference pointed out: "In the economic and social order . . . and especially in the political order, where a variety of concrete choices is offered, the priest, as priest, should not directly concern himself with decisions or leadership nor with the structuring of solutions" (Med-PR:19). And the 1971 Synod of Bishops stated: "Leadership or active militancy on behalf of any political party is to be excluded by every priest unless, in concrete and exceptional circumstances, this is truly required by the good of the community and receives the consent of the bishop after consultation with the priests' council and, if circumstances call for it, with the episcopal conference" ("The Ministerial Priesthood," Part Two, no. 2). Certainly the present thrust of the Church is not in that direction.

By virtue of the way in which they follow Christ, and in line with the distinc-   **528**
tive function that is theirs within the Church's mission because of their specific charism, religious also cooperate in the evangelization of the political order. Living in a society that is far from fraternal, that is taken up with consumptionism, and that has as its ultimate goal the development of its material forces of production, religious will have to give testimony of real austerity in their lifestyle, of interhuman communion, and of an intense relationship with God. They, too, will have to resist the temptation to get involved in party politics, so that they do not create confusion between the values of the Gospel and some specific ideology.

Close reflection upon the recent words of the Holy Father addressed to   **529**
bishops, priests, and religious will provide valuable guidance for their service in this area: "Souls that are living in habitual contact with God and that are operating in the warm light of his love know how to defend themselves easily against the temptations of partisanship and antithesis that threaten to create painful divisions. They know how to interpret their options for the poorest and for all the victims of human egotism in the proper light of the Gospel, without succumbing to forms of sociopolitical radicalism. In the long run such radicalism is untimely, counterproductive, and generative of new abuses. Such souls know how to draw near to the people and immerse themselves in their midst without calling into question their own religious identity or obscuring the 'specific originality' of their own vocation, which flows from following the poor, chaste, and obedient Christ. A measure of real adoration has more value and spiritual fruitfulness than the most intense activity, even apostolic activity. This is the most urgent kind of 'protest' that religious should exercise against a society where efficiency has been turned into an idol on whose altar even human dignity itself is sometimes sacrificed" (RMS).

Lay leaders of pastoral action should not use their authority in support of   **530**
parties or ideologies.

5.4. Reflections on Political Violence

Faced with the deplorable reality of violence in Latin America, we wish to   **531**
express our view clearly. Condemnation is always the proper judgment on physical and psychological torture, kidnapping, the persecution of political dissidents or suspect persons, and the exclusion of people from public life

because of their ideas. If these crimes are committed by the authorities entrusted with the task of safeguarding the common good, then they defile those who practice them, notwithstanding any reasons offered.

532 The Church is just as decisive in rejecting terrorist and guerrilla violence, which becomes cruel and uncontrollable when it is unleashed. Criminal acts can in no way be justified as the way to liberation. Violence inexorably engenders new forms of oppression and bondage, which usually prove to be more serious than the ones people are allegedly being liberated from. But most importantly violence is an attack on life, which depends on the Creator alone. And we must also stress that when an ideology appeals to violence, it thereby admits its own weakness and inadequacy.

533 Our responsibility as Christians is to use all possible means to promote the implementation of nonviolent tactics in the effort to re-establish justice in economic and sociopolitical relations. This is in accordance with the teaching of Vatican II, which applies to both national and international life: "We cannot fail to praise those who renounce the use of violence in the vindication of their rights and who resort to methods of defense which are otherwise available to weaker parties too, provided that this can be done without injury to the rights and duties of others or of the community" (GS:78).

534 "We are obliged to state and reaffirm that violence is neither Christian nor evangelical, and that brusque, violent structural changes will be false, ineffective in themselves, and certainly inconsistent with the dignity of the people" (Paul VI, Address in Bogotá, 23 August 1968). The fact is that "the Church realizes that even the best structures and the most idealized systems quickly become inhuman if human inclinations are not improved, if there is no conversion of heart and mind on the part of those who are living in those structures or controlling them" (EN:36).

5.5. Evangelization and Ideologies

Here we shall consider the exercise of discernment with regard to the ideologies existing in Latin America and the systems inspired by them.

535 Of the many different definitions of ideology that might be offered, we apply the term here to any conception that offers a view of the various aspects of life from the standpoint of a specific group in society. The ideology manifests the aspirations of this group, summons its members to a certain kind of solidarity and combative struggle, and grounds the legitimacy of these aspirations on specific values. Every ideology is partial because no one group can claim to identify its aspirations with those of society as a whole. Thus an ideology will be legitimate if the interests it upholds are legitimate and if it respects the basic rights of other groups in the nation. Viewed in this positive sense, ideologies seem to be necessary for social activity, insofar as they are mediating factors leading to action.

536 But in themselves ideologies have a tendency to absolutize the interests they uphold, the vision they propose, and the strategy they promote. In such a case they really become "lay religions." People take refuge in ideology as an ultimate explanation of everything: "In this way they fashion a new idol, as it were, whose absolute and coercive character is maintained, sometimes unwittingly" (OA:28).

In that sense it is not surprising that ideologies try to use persons and institutions as their tools in order to achieve their aims more effectively. Herein lies the ambiguous and negative side of ideologies.

But ideologies should not be analyzed solely in terms of their conceptual content. In addition, they are dynamic, living phenomena of a sweeping and contagious nature. They are currents of yearning tending toward absolutization, and they are powerful in winning people over and whipping up redemptive fervor. This confers a special "mystique" on them, and it also enables them to make their way into different milieus in a way that is often irresistible. Their slogans, typical expressions, and criteria can easily make their way into the minds of people who are far from adhering voluntarily to their doctrinal principles. Thus many people live and struggle in practice within the atmosphere of specific ideologies, without ever having taken cognizance of that fact. This aspect calls for constant vigilance and re-examination. And it applies both to ideologies that legitimate the existing situation and to those that seek to change it.   537

To exercise the necessary discernment and critical judgment with regard to ideologies, Christians must rely on "a rich and complex heritage, which *Evangelii Nuntiandi* calls the social doctrine, or social teaching, of the Church" (OAP:III,7).   538

This social doctrine or teaching of the Church is an expression of its "distinctive contribution: a global perspective on the human being and on humanity" (PP:13). The Church accepts the challenge and contribution of ideologies in their positive aspects, and in turn challenges, criticizes, and relativizes them.   539

Neither the Gospel nor the Church's social teaching deriving from it are ideologies. On the contrary, they represent a powerful source for challenging the limitations and ambiguities of all ideologies. The ever fresh originality of the gospel message must be continually clarified and defended against all efforts to turn it into an ideology.   540

The unrestricted exaltation of the State and its many abuses must not, however, cause us to forget the necessity of the functions performed by the modern State. We are talking about a State that respects basic rights and freedoms; a State that is grounded on a broad base of popular participation involving many intermediary groups; a State that promotes autonomous development of an equitable and rapid sort, so that the life of the nation can withstand undue pressure and interference on both the domestic and international fronts; a State that is capable of adopting a position of active cooperation with the forces for integration into both the continental and the international community; and finally, a State that avoids the abuse of monolithic power concentrated in the hands of a few.   541

In Latin America we are obliged to analyze a variety of ideologies:

a. First, there is capitalist liberalism, the idolatrous worship of wealth in individualistic terms. We acknowledge that it has given much encouragement to the creative capabilities of human freedom, and that it has been a stimulus to progress. But on the other side of the coin it views "profit as the chief spur to economic progress, free competition as the supreme law of economics, and private ownership of the means of production as an absolute right, having no limits nor concomitant social obligations" (PP:26). The illegitimate privileges stemming from the absolute right of ownership give rise to scandalous contrasts, and to a situation of dependence and oppression on both the national and   542 international levels. Now it is true that in some countries its original historical form of expression has been attenuated by necessary forms of social legislation and specific instances of government intervention. But in other countries capitalist liberalism persists in its original form, or has even retrogressed to more primitive forms with even less social sensitivity.

543   *b.* Second, there is Marxist collectivism. With its materialist presuppositions, it too leads to the idolatrous worship of wealth—but in collectivist terms. It arose as a positive criticism of commodity fetishism and of the disregard for the human value of labor. But it did not manage to get to the root of that form of idolatry, which lies in the rejection of the only God worthy of adoration: the God of love and justice.

544   The driving force behind its dialectics is class struggle. Its objective is a classless society, which is to be achieved through a dictatorship of the proletariat; but in the last analysis this really sets up a dictatorship of the party. All the concrete historical experiments of Marxism have been carried out within the framework of totalitarian regimes that are closed to any possibility of criticism and correction. Some believe it is possible to separate various aspects of Marxism—its doctrine and its method of analysis in particular. But we would remind people of the teaching of the papal magisterium on this point: "It would be foolish and dangerous on that account to forget that they are closely linked to each other; to embrace certain elements of Marxist analysis without taking due account of their relation with its ideology; and to become involved in the class struggle and the Marxist interpretation of it without paying attention to the kind of violent and totalitarian society to which this activity leads" (OA:34).

545   We must also note the risk of ideologization run by theological reflection when it is based on a praxis that has recourse to Marxist analysis. The consequences are the total politicization of Christian existence, the disintegration of the language of faith into that of the social sciences, and the draining away of the transcendental dimension of Christian salvation.

546   Both of the aforementioned ideologies—capitalist liberalism and Marxism—find their inspiration in brands of humanism that are closed to any transcendent perspective. One does because of its practical atheism; the other does because of its systematic profession of a militant atheism.

547   *c.* In recent years the so-called Doctrine of National Security has taken a firm hold on our continent. In reality it is more an ideology than a doctrine. It is bound up with a specific politico-economic model with elitist and verticalist features, which suppresses the broad-based participation of the people in political decisions. In some countries of Latin America this doctrine justifies itself as the defender of the Christian civilization of the West. It elaborates a repressive system, which is in line with its concept of "permanent war." And in some cases it expresses a clear intention to exercise active geopolitical leadership.

548   We fully realize that fraternal coexistence requires a security system to inculcate respect for a social order that will permit all to carry out their mission with regard to the common good. This means that security measures must be under the control of an independent authority that can pass judgment on violations of the law and guarantee corrective measures.

549   The Doctrine of National Security, understood as an absolute ideology, would not be compatible with the Christian vision of the human being as responsible

for carrying out a temporal project, and to its vision of the State as the adminis-
trator of the common good. It puts the people under the tutelage of military and
political elites, who exercise authority and power; and it leads to increased
inequality in sharing the benefits of development.

We again insist on the view of the Medellín Conference: "The system of liberal   550
capitalism and the temptation of the Marxist system would appear to exhaust the
possibilities of transforming the economic structures of our continent. Both
systems militate against the dignity of the human person. One takes for granted
the primacy of capital, its power, and its discriminatory utilization in the function of profit-making. The other, although it ideologically supports a kind of
humanism, is more concerned with collective humanity, and in practice becomes
a totalitarian concentration of state power. We must denounce the fact that Latin
America finds itself caught between these two options and remains dependent
on one or the other of the centers of power that control its economy" (Med-JU:10).

In the face of this situation, the Church chooses "to maintain its freedom with   551
regard to the opposing systems, in order to opt solely for the human being.
Whatever the miseries or sufferings that afflict human beings, it is not through
violence, power-plays, or political systems but through the truth about human
beings that they will find their way to a better future" (OAP:III,3). Grounded on
this humanism, Christians will find encouragement to get beyond the hard and
fast either-or and to help build a new civilization that is just, fraternal, and open
to the transcendent. It will also bear witness that eschatological hopes give
vitality and meaning to human hopes.

For this bold and creative activity Christians will fortify their identity in the   552
original values of Christian anthropology. The Church "does not need to have
recourse to ideological systems in order to love, defend, and collaborate in the
liberation of the human being. At the center of the message of which the Church
is the trustee and herald, it finds inspiration for acting in favor of brotherhood,
justice, and peace; and against all forms of domination, slavery, discrimination,
violence, attacks on religious liberty, and aggression against human beings and
whatever attacks life" (OAP:III,2).

Finding inspiration in these tenets of an authentic Christian anthropology,   553
Christians must commit themselves to the elaboration of historical projects that
meet the needs of a given moment and a given culture.

Christians must devote special attention and discernment to their involvement   554
in historical movements that have arisen from various ideologies but are distinct
from them. The teaching of *Pacem in Terris* (PT:55 and 152), which is reiterated in
Octogesima Adveniens, tells us that false philosophical theories cannot be equated
with the historical movements that originated in them, insofar as these historical
movements can be subject to further influences as they evolve. The involvement
of Christians in these movements imposes certain obligations to persevere in
fidelity, and these obligations will facilitate their evangelizing role. They include:

a. Ecclesial discernment, in communion with their pastors, as described in   555
Octogesima Adveniens (OA:4).

b. The shoring up of their identity by nourishing it with the truths of faith,   556
their elaboration in the social teaching or doctrine of the Church, and an enriching life of prayer and participation in the sacraments.

557   *c.* Critical awareness of the difficulties, limitations, possibilities, and values of these convergences.

5.6. The Danger of the Church and Its Ministers' Activity Being Used as a Tool

558   In propounding an absolutized view of the human being to which everything, including human thought, is subordinated, ideologies and parties try to use the Church or deprive it of its legitimate independence. This manipulation of the Church, always a risk in political life, may derive from Christians themselves, and even from priests and religious, when they proclaim a Gospel devoid of economic, social, cultural, and political implications. In practice this mutilation comes down to a kind of complicity with the established order, however unwitting.

559   Other groups are tempted in the opposite direction. They are tempted to consider a given political policy to be of primary urgency, a precondition for the Church's fulfillment of its mission. They are tempted to equate the Christian message with some ideology and subordinate the former to the latter, calling for a "re-reading" of the Gospel on the basis of a political option (OAP:1,4). But the fact is that we must try to read the political scene from the standpoint of the Gospel, not vice-versa.

560   Traditional integrism looks for the Kingdom to come principally through a stepping back in history and reconstructing a Christian culture of a medieval cast. This would be a new Christendom, in which there was an intimate alliance between civil authority and ecclesiastical authority.

561   The radical thrust of groups at the other extreme falls into the same trap. It looks for the Kingdom to come from a strategic alliance between the Church and Marxism, and it rules out all other alternatives. For these people it is not simply a matter of being Marxists, but of being Marxists in the name of the faith (see nos. 543–46 above).

5.7. Conclusion

562   The mission of the Church is immense and more necessary than ever before, when we consider the situation at hand: conflicts that threaten the human race and the Latin American continent; violations of justice and freedom; institutionalized injustice embodied in governments adhering to opposing ideologies; and terrorist violence. Fulfillment of its mission will require activity from the Church as a whole: pastors, consecrated ministers, religious, and lay people. All must carry out their own specific tasks. Joined with Christ in prayer and abnegation, they will commit themselves to work for a better society without employing hatred and violence; and they will see that decision through to the end, whatever the consequences. For the attainment of a society that is more just, more free, and more at peace is an ardent longing of the peoples of Latin America and an indispensable fruit of any liberative evangelization.

PART THREE
EVANGELIZATION IN THE
LATIN AMERICAN CHURCH:
COMMUNION AND PARTICIPATION

God calls us in Latin America to a life in Jesus Christ. We face the pressing task of   **563**
announcing this life to all our brothers and sisters. The evangelizing Church has this
mission: to preach conversion, to liberate human beings, and to direct them toward the
mystery of communion with the Trinity and with all their brothers and sisters, trans-
forming them into agents and cooperators in God's plan.

How is the Church to live its mission?

All baptized persons feel drawn by the Spirit of Love to go out of themselves to open   **564**
up to their brothers and sisters and to live in community. In our union with each other
the risen Jesus Christ makes his presence felt, celebrating his Easter in Latin America.

Let us see how the marvellous gift of new life becomes a reality in a surpassing way   **565**
in each local Church, and also increasingly in the family, small communities, and
parishes. From these centers of evangelization the People of God in history go on
growing in grace and holiness through the dynamism of the Spirit and the participation
of Christians. In their midst arise charisms and services. How do they diversify in their
evangelizing mission? And how do we integrate into the life of the Church the
hierarchical ministers, divinely consecrated men and women, and finally all the mem-
bers of God's People?

By what means do the baptized operate? The activity of the Spirit finds expression in   **566**
prayer and listening to the Word of God. It is deepened in catechesis, celebrated in the
liturgy, witnessed to in our lives, communicated through education, and shared in
dialogue. Through dialogue we seek to offer all our brothers and sisters the new life that
we receive in the Church through no merit of our own, as workers of the first hour.

It includes:

CHAPTER I
CENTERS OF COMMUNION AND PARTICIPATION

567   The mystery of the Church is that of a fraternal community of theological charity, the fruit of an encounter with the Word of God and of the celebration of the paschal mystery of Christ the Savior in the Eucharist and the other sacraments. It has been entrusted to the apostolic college, presided over by Peter, to evangelize the world. This whole mystery takes root and tends to unfold its dynamic transformation of human life, both personal and social, on various levels and in various circumstances. These constitute preferential centers or locales of evangelization, designed to build up the Church and promote its missionary diffusion.

1. The Family
2. Base-level Ecclesial Communities (CEBs), the Parish, and the Local Church.

1. The Family

568   To be truly a center of communion and participation, the Latin American family must find ways to achieve internal renewal and communion with the Church and the world.

569   We are delighted to broach the theme of the family as a subject and object of evangelization. Conscious of its complexity, but also obedient to the voice of the Lord rendered present by the Holy Father's words in his homily on the family here in Puebla (28 January 1979; see pp. 77–80 in this volume), we wish to share his concern: to help the family be faithful to its evangelizing mission at this time.

The family is a subject and object of evangelization, an evangelizing center of communion and participation.

1.1. Introduction

570   The Fathers of the Medellín Conference saw in our peoples' great feeling for family one of the primordial traits of Latin American culture: "Ten years having passed, the Church in Latin America feels happy about all that it has managed to accomplish on behalf of the family. But it humbly recognizes how much remains to be done; and it sees that pastoral care of the family, far from having lost its priority character, appears even more urgent today as an important element of evangelization" (HP:2).

1.2. The Situation of the Family in Latin America

571   The family is one of the institutions that has been most influenced by the process of change in recent times. As the pope reminded us, the Church is aware that the more negative results of underdevelopment have had their repercussions on the family: "truly depressing indications of unhealthiness, poverty and even misery, ignorance and illiteracy, inhuman housing conditions, chronic malnutrition, and countless other realities that are just as sad" (HP:3).

We must also recognize the fact that the reality of the family is no longer a 572
uniform one. For each family, independent of social class, is influenced differently by the factors associated with change. They include sociological factors
(social injustice, principally), cultural factors (the quality of life), political factors
(domination and manipulation), economic factors (wages, unemployment, multiple employment), and religious factors (secularist influence), among others.

The family also is the victim of those who turn power, wealth, and sex into 573
idols. Contributing to this are unjust structures, especially the communications
media. The media does so, not only with its messages about sex, profit, violence,
power, and ostentatious display, but also with its contribution to the propagation of divorce, marital infidelity, abortion, and the acceptance of free love and
pre-marital sex.

Not infrequently the disorientation of consciences is due to the lack of unity 574
among priests regarding the norms and application of papal doctrine on important aspects of family and social morality.

Rural families and those dwelling on the outskirts of our cities suffer especially 575
from the effects of international commitments by governments with regard to
family planning. This leads to the imposition of birth-control policies and experiments that do not take into account the dignity of the person or the authentic
development of peoples.

In these sectors of the common people, the chronic and generalized situation of 576
unemployment affects family stability, since the need for work imposes emigra-
tion, the absence of parents, and the scattering of the children.

On every social level the family also suffers from the deleterious impact of 577
pornography, alcoholism, drugs, prostitution, and white slavery as well as the
problem of unwed mothers and abandoned children. With the failure of chemical
and mechanical contraceptives, there has been a shift to human sterilization and
induced abortion, for which insidious campaigns are employed.

Diligent pastoral care is urgently required to avoid the evils resulting from lack 578
of education in love, lack of preparation for marriage, failure to evangelize the
family and to educate spouses for responsible parenthood. Moreover, we cannot
overlook the fact that a large number of families on our continent have not
received the sacrament of matrimony. Nevertheless, many of them live in in-
dubitable unity, fidelity, and responsibility. This situation poses theological
questions, and it demands an adequate pastoral accompaniment.

On the other side of the coin it is satisfying to see that every day there are more 579
Christians trying to live their faith in the family and its context. They are giving a
valuable evangelical witness, and they are even raising a reasonably large family
with dignity. There are also many engaged couples preparing themselves seriously for marriage and trying to give a real Christian meaning to their ceremony.
We can also note efforts to inject vigor into family pastoral care, and to make it
adequate to the challenges and circumstances of modern life.

In every country interesting initiatives have arisen to shore up the values and 580
spirituality of the family as a domestic Church committed to participating in the
local Church. In all this we see the result of the silent, ongoing activity of
Christian movements on behalf of the family.

Throughout Latin America we can visit "homes where food and well-being are 581
not lacking, but harmony and joy perhaps are; homes where families live rather

modestly, uncertain of the morrow, helping one another to live a difficult but dignified existence; poor habitations on the outskirts of your cities where there is much hidden suffering, though the simple joy of the poor dwells there; humble shanties of peasants, indigenous peoples, immigrants, etc." (HP:4). We will conclude by underlining the point that the very facts that point to the disintegration of the family end up revealing "the true character of this institution in one way or another" (GS:47). It "was not abolished, either by the penalty of original sin or by the punishment of the flood"(Liturgy of Matrimony); but it continues to suffer from the hardness of the human heart (Matt. 19:8).

1.3. Theological Reflection on the Family

582   The family is the image of God, who, "in his innermost mystery, is not a loneness but a family" (HP:2). The family is an alliance of persons arrived at through the loving call of the Father, who invites the spouses to an "intimate partnership of married life and love" (GS:48), the model of which is Christ's love for his Church. The law of conjugal love is communion and participation, not domination. It is an exclusive, irrevocable, and fruitful surrender to the person loved, without any loss of one's own identity. In its rich sacramental reality, a love so understood is more than a contract; it has the characteristics of the covenant (GS:48).

583   The couple sanctified by the sacrament of matrimony is a witness to the paschal presence of the Lord. The Christian family cultivates the spirit of love and service. Four fundamental relations of the person find their full development in family life: parenthood, filiation, brotherhood, and nuptial life. These same relationships make up the life of the Church: the experience of God as Father; the experience of Christ as our brother; our experience as children in, with, and through the Son; and the experience of Christ as the spouse of the Church. Family life reproduces these four basic experiences and shares them in miniature. They are four aspects of human love (GS:49).

584   In being born, Christ assumed the condition of the child: he was born poor, subject to his parents. Every child—an image of Jesus being born—ought to be welcomed with affection and kindness. In transmitting life to a child, conjugal love produces a new person—singular, unique, and unrepeatable. It is there that the ministry of evangelization begins for the parents. Their responsible parenthood should be grounded on it: Given the social, economic, cultural, and demographic circumstances in which we live, are the spouses capable of raising and evangelizing another child in the name of Christ? The response of judicious parents will be the result of right discernment, not of the opinion of other persons, or the latest fashion, or the impulses. Thus instinct and whim will give way to the conscious, free discipline of sexuality out of love for Christ, whose countenance appears on the countenance of the child that is desired and that is freely brought into life.

585   The slow and joy-filled raising of the family always represents a sacrifice reminiscent of the redeeming cross. But the intimate happiness that links the parents also recalls the resurrection. In this paschal spirit the parents evangelize their children and are evangelized by them in turn (EN:71). The acknowledgment of faults and the sincere manifestation of forgiveness are elements of permanent conversion and permanent resurrection. The paschal atmosphere flourishes in all

of Christian life and becomes prophetism upon contact with the divine Word. But evangelization is not just reading the Bible. It also means moving to offer a word of admiration, consolation, correction, enlightenment, and assurance.

Stability in the parent-child relationship speaks volumes. When other families see how they love one another, it gives rise to the desire for, and the practice of, a love that links families with each other as a sign of the unity of the human species (LG:1). There the Church grows through the integration of families by means of baptism, which makes all brothers and sisters. Where catechesis strengthens the faith, all are enriched by the testimony of the Christian virtues. A healthy atmosphere of inter-family ties is a unique locus of nourishment and physical and mental support for the children in their early years. There the parents are teachers, catechists, and the first ministers of prayer and divine worship. The image of Nazareth takes on fresh life: "Jesus, for his part, progressed steadily in wisdom and age and grace before God and men" (Luke 2:52).   **586**

To function well, society requires the same things as the home. It must form aware persons, united in the bonds of fraternity to foster their common development. Thus the prayer, work and educational activity of the family as a social cell must be geared to changing unjust structures through human communion and participation and through the celebration of the faith in daily life. "In the mutual interaction that takes hold in the course of time between the Gospel and the concrete personal and social life of the human being" (EN:29), the family learns how to read and live the explicit message concerning the rights and duties of family life. Hence it denounces and announces; it commits itself to changing the world in a Christian sense; and it contributes to progress, community life, the exercise of distributive justice, and peace.   **587**

In the Eucharist the family finds its full measure of communion and participation. It prepares for this through its yearning and quest for the Kingdom, purifying the soul of all that distances it from God. In the spirit of oblation it exercises the common priesthood and participates in the Eucharist. This is prolonged in life through dialogue, in which it shares conversation, concerns, and plans, thus deepening family communion. To live the Eucharist is to recognize and share the gifts we receive from the Holy Spirit through Christ. It is to accept the welcome we get from others and to let them come into our own lives. Once again the spirit of the covenant surges up, as we allow God to enter our lives and use them as he sees fit. At the center of family life there emerges the strong but gentle image of the crucified and resurrected Christ.   **588**

It is from this source that the family's mission arises. This domestic Church, converted by the liberating power of the Gospel into a "school of deeper humanity" (GS:52), knows that it is on pilgrimage with Christ and involved with him in service to the local Church. So it launches out into the future, ready to overcome the fallacies of the rationalism and worldly wisdom that are disorienting people today. Seeing reality as God sees it and governs it, and acting upon it accordingly, the family strives for greater fidelity to the Lord; it seeks to worship, not idols but the living God of love.   **589**

1.4. Pastoral Options

Basic option. Our option takes due note of the teachings of Medellín, Paul VI, and the recent teaching of John Paul II on the family: "Make every effort to ensure   **590**

that there is pastoral care for the family. Attend to this area of such priority importance, certain that evangelization in the future depends largely on the 'domestic Church' "(OAP:IVa). And so we confirm the priority of family pastoral care within the organic pastoral effort in Latin America.

We propose a basic outline of family pastoral care:

591 *a*. Family pastoral care fits admirably into the pastoral effort of the whole Church. It is evangelizing, prophetic, and liberative.

592 —It announces the Gospel of conjugal and family life as a paschal experience lived out in the Eucharist.

593 —It denounces the fallacies and abuses that cast shadows or obstacles in the way of the Gospel of conjugal and family love.

594 —It seeks ways to enable couples and families to move forward in their vocation of love and their mission to form persons, educate them in the faith, and contribute to development. In the numerous instances of incomplete families, it must find pastoral ways to provide them with adequate attention.

595 —It accepts couples and families, whatever may be their concrete, individual situation; and it accompanies them in the footsteps of the Good Shepherd, understanding their weakness and respecting the rhythm of their human poverty and ignorance.

596 *b*. The agents of this pastoral effort are those who are committed to living the Gospel of the family, and who promote small or large ecclesial communities on the family level.

597 *c*. These agents elaborate a family pastoral effort at the moments in the lives of couples and families that are fraught with salvific grace: courtship, engagement, marriage, parenthood, child-rearing, anniversaries, baptisms, First Communions, family festivals and celebrations, and not excluding crisis-moments in family life or painful times such as illness and death.

598 This family pastoral effort is intimately bound up with the social pastoral effort:

—in the effort to create structures and environments that will make family life possible;

—in recreation, when people try to provide safe and constructive circumstances for their children and all young people;

—in cultural training, when people transmit values received from family and local history;

—in the apostolate, when people are joined as communities intimately associated with the hierarchy and involved with their local Church.

599 *d*. With the Word as point of departure, the family pastoral effort offers principles and guidelines for action: giving preference to "being more" over the tendency to possess, know, or exert power "more" without serving more; giving more than receiving.

600 *e*. Family pastoral care is elaborated:

—in an atmosphere of trust in the truth;

—through the integration of natural family values with the faith;

—with Christian discernment of the circumstances surrounding decision-making.

As *courses of action* we propose:

601 *a*. To enrich and systematize the theology of the family so that people may

come to know and appreciate it more profoundly as the "domestic Church" (LG:11)—the aim being to shed light on the new situations facing Latin American families.

b. To affirm that in all family pastoral care the family itself is to be viewed as a subject and irreplaceable agent of evangelization and as the basis for societal communion. **602**

c. To promote within families a profound sense of communion between the family members and expressions of open-hearted, generous, mutual service, thus fostering the realization of the Good News. **603**

d. To underline the need to educate all family members in justice and love so that they can be responsible, solidary, and effective agents in promoting Christian solutions for the complex social issue in Latin America. **604**

e. To consider pre-sacramental catechesis and the liturgical celebration of the sacraments as privileged moments for proclaiming and responding to the Gospel of conjugal and family love. **605**

f. To provide for sex education as an important part of progressive education in love. Sex education should be complete and opportune, enabling people to discover the beauty of love and the human value of sex. **606**

g. To stay by the side of spouses in order to help them grow in the faith and probe deeper into the mystery of Christian marriage. In this way we will help them to be happy, teaching them to cultivate love, enter into dialogue, display sensitivity and attention, and focus all their life-interests in the home. **607**

h. To pay heed, out of a profoundly evangelical pastoral outlook, to the sensitive problem of de facto marital unions, of incomplete families, in a profound spirit of understanding prudence. **608**

i. To give preferential attention to educating married couples for responsible parenthood. This would equip them not only to exercise a proper regulation of fertility and to enjoy their complementarity more, but also to become good educators of their children. **609**

j. In the face of birth-control campaigns promoted by the government or by foreign countries, to provide families with adequate information about the manifold negative effects of the techniques prevalent in neo-Malthusian philosophies; and to continue to apply fully the clear and often reiterated ethical norms of the magisterium. **610**

To achieve a proper regulation of fertility, we must promote the existence of centers where people will be taught scientifically the natural methods of birth control by qualified personnel. This humanistic alternative avoids the ethical and social evils of anti-conception techniques and sterilization, which historically have been forerunners of legalized abortion. **611**

k. Not to restrict pastoral concern about respect for the basic right to life to the abominable crime of abortion, but to extend it to defending integrity and health in all the other moments and circumstances of human existence. **612**

l. To follow faithfully this recommendation of John Paul II: "In defense of the family . . . the Church pledges its help; and it invites governments to adopt, as a key point of their action, a socio-family policy that is intelligent, bold, and persevering—recognizing that herein undoubtedly lies the future, the hope, of the continent" (HP:3). **613**

m. To provide—in seminaries, religious institutes, and other centers—ade- **614** quate training in family pastoral care; and to do the same later in the ongoing training of priests and other agents of evangelization.

615   *n.* To promote and strengthen movements and forms of pastoral care for the family, respecting their own proper charisms within the overall pastoral effort.

616   *o.* To create or give new life to coordinating centers of family pastoral care, in order to ensure the success of these courses of action. This would involve centers on the diocesan, national, and continental levels; and it would involve the participation of parents.

2. Base-Level Ecclesial Communities (CEBs), the Parish, and the Local Church

617   *Besides the Christian family, the first center of evangelization, human beings live their fraternal vocations in the bosom of the local Church, in communities that render the Lord's salvific design present and operative, to be lived out in communion and participation.*

Thus within the local Church we must consider the parishes, the CEBs, and other ecclesial groups.

618   *The Church is the People of God, which expresses its life of communion and evangelizing service on various levels and under various historical forms.*

2.1. The Situation

619   *In general* we can say that in our Latin American Church today we find a great longing for deeper and more stable relationships in the faith, sustained and animated by the Word of God. We see an intensification in common prayer and in the effort of the people to participate more consciously and fruitfully in the liturgy.

620   We note an increase in the co-responsibility of the faith, both in organization and in pastoral action.

621   There is more wide-ranging awareness and exercise of the rights and duties appropriate to lay people as members of the community.

622   We notice a great yearning for justice and a sincere sense of solidarity, in a social milieu characterized by growing secularism and other phenomena typical of a society in transformation.

623   Bit by bit the Church has been dissociating itself from those who hold economic or political power, freeing itself from various forms of dependence, and divesting itself of privileges.

624   The Church in Latin America wishes to go on giving witness of unselfish and self-denying service in the face of a world dominated by greed for profit, lust for power, and exploitation.

625   In the direction of greater participation, there has been an increase of ordained ministries (such as the permanent diaconate), non-ordained ministries, and other services such as celebrators of the Word and community animators. We also note better collaboration between priests, religious, and lay people.

626   More clearly evident in our communities, as a fruit of the Holy Spirit, is a new style of relationship between bishops and priests, and between them and their

people. It is characterized by greater simplicity, understanding, and friendship in the Lord.

All this is a process, in which we still find broad sectors posing resistance of various sorts. This calls for understanding and encouragement, as well as great docility to the Holy Spirit. What we need now is still more clerical openness to the activity of the laity and the overcoming of pastoral individualism and self-sufficiency. On the other hand, the impact of the secularized milieu has sometimes produced centrifugal tendencies in the community and the loss of an authentic ecclesial sense.	627

We have not always found effective ways to overcome the meagre education of our people in the faith. Thus they remain defenseless before the onslaughts of shaky theological doctrines, sectarian proselytism, and pseudo-spiritual movements.	628

In particular we have found that small communities, especially the CEBs, create more personal inter-relations, acceptance of God's Word, re-examination of one's life, and reflection on reality in the light of the Gospel. They accentuate committed involvement in the family, one's work, the neighborhood, and the local community. We are happy to single out the multiplication of small communities as an important ecclesial event that is peculiarly ours, and as the "hope of the Church" (EN:58). This ecclesial expression is more evident on the periphery of large cities and in the countryside. They are a favorable atmosphere for the rise of new lay-sponsored services. They have done much to spread family catechesis and adult education in the faith, in forms more suitable for the common people.	629

But not enough attention has been paid to the training of leaders in faith-education and Christian directors of intermediate organisms in the neighborhoods, the world of work, and the rural farm areas. Perhaps that is why not a few members of certain communities, and even entire communities, have been drawn to purely lay institutions or have been turned into ideological radicals, and are now in the process of losing any authentic feel for the Church.	630

The parish has been going through various forms of renewal that correspond to the changes in recent years. There is a change in outlook among pastors, more involvement of the laity in pastoral councils and other services, ongoing catechetical updating, and a growing presence of the priest among the people, especially through a network of groups and communities.	631

In the area of evangelization the parish embodies a twofold relationship of communication and pastoral communion. On the diocesan level parishes are integrated into regions, vicarages, and deaneries. And within the parish itself pastoral work is diversified in accordance with different areas, and there is greater opening to the creation of smaller communities.	632

But we still find attitudes that pose an obstacle to the dynamic thrust of renewal. Primacy is given to administrative work over pastoral care. There is routinism and a lack of preparation for the sacraments. Authoritarianism is evident among some priests. And sometimes the parish closes in on itself, disregarding the overall apostolic demands of a serious nature.	633

On the level of the local Church we note a considerable effort to arrange the territory so that greater attention can be paid to the People of God. This is being	634 done by the creation of new dioceses. There is also concern to provide the Churches with organisms that will foster co-responsibility through channels suited for dialogue: e.g., priest councils, pastoral councils, and diocesan committees. These are to inspire a more organic pastoral effort suited to the specific reality of a given diocese.

635 Among religious communities and lay movements we also see a greater awareness of the necessity of being involved in the mission of the local Church and evincing an ecclesial spirit.

636 *On the national level* there is a noticeable effort to exercise greater collegiality in episcopal conferences, which are continuously being better organized and fitted with subsidiary organisms. Deserving of special mention is the growth and effectiveness of the service that CELAM offers to ecclesial communion throughout Latin America.

637 *On the worldwide level* we note the fraternal interchange promoted by the sending of apostolic personnel and economic aid. These relationships have been established with the episcopates of Europe and North America, with the help of CAL; their continuation and intensification offer ampler opportunities for interecclesial participation, which is a noteworthy sign of universal communion.

2.2. Doctrinal Reflection

638 The Christian lives in community under the activity of the Holy Spirit. The Spirit is the invisible principle of unity and communion, and also of the unity and variety to be found in states of life, ministries, and charisms.

639 In their families, which constitute domestic Churches, the baptized are summoned to their first experience of communion in faith, love, and service to others.

640 In small communities, particularly those that are better organized, people grow in their experience of new interpersonal relationships in the faith, in deeper exploration of God's Word, in fuller participation in the Eucharist, in communion with the pastors of the local Church, and in greater commitment to justice within the social milieu that surrounds them.

One question that might be raised is: When can a small community be considered an authentic base-level ecclesial community (CEB) in Latin America?

641 As a community, the CEB brings together families, adults and young people, in an intimate interpersonal relationship grounded in the faith. As an ecclesial reality, it is a community of faith, hope, and charity. It celebrates the Word of God and takes its nourishment from the Eucharist, the culmination of all the sacraments. It fleshes out the Word of God in life through solidarity and commitment to the new commandment of the Lord; and through the service of approved coordinators, it makes present and operative the mission of the Church and its visible communion with the legitimate pastors. It is a base-level community because it is composed of relatively few members as a permanent body, like a cell of the larger community. "When they deserve their ecclesial designation, they can take charge of their own spiritual and human existence in a spirit of fraternal solidarity" (EN:58).

642 United in a CEB and nurturing their adherence to Christ, Christians strive for a more evangelical way of life amid the people, work together to challenge the egotistical and consumeristic roots of society, and make explicit their vocation to communion with God and their fellow humans. Thus they offer a valid and

worthwhile point of departure for building up a new society, "the civilization of love."

The CEBs embody the Church's preferential love for the common people. In them their religiosity is expressed, valued, and purified; and they are given a concrete opportunity to share in the task of the Church and to work committedly for the transformation of the world. **643**

The *parish* carries out a function that is, in a way, an integral ecclesial function because it accompanies persons and families throughout their lives, fostering their education and growth in the faith. It is a center of coordination and guidance for communities, groups, and movements. In it the horizons of communion and participation are opened up even more. The celebration of the Eucharist and the other sacraments makes the global reality of the Church present in a clearer way. Its tie with the diocesan community is ensured by its union with the bishop, who entrusts his representative (usually the parish priest) with the pastoral care of the community. For the Christian the parish becomes the place of encounter and fraternal sharing of persons and goods; it overcomes the limitations inherent in small communities. In fact, the parish takes on a series of services that are not within the reach of smaller communities. This is particularly true with respect to the missionary dimension and to the furthering of the dignity of the human person. In this way it reaches out to migrants, who are more or less stable, to the marginalized, to the alienated, to nonbelievers, and in general to the neediest. **644**

In *the local Church*, which is shaped in the image of the universal Church, we find the one, holy, catholic, and apostolic Church of Christ truly existing and operating (LG:23; CD:11). The local Church is a portion of the People of God, defined by a broader sociocultural context in which it is incarnated. Its primacy in the complex of ecclesial communities is due to the fact that it is presided over by a bishop. The bishop is endowed, in a full, sacramental way, with the threefold ministry of Christ, the head of the mystical body: prophet, priest, and pastor. In each local Church the bishop is the principle and foundation of its unity. **645**

Because they are the successors of the apostles, bishops—through their communion with the episcopal college and, in particular, with the Roman pontiff—render present the apostolicity of the whole Church. They guarantee fidelity to the Gospel. They make real the communion with the universal Church. And they foster the collaboration of their presbytery and the growth of the People of God entrusted to their care. **646**

It will be up to the bishop to discern the charisms and promote the ministries that are needed if his diocese is to grow toward maturity as an evangelized and evangelizing community. That means his diocese must be a light and leaven in society as well as a sacrament of unity and integral liberation. It must be capable of interchange with other local Churches and animated by a missionary spirit that will allow its inner evangelical richness to radiate outside. **647**

2.3. Pastoral Lines of Approach

As pastors, we are determined to promote, guide, and accompany the CEBs in the spirit of the Medellín Conference (Med-JPP:10) and the guidelines set forth by *Evangelii Nuntiandi* (no. 58). We will also foster the discovery and gradual training **648** of animators for these communities. In particular, we must explore how these small communities, which are flourishing mainly in rural areas and urban peripheries, can be adapted to the pastoral care of the big cities on our continent.

649   We must continue the efforts at parish renewal: getting beyond the merely administrative aspects; seeking greater lay participation, particularly in pastoral councils; giving priority to organized forms of the apostolate; and training lay people to assume their responsibilities as Christians in the community and the social milieu.

650   We must stress a more determined option for an overall, coordinated pastoral effort, with the collaboration of religious communities in particular. We must promote groups, communities, and movements, inspiring them to an ongoing effort at communion. We must turn the parish into a center for promoting services that smaller communities cannot surely provide.

651   We must encourage experiments to develop the pastoral activity of all the parish agents, and we must support the vocational pastoral effort of ordained ministers, lay services, and the religious life.

652   Worthy of special recognition and a word of encouragement are priests and other pastoral agents, to whom the diocesan community owes support, encouragement, and solidarity. This holds true also for their fitting sustenance and social security, within the spirit of poverty.

653   Among priests we want to single out the figure of the parish priest. He is a pastor in the likeness of Christ. He is a promoter of communion with God, his fellow humans to whose service he dedicates himself, and his fellow priests joined around their common bishop. He is the leader and guide of the communities, alert to discern the signs of the time along with his people.

654   In the realm of the local Church efforts should be made to ensure the ongoing training and updating of pastoral agents. Spirituality and training courses should be provided by retreat centers and days of recollection. It is urgent that diocesan curias become more effective centers of pastoral promotion on three levels: that of catechetics, liturgy, and services promoting justice and charity. The pastoral value of administrative service should also be recognized. A special effort should be made to coordinate and integrate pastoral diocesan councils and other diocesan organisms. For even though they present problems, they are indispensable tools in planning, implementing, and keeping up with the pastoral activity in diocesan life.

655   The local Church must stress its missionary character and its aspect of ecclesial communion, sharing values and experiences as well as fostering the interchange of personnel and resources.

656   Through its pastors, episcopal collegiality, and union with the Vicar of Christ, the diocesan community ought to intensify its intimate communion with the center of church unity. It should also shore up its loyal acceptance of the service that is offered through the magisterium, nurturing its fidelity to the Gospel and its concrete life of charity. This would include collaboration on the continental level through CELAM and its programs.

657   We pledge to make every effort to ensure that this collegiality—of which this conference in Puebla and the two previous conferences are privileged instances —will be an even stronger sign of credibility for our proclamation of the Gospel and our service to it; that it will thereby foster fraternal communion in all of Latin America.

CHAPTER II
AGENTS OF COMMUNION AND PARTICIPATION

We now turn our attention to the principal agents of evangelization.

With them we wish to reflect, to take new heart, and to assume new options for carrying out our pastoral task.

We are responsible for the difficult but honorable mission of evangelizing every person and every milieu.   **658**

We are referring to priests, deacons, religious men and women, and committed lay people. We begin with ourselves, the bishops.

1. The Hierarchical Ministry
2. The Consecrated Life
3. Lay People
4. Pastoral Work on Behalf of Vocations

1. The Hierarchical Ministry

The hierarchical ministry, the sacramental sign of Christ, the Pastor and Head   **659**
of the Church, is chiefly responsible for building up the Church and its communion, and for giving impetus to its evangelizing activity.

1.1. Introduction

In recent years there has been much theological reflection on priestly identity.   **660**
It has been spurred by the crises and maladjustments that have struck priestly identity with a certain force. So there is a need for such reflection. We invite theologians and pastoralists to explore this important field more deeply, following the directives of the magisterium, particularly those of Vatican II, the Medellín Conference, the 1971 Synod of Bishops, and the Directory for the Pastoral Ministry of Bishops. A synthesizing vision, which will bring together elements that are sometimes presented as antithetical, is of the utmost interest.

By virtue of its sacramental participation in Christ, the Head of the Church, the   **661**
priesthood is a service for unity in the community through the Word and the Eucharist (Eph. 4:15–17). Ministry to the community implies a sharing in the power and authority that Christ communicates through ordination. It establishes the priest in the threefold dimension of Christ's own ministry as prophet, liturgical priest, and king. The priest becomes one who acts in Christ's name in the service of the community.

In the identity of his service, the being and work of the priest is referred to the   **662**
Eucharist. The Eucharist is the root and pivot of the whole community (PO:6), the center of the sacramental life toward which the Word leads. Hence one can say that where the Eucharist is, there the Church is. And since the latter is served by the bishop, in union with his priests, it is equally correct to say that "where the bishop is, there the Church is."

By virtue of sacramental fraternity, full unity between the ministers of the   **663**
community is already an evangelizing reality. The need for this unity was

recalled by John Paul II in his Opening Address to this conference (OAP:II, 1 and 2). Pastoral unity itself derives from this source.

1.2. The Situation

664   In line with the needs of the day, we notice a change in outlook and attitude among the hierarchical ministers, and hence a change in their image.

665   We see a deeper and growing awareness of the evangelizing, missionary character of the pastoral task.

666   The lifestyle of many pastors has grown in simplicity and poverty, in mutual affection and understanding, in closeness to the people, openness to dialogue, and shared responsibility.

667   Ecclesial communion has been firmed up between the bishops and the Holy Father; between the bishops themselves; between priests and religious and their bishops; and between various ecclesial families. Deserving of special recognition are the local Churches of various countries that not only have augmented our evangelizing work by sending priests, religious, and other pastoral agents but also have made generous, Christian contributions of their resources.

668   It is moving and inspiring to see the spirit of sacrifice and abnegation with which many pastors exercise their ministry in the service of the Gospel. They do so by preaching, celebrating the sacraments, or defending human dignity in the face of loneliness, isolation, incomprehension, and sometimes persecution and death (PO:13).

669   In almost all ministers we find a growing concern to update themselves, not only intellectually but also spiritually and pastorally, and to make use of all the means that will further this end.

670   We note greater clarification with regard to priestly identity. This has led to a new affirmation of the spiritual life of the hierarchical ministry, and a preferential service of the poor.

671   Pastors have contributed noticeably to heightened awareness in the activity of the laity, both with respect to their specific vocation as lay people and their more responsible participation in the life of the Church. This has even included different types of ministry.

672   A stimulating phenomenon is that of the permanent deacons and their varied forms of ministry, particularly in rural parishes and peasant areas. But we do not want to overlook the CEBs and other groups of faithful. In any case there must be further theological reflection on the figure of the deacon so as to win greater acceptance of his ministry.

     Within this encouraging panorama we also find negative aspects. Here we present a few of them.

673   *a*. There is a lack of unity regarding the basic criteria of pastoral work. The results are "tensions" over obedience and serious repercussions in the "overall, coordinated pastoral effort" [*pastoral de conjunto*].

674   *b*. Despite a recent increase in vocations, there is a disconcerting dearth of ministers. One of the reasons for this is a deficient missionary consciousness.

675   *c*. The distribution of the clergy throughout the continent is inadequate. In some cases this situation is aggravated by the fact that priests fill in for others in performing other tasks.

d. There is not enough pastoral, spiritual, and doctrinal updating. This pro- 676
duces feelings of insecurity in the face of theological advances and erroneous
doctrines. It provokes feelings of pastoral frustration and even a certain crisis of
identity.

e. Sometimes inadequate support and the absence of a modicum of social 677
security for priests prompt them to go out looking for paid work, to the detriment
of their ministry.

f. Sometimes we find an absence of timely prophetic and magisterial intervention by the bishops, and of better collegial consistency.

1.3. Enlightenment from Pastoral Theology

The great ministry or service that the Church offers to the world and human 679
beings in it is evangelization, which is offered in words and deeds (DV:2). It is
the Good News that the Kingdom of God, a kingdom of justice and peace, reaches
human beings in Jesus Christ.

From the very beginning there were different ministries in the Church for the 680
work of evangelization. The New Testament writings depict the vitality of the
Church finding expression in many types of service. St. Paul mentions the
following, among others: prophecy, ministry, teaching, exhortation, almsgiv-
ing, ruling, works of mercy (Rom. 12:6–8). In other contexts Paul talks about
other ministries: wisdom in discourse, discernment of spirits, and so forth (1
Cor. 12:8–11; Eph. 4:11–12; 1 Thess. 5:12f.; Phil. 1:1). Various ministries are also
described in other New Testament writings.

"The divinely established ecclesiastical ministry is exercised on different levels 681
by those who from antiquity have been called bishops, priests, and deacons"
(LG:28). They constitute the hierarchical ministry, which they receive in the
sacrament of orders through "the laying on of hands." As Vatican II teaches,
through the sacrament of orders—episcopal and priestly—there is conferred a
ministerial priesthood that is essentially distinct from the common priesthood
shared by all the faithful through the sacrament of baptism (LG:10). Those who
receive the hierarchical ministry are made "pastors" in the Church "in accordance with their function." Like the Good Shepherd (John 10:1–16), they go before
the flock; they give their lives so that the flock may have life and have it in
abundance; they know their flock and are known by them in turn.

"Going before the flock" means being alert to the paths that the faithful are 682
travelling so that they, united in the Spirit, may bear witness to the life, suffering,
death, and resurrection of Jesus Christ. Jesus, poor among the poor, announced
that we all are children of the same Father and hence brothers and sisters.

"Giving their lives" is the gauge of "hierarchical ministry" and the proof of 683
greater love. That is how Paul lived, dying daily to carry out his ministry (2 Cor.
4:11).

"Knowing their flock and being known by them" does not simply mean 684
knowing the needs of the faithful. It means investing one's own being in them
and loving as one who came to serve rather than be served (Matt. 20:25–28).

We reaffirm our adherence to all the teachings about pastors that have been 685
given to us by Vatican II, the 1971 Synod of Bishops, the Medellín Conference,
and the Episcopal Directory. Now, because we think it will be useful for

evangelization in Latin America's present and future, we offer some "reflections" on the ministry of bishops, priests, and deacons.

686   As a member of the episcopal college presided over by the pope, the bishop is a successor of the apostles. Through his full participation in Christ's priesthood, he is a visible and efficacious sign of Christ, for whom he substitutes as teacher, shepherd, and high priest (LG:21). This threefold, inseparable function is meant to serve the unity of his local Church. It creates obligations of a spiritual and pastoral character that deserve to be stressed today.

687   The bishop is a teacher of truth (OAP:I,6). In a Church totally dedicated to the service of the Word, he is the first and foremost evangelizer and catechist. No other task can exempt him from this sacred mission. He ponders the Word religiously, keeps himself up-to-date doctrinally, and preaches it personally to the people. He sees to it that his community keeps moving forward in its knowledge and practice of the Word of God, encouraging and guiding all those who teach in the Church (in order to avoid "parallel magisteria" of persons or groups). He encourages the collaboration of theologians, who exercise their specific charism within the Church from the standpoint of theology's own specific methodology; to do this, he tries to keep up to date theologically so that he can discern the truth and maintain dialogue with them. And he does all this in communion with the pope and his fellow bishops, particularly those in his own episcopal conference.

688   The bishop is a sign and constructor of unity (OAP:II,1). His authority, exercised evangelically, is put in the service of unity. He promotes the mission of the whole diocesan community. He fosters participation and co-responsibility on different levels. He infuses confidence into his collaborators—especially priests, to whom he is supposed to be a father, brother, and friend (LG:28). In his diocese he creates a climate of organic, spiritual, ecclesial communion that will enable all religious men and women to live out their own specific way of belonging to the diocesan family. He discerns and appreciates the multiplicity and variety of the charisms poured out on the members of his Church, in such a way that they effectively work together for its growth and vitality. He makes his presence felt in the major circumstances surrounding the life of his local Church.

689   The bishop is a high priest and sanctifier. He personally exercises his function of presiding over the liturgy and promoting it. Grounded on his own personal witness, he fosters the holiness of all the faithful as the first tool of evangelization (EN:21,41,69). He looks to the grace of the sacrament of orders as the basis for an ongoing cultivation of the spiritual life. Based in personal love for Christ, this gives impetus to his love for the Church and his generous, self-denying pastoral care of his flock. He shows concern for the spiritual life of his priests and religious. His life—joyous, austere, simple, and as close to his people as possible—becomes a witness to Christ the Pastor and a medium of dialogue with all human beings.

690   Through the sacrament of orders priests become the principal co-workers of the bishops in their threefold ministry. They render Christ the Head present in the community (PO:2). Joined with their bishop and united in intimate sacramental fraternity, they form a single presbytery dedicated to a variety of tasks to serve the Church and the world (LG:28). These realities make them "central pieces in the ecclesial task" (AP:1).

691   Since they are inseparable from their bishops, the above mentioned traits of

pastoral spirituality apply to priests as well. Given the current situation of the Church in Latin America, the following items are of priority importance:

The priest announces the Kingdom of God, which begins in this world and will reach its fulfillment when Christ comes at the end of time. To serve this Kingdom, the priest abandons everything to serve his Lord. A sign of this radical oblation is ministerial celibacy, a gift of Christ himself and a guarantee of generous, freely proffered dedication to the service of human beings. **692**

The priest is a man of God. He can be a prophet only insofar as he has had experience of the living God. Only this experience will make him the bearer of a powerful Word who can transform the personal and social life of human beings to conform with the Father's plan. **693**

Prayer in all its forms—especially the canonical hours of the breviary entrusted to him by the Church—will help him to maintain this experience of God that he is supposed to share with his brothers and sisters. **694**

Like the bishop and in communion with him, the priest evangelizes, celebrates the holy sacrifice, and serves unity. **695**

As a pastor committed to the integral liberation of the poor and the oppressed, the priest always operates with evangelical criteria (EN:18). He believes in the force of the Spirit so as not to fall into the temptation of becoming a political leader, social director, or functionary of some temporal authority. For that would prevent him from being "a sign and factor of unity and fraternity" (AP:8). **696**

The deacon, a co-worker of the bishop and the priest, receives his own specific sacramental grace. The charism of the diaconate, a sacramental sign of "Christ the servant," is very effective in bringing about a poor, servant Church that exercises its missionary function for the integral liberation of the human being. **697**

The deacon's mission and function are not to be measured by merely pragmatic criteria, by various actions that could be exercised by nonordained ministers (EN:73) or any baptized person. Nor is his mission and function to be viewed solely as a solution to the numerical scarcity of priests (LG:29) affecting Latin America. The suitability of the deacon resides in his effectively contributing to the Church's better execution of its salvific mission (AG:16), thanks to more adequate attention to its evangelizing task. **698**

The establishment of the permanent diaconate, already requested of the Holy See by most of our episcopal conferences, should involve a mixture of "the new and the old." It is not simply a matter of restoring the diaconate of an earlier age. It is a matter of delving into the tradition of the universal Church and the specific realities of our own continent. Through attention to these two aspects (EN:73), we must nurture fidelity to the patrimony of the Church as well as a sound pastoral creativity with evangelizing ramifications. **699**

The ministerial spirituality common to all the members of the hierarchy must center around the Eucharist and be characterized by authentic devotion to the Most Blessed Virgin Mary. This devotion is deeply rooted in the people we are evangelizing. It is a guarantee of ongoing fidelity, a key characteristic of the evangelizer (HM). **700**

1.4. Pastoral Orientations

Bishops. We bishops pledge:

To continually carry out the ministry of evangelization with joy, fearlessness, **701** and humility. We shall regard it as the priority task of our episcopal office, following the road opened up and illuminated by the outstanding pastors and missionaries on this continent.

702   To take on episcopal collegiality in all its dimensions and consequences on both the regional and universal levels.

703   To promote the unity of the local Church at any cost, using spiritual discernment so as not to extinguish or standardize the rich variety of charisms. And we will give special importance to promoting an organic pastoral effort and to inspiring communities.

704   To give priestly and pastoral councils, and other pastoral organisms, the consistency and functioning capability demanded by Vatican II; and to be concerned about fostering the spiritual and pastoral growth of our priests.

705   To look for ways to bring together priests living in remote regions, in order to preclude their isolation and to foster greater pastoral effectiveness. In particular, we shall give consideration to "military chaplains," trying to make sure that they are pastorally integrated into the diocesan presbytery in places where they perform their priestly ministry.

706   To make every effort to promote justice and to defend the dignity and the rights of the human person, in line with the demands of the Gospel and our own mission (OAP:III).

707   To make clear through our lives and our attitudes that our preference is to evangelize and serve the poor, while remaining totally faithful to the Gospel and not losing sight of our charism as signs of unity and shepherds.

708   To give preferential attention to the seminary, given its importance in training the priests on whom will depend, in large measure, "the wished-for renewal of the whole Church" (OT: Preface). We will strive to give them the best possible priests, priests adequately trained. In every way possible we will try to come to a better knowledge of the teachers and the students, and to establish greater contact with them.

709   To look effectively for a solution to the difficult economic plight of priests by offering them adequate remuneration and social security. If necessary, we will resort to initiatives beyond the diocesan level, be they national or international, in the Christian spirit of sharing resources.

710   To study objectively the phenomenon of priests leaving their ministry, its causes and its repercussions on the life of the Church. We will keep in mind the criterion spelled out by the 1971 Synod of Bishops: "A priest who leaves the ministry should receive just and fraternal treatment; but even though he can assist in the service of the Church, he is not to be admitted to the exercise of priestly activities" ("The Ministerial Priesthood," Part Two, 4d).

711   *Priests.* In their ministry let priests give priority to the proclamation of the Gospel, most especially to the neediest (workers, peasants, indigenous peoples, the marginalized, and Afro-American groups), including the promotion and defense of their human dignity.

712   The missionary vitality of priests should be renewed. They should be trained in an attitude of generous availability, so that we can effectively respond to the unequal distribution of clergy that exists at present.

713   Priests should give priority to evangelizing work among families and young people, and to the fostering of priestly and religious vocations.

Priests should devote themselves to incorporating the laity and religious **714**
women more and more actively into pastoral activity, accompanying them with
the needed spiritual and doctrinal support.

Permanent deacons. The deacon should be fully inserted into the community he **715**
serves. He should continuously nurture communion between his community
and the priests and the bishop. In addition, he should respect and foster the
ministries exercised by the laity.

The community should play an important role in carefully selecting candidates **716**
for the diaconate. The training of deacons should be adequate and ongoing. In
addition, their own families, the communities that receive them, the presby-
teries, and the laity should be properly prepared.

Provisions should be made for the fair remuneration of permanent deacons **717**
dedicated completely to the pastoral ministry.

Studies should be promoted to explore the theological, canonical, and pastoral **718**
aspects of the permanent diaconate. And efforts should be made to ensure
satisfactory diffusion of such studies.

Ongoing formation. The grace received at ordination, which must be revivified **719**
continually (2 Tim. 1:6–7), and the mission of evangelization require that hierarchical ministers receive serious, ongoing training. Such training cannot be limited to the intellectual sphere; it must extend to every aspect of life.

This training will take due account of the age and condition of the persons **720**
involved. Its aim must be to train the hierarchical ministers so that they, in line
with the demands of their vocation and mission as well as the reality of Latin
America, will live personal and community lives in an ongoing process that
makes them pastorally competent to exercise their ministry.

2. The Consecrated Life

The consecrated life is, in itself, an evangelizing life designed to promote **721**
communion and participation in Latin America.

2.1. Tendencies of the Consecrated Life in Latin America

It is a joy for us bishops to verify the presence and dynamic activity of so many **722**
consecrated persons in Latin America. They are dedicating their lives to the
mission of evangelization even as they did in the past. We can echo the words of
Paul VI: "Not infrequently we find them in the vanguard of the Church's mission, confronting the greatest risks to their holiness and their very lives. Yes, the
Church does indeed owe them a very great deal" (EN:69). This leads us to foster
and accompany the consecrated life, in line with its characteristic features
(MR:9).

From the experience of the religious life in Latin America we wish to select only **723**
the most significant and renewal-oriented tendencies that the Spirit is promoting
in the Church. We also wish to point out some of the difficulties brought to light
by the crisis in recent years.

While we are referring here directly to the religious life, we wish to point out to **724**
secular institutes and other forms of consecrated life that many of these ideas and
experiences relate to them as well (on secular institutes, see nos. 774–76 below).

The Church of Latin America has high esteem for the stimulus they provide for consecration to God, and for their "secularity" as an especially valuable way of carrying Christ's presence and message to every sort of human milieu.

725 The religious life as a whole constitutes the specific mode of evangelization peculiar to religious. So in pointing out these aspects, we are summing up the contribution of religious to evangelization. We find the following tendencies in particular:

726 *a. Experience of God.* There are certain signs that express a desire to deepen and interiorize one's living of the faith, in the realization that there can be no convincing and persevering evangelization without contact with the Lord.

727 There is an effort to assure that prayer becomes an attitude toward life, so that prayer and life mutually enrich each other. Thus prayer would lead people to involve themselves in real life, and real-life experience of reality would call for intense moments of prayer. Besides the quest for private prayer, there is a particular concern for community prayer: for sharing one's experience of the faith, exercising discernment of reality, and praying together with the people.

728 This prayer must be visible and stimulating. People are also rediscovering the significance of the Church's great tradition of using psalms and liturgical texts for prayer, particularly in shared celebration of the Eucharist. The same is happening with other traditional devotions, such as the Rosary.

729 It must be admitted that some religious have not successfully integrated prayer and real life. This is particularly true if they are absorbed in activities, if they lack private space for the inner life in their involvement, or if they are living a false kind of spirituality.

730 *b. Fraternal community.* There is an effort to emphasize fraternal relations. These are interpersonal relationships in which value is put on friendship, sincerity, and maturity as an indispensable human basis for living together; they have a dimension of faith, since it is the Lord who summons us. All this involves a simpler and more receptive lifestyle and entails dialogue and participation.

731 We see different kinds of community life. There are many communities corresponding to particular kinds of works and the various foundational charisms. We also see "small communities" arising, usually out of a desire to be involved in modest neighborhoods or the countryside, or to undertake a specific mission of evangelization. Experience proves that these small communities must meet certain conditions if they are to be successful. There must be evangelical motivation, personal sharing, community prayer, apostolic work, evaluation processes, and integration into the religious institute and the diocese through the indispensable service of authorities.

732 Today personal closeness and the diversity of outlooks raise special difficulties when one's sense of faith is diminished or when there is no respect for a proper range of pluralism.

733 *c. Preferential option for the poor.* Pastoral openness in one's labors and a preferential option for the poor represent the most noticeable tendency of religious life in Latin America. Indeed religious increasingly find themselves in difficult, marginalized areas; in missions to the indigenous peoples; and in silent, humble labors. This option does not imply exclusion of anyone, but it does imply a preference for the poor and a drawing closer to them.

734 This has led to a re-examination of traditional works in order to respond better

to the demands of evangelization. It has also shed clearer light on their relationship with the poverty of the marginalized. Now this does not imply simply interior detachment and community austerity; it also implies solidarity with the poor, sharing with them, and in some cases living alongside them.

But this option entails negative effects when there is a lack of adequate preparation, of community support, of personal maturity, or of evangelical motivation. Not infrequently this option has involved the risk of being misinterpreted.

735

d. Integration into the life of the local Church. One notices a rediscovery and a conscious experience of the mystery of the local Church, as well as a growing desire to participate and to contribute the riches of one's own vocational charism. This leads to greater integration into the overall, organized pastoral effort, and to fuller participation in diocesan and supradiocesan organisms and activities.

736

But there are tensions: sometimes within the communities; sometimes between them and the bishops. The pastoral mission of the bishop or the specific charism of the religious institute may be lost sight of. There may be an absence of dialogue and joint discernment when it comes to re-examining projects and making personnel changes in the service of the diocese. We are concerned about the thoughtless abandonment of labors that have traditionally been in the hands of religious communities: e.g., schools, hospitals, and so forth.

737

Contemplative communities constitute what might be called the heart of the religious life. They inspire and stimulate all to intensify the transcendent sense of the Christian life. They, too, evangelize because "being contemplative does not mean making a radical break with the world, with the apostolate. The contemplative must find his or her specific way of understanding the Kingdom of God" (ARG:2).

738

2.2. Criteria

a. God's design. The consecrated life, with deep, age-old roots among the peoples of Latin America, is a gift conferred unceasingly on the Church by the Spirit as "a privileged means of effective evangelization" (EN:69).

739

In deciding to liberate our history from sin, the seed of indignity and death, the Father chooses baptized men and women in his Son, through the Spirit. They are chosen for a radical following of Jesus Christ within the Church.

740

And since the universal Church is made real in the local Churches (CD:11), it is in the latter that the consecrated life discovers the reality of the relationship between vital community and the ecclesial commitment to evangelization. With the local Churches consecrated people share the struggles, sufferings, joys, and hopes of building up the Kingdom; in them overflow the riches of their specific charisms as a gift of the evangelizing Spirit. In the local Churches they encounter their brothers and sisters, presided over by the bishop who exercises "the ministry of discernment and harmonization" (MR:6).

741

b. Called to a radical following of Christ. Called by the Lord (Matt. 4:18–21), they pledge to follow him in a radical way. They identify with him on the basis of the Beatitudes. As the pope has put it: "Never forget that if you are to maintain a clear concept of the value of your consecrated life, you will need a profound vision of faith that is nurtured and preserved by prayer (PC:6). That will enable you to overcome all uncertainty about your specific identity. It will keep you loyal

742

to the vertical dimension you need to identify yourselves with Christ on the basis of the Beatitudes, and to be authentic witnesses to God's Kingdom for the benefit of people today" (AR:4).

743   Thanks to their consecration, and on the basis of their communion with the Father, they joyously accept the mystery of self-emptying and paschal exaltation (Phil. 2:3–11). Radically denying themselves, they accept the Lord's cross as their own (Matt. 16:24) and shoulder it. They accompany those who are suffering from injustice, from a lack of deeper meaning in their lives as human beings, and from a thirst for peace, truth, and life. Sharing in the death of those who suffer, they joyously rise with them to newness of life. Becoming all things to all human beings, they regard the poor as privileged beings, as the Lord's favorites.

744   They are called in a special way to live in intense communion with the Father. He fills them with his Spirit, urging them on to fashion ever renewed communion between human beings. Thus the consecrated life is a prophetic affirmation of the supreme value of communion with God and between human beings (ET:53). It is also a "splendid and striking testimony that the world cannot be transfigured and offered to God without the spirit of the beatitudes" (LG:31).

745   Taking Mary as their model of consecration and their intercessor, the consecrated will flesh out the Word of God in their lives. Like her and with her, they will offer that Word to human beings in an ongoing process of evangelization.

746   Their radical consecration is made to God, as the one loved above everything else, and hence to the service of human beings. It is expressed and realized through the evangelical counsels, which are assumed as vows, or through other sacred bonds which unite them "to the Church and her mystery in a special way" (LG:44).

747   Living in poverty as the Lord did, and knowing that the only Absolute is God, they share their goods, proclaim the gratuitous generosity of God and his gifts, and thus inaugurate the new justice. In a special way they proclaim "that the Kingdom of God and its overmastering necessities are superior to all earthly considerations" (LG:44). With their witness they are an evangelical denunciation of those who serve money and power, who egotistically keep back for themselves the goods that God has given to humanity for the benefit of the whole community.

748   Their consecrated obedience is lived in a courageous, self-denying way as "a sacrifice of themselves" (PC:14). It expresses their communion with the salvific will of God and their denunciation of any historical project that diverges from the divine plan and does not help human beings to grow in their dignity as children of God.

749   In a world where love is being emptied of its full measure, where disunion increases distances everywhere, and where pleasure-seeking is erected into an idol, those who belong to God in Christ through consecrated chastity will bear witness to God's liberating covenant with humanity. In the bosom of their local Church they will serve as the presence of the love of Christ for the Church: "Christ loved the Church. He gave himself up for her" (Eph. 5:25). Finally, they will be to all a luminous sign of eschatological liberation, a liberation lived out in surrender to God and in new, universal solidarity with human beings.

750   Thus "this silent testimony of poverty and detachment, of purity and transparency, of self-abandonment in obedience, can be both a summons to the world

and the Church itself and an eloquent sermon, capable of touching even non-Christians of good will who are sensitive to certain values" (EN:69).

Living a life of continuous prayer, they are called to show their brothers and sisters the supreme value and apostolic efficacy of union with the Father (RMS). 751

Fraternal communion lived out in obedience to all its demands, to which religious are called, is the sign of the transforming love that the Spirit pours into their hearts and that is stronger than any ties of flesh and blood. 752

Different persons, sometimes of different nationalities, share the same kind of life and mission in intimate fraternity. In this way they bear eloquent witness to the life of the triune God in his Church, working in a spirit of ecclesial communion and acting as a leaven for communion between human beings and for co-sharing in the gifts of God. 753

If all the baptized have been called to share in Christ's mission, to open up to their brothers and sisters, and to work for unity (Gal. 3:26–28) inside and outside the ecclesial community, this is far truer of those whom God has consecrated to himself. The latter are invited to live the new commandment through gratuitous self-giving to all human beings. And they are to do this "with a love that is non-partisan and that excludes no one, even though it is directed to the poorest by way of preference" (AP:7). 754

Thus we get the services initiated by the Spirit as a salvific expression of Jesus Christ (1 Cor. 12:4–14; Eph. 4:10; Rom. 12:4). Though carried out individually, these services are assumed by the whole community. Urged on by love for Christ, religious serve to stimulate missionary awareness within the ecclesial community insofar as they display their readiness to be sent into places and situations where the Church needs more help of a generous nature (EN:69). 755

The wealth of the Spirit is manifested in the charisms of the founders. These charisms spring up in his Church throughout the ages, expressing the power of his love to respond solicitously to human needs (LG:46). 756

Fidelity to one's own charism, then, is a concrete form of obedience to the saving grace of Christ, and of sanctification with him in order to redeem his brothers and sisters. It may have to do with education, health or social services, the parochial ministry, culture, art, or whatever. This renders the Spirit present, to evangelize human beings with his manifold richness. 757

2.3. Options for a Consecrated Life That Is More Evangelizing

Given direction by the teachings of *Evangelii Nuntiandi*, *Evangelica Testificatio*, and *Mutuae Relationes*, we pledge to work together with Major Superiors to implement the following options: 758

a. Deeper consecration. We pledge to use the most suitable means to intensify the living out of total, radical consecration to God. Such consecration involves two inseparable, complementary aspects: generous, total surrender and dedication to God; and service to the Church and all humanity. 759

We pledge to foster the attitude of prayer and contemplation that is born of the Word of the Lord, heeded and lived in the concrete circumstances of our history. 760

We pledge to set high value on the evangelizing witness of the consecrated life as a vital expression of the gospel values proclaimed in the Beatitudes. 761

We pledge to revitalize the consecrated life through fidelity to its specific 762 charism and the spirit of religious founders, responding to the new needs of the People of God.

763 We pledge to foster a vocational choice that will allow for a full, conscious decision and that will equip people for evangelizing service suited to the present and future of Latin America. To this end we will encourage serious training both at the start and as an ongoing program, a training that is adapted to the specific, changing circumstances of our real situation.

764 *b. Consecration as an expression of communion.* We pledge to increase fraternity in the communities, encouraging interpersonal relations within them that will foster integration and lead to greater communion and missionary collaboration. We pledge to encourage openness to inter-congregational relations which, while respecting the pluralism of specific charisms and the dispositions of the Holy See, will increase unity.

765 In our dioceses we pledge to create a climate of organic, spiritual ecclesial communion around the bishop that will enable religious communities to live out their specific form of membership in the diocesan family. In particular we want it to help priest religious to realize that they are co-workers of the episcopal order and that in a certain way they are part of the clergy of the diocese (CD:34). To that end, we propose to join together in studying ecclesial documents, particularly *Mutuae Relationes*, which deals with relations between bishops and religious in the Church.

766 We pledge to promote complete adherence to the Church's magisterium, avoiding any doctrinal or pastoral outlook that diverges from its guidelines (OAP:I,7).

767 We pledge to further knowledge of the theology of the local Church among religious and of the theology of the religious life among the diocesan clergy. The aim of this would be to shore up an authentic, organic pastoral effort at the diocesan level and in our episcopal conferences (MR:36–37).

768 We pledge to set up institutionalized relationships between episcopal conferences and other ecclesial organisms on the one hand and the national conferences of religious superiors and other organisms of religious men and women on the other. This would be in line with the criteria set down by the Holy See for relations between bishops and religious in the Church.

769 *c. A more committed mission effort.* We pledge to encourage religious to assume a preferential commitment to the poor, keeping in mind the words of John Paul II: "You are priests and religious; you are not social directors, political leaders, or functionaries of some temporal authority. So I repeat: Let us not entertain the delusion that we are serving the Gospel if we are trying to 'dilute' our charism through an exaggerated interest in the broad field of temporal problems" (AP:8).

770 We pledge to stimulate religious men and women to see to it that their evangelizing activity reaches into the fields of culture, art, social communication, and human promotion. In this way they will be able to make their specific evangelical contribution in accordance with their vocation and their specific situation in the Church.

771 We pledge to encourage the willingness and readiness of consecrated religious to assume the role of an evangelizing vanguard within the local Church (EN:69), while remaining in loyal communion with their pastors and their community and maintaining fidelity to the charism of their founders.

We pledge to encourage their fidelity to their original charism, and also its 772
adaptation and implementation in line with the needs of God's People. In this
way their works may have greater evangelical impact and effect.

We pledge to rekindle the missionary vitality of religious and their attitude of 773
generous-hearted availability. This will prompt them to give concrete, effective
responses to the problem of unequal distribution of evangelizing resources that
now exists.

2.4. Secular Institutes

Insofar as the Secular Institutes are concerned specifically, it is important to 774
recall that their particular charism is to respond directly to the great challenge
being posed to the Church by current cultural changes. They are to move toward
forms of secularized life required by the urban-industrial world, but without
allowing secularity to turn into secularism.

In our day the Spirit has brought into being this new type of consecrated life 775
represented by the Secular Institutes. They are somehow meant to help resolve
the tension existing between real openness to the values of the modern world
(authentic Christian secularity) and full, thoroughgoing submission of heart to
God (the spirit of consecration). Situated right in the center of this conflict, such
Institutes can be a valuable pastoral contribution to the future. They can help to
open up new pathways of general validity for the People of God.

On the other hand the very set of issues they seek to tackle, as well as their lack 776
of roots in an already tried and tested tradition, exposes them more than other
forms of the consecrated life to the crisis of our day and the contagion of
secularism. The hopes and the risks entailed in this way of life should spur the
Latin American episcopate to show special solicitude in fostering and supporting
their growth.

3. Lay People

*Here we deal with the participation of lay people in the life of the Church and in
its mission in the world.*

3.1. The Situation

Within the Latin American Church there is a growing awareness of the need for 777
the presence of the laity in the mission of evangelization. Recognizing this fact,
we offer our encouragement to the many lay people who, through their witness of
Christian commitment, help to carry out the task of evangelization and to present
the face of a Church committed to the work of promoting justice among our
peoples.

In our continent's present situation a particular challenge is posed to the laity 778
by the configuration that systems and structures are assuming. As a result of an
unequal process of industrialization, urbanization, and cultural transformation,
socioeconomic differences are deepening. This chiefly affects the masses of the
common people, leading to growing oppression and marginalization.

In trying to face up to these challenges since Vatican II and the Medellín 779

Conference, the Church in Latin America has had overall positive experiences and taken steps forward, as we noted in nos. 10ff. It has also encountered difficulties and crises (see nos. 16–27).

780   Some crises have naturally affected the Latin American laity, particularly the organized laity. They have suffered from the conflict-ridden assaults, not only of society itself (repression by groups with power), but also of a forceful process of ideologization and of distrust among themselves or among the institutions to which they belong. This has even gone so far as painful ruptures between the lay movements themselves, or between them and their pastors.

781   Today, however, we are seeing another aspect of the crisis and its positive consequences. There has been a progressive growth in serenity, maturity, and realism. This is expressed in open aspirations to promote structures of dialogue, participation, and coordinated pastoral action within the Church. It is also expressed in greater awareness of being a member of the Church.

782   This growing optimism in lay movements does not disregard the tensions that persist, however. Such tensions persist, both with respect to understanding the import of the lay person's commitment today in Latin America and with respect to the appropriate kind of involvement in ecclesial activity.

783   Whereas these tensions chiefly affect those participating in lay movements, large segments of the Latin American laity have not taken full cognizance of their membership in the Church. Their lives reveal an inconsistency between the faith they claim to profess and practice on the one hand and the real-life involvement they assume in society on the other hand. This divorce between faith and life is aggravated by secularism and by a system that gives priority to possessing more over being more.

784   Similarly, the effective advancement of the laity is often blocked by the persistence of a certain clerical mentality among many pastoral agents, among clergy, and even among lay people.

785   As just described, the social and ecclesial context has posed obstacles to the active, responsible participation of the laity in such important fields as politics and social and cultural activity, particularly among laborers and peasants.

3.2. Doctrinal Reflection

786   *The laity in the Church and in the world.* The mission of the laity finds its roots and meaning in their innermost being, which Vatican II was concerned to stress in some of its documents:

—Baptism and confirmation incorporate them into Christ and make them members of the Church.

—In their own way they share in Christ's function as prophet, priest, and king; and they exercise this function in terms of their own condition.

—Fidelity to, and consistency with, the resources and demands of their being give them their identity as human beings of the Church in the midst of the world, and human beings of the world living within the Church (LG:chap. IV).

787   The fact is that lay people, by virtue of their vocation, are situated in the Church and in the world. Members of the Church, loyal to Christ, they are pledged to the construction of the Kingdom in its temporal dimension.

788   In deep intercourse with their fellow lay persons and their pastors, in whom

they see their teachers in the faith, lay people help to build up the Church as a community of faith, prayer, and fraternal charity. They do this through catechesis, the sacramental life, and aid to their fellows.

Hence the multiplicity of the forms of the apostolate, each of which stresses one of the aforementioned aspects.

But it is in the world that the laity find their specific field of activity (EN:73). 789 Through the witness of their lives, timely speaking out, and concrete action, the laity have the responsibility of giving order to temporal realities and placing them in the service of the task of establishing God's Kingdom.

In the vast and complicated realm of temporal realities, some require the 790 special attention of the laity: the family, education, and social communications.

Among these temporal realities we cannot fail to place special emphasis on 791 political activity. This covers a wide range of activities: from voting, becoming politically active, and exercising party leadership, to holding public offices on various levels.

In every instance lay people should strive to seek and promote the common 792 good: defending the dignity of human beings and their inalienable rights; protecting those who are weakest and most in need; fashioning peace, freedom, and justice; and creating more just and fraternal structures.

So on our Latin American continent, which is characterized by serious prob- 793 lems of injustice that have grown even more acute, lay people cannot excuse themselves from a serious commitment to promote justice and the common good (AA:14). In undertaking this commitment they will always accept enlightenment from the faith and guidance from the Gospel and from the social doctrine of the Church; but they will also be guided by intelligence and aptitude geared toward effective action. "It is not enough for Christians to denounce injustices. They are also required to be truly witnesses to, and agents of, justice" (AWG:2).

As the participation of lay people in the life of the Church and its mission in the 794 world grows, there is an increasingly urgent need for them to acquire a solid overall human formation. This formation must be doctrinal, social, and apostolic. Lay people have the right to get this formation first and foremost in their own movements and associations, but also in adequate institutes and in contact with their pastors.

By the same token, lay people should contribute to the Church as a whole their 795 own experience of sharing in the problems, challenges, and urgent needs of their "secular world"—their world of persons, families, social groups, and peoples. This will ensure that ecclesial evangelization takes vigorous root. In this respect the laity, by virtue of their life experiences, their scholarly, professional, and work competence, and their Christian understanding, can make a precious contribution by offering all they can to examining, investigating, and developing the social teaching of the Church.

An important aspect of this formation has to do with delving deeper into a 796 spirituality that is more suited to the status of the lay person. Some of the essential dimensions of such a spirituality are the following:

—Lay people are not to flee from temporal realities in order to seek God. They 797 are to remain present and active amid those realities, and there find the Lord.

—To this presence and activity they are to add the inspiration of faith and a sense of Christian charity.

—Through the light of faith, they are to discover the presence of the Lord in that reality.

798 —In their mission, often riddled with conflict and tensions for their faith, they must strive to revitalize their Christian identity through contact with the Word of God, intimacy with Christ in the Eucharist, celebration of the other sacraments, and prayer.

799 Such a spirituality should be able to provide the Church and the world with "Christians who have a vocation to holiness—solid in their faith, secure in the doctrine proposed by the authentic magisterium, firm and active in the Church, grounded in a deep spiritual life, . . . persistent in evangelical witness and activity, consistent and courageous in their temporal commitments, constant as promoters of peace and justice in the face of all violence or oppression, keen in their critical-minded discernment of situations and ideologies in the light of the social teachings of the Church, and confident in their hope in the Lord" (ALP:6).

800 *The organized laity.* We express our confidence in, and our determination to give encouragement to, the organized forms of the lay apostolate because:

801 —Such organization is a sign of communion and participation in the life of the Church. It allows for the growth and transmission of experiences and the ongoing training and preparation of the members.

802 —The apostolate often requires joint action, both in church communities and various milieus.

803 —In a society where planning and structure is constantly increasing, the efficacy of apostolic activity will also depend on organization.

804 *Diversified ministries.* In carrying out its mission, the Church relies on a diversity of ministries (AA:21). Alongside the hierarchical ministries, the Church acknowledges there is a place for nonordained ministries. So the laity, too, can feel called or be called to collaborate with their pastors in service to the ecclesial community. For the life and growth of the community they may exercise various ministries, depending on the grace and charisms that the Lord gives them (EN:73).

805 The ministries that can be conferred on lay people are those services that relate to truly important aspects of ecclesial life: dealing, for example, with the word of God, the liturgy, or the direction of the community. These ministries are exercised by the laity in a stable way. They must be publicly recognized and conferred by those who hold responsibility in the Church.

3.3. Pastoral Criteria

806 *Criteria governing the laity involved in the overall, organized pastoral effort.* A revitalized pastoral effort on the part of the organized laity requires the following:

a. missionary vitality, including initiative and boldness to discover new fields for the evangelizing activity of the Church;

b. openness to coordinate one's activity with organizations and movements, in the realization that none of them enjoys exclusive claim to the Church's activity;

c. permanent and systematic channels of doctrinal and spiritual formation, involving updating of content and adequate pedagogy.

807 The diversity of the organized forms of the lay apostolate requires their pres-

ence and participation in the overall, coordinated pastoral effort. This is required both by the very nature of the Church, which is a mystery of communion between different members and ministers, and for the efficacy of pastoral activity, which demands the coordinated participation of all.

The participation of the laity is needed, not only in the execution of the overall pastoral effort, but also in the planning of that activity and in the decision-making organisms. 808

Lay involvement in the overall pastoral effort will ensure that the organized forms of the lay apostolate are related, as they must be, to the pastoral effort aimed at the great masses of the People of God. 809

The organized forms of the lay apostolate should give their members help, support, and enlightenment with regard to their political involvement. It is clear, however, that there are difficulties involved when leaders of apostolic movements also are active in political parties. These difficulties must be resolved with pastoral prudence, due account being taken of the principle that their apostolic movement should avoid commitment to a specific political party. 810

Pastoral criteria governing the ministries. The ministries that can be given to lay people should have the following characteristics:

—They are not to be clericalized. Those who receive them continue to be lay people, whose fundamental mission is to be present in the world. 811

—They require a vocation or aptitude that is ratified by the pastors. 812

—They are geared toward the life and growth of the ecclesial community, but they are not to lose sight of the service that the community must offer to the world. 813

—They are varied and diverse, in accordance with the charisms of those who are called and the needs of the community. But this diversity must be coordinated, by virtue of its relationship with the hierarchical ministry. 814

In the exercise of these ministries it would be well to avoid the following dangers:

a. The tendency to clericalize the laity or to reduce the lay commitment of those who receive such ministries. For that would overlook the fundamental mission of lay people, which is their involvement in temporal realities and their family responsibilities. 815

b. Such ministries are not to be promoted as a purely individual incentive, outside of a community context. 816

c. The exercise of ministries by some lay people cannot diminish the active participation of the rest. 817

3.4. Evaluation

To analyze and evaluate the current situation and the perspectives of the laity, we must do two things: (1) pinpoint the reality of their active presence in the various sectors that make up the social dynamics; (2) make clear the "caliber" of this presence. 818

To this end, we will use a frame of reference that has two dimensions:

The first, which allows us to quantify the presence of the laity, is the growth of functional realms (the realm of culture, work, etc.) vis-à-vis territorial areas (the neighborhood, the parish, etc.) as a result of the processes of industrialization and urbanization. 819

820   The second enables us to determine the quality of the laity's presence. In this case the indicative factor is how they understand the social reality, the being and mission of the Church.

Under the first dimension we may note:

821   —the existence of many lay people and lay movements in the local area (the neighborhood, the parish);

822   —the appreciable presence of lay people in the area of "pastoral support," though with deficiencies in training services. This would include services in providing doctrinal training for the laity, in inviting them to get involved and to nurture spirituality, etc.

823   —a very poor presence of the laity in the area of "constructing society" (workers, peasants, businesspeople, technical people, politicians, etc.). There is an almost total absence of lay people in the area of cultural creation and diffusion (intellectuals, artists, educators, students, and members of the social communications media).

Under the second dimension we may note:

824   —the persistence of lay people and lay movements that have not adequately undertaken the social dimension of their commitment, either because they are wedded to their own concerns for economic advantage and power, or because they are deficient in understanding and accepting the Church's social teaching. We also note other lay people and lay organizations that have stripped their apostolate of essential evangelical dimensions by excessively politicizing their commitment.

825   —the existence of lay movements that are distorted by excessive dependence on the initiatives of the hierarchy; and of others that give themselves so much autonomy that they separate themselves from the ecclesial community.

826   Finally, a fact of particular seriousness is the insufficient effort invested in discerning the causes and conditionings of social reality, particularly with regard to the means and instruments for transforming society. This is needed to shed light on the activity of Christians if they are to avoid uncritical assimilation of ideologies on the one hand or a spirituality of evasion on the other. This also enables them to go beyond mere denunciation and to find courses of action.

3.5. Conclusions

827   We urgently appeal to the laity to commit themselves to the evangelizing mission of the Church, of which the promotion of justice is an integral and indispensable part. This mission most directly relates to the activity of lay people, always performed in communion with their pastors.

828   We encourage the organized presence of the laity in the various areas of pastoral work. This would presuppose the integration and coordination of various movements and services within an overall, organic pastoral plan covering the lay sector.

829   We urge that special consideration be given to the organized laity with respect to ecclesial activity. They should be given adequate pastoral attention, and due appreciation should be shown for their role in the overall pastoral work of the Church.

830   In particular, special importance should be attached to establishing or activating diocesan or national departments of the laity, or other organs of coordination

and inspiration. Equally urgent attention should be paid to shoring up Latin American organs of lay movements, relying on the help that is being provided in this area by CELAM's Department of the Laity.

We also want to stress the important role that can be played by lay people who are called individually to service in the Church's institutions. This would apply particularly to educational institutions, organs of human and social promotion, and work in mission areas. **831**

We ask that centers or services be encouraged for the integral training of lay people and that such organisms put adequate emphasis on an active pedagogy that is complemented by systematic training in the fundamentals of the faith and the social teaching of the Church. We would also view organized movements as training tools—with their projects, experiences, work agendas, and evaluations. **832**

In Latin America, particularly in areas where hierarchical ministers are not in sufficient supply, special creativity should be encouraged, under the responsibility of the hierarchy, to establish ministries or services that can be exercised by the laity to meet the demands of evangelization. Special care should be invested in training the candidates adequately. **833**

3.6. Women

Though various parts of this document talk about women—as a nun, in the home, etc.—here we want to consider women in terms of their concrete contribution to evangelization in Latin America's present and future.

The situation. As is well known, women have been pushed to the margins of society as the result of cultural atavisms—male predominance, unequal wages, deficient education, etc. This is manifest in their almost total absence from political, economic, and social life. To these are added new forms of marginalization in a hedonistic consumer society, which even go to the extreme of transforming the woman into an object of consumption. This exploitation is camouflaged under the pretext that times are changing, a pretext disseminated by advertising, eroticism, pornography, etc. **834**

In many of our countries female prostitution is on the increase, due either to the stifling economic situation or to the acute moral crisis. **835**

In the work sector we note the evasion of, or non-compliance with, laws that protect women. Faced with this situation, women are not always organized to demand respect for their rights. **836**

In families women are overburdened, not only with domestic tasks but with professional work as well. In quite a few cases they must assume all the responsibilities because the man has abandoned the home. **837**

We must also consider the sad situation of female domestic employees. They are often subjected to maltreatment and exploitation by their employers. **838**

In the Church itself there has sometimes been an undervaluation of women and minimal participation by them in pastoral initiatives. **839**

But there are also positive signs that must be noted: the slow but increasing influx of women into tasks dealing with the construction of society and the resurgence of women's organizations working to advance women and to incorporate them into all areas. **840**

Reflection. First, we must consider *the equality and dignity of the woman*. Like **841**

the man, the woman is the image of God: "God created man in his image; in the divine image he created him; male and female he created them" (Gen. 1:27). Thus the task of ruling the world, continuing the work of creation, and being God's co-creators is woman's as much as man's.

842   Second, we must consider *the mission of woman in the Church*. As far back as the Old Testament we find that women played significant roles in the People of God. For example, there was Miriam, the sister of Moses; Anna; the prophetesses, Deborah and Hulda (2 Kings 22:14); Ruth; Judith; and others.

843   In the Church, women share in Christ's gifts and spread his witness through a life of faith and charity. Such were the Samaritan woman (John 4); the women who accompanied the Lord and served him with their goods (Luke 8:2); the women present on Calvary (John 19:25); the women who were sent by the Lord to tell the apostles that he had risen (John 20:17); and the women in the first Christian communities (Acts 1:14; Rom. 16:1–15).

844   But the prime example is Mary. At the Annunciation she unconditionally accepted the Word of God (Luke 1:26ff.). At the Visitation she went to serve and announced the presence of the Lord (Luke 1:39–45). In the Magnificat she prophetically sung of the freedom of the children of God and the fulfillment of the promise (Luke 1:46f.). At the Nativity she gave birth to the Word of God and offered him to the adoration of all those seeking him, whether simple shepherds or wise men from distant lands (Luke 2:1–8). In the flight into Egypt she accepted the consequences: the suspicion and persecution of which the Son of God was the object (Matt. 2:13–15). She accepted the mysterious and adorable behavior of the Lord, storing up everything in her heart (Luke 2:51). Present and attentive to human needs, she called forth the "messianic sign" that brought joy to the wedding feast (John 2:1–11). By the side of the cross she was strong and faithful, open to accepting a universal motherhood. She waited ardently for the fullness of the Spirit, along with the whole Church (Acts 1–2). And her Assumption is commemorated in the liturgy by the figure of the woman, the symbol of the Church in the Book of Revelation (Rev. 12).

845   With her specific aptitudes, the woman should make a real contribution to the Church's mission, participating in organisms for pastoral planning, pastoral coordination, catechesis, etc. (MR:49–50). The possibility of entrusting non-ordained ministries to women will open up new ways for them to participate in the Church's life and mission.

846   We wish to underline the fundamental role of the woman as mother, the defender of life and the home educator.

    Finally, there is *the mission of the woman in the world* (communion and participation, the common task).

847   —Our's peoples' aspirations for liberation include the human advancement of the woman as an authentic "sign of the times," which is supported by the biblical concept of the lordship of the human being, who was created "male and female."

848   —Women ought to be present in temporal realities, contributing their specific reality as women and participating with men in the transformation of society. The value of women's work should not be solely the satisfaction of economic needs. Work should also be an instrument for achieving personalization and building a new society.

849   *Conclusion.* The Church is summoned to contribute to the human and Christian advancement of women, thus helping them to move out of marginalized

situations in which they may now find themselves and equipping them for their mission in the ecclesial community and the world.

4. Pastoral Work on Behalf of Vocations

Pastoral work on behalf of vocations is a duty of the whole Church. We now consider this topic as well as the validity of seminaries.

4.1. The Situation

Some positive data. There is greater awareness of the problem of vocations and greater theological clarity about the unity and diversity of the Christian vocation. 850

There has been a successful increase in courses, meetings, workshop days, and conferences.

In most instances all this has taken place with collaboration between the diocesan clergy, religious men and women, and the laity. And it has been linked with pastoral work among young people, seminaries, and houses of formation.

In many countries apostolic youth groups and CEBs have been effective centers of pastoral work on behalf of vocations.

One visible fruit of this effort is the fact that in many countries we find a planned pastoral effort on behalf of vocations both on the national and the diocesan levels. This corresponds to the initiatives of the Sacred Congregation for Catholic Education.

In recent years there has been a noticeable increase in vocations to the priesthood and the consecrated life, even though it is not enough to meet our own needs and our missionary obligation to other Churches in greater need.

Among the laity, too, we note in recent years a growing advertence to their own specific vocation.

Some negative data. We are not adequately accompanying the laity in the discovery and maturation of their own specific Christian vocation. 851

A negative influence is being exercised by the "milieu," which is becoming more and more secularist, and more and more given to consumptionism and eroticism.

We see many shortcomings in the family.

We see great marginalization of the masses.

We see a lack of witness on the part of some priests and religious.

Among some priests, religious men and women, and lay people we see a lack of interest and an indifference insofar as pastoral work on behalf of vocations is concerned.

We see doctrinal deviations.

We see that pastoral work on behalf of vocations is not deeply integrated into family pastoral care, educational pastoral efforts, and the overall, coordinated pastoral effort.

4.2. Reflection and Criteria

The human vocation, Christian vocation, and specific Christian vocation. God calls each and every human being to faith. Through faith, all are called to enter the People of God by means of baptism. This summons through baptism, confirma- 852 tion, and the Eucharist to be God's People is a call to *communion and participation* in the life and mission of the Church, and hence in the evangelization of the world.

853   However, not all of us are sent out to serve and evangelize on the basis of the same function. Some do it as hierarchical ministers, some as lay people, and some as people dedicated to the consecrated life. Complementing each other, we all construct the Kingdom of God on earth.

854   According to God's plan, all of us Christians are to find fulfillment as human beings. This is our *human vocation*. We also are to find fulfillment as Christians, living out our baptism and its summons to be holy (communion and cooperation with God), to be active members of the community, and to bear witness to the Kingdom (communion and cooperation with others). This is our *Christian vocation*. Finally, we must discover the concrete vocation (as lay person, consecrated religious, or hierarchical minister) that will enable us to make our specific contribution to the construction of the Kingdom. This is our *specific Christian vocation*. In this way we will carry out our evangelizing mission in a full and organic way.

855   *Diversity in unity.* The hierarchical ministry (bishops, priests, and deacons) gives unity and authenticity to ecclesial service as a whole in its great task of evangelization.

856   The consecrated life in all its forms, with explicit mention of the contemplative life, is in itself "a privileged means of effective evangelization" (EN:69) by virtue of the radical nature of its witness.

857   With their special function in the world and society, lay people face a huge task of evangelization in the present and future of our continent.

858   Moreover, today the Holy Spirit is raising up a variety of ministries in the Church. These ministries, also exercised by lay people, are capable of rejuvenating and reinforcing the evangelical dynamism of the Church (EN:73).

859   Insofar as vocations to the priesthood and the consecrated life in the concrete are concerned, we make our own the words of John Paul II: "Despite an encouraging revival of vocations, the lack of vocations is a grave and chronic problem in most of your countries. . . . Lay vocations, indispensable as they are, cannot be a satisfactory compensation. What is more, one of the proofs of the laity's commitment is the abundance of vocations to the consecrated life" (OAP: IVb).

860   *God, community, and the individual.* Finding one's ministerial and evangelizing place in the Church does not depend solely on one's personal initiative. It is first and foremost a gratuitous call from God, a divine vocation. It must be perceived, through discernment, by listening to the Holy Spirit, standing before the Father through Christ, and confronting the concrete, historical community that is to be served. It is also the fruit and expression of the whole ecclesial community's vitality and maturity (OAP: I,7).

861   So any authentic pastoral work on behalf of vocations that attempts to help human beings in this process will have to be centered around the initial call, its subsequent maturation, and perseverance, engaging the whole community in this service.

862   *Prayer in pastoral work on behalf of vocations.* In the complex problem of vocations there must be uninterrupted recourse to personal and community prayer at every moment and on every level. It is God who calls; it is God who

gives efficacy to evangelization. Christ himself told us: "The harvest is rich but the workers are few; . . . ask the harvest-master to send workers to his harvest" (Luke 10:2).

An incarnate, differentiated pastoral effort. Because pastoral work on behalf of vocations is an evangelizing action and has that mission of the Church as its aim, it must be incarnate and differentiated. That is to say, it must offer a response, based on faith, to the concrete problems of each nation and region; and it must reflect the unity and variety of functions and services that are part of this diversified body whose head is Christ.   863

Today Latin America is engaged in trying to overcome its situation of under-development and injustice (see nos. 27–50 above). It is tempted by anti-Christian ideologies and coveted by extremist leaders and power centers. So it needs persons aware of their dignity and their historical responsibility. And it needs Christians jealous of their identity who, in line with their commitment, will be builders of a "more just, humane, and habitable world that will not close in on itself but rather open up to God" (HSD:3). Each person must do this in terms of his or her own place and function, and all must do it in communion and participation. This is the great challenge and service of evangelization in our continent's present and future; and it is also the great responsibility incumbent on our pastoral work on behalf of vocations. Here and now we praise and give our unqualified support to all those who are working in this area with faith, hope, and love.   864

The setting of pastoral work on behalf of vocations and its privileged locales. The period of youth is a privileged time for one's vocational option, though it is not the only time. Hence all pastoral work among youth should also be pastoral work on behalf of vocations. "An intensive pastoral effort must be reactivated. Starting off from the Christian vocation in general and an enthusiastic pastoral effort among young people, such an effort will give the Church the servants it needs" (OAP:IVb).   865

Pastoral work on behalf of vocations is also an essential dimension of family pastoral work and educational pastoral work. It should hold a place of priority in the overall, coordinated pastoral effort.   866

Privileged locales for pastoral work on behalf of vocations are the local Church, the parish, CEBs, the family, apostolic movements, youth groups and move-ments, educational centers, catechesis, and vocation efforts.   867

Likewise, special attention should also be paid to those who hear the call of the Lord to a specific Christian vocation in adulthood.   868

4.3. Seminaries

Most of our Churches see the need to ensure a solid human and Christian formation and a special religious formation (OT:3) prior to the major seminary.   869

Thoroughly renovated, the minor seminary must try to respond to this need. Indeed in some areas there has already been a positive response to this whole problem. In other areas we find training centers for the major seminary or similar initiatives.   870

One constant thing should be pursued in all of them: that young people do not lose contact with reality or get uprooted from their social context. It is worth   871 noting that all these formulas are an integral part of pastoral work on behalf of vocations among young people. Hence they should be closely tied up with the family, and they should lead young people to make a pastoral commitment that is suitable for their age.

872 Finally, all this should result in the young person acquiring a solid spirituality and making a free, mature choice.

873 The maturing and training process for the priestly vocation finds it most auspicious atmosphere in the "major seminary" or "house of formation," which Vatican II declared to be necessary for priestly formation (OT:4).

874 Insofar as seminaries are concerned, we see a strong spirit of renewal in Latin America that augurs much hope and promises a response to the whole problem of training. However, other formulas for the training of seminarians are required. They would not be parallel forms of training but rather experiments or experiences carried out with the approval of the episcopal conference and the Holy See for special situations (see the Circular of the Sacred Congregation for Catholic Education, 16 July 1976).

875 The major seminary, integrated into the life of the Church and the world in line with norms and specific guidelines from the Holy See, aims to accompany the full development of the future pastors' whole personality—human, spiritual, and pastoral. They are to have a strong experience of God and a clear-eyed vision of the reality they face in Latin America. In intimate communion with their bishop, the teacher of truth, and with other priests, they must be the ones who evangelize, inspire, and coordinate the different charisms of the People of God for the building up of the Kingdom (OAP:passim). The formation of pastors should be the constant concern giving direction to studies and the spiritual life. Pastoral activities should be re-examined in the light of faith, due counsel being taken with their educators.

876 Guided by sound spiritual direction, the seminarian will acquire experience of God, living constantly in communion with him in prayer, the Eucharist, and a solid, filial devotion to the Virgin Mary.

877 Insofar as studies are concerned, attention must be given to a deep doctrinal formation that corresponds to the Church's magisterium and to an adequate vision of reality.

878 In seminaries stress must be placed on austerity, discipline, responsibility, the spirit of poverty, and an atmosphere of authentic community life. Future priests must be trained for celibacy in a responsible way. All this is required by the renunciation and self-surrender demanded of the priest.

879 We want to stress the value of common centers of formation for the diocesan clergy and religious, in line with the norms of the Holy See. They are worthwhile for the communitarian sense they embody, and for their contribution to an integrated overall pastoral effort.

880 In lamenting the lack of trainers of priests, it is our duty to acknowledge and encourage all those who work at training future priests.

4.4. Options and Courses of Action

881 We must motivate, coordinate, and assist in the advancement and maturation of all vocations, especially vocations to the priesthood and the religious life, giving real priority to this task.

We must encourage campaigns of prayer so that the people will take cogni- 882
zance of existing needs. The vocation is the response of a provident God to the
praying community.

We must accompany all those who feel the summons of the Lord in the process 883
of discernment and help them to cultivate the dispositions that are basic to
vocational maturation.

All pastoral work on behalf of vocations must be fleshed out in the present 884
historical moment of Latin America. It must also be differentiated. That is to say,
it must reflect and promote a diversity of vocations in the unity of the Church's
mission and evangelizing service.

Pastoral work on behalf of vocations must be given the priority it rightfully 885
possesses in the overall pastoral effort and, more concretely, in pastoral work
among families and young people.

Special effort must be invested in promoting vocations among peasants, labor- 886
ers, and marginalized ethnic groups. Their later training must be planned out so
that it may be adequate (see the Circular of the Sacred Congregation for Catholic
Education, 16 July 1976).

At the same time more intense effort must be given to promoting priestly and 887
religious vocations in cities, among professionals, university students, etc.

We must faithfully implement the norms and guidelines of the Holy See and 888
the episcopal conferences with regard to seminaries. With the necessary adaptations, these norms and guidelines must also be observed by religious communities in the training of their priests.

We must train personnel who will dedicate themselves full-time to pastoral 889
work on behalf of vocations. And we must point out to them that their principal
mission is to inspire our whole pastoral effort along this line.

We must create advanced-training institutes for educators of priests on the 890
local and continental level; and we must also take advantage of international
institutes, particularly those in Rome.

We must arouse, promote, and give direction to missionary vocations, en- 891
visioning centers or seminaries for this specialized purpose.

CHAPTER III
MEDIA OF COMMUNION AND PARTICIPATION

As the people responsible for the ministry of evangelization, we are concerned 892
to know how to reach Latin Americans with the Word of God in such a way that it
will be heeded, assimilated, incarnated, and celebrated by them, and then
transmitted to their fellow human beings.

We know that it is God who ensures growth (1 Cor. 3:6–7), but the Lord of the 893
harvest expects collaboration from his servants. So we want to ponder the
principal means of evangelization through which the Church creates communion
and invites human beings to the service of their brothers and sisters.

The community, which joyfully celebrates the Lord's Pasch in the liturgy, has a 894
commitment to bear witness, catechize, educate, and communicate the Good
News through all the means at its disposal.

It also feels the need to enter into communion and dialogue with those human beings on our continent who are seeking truth.

1. Liturgy, Private Prayer, Popular Piety
2. Witness
3. Catechesis
4. Education
5. Social Communication

1. Liturgy, Private Prayer, Popular Piety

895   *Private prayer and popular piety, present in the soul of our people, constitute evangelization values. The liturgy is the privileged moment of communion and participation for an evangelization that leads to integral, authentic Christian liberation.*

1.1. The Situation

896   *a. Liturgy.* Liturgical renewal in Latin America is providing generally positive results. This is because we are rediscovering the real place of the liturgy in the Church's evangelizing mission, because the new liturgical books are encouraging greater comprehension and participation among the faithful, and because pre-sacramental catechesis is spreading.

897   All this has been inspired by the documents of the Holy See and episcopal conferences, as well as by meetings on various levels in Latin America—regional, national, etc.

898   This renewal has been facilitated by a common language, a rich cultural heritage, and popular piety.

899   We sense the need to adapt the liturgy to various cultures and to the situation of our people—young, poor, and simple (SC:37–40).

900   The lack of ministers, the scattered population, and the geographical situation of our continent have prompted us to take greater cognizance of the usefulness of celebrations of the Word, and of the importance of utilizing the media of social communication (radio and television) to reach all.

901   But our observation is that we have not yet given pastoral work devoted to the liturgy the priority it deserves within our overall pastoral effort. Much harm is still being done by the opposition evident in some sectors between evangelization on the one hand and sacramentalization on the other. The liturgical training of the clergy is not being deepened as it should be, and we note a marked absence of liturgical catechesis designed for the faithful.

902   Participation in the liturgy does not have an adequate impact on the social commitment of Christians. Sometimes the liturgy is used as a tool in ways that disfigure its evangelizing value.

903   The failure to observe liturgical norms and their pastoral spirit has also been harmful, leading to abuses that cause disorientation and division among the faithful.

904   *b. Private prayer.* The popular religiosity of Latin Americans contains a rich heritage of prayer. Rooted in the native cultures, it was later evangelized by the forms of Christian piety introduced by missionaries and immigrants.

The age-old custom of coming together to pray at festivals and on special occasions is one that we regard as a rich treasure. More recently this prayer-life has been enriched by the biblical movement, new forms of contemplative prayer, and the prayer-group movement. 905

Many Christian communities that have no ordained minister accompany and celebrate events and feasts by coming together for prayer and song. These meetings simultaneously evangelize the community and imbue it with an evangelizing dynamism. 906

In large areas family prayer has been the only form of worship in existence. In fact, it has preserved the unity and faith of the family and the common people. 907

The invasion of the home by radio and TV has jeopardized the pious practices carried out in the bosom of the family. 908

Even though prayer often arises from merely personal needs and finds expression in traditional formulas that have not really been assimilated, people must not overlook the fact that the vocation of Christians should lead them to a moral, social, and evangelizing commitment. 909

c. Popular piety. A popular piety, a piety of the common people, is evident among all the Catholic people of Latin America. It is evident on every level and it takes quite a variety of forms. We bishops must not overlook this piety. It must be scrutinized with theological and pastoral criteria so that its evangelizing potential may be discovered. 910

Latin America is insufficiently evangelized. The vast majority of the people express their faith predominantly in forms of popular piety. 911

The forms of popular piety are quite diverse, and they are both communal and personal in character. Among them we find the cultic worship of the suffering, crucified Christ; devotion to the Sacred Heart; various devotions to the Most Blessed Virgin Mary; devotion to the saints and the dead; processions; novenas; feasts of patron saints; pilgrimages to sanctuaries; sacramentals; promises; and so forth. 912

Popular piety presents such positive aspects as a sense of the sacred and the transcendent; openness to the Word of God; marked Marian devotion; an aptitude for prayer; a sense of friendship, charity, and family unity; an ability to suffer and to atone; Christian resignation in irremediable situations; and detachment from the material world. 913

But popular piety also presents negative aspects: lack of a sense of belonging to the Church; a divorce between faith and real life; a disinclination to receive the sacraments; an exaggerated estimation of devotion to the saints, to the detriment of knowing Jesus Christ and his mystery; a distorted idea of God; a utilitarian view of certain forms of piety; an inclination, in some places, toward religious syncretism; the infiltration of spiritism and, in some areas, of Oriental religious practices. 914

Too often forms of popular piety have been suppressed without valid reasons, or without replacing them with something better. 915

1.2. Doctrinal and Pastoral Criteria

a. The liturgy. All this renewal must be guided by an authentic theology of the liturgy. The theology of the sacraments is an important component of such a theology. This will help people to get beyond a neo-ritualistic outlook. 916

917   Through Christ and in the Spirit, the Father sanctifies the Church. He then sanctifies the world through the Church. And then the world and the Church, through Christ and in the Spirit, give glory to the Father.

918   As an action of Christ and the Church, the liturgy is the exercise of the priesthood of Jesus Christ (SC:7). It is the summit and source of ecclesial life (SC:10). It is an encounter with God and one's fellows; a banquet and sacrifice realized in the Eucharist; a feast of ecclesial communion. In it the Lord Jesus, through his paschal mystery, assumes and liberates the People of God and, through that People, all humanity. Their history is converted into a salvation history designed to reconcile human beings with each other and with God. The liturgy is also a force operative in our wayfaring pilgrimage so that we, through a life-transforming commitment, can bring about the full realization of the Kingdom in accordance with God's plan.

In the local Church "the bishop is to be considered the high priest of his flock. In a certain sense it is from him that the faithful who are under his care derive and maintain their life in Christ" (SC:41).

920   Human beings are sacramental beings. On the religious level human beings express their relationship with God through a complex of signs and symbols. God likewise uses signs and symbols in communicating with human beings. In a certain sense all creation is a sacrament of God because it reveals God to us (Rom. 1:19).

Christ "is the image of the Invisible God" (Col. 1:15). As such, he is the primordial, radical sacrament of the Father: "Whoever has seen me has seen the Father" (John 14:9).

922   The Church in turn is the sacrament of Christ (LG:1), designed to communicate the new life to human beings. The seven sacraments of the Church concretize and actualize this sacramental reality for the different situations of life.

923   So it is not enough to receive them in a passive way. They must be received in a lively spirit and in the context of ecclesial communion. Through the sacraments Christ continues to meet human beings and save them, thanks to the activity of the Church.

The Eucharistic celebration, the center of the sacramental life of the Church and the fullest presence of Christ in humanity, is the center and summit of the whole sacramental life (SC:10).

924   Liturgical renewal must be guided by pastoral criteria that are grounded in the very nature of the liturgy and its evangelizing function.

925   Liturgical renewal and reform encourage the participation that leads to communion. Fully conscious and active participation in the liturgy is the primary and necessary wellspring of a truly Christian spirit (SC:14). So pastoral considerations, while always respecting the observance of liturgical norms, should move beyond simple rubricism.

926   The signs are important in all liturgical action. They should be employed in a vital and fitting way, and they presuppose an adequate catechesis. The adaptations envisioned in the conciliar decree *Sacrosanctum Concilium* and in subsequent pastoral norms are indispensable for achieving a rite that is suited to our needs. This is particularly true in the case of plain, simple people, whose legitimate cultural expressions must be taken into account.

927   No pastoral activity can be carried out without reference to the liturgy. Liturgical celebrations presuppose initiation into the faith through evangelical procla-

mation, catechesis, and biblical preaching. This is the underlying reason for pre-sacramental courses and encounters.

On the other hand, every celebration should have an evangelizing and catechetical thrust, adapted to the various kinds of assemblies of the faithful—small groups, children, popular groups, etc. **928**

Celebrations of the Word, with numerous, varied, and well-chosen readings from Sacred Scripture (SC:35 [4]), are of great benefit to the community—particularly in the absence of priests, and especially in the carrying out of Sunday worship. **929**

As part of the liturgy, the homily is a privileged occasion for discussing the mystery of Christ in the here and now of the community's life. It should start off from the sacred texts, relate them to the sacrament, and apply them to concrete life. Care should be taken in preparing the homily, and its length should be in due proportion to other parts of the celebration. **930**

The one who presides over the celebration is the director [*animador*] of the community. By his work he fosters the participation of the faithful. This explains the importance of a worthy and proper form of celebrating the liturgy. **931**

b. Private prayer. First let us consider the example of Christ at prayer. The Lord Jesus, who went about on earth doing good and proclaiming the Word, dedicated many hours to prayer under the impulse of the Spirit. He spoke to the Father with filial trust and in an incomparably intimate way. He gave an example to his disciples, whom he expressly taught how to pray. Moved by the Holy Spirit, Christians will make prayer a motif of their daily life and work. Prayer creates in them an attitude of praise and thanks to the Lord; increases their faith; confirms them in an active hope; induces them to give themselves to their brothers and sisters and to be faithful to the apostolic task; and equips them to form a community. The Church, praying in its members, is joined in oneness to the prayer of Christ. **932**

Then there is family prayer. As both evangelized and evangelizer, the Christian family must follow the example of the praying Christ. The family's prayer manifests and sustains the life of the domestic Church, where the seed of the Gospel is received with a welcome. That seed grows to qualify all the members as apostles, and to turn the family into a nucleus of evangelization. **933**

The liturgy does not exhaust all the activity of the Church. Also to be recommended are the pious exercises of the Christian people, provided that they accord with the Church's norms and laws. In a certain way these exercises are derived from the liturgy and lead back to it (SC:13). The mystery of Christ is one; but in its richness it shows various forms and ways of reaching human beings. Thanks to their rich religious heritage, and due to the pressure of temporal and spatial circumstances, Christian communities become active evangelizers by living a life of prayer. **934**

c. Popular piety. The piety of the common people leads to love for God and human persons. It also helps persons and peoples to take cognizance of their responsibility in realizing their own destiny (GS:18). Authentic popular piety, grounded in the Word of God, contains evangelical values that help to deepen the faith of the people. **935**

The expression of popular piety should respect native cultural elements (see nos. 444ff. above). **936**

To be an effective element of evangelization, popular piety needs constant **937** purification and clarification. It must lead people, not only toward belonging to the Church, but also toward living the Christian life and commiting oneself to one's fellow human beings.

1.3. Conclusions

938   *a. The liturgy.* We wish to give the liturgy its true dimensions as the summit and source of the Church's activity (SC:10).

939   We wish to celebrate our faith in the liturgy as an encounter with God and our brothers and sisters; as a feast of ecclesial communion; as a source of strength for our pilgrimage; and as a commitment to our Christian way of life. We particularly wish to give special importance to the Sunday liturgy.

940   We wish to give full value once again to the force of "signs" and their theology.

We wish to celebrate our faith in the liturgy with cultural expressions that display a sound creativity. We wish to foster suitable adaptations, particularly with respect to ethnic groups and the simple folk (popular groups). But we also want to take care that the liturgy is not expropriated for aims that are alien to its nature, that the norms of the Holy See are faithfully kept, and that all arbitrariness is avoided in liturgical celebrations.

941   We wish to study the catechetical and evangelizing function of the liturgy.

942   We wish to promote the training of agents involved in pastoral efforts on behalf of the liturgy, to offer them an authentic theology that will lead them to a living commitment.

943   We want to try to provide those who preside over liturgical celebrations with conditions that will improve their function and lead to lively communication with the assembly. Special effort should be put into the preparation of the homily, which has great value for evangelization.

944   We wish to foster celebrations of the Word that are directed by deacons or lay people (men and women).

945   Care should be put into preparing and carrying out the liturgy of the sacraments, of the great feasts, and of the ceremonies held in sanctuaries.

946   The celebration of the Word at funerals and in acts of popular devotion should be utilized as a propitious occasion for evangelization.

947   We propose to promote sacred music as an eminent service that is consistent with the character of our people.

948   We propose to respect our patrimony of religious art, and to encourage artistic creativity suited to the new liturgical forms.

949   We propose to increase the number of celebrations carried by radio and television, taking due account of the nature of the liturgy and the character of the particular communications media being utilized.

950   We propose to encourage meetings in preparation for the celebration of the sacraments.

951   We propose to utilize the potential offered by the new rituals of the sacraments. Priests will dedicate themselves in a special way to administering the sacrament of reconciliation.

952   *b. Private prayer.* The diocese in its overall pastoral effort, the parish, and smaller communities (CEBs and families) will integrate personal and community prayer into their programs of evangelization.

953   We shall try to make sure that all the activities of the Church (meetings, use of

the media of social communication, social works, etc.) are an occasion for, and a school of, prayer.

We propose to use seminaries, monasteries, schools, and other training centers as privileged locales for praying, radiating a life of prayer, and forming teachers of prayer. 954

Priests, religious, and committed lay people should distinguish themselves in prayer, and in teaching prayer to the People of God. 955

We should promote works that foster the sanctification of work and the prayer of the sick and the disabled. 956

We must foster those forms of popular piety that help to promote personal, family, group, and community prayer. 957

We must integrate prayer groups into the organic pastoral effort so that they lead their members to the liturgy, evangelization, and social involvement. 958

c. Popular piety. Pastoral agents must try to recover the evangelizing values of popular piety in its varied personal and mass manifestations. 959

Popular piety will be used as a starting point in trying to make sure that the faith of the people acquires maturity and depth. To this end, popular piety is to be based on the Word of God and on a sense of membership in the Church. 960

The people are not to be deprived of their expressions of popular piety. Where changes are necessary, we should proceed gradually and there should be prior catechesis so as to arrive at something better. 961

The sacramentals are to be geared toward helping people to acknowledge the gifts of God and to become increasingly aware of the commitment the Christian has in the world. 962

Devotion to Mary and the saints is to be presented as the realization of Christ's Pasch in them (SC:104). People are to be reminded that such devotion should lead them to live out the Word and to bear witness in their lives. 963

2. Witness

2.1. The Situation

Throughout its history, the Church in Latin America has borne witness to its beliefs in various ways. Its fidelity to the Vicar of Christ, mutual aid among the local Churches, and the existence and labors of CELAM are signs of the communion in which it lives. 964

Thanks to countless priests, religious men and women, missionaries, and lay people, the Church has been present among the poorest and neediest: preaching the Christian message; fleshing out the charity that the Spirit pours out in it for the integral promotion of the human being; and bearing witness that the Gospel has the power to elevate and dignify humanity. 965

Not all the members of the Church, however, have shown respect for human beings and their culture. Many have demonstrated a faith with little strength to overcome their egotism, their individualism, and their greedy hold on riches. They have acted unjustly and injured the unity of society and the Church itself. 966

2.2. Doctrinal Criteria

Christ, the first evangelizer and faithful witness (Rev. 1:5), evangelizes by bearing truthful witness to what he has seen in the Father's presence. He does 967 what he sees the Father doing (John 5:19). His actions testify that he has come from the Father.

968   Authentic Christians, united with Jesus, bear this same witness in their own turn. Through their actions they testify to the love that the Father has for human beings, to the saving power with which Jesus Christ liberates people from sin, and to the love that has been poured out by the Spirit that dwells in them. This love is capable of creating authentic communion with the Father and their fellow human beings.

969   The works of Christians guided by the Spirit are love, communion, participation, solidarity, self-mastery, joy, hope, justice achieved in peace (James 3:18), chastity, unselfish giving of self—in a word, all that goes to make up holiness. This is to be accompanied by reception of the sacraments, prayer, and intense devotion to Mary.

970   The true witness of Christians, then, is the manifestation of the works that God is carrying out in human beings. The witness given by human beings is not based on their own capacities. It is based on their confidence in the power of God that transforms them and in the mission God confers on them.

2.3. Pastoral Criteria

971   Witness is a primary element of evangelization and an essential condition for the real-life efficacy of preaching (EN:21, 49, 76). Hence it must always be present in the life and evangelizing activity of the Church. It is only in this way that witness, in the context of life in Latin America, will be a "sign" that leads people to a desire to know the Good News and that bears witness to the Lord's presence among us.

972   Given the situation in which our peoples live, the fruits of the Spirit that make up the core of our witness involve certain implications for us. All of us— hierarchy, laity, and religious—must live in an ongoing process of self-criticism, in the light of the Gospel, on the personal, group, and community levels. This we must do if we are to rid ourselves of every attitude that is not evangelical and that disfigures the visage of Christ (DT:607).

973   This is our first pastoral option: the Christian community itself—its lay people, pastors, ministers, and religious—must be converted more and more to the Gospel so that they will be able to evangelize others.

974   Above all, it is important that we, as a community, re-examine our communion and involvement with the poor, the lowly, and the common people. That means we must hear them, accept their deepest aspirations, esteem them, and offer discernment, encouragement, and correction. We must allow the Lord to guide us so that we can truly effect unity with them in one same body and one same spirit.

975   This imposes on us a more assiduous prayer life; deeper meditation on the Scriptures; real, inner, Gospel-based divestiture of our privileges, ways of thinking, ideologies, preferential relationships, and material goods (EN:76); greater simplicity of life; real commitment to the task of carrying out such important things as the complete payment of the "social mortgage" on property; the Christian sharing of material and spiritual goods; collaboration in community activities on behalf of human advancement; and a broad range of charitable works

whose minimal demand is justice, along with the greatest amount of freedom vis-à-vis perverted criteria and centers of power.

On the continental level it is also important that the Church move forward in carrying out the signs that witness to its interior vitality. These signs include greater solidarity with the local Churches and better pastoral coordination through CELAM. The latter organization must go on serving episcopal collegiality and intraecclesial communion in Latin America.

976

3. Catechesis

Catechesis, "which consists in ordered and progressive education in the faith" **977**
(1977 Synod of Bishops, Message on Catechesis:1), must be a priority activity in Latin America if we wish to achieve a deep-rooted renovation of the Christian life, that is to say, if we wish to arrive at a new civilization that signifies communion and sharing between persons in the Church and in society.

3.1. the Situation

From a historical standpoint, we can note positive and negative aspects in catechesis since the Medellín Conference.

Positively speaking, we find a flowering of catechetical activity in new and rich **978**
experiences in different countries. For example:

—A sincere effort to integrate faith and life, human history and salvation **979**
history, the human condition and revealed doctrine, so that human beings may achieve their true liberation.

—A positive catechetical pedagogy that starts off from the person of Christ and **980**
moves on to his precepts and counsels.

—A more refined love for Sacred Scripture as the principal source of catechesis. **981**

—An education focusing on the constructive, critical meaning of the person **982**
and the community in the framework of a Christian vision.

—A rediscovery of the community dimension, with the result that the ecclesial **983**
community is assuming responsibility for catechesis at every level. That would include the family, the parish, CEBs, the school community, and diocesan and national organization.

—An ever-increasing realization that catechesis is a dynamic, gradual, on- **984**
going process of education in the faith.

—An increase of institutes for the training of catechists in many areas and on all **985**
levels—diocesan, national, and international.

—A proliferation of catechism texts. This is sometimes positive and sometimes **986**
negative. It is the latter insofar as the texts are partial or unrevised.

We find the following negative aspects:

—Catechesis does not reach all Christians to a sufficient degree. Nor does it **987**
reach all sectors and situations: e.g., broad segments of young people, intellectual elites, peasants and workers, the Armed Forces, old people, the sick, and so forth.

—There is a tendency to succumb frequently to various forms of dualism and **988**
false antitheses: e.g., between a catechesis of the sacraments and a catechesis of real life, or between a catechesis focusing on the real-life situation and a

catechesis focusing on doctrines. Failing to find a proper balance, some have fallen into formulism while others have concentrated on real life without presenting doctrines. And some have moved from total emphasis on memorization to a total neglect of the use of memory.

989 —We find catechists who disregard initiation into prayer and the liturgy.

990 —Sometimes there is no real respect for the proper area of competence of theologians and catechists (OAP:I,4), in harmony with the Church's magisterium. This has meant that concepts based on theological or scholarly hypotheses have been spread among catechists.

991 —We find that catechetical attitudes with regard to ecumenism display a certain amount of disorientation.

3.2. Theological Criteria

992 *a. Communion and participation.* The work of evangelization carried out in catechesis demands communion between all. It demands that there be no divisions and that persons encounter each other in an adult faith and an evangelical love (DT:611, 612). One of the goals of catechesis is precisely the building up of the community.

993 The collaboration of all the members of the ecclesial community is required, each in accordance with his or her own ministry and charism. Apostolic and missionary responsibilities cannot be evaded if the Church is to build up the Church in catechesis (EN:13–14). The Church is evangelized and evangelizing in a constant, ongoing way.

994 *b. Fidelity to God.* Fidelity to God finds expression in catechesis as fidelity to the Word given in Jesus Christ. Catechists preach Jesus Christ, not themselves, in fidelity to his Word (DT:632,633; EN:8,9,22,27,42) and his whole message.

995 *c. Fidelity to the Church.* All catechists know that fidelity to Jesus Christ is indissolubly bound up with fidelity to the Church (EN:16); that their labor continually builds up the community and transmits the image of the Church (DT:631); and that this should be done in union with the bishops and the mission received from them.

996 *d. Fidelity to the Latin American.* Fidelity to the human beings of Latin America requires that catechesis penetrate, take up, and purify the values of their culture (DT:417). This means that every effort must be made by the catechists to focus on the use and adaptation of their idiom.

997 So catechesis should shed the light of God's Word on human situations and the happenings of real life, to help people discover in them the presence or absence of God.

998 *e. Conversion and growth.* Catechesis should lead to a process of ongoing, progressive conversion and growth in the faith.

999 *f. An integrative catechesis.* "In any integral catechesis we should always find the following things brought together in an inseparable way:
—knowledge of the Word of God;
—the celebration of faith in the sacraments;
—the profession of faith in day-to-day life" (1977 Synod of Bishops, Message on Catechesis:11).

3.3. Pastoral Projects

To carry out its evangelizing mission in Latin America, catechesis will have to keep the following obligations in mind:

a. The obligation to form human beings who are personally committed to Christ, capable of participation and communion within the Church, and dedicated to serving the world in a salvific way. **1000**

b. The obligation to take sacred Scripture as our principal source, reading it in the context of life and in the light of tradition and the Church's magisterium, and also transmitting the creed of faith. So importance will be attributed to the biblical apostolate. We will spread the Word of God, form Bible groups, etc.* **1001**

c. The obligation to give pastoral priority to the adequate training of catechists in different institutes. We will take care that they receive specialized training for the differing situations, ages, and regions of those being catechized: e.g., small children, teenagers, peasants, laborers, members of the Armed Forces, elites, sick people, the retarded, convicts, etc. **1002**

d. The urgent obligation to adapt the *ratio studiorum* in training institutes for priests and religious, in order to teach them more intensively how to transmit the gospel message in an adequate and contemporary way. **1003**

Catechists will endeavor to do the following:

—To proclaim the whole, integral Word of God in order to get beyond dualism, false antitheses, and one-sidedness; **1004**

—To initiate their pupils into prayer and the liturgy, witness and apostolic commitment; **1005**

—To impart a catechesis that is vocationally oriented, explaining the vocation of the lay person as well. They will try to evoke a commitment suited to people's different ages, from early childhood to adulthood. **1006**

—As educators of persons and communities in the faith, to concentrate on a methodology that takes the form of a steady, ongoing process. This would entail various stages, including conversion, faith in Christ, life in community, the sacramental life, and apostolic commitment (Acts 2:38–42). **1007**

—To provide an integral education in their faith that would include the following aspects: equipping Christians to give reasons for their hope (1 Pet. 3:15); a capacity to dialogue ecumenically with other Christians; a solid formation for the moral life, lived as the following of Christ, with stress laid on practicing the Beatitudes; gradual training for a positive, Christian sexual ethics; training for political life and for the social doctrine of the Church. **1008**

Methodology. Catechists will take into account the importance of memory. As Paul VI put it, people should "memorize the most important sentences of the Bible, especially those of the New Testament, as well as the liturgical texts that are used for prayer in common and to facilitate the profession of faith" (Address at the close of the 1977 Synod of Bishops). They will also give importance to audiovisual techniques: pictures, mini-media, dramatizations, songs, etc. **1009**

Catechetical activity. It will be aimed simultaneously at groups and large **1010**

---

*This was the aim behind the establishment of the Catholic World Biblical Federation.

crowds. Insofar as the latter are concerned, there is great effectiveness in popular missions that are suitably revised to meet the needs of evangelization.

1011 Ongoing, permanent catechesis from early childhood to old age will be fostered. To this end, the communities or institutions that engage in catechesis will be fully integrated with each other: i.e., the family, the school, the parish, various movements, and diverse communities or groups.

4. Education

1012 *In the eyes of the Church, educating the human being is an integral part of its evangelizing mission, a continuation of Christ's mission as Teacher (EC:9).*

1013 *When the Church evangelizes and effects the conversion of human beings, it also educates them. For salvation (a gratuitous divine gift), far from dehumanizing human beings, perfects them, ennobles them, and helps them to grow in humanness (PP:15–17). In that sense evangelization is education. But education as such, rather than being part of the essential content of evangelization, is more a part of its complete, overall content.*

4.1. The Situation

1014 In our region the work of education is being carried out in a situation characterized by sociocultural change. Its features include the secularization of culture, influenced by the media of mass communication and by quantitative economic growth. Though such growth has represented some progress, it has not given rise to the changes required to produce a more just and balanced society. The situation of poverty that affects the great majority of our peoples displays a significant correlation with the educational processes. The downtrodden sectors have the highest rates of illiteracy and dropping out of school, and the least chances for getting a job.

1015 A real problematic situation in some countries is the presence of aboriginal groups. Despite their cultural values (forms of social organization, symbolic systems, customs, community celebrations, arts, and manual skills), they lack structured forms of education, writing, certain aptitudes and mental habits. These circumstances marginalize them and place them at a disadvantage. As a result, conventional educational institutions strike them, not only as alien but also as non-functional, because they uproot them from the community.

1016 Population growth has accelerated the demand for education at every level— elementary school, high school, and beyond. This has been matched by a considerable increase in the education offered, especially by the state sector. But the distribution of fiscal resources tends to be governed by political criteria rather than a preference for the less favored segments of the population. Despite difficulties, private initiatives and institutions attached to the Church have helped to increase the available educational possibilities.

1017 Relations between Church and State on educational matters vary from country to country. In some we find legal or de facto forms of real cooperation. In others we find situations of conflict, especially where the State has a monopoly on education. In general, dialogue depends on the political situation. Some governments have come to regard certain features and contents of Christian education as subversive.

The growing demand for education of various sorts also poses new challenges to the Church. This holds true in the area of conventional education (schools and universities), and also in other areas: adult education; informal, unsystematic home education from a distant source—this development being closely bound up with the notable development of the modern media of communication; and finally, the broad possibilities opened up by continuing education. 1018

Religious educators are raising questions about the Catholic school institution: because it is alleged to foster elitism and class-attachments; because the results seem to be meager with regard to education in the faith and social changes; because there are financial problems; and so forth. This is one of the reasons why many religious have abandoned the field of education for a type of pastoral activity that they regard as more direct, worthwhile, and urgent. 1019

We note with satisfaction the growing presence of lay people in the Church's educational institutions and the involvement of responsible Christians in every area of education. 1020

We discern ideological influences in the way that education, even Christian education, is conceived. One conception is utilitarian and individualistic. It views education simply as a means to ensure oneself a good future, an investment in tomorrow. Another view seeks to turn education into a tool, not for individualistic ends but for the benefit of a certain kind of sociopolitical project, be it statist or collectivist. 1021

Difficulties are being encountered in coordinating the agents and agencies of church education, with each other and with the bishops, either because the leadership of the latter is not fully accepted or because a real concern and commitment to education is missing among the pastors. As a result, one can also see deficiencies in educational planning and a certain inability to determine objectives. 1022

The idea of an "educational community, or polity" is growing. It means integrating all the actual or potential educational facilities of the community, starting with the family and placing special stress on it. This conception is transforming some schools into real agents of evangelization. 1023

4.2. Principles and Criteria

Education is a human activity in the cultural order. Culture has an essentially humanizing aim (GS:53, 55, 56, 59, 61). So it is obvious that the aim of all genuine education is to humanize and personalize human beings. Rather than putting them on the wrong track, education should effectively point them toward their ultimate goal (DIM:3; GE:1), which transcends the essential finiteness of the human being. Education is more humanizing to the extent that it is more open to transcendence: i.e., to truth and the Supreme Good. 1024

Education humanizes and personalizes human beings when it ensures that they fully develop their thinking and their freedom and that these bear fruit in habits of understanding and communion with the totality of the real order. It is 1025 through such habits that human beings humanize their world, produce culture, transform society, and construct history (GS:55).

1026   Evangelizing education assumes and completes the notion of liberating education. For it should contribute to the conversion of the total human being—not just the innermost, individual ego of the person but also that person's peripheral and social ego. It should radically orient human beings to genuine Christian freedom, which opens them to full participation in the mystery of the risen Christ: i.e., to filial communion with the Father and to fraternal communion with all their fellow beings (EN:27,29–30,33; Med-ED:8).

So this evangelizing education should include the following characteristics among others:

1027   **a.** It should humanize and personalize human beings, creating in them a place where the Good News about the Father's saving plan in Christ and his Church can be revealed and heeded.

1028   **b.** It should be integrated into Latin America's social process. That process has been impregnated by a radically Christian culture; but this culture contains both values and anti-values, lights and shadows, and hence must be constantly evangelized over again.

1029   **c.** It should exercise the critical function proper to any authentic education. From an educational standpoint it should try to keep regenerating the cultural standards and the norms of social interaction that will enable people to create a new society that is truly fraternal and participative. In short, it should be education for justice.

1030   **d.** It should turn the pupils into active subjects, not only of their own development, but also of service dedicated to the development of the community. It should be education for service.

With what was said above in mind, we enumerate the following criteria:

1031   **a.** Catholic education is part of the Church's evangelizing mission (EC:9), and it should explicitly announce Christ the Liberator (EN:22).

1032   **b.** Catholic education must not lose sight of the concrete, historical situation in which human beings find themselves: i.e., a sinful situation on both the individual and social level. Hence the aim must be to form strong personalities who are capable of resisting any debilitating relativism and of living out the demands of baptism in a consistent way (EC:12).

1033   **c.** Catholic education must produce the agents who will effect the permanent, organic change that Latin American society needs (Med-ED:8). This is to be done through a civic and political formation that takes its inspiration from the Church's social teaching (OAP:I,9).

1034   **d.** As persons, all human beings have an inalienable right to an education that accords with their goal, character, and sex, and that is adapted to the culture and traditions of their homeland (GE:1). Those who do not receive this education should be regarded as the poorest of the poor (PP:35; AY:4), and hence most in need of the Church's educational work.

1035   **e.** The Christian educator performs a humane and evangelizing mission. The educational institutions of the Church receive an apostolic mandate from the hierarchy (EC:71).

1036   **f.** The family is primarily responsible for education. All educational work must equip the family so that it can exercise this mission.

g. The Church proclaims freedom of education, not to foster privileges or private profit, but as a right to the truth belonging to persons and communities (GE:6; EC:11).   1037

At the same time the Church is ready to collaborate in the educational task of our pluralistic society (EC:14).

h. In line with the two aforementioned principles, the State should distribute its budget fairly among non-governmental educational services so that parents, who also are contributors, can freely choose the education they want for their children.   1038

4.3. Pastoral Suggestions

To promote, together with the agents of family pastoral work, the responsibility of the family, especially the parents, in every aspect of the educational process.   1039

Without forgetting other responsibilities of the Church in the area of education, to reaffirm effectively the importance of the Catholic school at every level. Efforts should be made to further its democratization and to transform it into the following, in line with the guidelines proposed by the Sacred Congregation for Catholic Education: 1040

—an effective medium for the critical, systematic, and integrative assimilation of knowledge and general culture;

—a more suitable locale for dialogue between the faith and scholarly science;

—a privileged milieu for fostering and stimulating growth in the faith; this would not depend solely on programmed courses in religion (EC:50);

—a valid alternative for educational pluralism.

To help religious educators, especially young ones, to rediscover and deepen the pastoral meaning of their school work, in accordance with their specific charism; and to help them in this difficult task.   1041

To encourage Christian educators, particularly lay people, to assume their membership and role in the Church as people called to share the Church's evangelizing mission in the field of education.   1042

To give priority in the educational field to the many poor segments of our population, who are materially and culturally marginalized. By way of preference, the educational services and resources of the Church should be geared toward them, with the agreement of the Ordinary of the area.   1043

Of equal priority is the education of leaders and agents of change.   1044

To combine literacy training of marginal groups with educational activities that will help them to communicate effectively; to take cognizance of their rights and duties; to understand the situation in which they are living and its causes; to organize effectively in the fields of civil life, labor, politics, and government power; and hence to participate fully in the decision-making processes that affect them.   1045

Without disregarding current educational commitments in the school sector, it is urgent that educators respond generously and imaginatively to the challenges that confront the Latin American Church in the present and the future. These new forms of educational activity cannot be the product of improvisation or whimsy. Their agents must be properly trained. They must be based on objective   1046 diagnoses of needs and on an inventory and evaluation of resources. The use of participatory methods would be advisable.

1047   To promote popular education (informal education) in order to revitalize our popular culture. Use should be made of picture and sound media that creatively bring out the profoundly Christian values and symbols of Latin American culture.

1048   To stimulate every sector of the civic community. To this end frank and receptive dialogue must be established so that the community will assume its educational responsibilites and succeed in transforming itself, along with its institutions and resources, into an authentic "educational polity."

1049   To foster the coordination of educational tasks, agents, and institutions in the pastoral activity of the local Church by means of a competent organism under the bishop. Planning and evaluation will be under its charge. There must be an objective evaluation of activities, structures, and situations that will ensure a better utilization of resources. It might entail altering, eliminating, or creating institutions and programs.

1050   To develop the Christian doctrine or theory of education, especially on the level of episcopal commissions. This theory is based on the teachings of the Church and on pastoral experience. In the light of that doctrine we could then examine the objectives, principles, and methods of the existing educational systems in order to interpret them satisfactorily and evaluate their results critically. We have an urgent obligation to elaborate, on the basis of this theory, a Christian educational project (EC:4) on the national or continental level. This should provide the inspiration for the concrete philosophy of various educational institutions to.

4.4. Universities

1051   In the last ten years there has been an enormous demand for higher education. There has been a massive enrollment of young Latin Americans in universities, prompted in large part by the accelerated development of our countries. This phenomenon has brought a serious problem to light: the inability of our educational and social system to satisfy the demands placed on it. This inability frustrates thousands of young people. Many never get into a university, and many of those who do get in find themselves unemployed when they graduate.

1052   The secularization of culture, the progress of technology, and the advances made in the social and anthropological disciplines pose a series of questions about the human being, God, and the world. This results in confrontations between scientific knowledge and faith, technology and the human being—particularly for the faithful.

1053   The ideologies that are in vogue know that universities are an ideal place for them to infiltrate and to gain control over culture and society.

1054   The university should train real leaders and builders of a new society. Insofar as the Church is concerned, this means promulgating the gospel message in this milieu in an effective way, respecting academic freedom, inspiring its creative function, taking part in the political and social education of its members, and shedding light on scientific investigation.

1055   That is why we should devote our attention to the intellectual and university milieu. It could be said that this is a key, functional option with respect to evangelization. Otherwise we would lose a decisive field for shedding light on structural change.

Since results cannot be measured in the short term, one might get the impression that failure and ineffectiveness predominate. However, this should not diminish the hopes and efforts of Christians working in the university field. For despite difficulties, they are collaborating in the evangelizing mission of the Church. **1056**

It is important to evangelize the university milieu (teachers, researchers, and students) through timely contacts and pastoral services within non-ecclesial institutions of higher education. **1057**

In particular, we must say that the Catholic university, the vanguard of the Christian message in the university world, is called upon to render outstanding service to the Church and society. **1058**

In a pluralistic world it is not easy for the Catholic university to maintain its identity. As a Catholic institution, it will carry out its function by finding "its deeper, ultimate significance in Christ and his salvific message, which embraces human beings in their totality" (AU:2). As a university, it will try to stand out by virtue of its scholarly earnestness, its commitment to truth, its training of competent professionals for the world of work, and its quest for solutions to the most keenly felt problems facing Latin America. **1059**

Its primordial educational mission will be to foster an integral culture that is capable of producing people who stand out by virtue of their thorough scholarly and humanistic knowledge; by their witness of the faith to the world" (GE: 10); by their sincere practice of Christian morality and their commitment to create a new, more just and fraternal Latin America. It will thus contribute actively and effectively to the creation, renewal, and transformation of our culture through the force of the Gospel. It will help to effect a greater harmonization of national, human, and Christian elements. **1060**

Besides fostering interdisciplinary dialogue (particularly between other disciplines and theology), the quest for truth as a joint undertaking of professors and students, and the integration and participation of all in the life and activity of the university according to their competence, the Catholic university itself should be an example of living, operative Christianity. All the members of the university, even those who accept and respect these ideals without being Catholics, should form one "university family"(AU:3). **1061**

In carrying out this mission of service, the Catholic university will have to engage in ongoing self-analysis and to make its operational structure flexible. This it must do if it is to confront the challenges of its region or nation. It must offer specialized short-term courses, continuing education for adults, and extension services for the poor and other marginalized groups. **1062**

5. Social Communication

Evangelization, the proclamation of the Kingdom, is communication. Hence social communication must be taken into account in every aspect of the transmission of the Good News. **1063**

As a vital social act, communication arises with human beings themselves. In the modern age it has been rendered much more effective by powerful technolog- **1064** ical resources. Today, then, evangelization cannot prescind from the media of communication (EN:45; CP:1).

5.1. The Situation

1065   *Overview of the real situation in Latin America.* Social communication represents a broad and deep dimension of human relations. Thanks to it, human beings are brought into interrelationship individually and collectively; at the same time they are exposed to the influence of audio-visual civilization and to the contamination of "noise pollution" (CP:8).

1066   Thanks to the diversity of the existing media (radio, television, the movies, the press, the theater, and so forth), which operate simultaneously and in mass terms, social communication has an impact on every aspect of human life and exercises a decisive influence on human beings, either consciously or subliminally (CP:6).

1067   Social communication is conditioned by the sociocultural reality of our countries. It, in turn, is one of the determining factors in maintaining that reality.

1068   We recognize that the media of social communication are factors for communion; that they contribute to the integration of Latin America and to the expansion and democratization of culture; that they also contribute to the entertainment of people, particularly those who live outside the great urban centers; and that they increase people's capacity for perception and sensory acuteness through auditory and visual stimuli.

1069   Despite these positive aspects, we must denounce the control and ideological manipulation of these media of social communication exercised by political and economic power-groups. They seek to maintain the status quo, or even to create a new order of dependence and domination; or else they seek to subvert the existing order and to create one that is the very antithesis of it. Exploitation of passions, feelings, violence, and sex for consumeristic purposes constitutes a flagrant violation of individual rights. The same is true of indiscriminate use of messages, either subliminal or repetitive, which show little respect for the person—the family in particular.

1070   Journalists are not always objective and honest in transmitting news. Thus it is they themselves who sometimes manipulate information—by concealing, altering, or inventing the content of the news and thus greatly misleading public opinion.

1071   Monopolistic control over information, either on the part of government or private interests, permits the arbitrary use of the information media. It allows for the manipulation of messages on the basis of factional interests. Particularly serious is the manipulation by multinational enterprises and interests of information coming to or destined for our countries.

1072   The programming schedule, largely of foreign provenience, produces transculturation that is non-participatory, and that may even destroy autochthonous values. The advertising system as it stands, and the improper use of sports as an escape mechanism, make them factors promoting alienation. Their mass-oriented and compulsive impact can lead to the isolation and even the disintegration of the family community.

1073   The media of social communication are often turned into propaganda vehicles for the prevailing materialism, which is pragmatic and consumption-oriented. In our people they create false expectations, fictitious needs, serious frustrations, and an unsound spirit of competition.

Overview of the real situation in the Latin American Church. There is a certain **1074** awareness of the importance of social communication in the Latin American Church. But it is not perceived as an all-pervasive phenomenon that affects all human relations and pastoral work itself; nor is there adequate perception of the specific idiom of the media.

The Church has explicitly proposed its teaching about the media of social **1075** communication. It has published numerous documents on the subject, but it has been tardy in implementing these teachings.

The Church has not taken sufficient advantage of the opportunities offered it to **1076** communicate via non-Church-owned media, nor has it adequately utilized its own media or those under its influence. Furthermore, its own media are not integrated with each other or with the overall pastoral effort.

Except for rare exceptions, there is as yet no real concern in the Latin American **1077** Church to train the People of God in social communication; to equip them to adopt a critical-minded attitude toward the bombardments launched by the mass media; and to counteract the impact of the media's alienating messages—be they ideological, cultural, or promotional. This situation is aggravated by the minimal use made of organized courses in this field, by the meager budget assigned to the media of social communication in the task of evangelization, and by failure to devote due attention to the owners and technicians of these media.

Here we must mention two very positive phenomena: the rapid growth of the **1078** Media of Group Communication (MCG), and of small media producing an increasing amount of material for evangelization. Pastoral agents are employing these media more and more every day, thus fostering greater capacity for dialogue and contact in this area.

In recent years the Latin American Church has done much to improve com- **1079** munication within the Church. In many cases, however, the results have not measured up to the demands of the moment. The flow of experiences and legitimate opinions, as a public expression of views within the Church, is restricted to sporadic and hence inadequate manifestations that have little influence on the ecclesial community as a whole.

5.2. Options

Criteria. **1080**
   a. To integrate communication into the overall pastoral effort.
   b. Among the tasks to be carried out in this field, to give priority to training **1081** both the public in general and pastoral agents at every level in social communication.
   c. To respect and foster freedom of expression and its correlate, freedom of **1082** information. They are essential presuppositions of social communication and its function in society. They should be fostered within the bounds of professional ethics, in line with Paul VI's exhortation *Communio et Progressio.*

Pastoral proposals. In the light of all the issues facing Latin America today, and in the light of the phenomenon of social communication and its implications for evangelization, it seems proper to formulate the following pastoral proposals:
   a. It is urgently necessary that the hierarchy and pastoral agents in general, all **1083**

of us, become acquainted with the phenomenon of social communication, understand it, and gain a deeper experiential contact with it. In this way we can adapt our pastoral responses to this new reality and integrate communications into our overall, coordinated pastoral effort.

1084   *b*. If pastoral work with communications is to be successfully coordinated with the overall, organic pastoral effort, we must create a specific department or organism for social communication where there is none. Such a department would be both diocesan and national. Where such departments do exist, they must be upgraded and correlated with activities in all pastoral areas.

1085   *c*. The task of providing training in the field of social communication is a priority one. Hence we must train all the agents of evangelization in this field.

Candidates for the priesthood and the religious life must have such training integrated into their curricula and their pastoral training.

Systems of ongoing training must be planned for priests, religious men and women, pastoral agents, and those in charge of national and diocesan organisms concerned with pastoral work in the field of social communication.

Special attention should be devoted to professionals in the communications field and to the training of those who cover religious information.

1086   *d*. Within the framework of liturgical norms, each local Church should determine the most suitable way to introduce into the liturgy, which itself is communication, the audio-visual resources, symbols, and forms of expression most suited to represent our relationship with God in such a way as to facilitate greater and more adequate participation in liturgical acts.

1087   A careful handling of sound in places of worship is to be recommended.

1088   *e*. We must educate the public audience to adopt a critical attitude toward ideological, cultural, and promotional messages and their impact. These messages bombard us continually. Our aim must be to counteract the negative effects of manipulation and massification.

1089   It is advisable that the ecclesial organisms that operate on a continental scale (UNDA, OCIC, UCLAP) devote special attention to training the public audience and the other persons mentioned above.

1090   *f*. Without neglecting the necessary and urgent presence of the mass-oriented media, it is urgent that we intensify our use of the Media of Group Communication (MCG). Besides being less costly and easier to handle, they offer the possibility of dialogue and they are more suited to a person-to-person type of evangelization that will evoke truly personal adhesion and commitment (EN:45–46).

1091   *g*. For greater efficacy in transmitting the divine message, the Church should utilize a language that is up-to-date, concrete, direct, clear, and at the same time judicious. This language must be close to the reality that confronts the people, their outlook, and their religiosity, so that it can be easily grasped. To this end, we must consider the systems and resources of audio-visual language that are peculiar to people today.

1092   *h*. The Church must use the Gospel to shed light on everyday events and try to accompany Latin Americans on the basis of sound knowledge of their daily tasks and the events that have an impact on them. To this end, the Church must take pains to have its own channels of information and news that will ensure intercommunication and dialogue with the world. This is all the more urgent to the extent that experience reveals the continuing distortion of the thoughts and deeds of the Church by various agencies.

The presence of the Church in the world of social communication requires significant economic resources, which are to be provided for by the Christian community.

1093

i. Knowing the situation of poverty, marginalization, and injustice in which large masses of Latin Americans are immersed, and also being aware of the violations of human rights, in its use of its own media the Church must more and more each day become the voice of the dispossessed, even at the risk entailed.

1094

j. The limitations we have had on this continent force us to ratify the social right to information, with its correlative obligations within an ethical framework that calls for respect for personal privacy and the truth. These principles have even more validity within the Church itself.

1095

CHAPTER IV
DIALOGUE FOR COMMUNION AND PARTICIPATION

To step up ecumenical dialogue between religions and with non-believers, for the sake of communion, seeking areas for participating in the universal proclamation of salvation.

1096

1.1. Introduction

Evangelization has a universality that knows no bounds: "Go into the whole world and proclaim the good news to all creation" (Mark 16:15). The Church, the trustee of the Good News and an evangelizer, begins by evangelizing itself (EN:15). This mandate of the Lord, of which all Christians are trustees, prompts a common effort under the impetus of the Holy Spirit to bear witness to our hope "before the whole world" (UR:12). Faced with the responsibility of evangelization, the Catholic Church opens up to a dialogue of communion, seeking areas for sharing in the universal proclamation of salvation.

1097

This presupposes that evangelization and dialogue are intimately related. The areas of interchange opening up to the Church are many and varied. Here, in line with Vatican II and the encyclical *Ecclesiam Suam* (ES:60ff.), we have focused on three groups: non-Catholic Christians; non-Christians; and non-believers.

1098

From the time of its discovery the Latin American continent was evangelized in the Catholic faith. This is a fundamental feature of the identity and unity of the continent; it is also a permanent task. For various reasons a growing religious and ideological pluralism is appreciated today.

1099

1.2. The Situation

In Latin America the Catholic Church constitutes the vast majority. This is not only a sociological fact but also a theological fact of great relevance.

1100

Besides the Catholic Church we find Eastern Churches and other Western Churches and communities.

1101

We also find what people now are wont to call "free religious movements" (or, in popular language, "sects"). Some of them remain within the bounds of a

1102

basically Christian profession of faith. Others, however, cannot be considered as such.

1103   Judaism is present, with all the varying currents and tendencies that are proper to it.

1104   We find Islam and other non-Christian religions.

1105   We also note other religious or para-religious forms, differing greatly in outlook among themselves, which do accept some superior reality ("spirits," "occult forces," "heavenly bodies," etc.), with which they understand themselves to be in communication to obtain help and norms for living.

1106   "Non-belief" is a phenomenon that covers very diverse realities. It manifests itself in explicit rejection of the divine—its most extreme form—and more frequently in distorted ideas about God and religion, which are viewed as alienating. This view finds a fairly good reception among intellectuals, university people, young people, and laborers. Others make religions equal and restrict them to the private sphere. Finally, a growing number of people show no concern for religion, at least in their practical life.

1107   *Positive and negative aspects.* There has been a growing interest in ecumenism among us, especially since Vatican II. We find proof of this in joint efforts to promote knowledge, appreciation, and the spread of Sacred Scripture; in increasingly frequent private and public prayers for unity, which find particular expression in the week dedicated to prayers for unity; in inter-confessional meetings and reflection groups; in joint efforts for the advancement of human beings, the defense of human rights, and the construction of justice and peace. In some places people have reached the stage of bilateral or multilateral church councils on various levels.

1108   However, ignorance or distrust of ecumenism persists among many Christians. In our communities the distrust is largely due to proselytism, which is a serious obstacle to real ecumenism. Another negative influence is the existence of alienating tendencies in some religious movements, which dissociate human beings from their commitment to their neighbor. But we also find that the pretext of ecumenism is used for political forms of co-optation and manipulation that vitiate the nature of dialogue.

1109   The "free religious movements" frequently evince a desire for community, participation, and a vital liturgy that must be taken into account. But we cannot fail to notice that these groups indulge in marked forms of proselytism, biblical fundamentalism, and strict literalism with respect to their own doctrines.

1110   On the continental level, and in some nations in particular, we see the beginnings of a structured dialogue with Judaism. But we also can see the persistence of ignorance with regard to its perduring values and of certain attitudes deplored by Vatican II (NA:4).

1111   The monotheism of Islam, the quest for the Absolute and for answers to the enigmas of the human heart—all characteristics of the great non-Christian religions—are starting points for a dialogue. That dialogue has begun in some places.

1112   In other religious or para-religious forms we can notice a search for answers to concrete human needs, a desire to make contact with the realm of the transcendent and the spiritual. But we also notice in them, besides a heavy stress on proselytism, a tendency to subjugate the spiritual transcendence of the human being to pragmatic considerations.

If we are to show adequate discernment of the phenomenon of non-belief in order to engage in effective dialogue, we must keep in mind the variety of causes and motives underlying it. They would include the deep-rooted inter-relationships between the objectifications of sin in the economic, social, politi-cal, and ideologico-cultural orders as well as the areas of ambivalence in any sincere search for truth or the advancement of freedom. Perhaps the Church itself cannot be considered blameless in this area (GS:19). Frequently non-believers distinguish themselves in the practice of human values that are in line with the Gospel. But the epoch is no stranger to various forms of militant atheism and humanism that block the integral development of the person. **1113**

1.3. Doctrinal Criteria

Evangelization and dialogue. All evangelization resonates the word of Christ, who in turn is the Word of the Father. This word seeks the response of faith (Luke 8:12). But this word, proclaimed by the Church, seeks to enter into a fruitful interchange with the religious and cultural manifestations that characterize our pluralistic world of today (GS:60ff.). This is dialogue, which always has a tes-timonial character, in an atmosphere of maximum respect for the person and identity of one's interlocutor. Dialogue imposes obligations of loyalty and integ-rity on both parties. It is not in opposition to the universal proclamation of the Gospel. Rather it completes that task in another way, always safeguarding the Church's obligation to share the Gospel with all (EN:53ff.). It is worth pointing out that the concern for ecumenism, prompted by the grace of the Holy Spirit, arose in the last century precisely within the framework of mission (UR:1); we cannot preach a divided Christ (John 17:21; EN:77). **1114**

That being the case, at Vatican II the Church exhorted pastors and all the faithful "to recognize the signs of the times and to participate skillfully in the work of ecumenism." The aim is to foster "unity among Christians" (UR:4), which was one of the principal aims of Vatican II (UR:4; SC:1). **1115**

With respect to Judaism, Vatican II "recalls the spiritual bond linking the people of the New Covenant with Abraham's stock." Hence it wishes to recom-mend and foster "mutual understanding and respect" between the faithful of the two religions (NA:4). **1116**

God's universal salvific will embraces all human beings (1 Tim. 2:4). Since Christ died for all, and since the ultimate vocation of the human being is one and divine, the Church is convinced that the Holy Spirit offers to all the possibility of being associated with the paschal mystery in some way, a way known only to God (GS:22,10). Since personal faith is a free act, the Church in dialogue must approach non-believers with the greatest respect for their personal freedom and try to comprehend their reasons and motivations. What is more, non-belief is a summons and a challenge to the fidelity and authenticity of believers and the Church (GS:19). **1117**

1.4. Pastoral Aspects

To foster a more simple, humble, and self-critical attitude in the Church and in Christians as a prerequisite for fruitful religious dialogue. **1118**

To promote in the various sectors and on the various levels where dialogue is **1119** occurring a firm common commitment to the defense and advancement of the basic rights of each and every human being, especially those most in need; and to collaborate in building a new society that is more just and free.

1120 To obtain an adequate exposition of Catholic doctrine, one that will provide a correct " 'hierarchy' of truths" (UR:11) and a valid response to the problems posed by the concrete situation of Latin America; likewise, to ensure the needed education, formation, and information with respect to ecumenism and religious dialogue in general, especially for pastoral agents.

1121 To foster joint witness, along ecumenical lines, by means of prayer, unity week exercises, joint biblical activity, groups for study and reflection, and interconfessional committees and councils at various levels, where possible.

1122 To study diligently the phenomenon of "free religious movements" and the reasons for their rapid growth; the aim would be to offer a response in our ecclesial communities to the yearning and questioning that such movements are attempting to meet: i.e., a lively liturgy, a real feeling of fraternity, and active missionary participation.

1123 To encourage religious dialogue with the Jews, keeping in mind the principles and points contained in the "Guidelines and Suggestions for Applying the Conciliar Declaration *Nostra Aetate*."

1124 On the basis of clear-eyed discernment, to inform and guide our communities about the aforementioned religious or para-religious forms and the distortions they embody for living out the Christian faith.

1125 To establish a more determined presence in centers where cultural trends arise and new protagonists emerge; so we need an organic pastoral approach to culture, worker movements, and young people.

1126 To take cognizance of the reality and extent of the phenomenon of non-belief; our aim should be to purify the faith of believers, to foster coherence between faith and life, and to ensure collaboration "in order to build up the world in genuine peace" (GS:92).

1127 Finally, to view the area of ecumenism, as well as openness to dialogue with non-Christians and non-believers, not just as specific sectors of evangelization but as an overall framework for our evangelizing activity.

PART FOUR
A MISSIONARY CHURCH SERVING
EVANGELIZATION IN LATIN AMERICA

The Spirit of the Lord prompts the People of God in history to discern the signs of the times and to discover, in the deepest yearnings and problems of human beings, God's plan regarding the human vocation in the building up of society, making it more humane, just, and fraternal. **1128**

Thus in Latin America we see poverty as the palpable seal stamped on the vast majority. At the same time, however, the poor are open, not only to the Beatitudes and to the Father's predilection, but also to the possibility of being the true protagonists of their own development. **1129**

For Jesus, the evangelization of the poor was one of the messianic signs. For us, too, it will be a sign of evangelical authenticity. **1130**

Furthermore, the young people of Latin America wish to construct a better world and, sometimes without even knowing it, they are seeking the evangelical values of truth, justice, and love. Evangelization of them will not only fulfill their generous yearnings for personal fulfillment but also guarantee the preservation of a vigorous faith on our continent. **1131**

Thus poor people and young people constitute the treasure and the hope of the Church in Latin America, and so evangelization of them is a priority task. **1132**

The Church also calls upon all its children, working within the framework of their own specific responsibilities, to be a leaven in the world and to share in building a new society on both the national and international levels. On our continent in particular, since it is Christian for the most part, people should be a source of growth, light, and transforming power. **1133**

It includes:

Chapter I: A Preferential Option for the Poor
Chapter II: A Preferential Option for Young People
Chapter III: Church Collaboration with the Builders of a Pluralistic Society
                in Latin America
Chapter IV: Church Activity on Behalf of the Person in National and Inter-
                national Society

263

CHAPTER I
A PREFERENTIAL OPTION FOR THE POOR

1.1. From Medellín to Puebla

1134   With renewed hope in the vivifying power of the Spirit, we are going to take up once again the position of the Second General Conference of the Latin American episcopate in Medellín, which adopted a clear and prophetic option expressing preference for, and solidarity with, the poor. We do this despite the distortions and interpretations of some, who vitiate the spirit of Medellín, and despite the disregard and even hostility of others (OAP:Intro.). We affirm the need for conversion on the part of the whole Church to a preferential option for the poor, an option aimed at their integral liberation.

1135   The vast majority of our fellow humans continue to live in a situation of poverty and even wretchedness that has grown more acute.* We wish to take note of all that the Church in Latin America has done, or has failed to do, for the poor since the Medellín Conference. This will serve as a starting point for seeking out effective channels to implement our option in our evangelizing work in Latin America's present and future.

1136   We see that national episcopates and many segments of lay people, religious men and women, and priests have made their commitment to the poor a deeper and more realistic one. This witness, nascent but real, led the Latin American Church to denounce the grave injustices stemming from mechanisms of oppression.

1137   The poor, too, have been encouraged by the Church. They have begun to organize themselves to live their faith in an integral way, and hence to reclaim their rights.

1138   The Church's prophetic denunciations and its concrete commitments to the poor have in not a few instances brought down persecution and oppression of various kinds upon it. The poor themselves have been the first victims of this oppression.

1139   All this has produced tensions and conflicts both inside and outside the Church. The Church has frequently been the butt of accusations, either of being on the side of those with political or socioeconomic power, or of propounding a dangerous and erroneous Marxist ideology.

1140   Not all of us in the Latin American Church have committed ourselves sufficiently to the poor. We are not always concerned about them, or in solidarity with them. Service to them really calls for constant conversion and purification among all Christians. That must be done if we are to achieve fuller identification each day with the poor Christ and our own poor.

---

*We referred to this in nos. 15ff. of this document. Here we would simply recall that the vast majority of our people lack the most elementary material goods. This is in contrast to the accumulation of wealth in the hands of a small minority, frequently the price being poverty for the majority. The poor do not lack simply material goods. They also miss, on the level of human dignity, full participation in sociopolitical life. Those found in this category are principally our indigenous peoples, peasants, manual laborers, marginalized urban dwellers and, in particular, the women of these social groups. The women are doubly oppressed and marginalized.

1.2. Doctrinal Reflection

Jesus evangelizes the poor. As the pope has told us, the evangelical commitment **1141**
of the Church, like that of Christ, should be a commitment to those most in need
(Luke 4:18–21; OAP:III,3). Hence the Church must look to Christ when it wants
to find out what its evangelizing activity should be like. The Son of God demonstrated the grandeur of this commitment when he became a human being. For he
identified himself with human beings by becoming one of them. He established
solidarity with them and took up the situation in which they find themselves—in
his birth and in his life, and particularly in his passion and death where poverty
found its maximum expression (Phil. 2:5–8; LG:8; EN:30; Med-JU:1,3).

For this reason alone, the poor merit preferential attention, whatever may be **1142**
the moral or personal situation in which they find themselves. Made in the image
and likeness of God (Gen. 1:26–28) to be his children, this image is dimmed and
even defiled. That is why God takes on their defense and loves them (Matt. 5:45;
James 2:5). That is why the poor are the first ones to whom Jesus' mission is
directed (Luke 4:18–21), and why the evangelization of the poor is the supreme
sign and proof of his mission (Luke 7:21–23).

This central feature of evangelization was stressed by Pope John Paul II: "I have **1143**
earnestly desired this meeting because I feel solidarity with you, and because
you, being poor, have a right to my special concern and attention. I will tell you
the reason: the pope loves you because you are God's favorites. In founding his
family, the Church, God had in mind poor and needy humanity. To redeem it, he
sent his Son specifically, who was born poor and lived among the poor to make us
rich with his poverty (2 Cor. 8:9)" (Address in the Barrio of Santa Cecilia, 30
January 1979).

In her Magnificat (Luke 1:46–55), Mary proclaims that God's salvation has to do **1144**
with justice for the poor. From her, too, "stems authentic commitment to other
human beings, our brothers and sisters, especially to the poorest and neediest,
and to the necessary transformation of society" (HZ:4).

Service to our poor brothers and sisters. When we draw near to the poor in order **1145**
to accompany them and serve them, we are doing what Christ taught us to do
when he became our brother, poor like us. Hence service to the poor is the
privileged, though not the exclusive, gauge of our following of Christ. The best
service to our fellows is evangelization, which disposes them to fulfill themselves
as children of God, liberates them from injustices, and fosters their integral
advancement.

It is of the utmost importance that this service to our fellow human beings take **1146**
the course marked out for us by Vatican II: "The demands of justice should first
be satisfied, lest the giving of what is due in justice be represented as the offering of a charitable gift. Not only the effects but also the causes of various ills
must be removed. Help should be given in such a way that the recipients may
gradually be freed from dependence on others and become self-sufficient"
(AA:8).

Commitment to the poor and oppressed and the rise of grassroots communities **1147**
have helped the Church to discover the evangelizing potential of the poor. For the
poor challenge the Church constantly, summoning it to conversion; and many of

the poor incarnate in their lives the evangelical values of solidarity, service, simplicity, and openness to accepting the gift of God.

1148   *Christian poverty.* For the Christian, the term "poverty" does not designate simply a privation and marginalization from which we ought to free ourselves. It also designates a model of living that was already in evidence in the Old Testament, in the type known as "the poor of Yahweh" (Zeph. 2:3; 3:12–20; Isa. 49:13; 66:2; Ps. 74:19; 149:4), and that was lived and proclaimed by Jesus as blessedness (Matt. 5:3; Luke 6:20). St. Paul spelled out this teaching, telling us that the attitude of the Christian should be that of a person who uses the goods of this world (whose makeup is transitory) without absolutizing them, since they are only means to reach the Kingdom (1 Cor. 7:29–31). This model of the poor life is one that the Gospel requires of all those who believe in Christ; so we can call it "evangelical poverty" (Matt. 6:19–34). Religious live this poverty, required of all Christians, in a radical way when they commit themselves by vows to live the evangelical counsels (see nos. 733–35 above).

1149   Evangelical poverty combines the attitude of trusting confidence in God with a plain, sober, and austere life that dispels the temptation to greed and haughty pride (1 Tim. 6:3–10).

1150   Evangelical poverty is also carried out in practice through the giving and sharing of material and spiritual goods. It is not forced on others but done out of love, so that the abundance of some might remedy the needs of others (2 Cor. 8:1–15).

1151   The Church rejoices to see many of its children, particularly the more modest members of the middle class, living this Christian poverty in concrete terms.

1152   In today's world this poverty presents a challenge to materialism, and it opens the way for alternative solutions to a consumer society.

1.3. Pastoral Guidelines

1153   *Objective.* The objective of our preferential option for the poor is to proclaim Christ the Savior. This will enlighten them about their dignity, help them in their efforts to liberate themselves from all their wants, and lead them to communion with the Father and their fellow human beings through a life lived in evangelical poverty. "Jesus Christ came to share our human condition through his sufferings, difficulties, and death. Before transforming day-to-day life, he knew how to speak to the heart of the poor, liberate them from sin, open their eyes to a light on the horizon, and fill them with joy and hope. Jesus Christ does the same thing today. He is present in your Churches, your families, and your hearts" (AWM:8).

1154   This option, demanded by the scandalous reality of economic imbalances in Latin America, should lead us to establish a dignified, fraternal way of life together as human beings and to construct a just and free society.

1155   The required change in unjust social, political, and economic structures will not be authentic and complete if it is not accompanied by a change in our personal and collective outlook regarding the idea of a dignified, happy human life. This in turn, disposes us to undergo conversion (Med-JV:1,3; EN:30).

1156   The gospel demand for poverty, understood as solidarity with the poor and as a rejection of the situation in which most people on this continent live, frees the poor person from being individualistic in life, and from being attracted and seduced by the false ideals of a consumer society. In like manner the witness of a poor Church can evangelize the rich whose hearts are attached to wealth, thus converting and freeing them from this bondage and their own egotism.

Means. To live out and proclaim the requirement of Christian poverty, the Church must re-examine its structures and the life of its members, particularly that of its pastoral agents, with the goal of effective conversion in mind. **1157**

Such conversion entails the demand for an austere lifestyle and a total confidence in the Lord, because in its evangelizing activity the Church will rely more on the being and power of God and his grace than on "having more" and secular authority. In this way it will present an image of being authentically poor, open to God and fellow human beings, ever at their disposal, and providing a place where the poor have a real chance for participation and where their worth is recognized. **1158**

Concrete actions. Committed to the poor, we condemn as anti-evangelical the extreme poverty that affects an extremely large segment of the population on our continent. **1159**

We will make every effort to understand and denounce the mechanisms that generate this poverty. **1160**

Acknowledging the solidarity of other Churches, we will combine our efforts with those of people of good will in order to uproot poverty and create a more just and fraternal world. **1161**

We support the aspirations of laborers and peasants, who wish to be treated as free, responsible human beings. They are called to share in the decisions that affect their lives and their future, and we encourage all to improve themselves (AO; AWM). **1162**

We defend their fundamental right "to freely create organizations to defend and promote their interests, and to make a responsible contribution to the common good" (AWM:3). **1163**

The indigenous cultures have undeniable values. They are the peoples' treasure. We commit ourselves to looking on them with sympathy and respect and to promoting them. For we realize "how important culture is as a vehicle for transmitting the faith, so that human beings might progress in their knowledge of God. In this matter there can be no differences of race or culture" (AO:2). **1164**

With its preferential but not exclusive love for the poor, the Church present in Medellín was a summons to hope for more Christian and humane goals, as the Holy Father pointed out (AWM). This Third Episcopal Conference in Puebla wishes to keep this summons alive and to open up new horizons of hope. **1165**

CHAPTER II
A PREFERENTIAL OPTION FOR YOUNG PEOPLE

To introduce young people to the living Christ as the one and only Savior so that they will be evangelized and evangelize in turn; so that they, in loving response to Christ, will contribute to the integral liberation of the human being and society by leading a life of communion and participation. **1166**

2.1. The Situation of Young People

1167   *Characteristics of young people.* Youth is not simply an age-group. It is also an attitude toward life in a stage that is not definitive but transitional. Young people display very characteristic traits.

1168   They are characterized by a non-conformity that calls everything into question; a spirit of risk that leads to radical commitments and situations; a creative capacity with new responses to a changing world, which they hope to keep on improving as a sign of hope. Their strongest and most personal aspiration is freedom, emancipated from all outside tutelage. They are a sign of joy and happiness. They are very sensitive to social problems. They demand authenticity and simplicity, and they rebelliously reject a society invaded by all sorts of hypocrisy and anti-values.

1169   This dynamism makes them capable of renewing cultures that otherwise would grow decrepit.

1170   *Young people in the social body.* The normal role played by young people in society is that of injecting dynamism into the social body. When adults are neither authentic nor open to dialogue with young people, they prevent the creative dynamism of young people from moving the social body forward. When they see that they are not taken seriously, young people move out in different directions. Some are vexed by various ideologies, particularly the most radicalized ones; sensitive to such ideologies by virtue of their natural idealism, they are not always sufficiently prepared for clear discernment. Some are indifferent to the existing system; or else they accommodate themselves to it with difficulty and lose their capacity to dynamize it.

1171   What disorients young people most is the threat to their need for authenticity by the adult environment, which is largely inconsistent and manipulative; by the generation-gap conflict; by a consumer civilization; by a certain instinct-oriented pedagogy; and by drugs, sexualism, and the temptation to atheism.

1172   Today young people are particularly manipulated in the political arena and in their use of "free time." Some young people have legitimate political anxieties and an awareness of social power. Lack of training in these areas and of balanced judgment leads them to radical or frustrating stances. They spend much of their "free time" in playing sports and using the media of social communication. For some, these are instruments of education and healthy recreation; for others they are factors fostering alienation.

1173   The family is the primary social body, in which young people are born and raised. Its stability, way of relating to young people, lifestyle, and openness to young people's values play a large role in the success or failure of young people to achieve fulfillment in society or in the Church (HP).

1174   Young women are going through an identity crisis, due to the prevailing confusion over woman's mission today. Negative features of women's liberation and a certain *machismo* still prevalent are blocking the sound advancement of women as an indispensable factor in the construction of society.

1175   *Young people in Latin America.* The youth of Latin America cannot be considered in the abstract. They differ, depending on their social situation or the sociopolitical experiences through which their respective countries are going.

If we focus on the social situation, we notice this: while some young people are growing up normally, due to their economic circumstances, many other young people are forced to work as if they were adults because of their poverty. The group would include indigenous peoples, peasants, miners, fishermen, and laborers. Beside young people who are living comfortably, we find students, particularly on the outskirts of urban areas, who are already faced with uncertainty about their future employment, or who have not found their own way because of lack of vocational guidance. **1176**

It also cannot be denied that some young people have been disillusioned by the lack of authenticity in some of their leaders; or that they have been disgusted by a consumer civilization. Other young people, by contrast, want to respond to the many different forms of egotism by constructing a world of peace, justice, and love. Finally, we find that not a few young people have experienced the joy of giving themselves to Christ, despite the many harsh demands imposed by his cross. **1177**

Young people and the Church. The Church sees in young people an enormous force for renewal, a symbol of the Church itself. This it does, not for tactical reasons but by virtue of its own vocation. For it is "called to constant self-renovation, that is to say, to repeated rejuvenation" (AY:2). Service to young people, carried out with humility, should effect a change in any inconsistency or mistrust within the Church vis-à-vis young people. **1178**

Right now, however, young people have different views of the Church. Some love it spontaneously for what it is, the sacrament of Christ. Some call it into question, demanding that it be authentic. Some are looking for a living Christ without his body, which the Church is. And then there is an indifferent mass, passively accommodated to a consumer civilization or some surrogate; they have no interest whatsoever in the demands of the Gospel. **1179**

Some young people are very disturbed over social issues, but they are repressed by the systems of government. They look to the Church as a space for freedom, as a place where they can express themselves without being manipulated and engage in social and political protest. Some, on the other hand, seek to utilize the Church as a tool of protest. Finally, a very active minority, influenced by their milieu or by materialistic and atheistic ideologies, deny and combat the Gospel. **1180**

Those young people who seek fulfillment in the Church can be disillusioned when there is no sound pastoral planning or programming to respond to the historical reality in which they are living. They also feel keenly the absence of well-prepared advisors, even though competent and self-sacrificing advisers are to be found in quite a few youth groups and youth movements. **1181**

2.2. Pastoral Criteria

We wish to respond to the situation of young people with the three criteria of truth proposed by John Paul II: the truth about Jesus Christ, the truth about the Church's mission, and the truth about the human being (OAP). **1182**

Even without realizing it, young people are moving toward an encounter with a Messiah, Christ; and he is moving toward them in turn. He alone makes young people really free. This is the Christ that should be presented to young people as **1183** the full and complete liberator (Gal. 5:1,13; 4:26,31; 1 Cor. 7:22; 2 Cor. 3:17). Through the spirit of the Beatitudes he enables all young people to be immersed in a process of ongoing conversion. He understands their frailties, and he offers them a very personal encounter with himself and the community in the sacraments of reconciliation and the Eucharist. Young people ought to experience Christ as a personal friend who never fails them, and as the way to total fulfillment. With him and through the law of love, young people journey toward our common Father and their brothers and sisters. In this way they experience true happiness.

1184   *Young people in the Church.* Young people should feel that they are the Church, experiencing it as a place of communion and participation. Hence the Church accepts their criticisms because it knows it has limitations in its members. The Church gradually develops their responsibility for its construction, eventually sending them out as witnesses and missionaries, particularly to the great mass of young people. In the Church young people come to feel that they are a new people: the people of the Beatitudes, with no security but Christ, with the heart of the poor; a contemplative people with an attitude of evangelical listening and discernment; builders of peace and the bearers of joy and a complete liberation project, aimed principally at their fellow young people. The Virgin Mary, the generous and loyal believer, educates young people to be Church.

1185   Young people who share the attitudes of Christ promote and defend the dignity of the human person. Through baptism they are the children of one single Father, brothers and sisters of all human beings; and they contribute to building up the Church. More and more they come to regard themselves as "citizens of the world," as instruments for building up the Latin American and world communities.

2.3. Pastoral Options

1186   *A preferential option.* The Church has confidence in young people (EN:72). They are a source of hope for it. In the young people of Latin America it sees a real potential for the present and future of its evangelization. Because they inject real dynamism into the social body, and especially the ecclesial body, the Church assumes a preferential option for young people in terms of its evangelizing mission on this continent (Med-Y:13).

1187   To this end we want to offer an overall pastoral approach. In line with an organic, differentiated pastoral effort, we seek to elaborate a pastoral effort to young people that will take due account of the social reality of the young people on our continent. We want to foster the growth and deepening of their faith for the sake of communion with God and human beings. We want to give direction to the vocational option of young people. We want to offer them the resources for becoming factors for change, and also effective channels for participating actively in the Church and in the transformation of society.

    That brings us to the following *concrete applications:*

1188   *Communion and commitment.* The evangelizing Church makes a strong appeal that young people seek and find in it the locale of their communion with God and human beings, so that they can build up "the civilization of love" and peace in justice. It invites them to commit themselves effectively to an evangelizing activity that excludes no one, that corresponds to the situation in which they live and shows a preference for the poorest.

Integration into the Church will be channeled mainly through youth movements or communities, which are to be integrated into the overall pastoral effort of the diocese and the nation. The further aim should be integration on the continental level, taking in all of Latin America. This integration will be achieved particularly by means of: 1189

—pastoral care for the family;

—the pastoral work of the Church on the diocesan and parochial level, which includes such various aspects as catechesis, education, vocations, etc.;

—the interrelating of various youth movements or communities; this will take into account their concrete social situation as high school students, college students, laborers, peasants, etc. They all have their own specific conditioning factors and needs insofar as the evangelizing process is concerned; and hence they require a specific pastoral effort.

Pastoral work aimed at movements and communities must take young people into account, and there should be a fruitful interrelationship. Groups should serve as a leaven in the mass and help to foster a total evangelization. 1190

Welcome and attention should be shown to young people who, for various reasons, must emigrate temporarily or permanently. Such young people are victims of loneliness, dislocation, marginalization, and so forth. 1191

Formation and participation. Involvement in the Church and the task of effectively committing oneself to constructing the new civilization of love and peace is a very demanding one. It calls for thorough formation and responsible participation. For this reason: 1192

Evangelization-oriented pastoral work among young people should be a real process of education in the faith that will lead to personal conversion and to a commitment to the work of evangelization. 1193

The basis of this education will be to introduce young people to the living Christ, who is both God and human being, and who is the model of authenticity, simplicity, and fraternity. It is he alone who saves people, liberating them from all sin and its consequences; who makes a commitment to the active liberation of his brothers and sisters through nonviolent means. 1194

Pastoral work with young people will seek to ensure that they grow in an authentic, apostolic spirituality. This would be based on the spirit of prayer, knowledge of the Word of God, and filial love for Mary Most Holy. This will unite them with Christ and place them in solidarity with their brothers and sisters. 1195

Pastoral work with young people will also help to train them gradually for sociopolitical action and for the work of changing less human structures into more human ones, in line with the social teaching of the Church. 1196

We will inculcate in young people a critical-minded attitude toward the media of social communication and the cultural counter-values that various ideologies try to impart, particularly liberal capitalism and Marxism. This will help to avoid the manipulation of young people. 1197

We will use a simple, adapted language, together with a pedagogy that keeps in mind the psychological differences between men and women and that is marked by mutual confidence and reciprocal trust. The aim will be to turn 1198 attention to the milieu in which they live and operate, so as to give focus to their dynamic evangelizing mission.

1199   We will stimulate the creative capabilities of young people so that they themselves will invent and discover all the varied and suitable means to incarnate in a constructive way the mission they have in society and the Church. Hence we will supply them with the means and the areas where they are to exercise their commitment. Among other things, we would recommend the missionary presence of young people in areas of dire need.

1200   Every effort should be made to give young people a sound spiritual orientation, so that their vocational option can mature—be it as a lay person, a religious, or a priest.

1201   Utmost importance should be attached to all those means that foster evangelization and growth in the faith: retreats, meetings, workshops, cursillos, live-ins, etc.

1202   As a major moment in the maturing of one's faith—which necessarily leads to apostolic commitment—we must mention the conscious, active celebration of the sacrament of confirmation. It should be preceded by a thorough catechesis, and be fully in line with the guidelines laid down by the Holy See and episcopal conferences.

1203   A priority task will be to train qualified youth directors—be they priests, religious, or lay people—to serve as guides and friends of youth. While preserving their own identity, they are to offer this service with human and Christian maturity.

1204   Youth as a group cannot be considered in the abstract, nor as an isolated group in the social body. So we need a well-articulated pastoral effort that will allow for effective communication between young people of various ages, and that will provide for continuing training and commitment as they move into adulthood.

1205   Pastoral work among young people will be a pastoral effort of joy and hope. It will transmit the joyous message of salvation to a world that is often sad, downtrodden, and devoid of hope in its quest for liberation (AY).

CHAPTER III
CHURCH COLLABORATION WITH THE BUILDERS OF A PLURALISTIC SOCIETY IN LATIN AMERICA

1206   *Through the proclamation of the Good News and through a radical conversion to justice and love, the Church collaborates in the work of transforming from within those structures of a pluralistic society that respect and promote the dignity of the human person, and that provide persons with the possibility of achieving their supreme vocation: communion with God and with each other (EN:18–20).*

3.1. The Situation

We will focus simply on a few aspects that present a more direct challenge to our pastoral activity. In a sense this will serve as a synthesis of questions treated elsewhere in this document.

Since the Medellín Conference in particular, two clear tendencies can be discerned:

a. On the one hand there is a thrust toward modernization, entailing strong economic growth, growing urbanization on our continent, and the increasingly technological character of economic, political, military, and other structures.

b. On the other hand the tendency is toward the pauperization and growing exclusion of the vast majority of Latin Americans from production. So the poor people of Latin America yearn for a society with greater equality, justice, and participation on every level.

These contradictory tendencies favor the appropriation by a privileged minority of a large part of the wealth as well as the benefits created by science and culture. On the other hand they are responsible for the poverty of a large majority of our people, who are aware of being left out and of having their growing aspirations for justice and participation blocked. Yet we also see that the middle classes are growing in many countries of Latin America.

So there arises a grave structural conflict: "The growing affluence of a few people parallels the growing poverty of the masses" (OAP:III,4).

3.2. Doctrinal Criteria

We live in a pluralistic society where we find differing religions, philosophical conceptions, ideologies, and value systems. Incarnated in different historical movements, they propose to construct the society of the future while rejecting the tutelage of any court of appeal that cannot be called into question.

We know that the Church, which has a valuable collaborative effort to make in the construction of society, does not claim any competence to propose alternative models (GS:42 and 76). So we adopt the following doctrinal criteria:

a. We do not claim any privilege for the Church. We respect the rights of all people and the sincerity of all convictions, having complete respect for the autonomy of terrestrial realities.

b. However, we demand for the Church the right to bear witness to its message and to use its prophetic word of annunciation and denunciation in an evangelical sense, i.e., to correct false images of society that are incompatible with the Christian vision.

c. We defend the rights of intermediary organisms under the principle of subsidiarity, including the rights of such organisms created by the Church itself, in collaborating to deal with everything that relates to the common good.

3.3. Pastoral criteria

We advocate the following:

a. Moving beyond the differentiation between pastoral care of elites and pastoral care of the common people. Our pastoral effort is one single effort. It penetrates evangelizing "cadres" or "elites." It affects all areas of social life. It gives dynamism to the life of society and at the same time it places itself in society's service.

b. The specific responsibility of lay people in building up temporal society, as *Evangelii Nuntiandi* proposes (EN:70).

1207

1208

1209

1210

1211

1212

1213

1214

1215

1216

1217   *c.* A preferential concern to defend and promote the rights of the poor, the marginalized, and the oppressed.

1218   *d.* A preferential concern for young people on the part of the Church, which sees in them a force for the transformation of society.

1219   *e.* The irreplaceable responsibility of the woman, whose collaboration is indispensable for the humanization of the processes of transformation. This is to guarantee that love is a dimension of life and change. Her involvement is also needed because her perspective is indispensable for the complete representation of the needs and hopes of the people.

3.4. Options and Courses of Pastoral Action

1220   We know that the common people, in their total dimension and their own particular way, construct the pluralistic society through their own organizations. Facing this challenge, we realize that the mission of the Church is not restricted to exhorting the various social groups and professional categories to fashion a new society for and with the common people. Nor is it solely to motivate each group to make its specific contribution in an honest, competent way. The Church must also urge them to serve as agents of a general consciousness-raising about the common responsibility, in the face of a challenge that requires the participation of all.

1221   We realize that structural transformation is the outward expression of inner conversion. We know that this conversion begins with ourselves. Without the witness of a converted Church, our word as pastors would be futile (EN:41).

1222   We assume the necessity of an organic pastoral effort in the Church as a unified source of dynamism, if it is to be effective in an ongoing way. This would include, among other things, guiding principles, objectives, options, strategies, and practical initiatives.

    Courses of pastoral action.

1223   —The defense and advancement of the inalienable dignity of the person.

1224   —The universal destiny of the goods created by God and produced by human beings. We cannot forget that "there is a social mortgage on all private property" (OAP:III,4).

1225   —Recourse to the sources of divine strength to be found in assiduous prayer, meditation on the Word of God which constantly calls things into question, and participation in the Eucharist by the constructors of society. With their enormous responsibilities, they are surrounded by temptations to lock themselves into the realm of earthly realities without opening up to the demands of the Gospel.

1226   —Led by the bishop, the Christian community must build a bridge of contact and dialogue with the builders of temporal society, in order to enlighten them with the Christian vision, stimulate them with significant gestures, and accompany them with effective actions (OA:4).

1227   —This contact and dialogue, marked by an attitude of sincere, receptive listening, should consider the problematic issues brought by the constructors of society from their own temporal sphere. In this way we will be able to find the criteria, norms, and approaches that will enable us to deepen and concretize the Church's social teaching. Here we are referring to the elaboration of a social ethics capable of formulating Christian answers to the major problems of contemporary culture (OA:4). We exhort all to combat economic corruption on every level, both in the area of public administration and in the area of private business; for such corruption causes grave damage to the vast majority of the people.

—This dialogue calls for initiatives that will permit encounter and close relationship with all those who are collaborating in the construction of society, so that they may discover their complementarity and convergence. To this end, priority must be placed on working with those who have decision-making power. This is not to rule out the recognition that social tensions can have constructive value. Within the demands of justice, such tensions help to guarantee people's freedom and rights, particularly those of the weakest.   **1228**

Insofar as *options, objectives, and strategies* are concerned, we would propose the following:

—To train people in the various pastoral sectors who will be capable of exercising leadership in them that can serve as a leaven of evangelization.   **1229**

—To elaborate, with people in each sector, norms of Christian conduct that will be the object of reflection and application and that will be subject to ongoing re-examination and revision.   **1230**

—To promote encounters that will bring together people from various pastoral sectors to share experiences and coordinate their activities.   **1231**

—To encourage the elaboration of viable alternatives in our evangelizing activity that will be geared toward the Christian renovation of social structures.   **1232**

—To promote the training of priests and deacons in specialized areas, and also new ministries entrusted to the laity that suit the pastoral needs of each sector.   **1233**

—To develop specialized movements that will bring together the elements available for the evangelization of particular milieus.   **1234**

—To be wise enough to value the resources of the poor, the lowly, the common people, and artisans for communicating the divine message.   **1235**

—To preserve the natural resources created by God for all human beings, in order to hand them down as an enriching heritage to future generations.   **1236**

Insofar as *practical initiatives* are concerned, the Church directs its word amicably and spontaneously to those whom it knows are among the people who need its guidance or encouragement and who are waiting for it. That is to say, it addresses those who elaborate, propagate, and implement ideas, values, and decisions: **1237**

—We remind politicians and people in government of the words of Vatican II: "God alone is the source of your authority and the foundation of your laws" (Closing Message to Rulers). And God is so through the mediation of the people. We affirm the nobility and dignity of involvement in an activity aimed at consolidating internal concord and external security. We encourage the sensible, intelligent activity of politicians to give the State better government, to achieve the common good, and to effectively reconcile freedom, justice, and equality in a truly participatory society. "In their proper spheres, the political community and the Church are mutually independent and self-governing. Yet, by a different title, each serves the personal and social vocation of the same human beings. This service can be more effectively rendered for the good of all, if each works better for wholesome mutual cooperation, depending on the circumstances of time and place" (GS:76).   **1238**

—We ask the intellectual and university world to act with spiritual freedom, to   **1239** carry out its creative function in an authentic way, to prepare itself for political education—which is quite distinct from mere politicization—and to satisfy the inner logic of reflection and the rigorous demands of scientific scholarship. For from this realm we expect to get projects and solid theoretical guidelines for the construction of the new society (Vatican II, Closing Message to Men of Thought and Science).

1240 —We ask scientists, technical people, and the creators of technological society to nurture their scientific spirit with love for the truth so that they may investigate the riddles of the universe and gain dominion over the earth. We ask them to avoid the negative effects of a hedonistic society and the technocratic temptation; to apply the power of technology to the creation of goods and the invention of means designed to rescue humanity from underdevelopment. In particular, we expect from them research and investigation designed to effect a synthesis between science and faith. We urge all thinkers who are aware of the value of wisdom—the first and last source of which is the *Logos*—and who are concerned about the creation of a new humanism, to take into account the magnificent statement of *Gaudium et Spes*: "The future of the world stands in peril unless wiser men are forthcoming" (GS:15). For this we need a major effort at interdisciplinary dialogue between theology, philosophy, and the sciences with a view to a new synthesis.

1241 —We urge those in charge of the communications media to draw up and respect a code of ethics governing information and communication; to realize that the instrumental neutrality of the media means they can be used for good or ill; and to serve the cause of truth, objectivity, education, and adequate knowledge about reality.

1242 —We urge creators in the arts to intuit the directions in which humankind is heading; to anticipate and interpret its crises; to open up the esthetic dimension of human life; and to contribute to the personalization of concrete human beings.

1243 —We ask jurists with their special expertise to reclaim and defend the value of the law in the relationship between rulers and ruled, and for the maintenance of proper discipline in society. We urge judges not to compromise their independence; to hand down fair, intelligent judgments; and, through their verdicts, to help educate the rulers and the ruled in the carrying out of their obligations and the knowledge of their rights.

1244 —To workers we say: In a world of growing urbanization and industrialization the role of workers becomes increasingly important as "the chief artisans of the prodigious changes which the world is undergoing today" (Vatican II, Closing Message to Workers). So workers should commit their real-life experience to the search for new ideas, thus renewing themselves and contributing even more decidedly to the construction of the Latin America of the future. They should not forget what Pope John Paul II told them in his talk. It is the right of workers "to freely create organizations to defend and promote their interests, and to contribute to the common good in a responsible way" (AWM:3).

1245 —To peasants we say: You are a dynamic force in the building of a more participatory society. Taking your side, John Paul II addressed the following words to those sectors who hold power: "To you, responsible officials of the people, power-holding classes who sometimes keep your lands unproductive when they conceal the food that so many families are doing without, the human conscience, the conscience of the peoples, the cry of the destitute, and above all the voice of God and the Church join me in reiterating to you that it is not just, it is not human, it is not Christian to continue certain situations that are clearly unjust. You must implement real, effective measures on the local, national, and international levels, following the broad line marked out by the encyclical *Mater et Magistra*. . . . Most beloved brothers and sisters and children: work for your advancement as human beings" (AO).

—We urge economists to contribute their creative thinking so that they can provide speedy answers for the basic demands of the human being and society. We urge business-owners to keep in mind the social function of business enterprises, to view them not only as elements of production and profit but also as communities of persons and elements of a pluralistic society, which are viable only when no excessive concentration of economic power exists. **1246**

—To those in the military we would reiterate what the Medellín Conference told them: "They have a mission to guarantee rather than inhibit the political liberty of citizens" (Med-PE). They should be mindful of their mission, which is to guarantee the peace and security of all. They should never abuse the force they possess. They should be defenders of the force of right and law. They should also foster a societal life that is free, participatory, and pluralistic. **1247**

—We urge public functionaries to carry out their work as a service. For the dignity of public life and public service lies in the fact that it is naturally directed to society, especially those who have less and thus are more dependent on the proper functioning of the public sector. **1248**

—Finally, we urge all to contribute to the normal functioning of society. We urge professional people and merchants to undertake their mission in a spirit of service to the people, who look to them for the defense of their lives and their rights and for the promotion of their well-being. **1249**

3.5. Conclusion

At the present juncture in Latin American history there can be rapid, thoroughgoing changes that will benefit all. In particular, they can benefit the poor, who are most affected, and young people, who will soon be responsible for the destiny of our continent. **1250**

To this end we propose that all people of good will be mobilized; that they join together with new hope for this immense task. We wish to hear them with keen sensitivity and to join them in their constructive work. **1251**

We look forward to combining forces with all our brothers and sisters who profess one and the same faith in Christ, even though they do not belong to the Catholic Church. We hope to elaborate points of convergence in an ongoing, progressive way so that we can hasten the arrival of the Kingdom of God. **1252**

To the children of the Church working hard in advanced outposts we wish to convey our confidence in their activity. They are to be our messengers of new hopes. We know that they will look to the Gospel, prayer, and the Eucharist as the sources of constant re-examination and revision in their lives and of God's strength to aid their work of transformation. **1253**

CHAPTER IV
CHURCH ACTIVITY ON BEHALF OF THE PERSON
IN NATIONAL AND INTERNATIONAL SOCIETY

4.1. Introduction

1254   Human dignity is an evangelical value, as John Paul II has reminded us; and the 1974 Synod of Bishops taught us that the promotion of justice is an integral part of evangelization.* Human dignity and the promotion of justice must be made real in the national and international order.

1255   In concerning ourselves with realities on the national and international scenes, we do so with an attitude of service as pastors rather than from an economic, political, or merely sociological standpoint. What we want to see between human beings is greater communion and sharing of all the goods that God has given us.

1256   So we want to look at the status of human dignity and of the promotion of justice in the real situation of our Latin America. We want to reflect on this matter in the light of our faith and in the light of principles grounded on human nature itself, in order to discover the criteria and services that will guide our pastoral activity today and in the near future.

4.2. Situation

On the national level. Let us recall some of the points that have already been brought up in other sections of this document:

1257   The people of Latin America continue to live in a social situation that contradicts the fact that they inhabit a continent which is Christian for the most part. The contradictions existing between unjust social structures and the demands of the Gospel are quite evident.

1258   There are many causes for this situation of injustice; but at the root of them all we find sin, both on the personal level and in structures themselves.

1259   We are deeply pained to see that the situation of violence—which can be called

---

*"Evangelization would not be complete if it did not take into account the mutual challenge that takes hold in the course of time between the Gospel and the concrete personal and social life of the human being. Precisely for this reason evangelization includes an explicit message, adapted to suit differing situations and fleshed out constantly, about the rights and duties of every human person; about family life, without which personal progress is hardly possible; about society's community life; about international life; about peace, justice, and development; and, in our day, a particularly forceful message about liberation" (EN:29).

"If the Church gets involved in defending or promoting human dignity, it does so in accordance with its mission. For even though that mission is religious in character, and not social or political, it cannot help but consider human persons in terms of their whole being. In the parable of the Good Samaritan, the Lord outlined the model way of attending to all human needs (Luke 10:30ff.); and he said that in the last analysis he will identify himself with the disinherited—the imprisoned, the hungry, and the abandoned—to whom we have offered a helping hand (Matt. 25:31ff.). In these and other passages of the Gospel (Mark. 6:35–44), the Church has learned that an indispensable part of its evangelizing mission is made up of works on behalf of justice and human promotion. It has learned that evangelization and human promotion are linked together by very strong ties of an anthropological, theological, and charitable nature" (OAP:III,2).

institutionalized violence (either as subversion or as repression)—has worsened. Human dignity is being abused, even in its most basic rights.

In particular we must note that since the decade of the fifties, and despite certain achievements, the ample hopes for development have come to nothing. The marginalization of the vast majority and the exploitation of the poor has increased. 1260

Failure to find fulfillment as human persons with fundamental rights begins even before birth. People are encouraged to avoid conception of children, and even to interrupt pregnancy by means of abortion. Lack of fulfillment continues with infant malnutrition, premature abandonment, and lack of medical attention, education, and housing. This fosters an ongoing situation of disorder, which not surprisingly leads to a proliferation of criminality, prostitution, alcoholism, and drug addiction. 1261

With access to social goods and social services blocked in this general context, as well as access to political decision-making, there is an intensification of attacks on freedom of opinion, religious freedom, and physical integrity. Assassinations, disappearances, arbitrary imprisonment, acts of terrorism, kidnappings, and acts of torture throughout the continent indicate a complete lack of respect for the dignity of the human person. And some try to justify themselves in this, even going so far as to appeal to the demands of national security. 1262

No one can deny the concentration of business ownership in the hands of a few, both in urban and rural areas; so there is an imperious need for real agrarian and urban reforms. Nor can anyone deny the concentration of power in the hands of civilian and military technocracies, which frustrate rightful claims for participation and guarantees in a democratic state. 1263

On the international level. Latin Americans see a society growing more and more unbalanced insofar as shared social life is concerned. There are "mechanisms that are imbued with materialism rather than authentic humanism, and that therefore lead on the international level to the ever increasing wealth of the rich at the expense of the ever increasing poverty of the poor" (OAP:III,4). These mechanisms manifest themselves in a society that is often programmed in terms of egotism; in manipulations of public opinion; in invisible expropriations; and in new forms of supranational domination, since the gap between the rich nations and the poor nations grows greater. And we must add that in many cases the power of multinational businesses overrides the exercise of sovereignty by nations and their complete control over their natural resources. 1264

Due to these new ways of operating, and to the exploitation caused by the organizational systems governing economics and international politics, the underdevelopment of our hemisphere can grow worse and even become permanent. We see it as a threat to the ideal of Latin American integration. This lamentable situation is motivated in large measure by nationalistic economic ambitions, by the paralysis of major plans for cooperation, and by new international conflicts. 1265

Sociopolitical imbalance on the national and international levels is creating many displaced people. Such, for example, are the emigrants, whose numbers can reach unexpected proportions in the near future. To them we must add people who have been displaced for political reasons: e.g., those in political asylum, refugees, exiles, and all the various people lacking proper documentary 1266 identification. Living in a situation of total neglect or abandonment are the aged, the underprivileged, vagabonds, and the vast masses of peasants and indigenous peoples, "almost always abandoned in an ignoble standard of living, and sometimes trapped and exploited severely" (Paul VI, Address to the Peasants, Bogota, 23 August 1968).

1267 Finally, an integral part of this complex social problem is the increase in arms expenditures and the artificial creation of superfluous needs imposed on poor nations from abroad (see no. 67 above).

4.3. Criteria

1268 *In national society.* The fulfillment of persons comes about through the exercise of their fundamental rights, as they are effectively recognized, protected, and promoted. Hence the Church, the expert in humanity, must be the voice of those who have no voice (of the person, of the community vis-à-vis society, and of the weak nations vis-à-vis the strong nations). Its proper role is one of teaching, denouncing, and serving in the interests of communion and participation.

1269 Faced with the situation of sin, the Church has a duty to engage in denunciation. Such denunciation must be objective, courageous, and evangelical. Rather than condemning, it attempts to save both the guilty party and the victim. Such denunciation, made after prior agreement has been reached between pastors, appeals to the internal solidarity of the Church and the exercise of collegiality.

1270 Enunciating the basic rights of the human person today and in the future is an indispensable part of the Church's evangelizing mission, and it will ever remain so. The Church proclaims the necessity of the following rights, among others, and their implementation:

1271 *Individual rights:* the right to life (to be born, to responsible procreation), to physical and psychic integrity, to legal protection, to religious freedom, to freedom of opinion, to participation in goods and services, to fashioning one's own destiny, to access to ownership "and other forms of private control over material goods" (GS:71).

1272 *Social rights:* the right to education, to association, to work, to housing, to health, to recreation, to development, to good government, to freedom and social justice, and to sharing in the decisions that affect the people and nations.

1273 *Emerging rights:* the right to one's own image, to a good reputation, to privacy, to information and objective expression, to conscientious objection "provided the just requirements of public order are observed" (DH:4), and to one's own vision of the world.

1274 However, the Church also teaches that recognition of these rights presupposes and imposes on the person "just as many respective duties. And rights as well as duties find their source, their sustenance, and their inviolability in the natural law, which grants or enjoins them" (PT:28).

1275 *In international society.* The imbalance in international society and the necessity of safeguarding the transcendent character of the human person in a new international order compels the Church to urge the proclamation of certain rights and active efforts *to turn them into a reality.* These would include:

1276 The right to a just form of international coexistence between nations, with full respect for their economic, political, social, and cultural self-determination.

1277 The right of each nation to defend and promote its own interests vis-à-vis multinational enterprises. On the international level there is now a need for a set of statutes that will regulate the activities of such enterprises.

The right to a new form of international cooperation that will re-examine the original terms and conditions of such cooperation. 1278

The right to a new international order with the human values of solidarity and justice. 1279

This new international order will avert a society built on neo-Malthusian criteria. It will be grounded on legitimate human social needs. It will provide for a healthy pluralism, and for the adequate representation of minorities and intermediary groups, so that it will not be a closed circle of nations. It will preserve the common patrimony of humanity, particularly the oceans. 1280

Finally, economic surpluses, the savings from disarmament, and all other wealth on which there is a "social mortgage," even on the international level, will have to be utilized for social purposes. They should ensure the free and direct access of the weakest to their integral development. 1281

Recognizing that the peoples of Latin America share many values, needs, difficulties, and hopes in common, there is a particular need to promote a legitimate form of continental integration. Such integration would move beyond various forms of egotism and narrow-minded nationalism, would respect the legitimate autonomy and territorial integrity of each people, and would encourage self-limitations on arms expenditures. 1282

4.4. Services

Besides proclaiming the dignity of human persons, their rights, and their duties, and besides denouncing violations of the human being, the Church must also engage in active service as an integral part of its evangelizing, missionary task. In common with all people of faith and good will, the Church should create an ethical conscience with regard to the major international problems. To this end: 1283

—The Church bears evangelical witness to God as present in history; and it awakens in human beings an attitude of openness to communion and participation. 1284

—In its own sphere it establishes organisms of social action and human promotion. 1285

—Insofar as it can, it steps in where public authorities and social organizations are absent or missing. 1286

—It summons the human community to re-examine and give new direction to international institutions, and to create new forms of protection based on justice that will ensure the authentically human advancement of the growing number of the needy. 1287

We recommend collaboration between episcopal conferences for the study of pastoral problems, particularly those relating to justice, which go beyond the national level. 1288

Insofar as the nameless and faceless members of society are concerned, the Church has a particular duty to take them in and help them; and also to restore their dignity and their human visage, "because when a human being's dignity is violated, the whole Church suffers" (Paul VI, January 1977). 1289

The Church must try to ensure that this floating segment of humanity is 1290 reintegrated into society without losing its own set of values. It must look after the full restoration of their rights. It must help to ensure that those who do not exist in legal terms get the necessary documentation, so that all may have access to the integral development that they deserve by virtue of their dignity as human beings and as children of God. In this way the Church will cooperate in the task of guaranteeing human beings a dignified existence, one that will equip them to find fulfillment both within the family and in society.

1291   Action by the Church is also needed so that the displaced and marginalized people of our time do not become permanent second-class citizens. For they are subjects with rights and with legitimate social aspirations. They have a right to adequate pastoral attention, in accordance with papal documents and the guidelines proposed at Latin American meetings dealing with pastoral aspects of migration.

1292   The Church makes an urgent appeal to the conscience of peoples and to humanitarian organizations, asking that:

—The right of asylum be strengthened and made general. This genuinely Latin American institution (Treaty of Rio de Janeiro, 1942) is the modern-day form of the protection once offered by the Church.

—Countries increase their quotas for immigrants and refugees, speeding up the implementation of agreements and mechanisms of integration relating to these matters.

—The occupational problem be attacked at its roots with specific policies for landholding, production, and commercialization. These policies should take care of the urgent needs of the population and give laborers stable places in their situations.

—Fraternal cooperation between nations in time of catastrophes be encouraged.

—Amnesty be facilitated as a sign of reconciliation in order to achieve peace, in line with Paul VI's invitation when he proclaimed the Holy Year of 1975.

—Centers for the defense of the human person be created. The aim of their work would be "to have the barriers of exploitation removed. These barriers are frequently the product of intolerable forms of egotism, against which [people's] best efforts at advancement are dashed" (AO).

1293   To all those persons who are afflicted and who are suffering from the violation of their rights, we send our words of understanding and encouragement. We urge those responsible for the common good to make a determined effort to remedy the causes of these situations and to create the conditions needed for an authentically human form of societal coexistence.

PART FIVE
UNDER THE DYNAMISM OF THE SPIRIT:
PASTORAL OPTIONS

The Spirit of the risen Jesus dwells in his Church. He is the Lord and giver of life. He is   **1294**
the power of God urging his Church toward fulfillment. He is God's Love, creating
communion and abundance. He is the Witness to Jesus who sends us out, as missionaries
with the Church, to bear witness to him among human beings.

We wish to be docile to this power and this love. So, under his urging, we seek   **1295**
communion and we desire to be servants of humanity. We have been sent out into the
world to transform it with God's gifts.

And, contemplating our pastoral tasks and plans, we desire to possess the creativity   **1296**
and dynamism of the Spirit, so that we may turn Latin American humanity into a new
humanity, in the image of the risen Christ, bearing new hope to his brothers and sisters.

PASTORAL OPTIONS

Examination of the foregoing themes has confronted us with the great chal-   **1297**
lenges that the Latin American continent poses to its present and future evangelization.

What response are we Christians called upon to give to this reality? What are   **1298**
the criteria and courses of a real and authentic evangelization for Latin America?
What are the basic pastoral options that will ensure that the Gospel, in all its
vitality and original force, becomes a real happening today?

Pastoral options are a choosing process. This process enables us, after ponder-   **1299**
ing and analyzing both positive and negative realities in the light of the Gospel,
to find and adopt the pastoral response to the challenges posed to evangelization.

In dealing with their specific topics, the various commissions have already   **1300**
provided a response. It is not necessary to repeat it. In this last section, by way of
conclusion, we simply wish to present the major lines or key options. It is
primarily a certain spirit, a characteristic outlook, that should mark evangelization on our continent. That continent is Christian down to its very core. Yet the
faith, as a norm of life and a total way of living together, does not have the desired

impact on the personal and social conduct of many Christians. Forms of injustice undermine and do violence to our societal life. They are especially evident in the extreme poverty, in the abuse of the dignity of the person, and in the violations of human rights. They prove clearly that faith has not yet attained full maturity among us. The living cultures on our continent and the new civilization arising under the influence of science and technology, with its strong secularistic tendency, call for greater evangelical commitment from Christians and an attitude of ongoing dialogue.

1301 　　We Christians, in our role as the People of God, are sent out to be a truly reliable seed of unity, hope, and salvation (LG:9). So today and tomorrow in Latin America we must be a community that lives its communion with the Trinity; that is the sign and presence of the crucified and risen Christ, who reconciles human beings with the Father in the Spirit, human beings with each other, and the world with its creator. "All these are yours, and you are Christ's and Christ is God's" (1 Cor. 3:22–23). "When, finally, all has been subjected to the Son, he will then subject himself to the One who made all things subject to him, so that God may be all in all" (1 Cor. 15:28).

　　We opt for:

1302 　　—A Church that is a sacrament of communion (LG:1), a Church that, in a history marked by conflicts, contributes irreplaceable energies to promote the reconciliation and solidary unity of our peoples.

1303 　　—A servant Church that prolongs down through the ages Christ, the Servant of Yahweh (Matt. 3:17; Isa. 42), by means of its various ministries and charisms.

1304 　　—A missionary Church that joyously proclaims to people today that they are children of God in Christ; that commits itself to the liberation of the whole human being and all human beings (service to peace and justice is an essential ministry of the Church); and that in solidarity immerses itself in the apostolic activity of the universal Church, in intimate communion with the successor of Peter. Being a missionary and an apostle is the very condition of the Christian.

1305 　　These attitudes, basic to the pastoral activity of our Churches on this continent, call for a Church engaged in an ongoing process of evangelization; an evangelized Church that heeds, explores, and incarnates the divine Word; and an evangelizing Church that proclaims, celebrates, and bears witness to this Word of God, the Gospel, Jesus Christ, in its life. This same evangelizing Church must also help to construct a new society in complete fidelity to Christ and humanity in the Holy Spirit: denouncing situations of sin; summoning people to conversion; and committing believers to world-transforming action.

Pastoral Planning

1306 　　The practical way to concretely carry out these fundamental pastoral options of evangelization is through a well-planned pastoral effort.

1307 　　A well-planned pastoral effort is the specific, conscious, deliberate response to the necessities of evangelization. It should be implemented through a process of participation at every level of the communities and persons concerned. They must be taught how to analyze reality, how to reflect on this reality from the standpoint of the Gospel, how to choose the most suitable objectives and means, and how to use them in the most sensible way for the work of evangelization.

The New Human Being

We must create in the people of Latin America a sound moral conscience, a **1308** critical-minded evangelical sense vis-à-vis reality, a communitarian spirit, and a social commitment. All that will allow for free, responsible participation, in a spirit of fraternal communion and dialogue, aimed at the construction of a new society that is truly human and suffused with evangelical values. That society must be modelled on the community of the Father, the Son, and the Holy Spirit; and it must be the response to the sufferings and aspirations of our peoples, who are filled with a hope that cannot be disappointed (Rom. 5:5).

Signs of Hope and Joy

Today, thank God, we find much evangelizing vitality on our continent. For **1309** example:

—The CEBs in communion with their pastors.

—Organized apostolic movements among the laity—married people, young people, and others.

—A keener awareness among lay people of their identity and ecclesial mission.

—New ministries and services.

—Intense communitarian pastoral activity by priests and religious men and women in the poorest areas.

—The ever increasing and more straightforward presence of bishops among the people.

—A more vital sense of episcopal collegiality.

—The hunger and search for God in prayer and contemplation, in imitation of Mary, who kept all the words and deeds of her son in her heart.

—The growing awareness of the dignity of the human being as understood in the Christian vision.

These are some of the many signs of hope and joy for those who are immersed in Christ's paschal mystery; who know that only the proclamation and living out of the Gospel, in imitation of him, leads to the authentic and complete liberation of humanity—"There is no other name in the whole world given to men by which we are to be saved" (Acts 4:12).

He is the fullness of all being (Col. 1:19). Only in Christ do human beings find **1310** their perfect happiness (John 17:13).

IV
BEYOND PUEBLA

THE SIGNIFICANCE OF PUEBLA
FOR THE CATHOLIC CHURCH
IN LATIN AMERICA

Jon Sobrino, S.J.

The Puebla documents represent one moment in the life-process of the Church in Latin America. I am going to comment on them in terms of this twofold point of view: their process character vis-à-vis Medellín and the future; and their ecclesial character as part of a more all-encompassing reality—the totality of the life of the Church. Thus this paper will be divided into two main parts. In the first part I shall examine the ongoing process of ecclesical reality as it eventually made its presence felt in Puebla. In the second part I shall offer some comments on the Puebla documents themselves.

The Presence of Ecclesial Reality in Puebla

The first thing to make its presence felt in Puebla was the ecclesial reality of Latin America. Needless to say, that reality was grasped differently by different spokespersons. To Puebla came the history of the Church since the Medellín Conference. To Puebla came Pope John Paul II. And in Puebla reality found its voice through the mouths of various bishops, theologians, journalists, and lay people.

Ecclesial History from Medellín to Puebla

We all are familiar with the documents and the spirit of Medellín and above all with the symbol into which that conference has been transformed. Here I am briefly going to recall some of the important points that will enable us to understand Puebla better. Medellín represented a happy convergence of several things: the expectations of our continent and of the Latin American Church; the new and incipient realizations of some groups within the Church; and the concrete Latin American implementation of Vatican II. The documents of Medellín, the most significant ones at least, came together within this real-life context in a deep way. They represented, as it were, the proclamation of a Good News for the continent. As Good News they were unexpected, precisely because of the intense, centuries-long expectation for a new and vigorous ecclesial life. Like all Good News, their impact was due to their own

289

content, not just to their authoritative nature as episcopal texts. Of course they were the message of the magisterium; but they were a message that itself bore the truth of reality. It was the reality of Christianity and Latin America that forced the bishops to speak. The message of Medellín was already in seedling form, and certainly in hope, the reality of the continent.

The Church appeared decisively in its missionary aspect, with decidedly concrete tasks to carry out. The denunciation of the sinfulness of the world, the annunciation of the good news of integral liberation, and the solemn commitment of the Church to carry out this liberation in partisan alliance with the poor: these were the words that had been awaited for so many years and that were suddenly spoken with the simple directness and conviction of someone who has found the right road. It represented an important twofold recovery of Latin American reality and of the gospel message. This recovery, a convergent and unifying one, went to make up the specificity and originality of the Latin American Church after centuries. No longer was the Church atemporal; no longer was it confined to traditional channels based on habit and custom.

The concrete implementations based on the Medellín Conference are well known. The Church began to make a decided commitment to the world. But this process was fleshed out in history along two fundamental lines. First of all, it was addressed to the vast majority, that is to say, to the poor multitudes who were being oppressed and had no voice. Second, it was addressed to them in terms of the process of conversion; in other words, it was directed against the reign of sin. The Church became the voice of those who had no voice, and it carried out a huge effort at prophetic denunciation. One need only recall the letter of the bishops and religious of Brazil: "I have heard the cries of my people." Or the initial remark of Bishop Romero when the Church of Aguilares was returned to him: "My job seems to be to go around picking up insults and corpses."

The Church began to be concerned about the historical efficacy of Christian love, encouraging thoroughgoing structural changes, calling for organized movements of the common people to defend their legitimate interests, and establishing solidarity with such movements. The Church began to be not only the People of God but also the People of God's Poor. It encouraged base-level communities, because they are at the roots of the people. It not only lent its voice to the poor but sought out their voice and let it sound out within the churches. It decentralized and gave up its worldly character by establishing solidarity with the poor. In many ecclesial groups it succeeded in establishing an unfamiliar degree of unity between bishops, priests, religious men and women, and the laity. It set up new ministries, not just to fill a gap, but to find new and rich resources in pastoral agents, peasants, laborers, and indigenous peoples. It bravely faced up to persecution and martyrdom, seeing all of them as privileged signs of its truth. The Church produced new forms of theological reflection, from grassroots thoughts to the fully articulated ideas of theologians. All of them were designed to be of service, both within the Church and in its mission.

In all that the Church has been glimpsing and discovering the "signs of the times." Herein lies the will of God for the Latin American Church today. Or, at the very least, this is the correct way to seek his will humbly, honestly, and effectively. In its liberating mission to the outside world the Church itself also could feel that it had been liberated within—to better hear and put into practice the word of God.

These positive accomplishments were also accompanied by difficulties, doubts, and even rejections on the part of some groups within the Church. To the initial surprise created by Medellín began to be added uncertainty and lack of knowledge. Either out of ignorance or in defense of their interests, lay people, priests, and bishops began to feel that they did not know where they fitted in or what they were supposed to do in this innovating Church. Practices, traditions, and doctrinal schemas are like old wineskins into which one cannot justifiably pour new wine. The unity focused around the mission effort became disunity for that very same reason. Yet both the unity and the disunity cut through all the various sectors of the Church. People began to talk about a "parallel magisterium," which did not exist in opposition to the hierarchy as such, but which mirrored the cross-sectional division. The theology of liberation, often not even read, much less understood, became a symbol of the dispute; or else it was disqualified in the name of an "authentic" theology of liberation propounded by the secretariat of CELAM. The search to make love effective in history presented new problems when people came into contact with various ideologies; in the concrete, this meant the ideology of Marxism. The religiosity of the common people (*religiosidad popular*) was viewed as ambiguous; and it was used in different ways by liberationist, populist, and traditionalist currents. Finally, the new political impact of the Church in many countries evoked serious conflicts with governments espousing national security, and with some nuncios and members of the hierarchy who were anxious to get back to less tense and more diplomatic approaches.

All these real-life problems—some more intraecclesial, others more social and political—prompted some people to reconsider the import of the Medellín Conference. Now if historical reality itself is the best exegesis of written texts, then it is obvious that maintaining Medellín is not simply a matter of orthodox, submissive acceptance of certain texts issuing from the magisterium; rather, it is a matter of upholding and accepting the history unleashed by the Medellín Conference. So people began to talk about ambiguities in the interpretation of Medellín, about various examples of reductionism, manipulation, and false interpretation. The preliminary consultative document (*documento de consulta*) and, to a lesser degree, the working draft (*documento de trabajo*) for the Puebla Conference sought to offer a different alternative to Medellín. Their interpretation was more culturalist, doctrinaire, and in accord with the western world, with which they sought to align Latin America. The surprising tack of Medellín was too much for some, and the proclamation of the Good News to the poor had proved to be too dangerous. What was necessary was an honorable retreat back to a Church which was more familiar, a Church where one knew right from the start what one was supposed to preach and do, how one should deal with the powerful of this world, and what the doctrinal answers were for almost any problem that might arise.

As the Puebla Conference drew nearer, however, there were other groups who wanted to uphold the surprising *éclat* of the Medellín Conference. They helped to prepare for the Puebla Conference with reflections at the grassroots level, with theological papers, and with meetings of priests and bishops. Upholding Medellín was not just a matter of stubbornness, self-love, or even the most traditional and orthodox understanding of the value of the episcopal magisterium. It was a matter of maintaining faith in a liberating God who heeds the cries of his people and of persevering in the following of Jesus. Though Medellín may have been followed by conflicts, obscurities, and even sound questionings, all that was viewed with the joy of a person who believes in a greater God and in a scandalous, crucified Christ. They would go to Puebla or work on behalf of Puebla in the hope of exploring and deepening Medellín, though of course this would mean going deeper into their theoretical analyses and into the pastoral and social practices of Christians. So it was amid this context that John Paul II arrived to open the Puebla Conference.

The Significance of John Paul II for Puebla

Four months into his pontificate, John Paul II decided to come to Puebla to inaugurate the Third Conference of the Latin American Episcopate. There were certainly risks involved. The Latin American Church is much too rich and complex for the pope to be able to have a thorough knowledge of it. The person or persons who advised him on his journey and in his discourses would play an important role. But the pope did come to Mexico and to Puebla, thus confirming a notion that was taking increasing hold in the consciousness of the universal Church: i.e., that both quantitatively and qualitatively Latin America is of fundamental importance for the universal Church. The quantitative aspect was symbolized by the incredible welcome that huge crowds gave the pope. The Church continues to play a most important part in the self-identity of the Latin American people who were present in Mexico. The welcome accorded the president of the United States three weeks later would seem ridiculous by comparison, both in terms of numbers and in terms of spontaneous popular demonstrations. The qualitative aspect has been acknowledged by many, thanks to the originality of the Latin American Church in recent years.

The whole context of the pope's visit and his discourses also pointed up something important which one group sought to water down in the preparations for Puebla. This was the fact that Latin America has its own texture and culture, which should not be a mirror-image of what is called western culture. The pope stressed this point forcefully when he spoke with great affection of the indigenous cultures and the realities that typified the life of peasants and laborers. At the very least, then, the pope's visit managed to reveal a particular people as it is, with its own hopes and problems that must be faced and resolved while maintaining its own proper identity. Both culturally and ecclesially the future of Latin America will depend basically on Latin America itself. It is not a question of artificially aping the more developed countries of the western world.

Besides this papal ratification of the Latin American continent as such, the pope's sojourn had a notable impact on Puebla. This was due in particular to the talks that he gave at various places in Mexico. This is not the moment to analyze them theologically or in detail. But I would like to point out what I regard as the main lines of those talks, which undoubtedly influenced the Puebla Conference, though in different ways. Granting the diversity and complexity of the pope's talks, we can group his ideas into three categories.

First of all, the pope reflected what seems to be most typical of himself by virtue of his own spiritual, human, and Christian experience. All that is obviously influenced by the country and the Church in which he spent his life: Poland and the Polish Catholic Church. Here we must mention his emphasis on devotion to Mary and fidelity to the Church. In a country like Poland even the mere formality of such things is important. In Latin America, however, the emphasis is more on the content to which the concrete Church must remain faithful. The pope also displayed his concern for the realm of spiritual values and the mystery of God; his natural compassion and his constant attention to children, the sick, and the aged; and his affection for, and frequent allusions to, the indigenous populations as bearers of a culture of their own.

Also characteristic of Pope John Paul II was his stress on maintaining the truth in its totality, without reservations or watering down. This was stressed on two levels. First, there was his insistence on proclaiming the value of the truth in itself, of the saving potentialities of a proclamation that is indeed truth: "The truth that comes from God ... includes the principle of authentic human liberation" (OAP:1). The second level had to do with fidelity to the truth as expounded by the Church's magisterium. He told the bishops assembled at Puebla that they must be teachers of the truth, "watching over purity of doctrine" (OAP:I,1). Insistence on the truth about Christ, the Church, and the human being—expounded in line with the tradition of the Church—constitutes the theoretical framework of the pope's Opening Address and of all his talks.

Secondly, the pope expressed fears and gave warnings about some aspects of ecclesial life. These are the remarks that captured many headlines in the press with its own interests. Though it is difficult to distinguish the pope's thoughts from those of his advisers in this area, it does seem that these remarks reflect the thought of his advisers more than his own. Why? Because these remarks deal with very concrete situations in Latin America, which the pope obviously had not had time to analyze in detail; because even some of the expressions used are typical expressions of the CELAM secretariat, not of the pope; and because in many instances they allude to resolving problems that are alleged to be touchy in Latin American theology when in fact they are not. These ideas would include: interpretations of Medellín "that are sometimes contradictory, not always correct, and not always beneficial for the Church" (HG:4); the "parallel magisterium" (AP); reductionist viewpoints in Christology (OAP:I,4); fears about a "new, people's" Church, or one theologically quite distinct from the Kingdom of God. Perhaps the pope also betrayed insufficient knowledge of the Latin American reality when, in urging explicit membership in the Church on people, he said: "It may not cost clear and direct persecution, but it could cost disdain, indifference, and marginalization" (HM). In many countries just the reverse is true.

The same insufficient knowledge may be evident when the pope, invoking the Virgin Mary on behalf of peace, generically enumerated the following triad as the evils opposing peace: "war, hatred, and subversion" (HG:5). No mention was made of a generalized state of repression. More his own seems to be his admonition to priests and religious men and women, urging them to deepen their spirituality rather than dedicating themselves to sociopolitical "radicalisms," or displaying an "exaggerated" interest in the temporal world, or becoming victims of ideological "radicalizations." I put some of his terms in quotes to show more objectively that his concern is for excessive exaggerations or radicalizations. That does not rule out sound efforts on behalf of integral liberation. Nor does it rule out the possibility that when proper discernment is used, and even in the temporal realm, "certain ways of substituting for them [i.e., the laity] retain their *raison d'être*" (OAP:III,7).

Third, the pope pointed out concretely what the integral liberation of the human being should be: i.e., the object of liberation. He stated it in programmatic terms in Part III of his Opening Address when he moved from dogmatic Christology to the Christology of the Synoptic Gospels. Alluding to Jesus' compassion on the multitude, his identification with the disinherited (Matt. 25), and the parable of the Good Samaritan, the pope drew this programmatic conclusion: "In these and other passages of the Gospel (Mark 6:35–44), the Church has learned that an indispensable part of its evangelizing mission is made up of works on behalf of justice and human promotion" (OAP:III,2). It is this section that clearly echoes Medellín, the pastoral letters of many Latin American bishops, and the language of numerous committed Christians. It is here that he talks about a "social mortgage on all private property." It is here that he says that peace is the fruit of justice, condemns consumptionism, and denounces the violation of human rights. He even alludes to the appearance of "collective violence" on our continent, which takes such forms as racial discrimination against individuals and groups and the physical or psychological torture of political prisoners and dissidents. It is here that he goes back to the theme of integral liberation; it certainly should be Christian, but in the last analysis it must be liberation. And it is here that the pope offers a deeply pastoral and people-oriented criterion: "Let us make no mistake about it: as if by some evangelical instinct, the humble and simple faithful spontaneously sense when the Gospel is being served in the Church and when it is being eviscerated and asphyxiated" (OAP:III,6).

In this programmatic part of his Opening Address we see the pope *in actu*, a pope who takes very much to heart the supreme and ultimate dignity of the human being. In the theological part of his talk he rightly grounds that dignity on the fact that the human being "is the image of God and cannot be reduced to a mere fragment of nature or to an anonymous element in the human city" (OAP:I,9). But in some of his other talks he has expressed the same point in sociopolitical terms: "May economics and politics never prevail over the human being" (HSD). Here we see a pope who is the custodian of the truth, to be sure, and indeed of the whole truth, but who is also a pastor and hence compassionate. His address to the indigenous peoples and peasants of Oaxaca on 29 January gives concrete expression to what he said in the closing part of the doctrinal section in his Opening Address. In the latter he tells us that in acting as defenders and promoters of human dignity "we come to the concrete, practical application of the themes we have touched upon in talking about the truth concerning Christ, about the Church, and about the human being" (OAP:III,1). In addressing the people of Oaxaca, he tells them that he would like to join with Paul VI and his views: "With him I would like to reiterate—with an even stronger emphasis in my voice, if that were possible— that the present pope wishes to be 'in solidarity with your cause, which is the cause of the humble people, the poor people.' . . . The pope chooses to be your voice, the voice of those who cannot speak or who have been silenced. He wishes to be the conscience of consciences, an invitation to action, to make up for lost time, which has frequently been a time of prolonged sufferings and unsatisfied hopes'' (AO).

To point up the concrete accent of the pope, of the universal pastor speaking to his people, I can think of nothing better than to cite some of the passages from his talk in Oaxaca:

> The disheartened world of field work, the laborers whose sweat waters their disheartened state as well, cannot wait any longer for their dignity to be recognized really and fully—a dignity no whit inferior to that of any other social sector. They have a right to be respected. They have a right not to be deprived of the little they have by maneuvers that sometimes amount to real plunder. They have a right not to be blocked in their desire to take part in their own advancement. . . .
>
> For their sake we must act promptly and thoroughly. We must implement bold and thoroughly innovative transformations. . . .
>
> The Church defends the legitimate right to private property in itself; but it is no less clear in teaching that there is always a social mortgage on all private property. . . . And if the common good demands it, there is no need to hesitate at expropriation itself, done in the right way. . . .
>
> To you, responsible officials of the people, power-holding classes who sometimes keep your lands unproductive when they conceal the food that so many families are doing without, the human conscience, the conscience of the peoples, the cry of the destitute, and above all the voice of God and the Church join me in reiterating to you that it is not just, it is not human, it is not Christian to continue certain situations that are clearly unjust.

Here we see a concrete connection being made between the Christology of the compassionate Jesus, the denouncer of injustice who is in solidarity with the poor, the ecclesiology of a Church in the service of God's Kingdom, and the essence and demands of human dignity. And that talk becomes all the more important if, as seems likely, the pope himself reworked it and gave it vital importance.

Thus the activity of John Paul II entailed a threefold task for the Puebla Conference: emphasis on a clear-cut doctrinal framework; an examination of conscience over the problems that have cropped up in the last ten years; and a clearly stated obligation to defend the dignity of human beings in Latin America. Puebla and its documents would take shape in terms of these guiding threads and the specific reality and diversity of the Latin American Churches.

The Presence of the Ecclesial Reality in Puebla

The problem of Puebla lay basically in this: in what way and with what intensity was the ecclesial reality of Latin America to make its presence truly felt? Obviously one had to take account of the varying ecclesial reality in different countries, as well as the varying evaluations of that reality, particularly by the bishops. In that sense Puebla was a struggle between the people who were more interested in watering down the novel and conflict-ridden aspects of that reality, and that reality itself as brought out by other spokespersons. While the immediate protagonists were the bishops, priests, and theologians, the real protagonist was the objective reality itself. Only from this standpoint, I feel, can one appreciate what happened at Puebla. Only thus can one understand the Final Document. The document represented at least a relative affirmation of the real Church over ecclesiastical figures who at first were more interested in offering opinions *about* the reality than in talking from within the heart of that reality. And those ecclesiastical figures had conservative tendencies for the most part, particularly in view of the way they were selected and invited to the conference.

If the ecclesial reality of Latin America managed to interject itself sufficiently despite everything, the reason lies in what has happened in the last ten years. Despite mistakes and limitations, which cannot be denied, there has been much dedicated Christian creativity; there have been various forms of Christian living and practice; there has been Christian witness sealed with much bloodshed—though this, unfortunately, was not brought out as it should have been; and there has been much faith in Jesus and much fortitude in the hardly easy task of following him. In the preparations for the Puebla Conference much effort was invested in channeling it toward neutral balance, disembodied calmness, and a prudent tone of advice and admonition concerning deviations and dangers. Yet, despite all that, it was not possible to stifle the cry of reality. At least some minimum strain of honesty, however unconscious, stopped people from silencing the hopes and anxieties of the people on our continent, the challenge facing the Church, and their contribution to a Church that they now called "new" because it seemed more like Jesus and was recovering the eternal novelty of the Gospel. That much honesty had to be shown to the people on our continent, the real protagonists of the Latin American Church.

The immediate protagonists and spokespersons of ecclesial life in Puebla were varied. The majority of the 360 members of the conference were what we could call centrist or conservative in tendency. The selection process helped to ensure that, giving the picture that the whole Church was more conservative than it actually is. But within the whole group there was a notable number of bolder figures. There were the Brazilian bishops as a group, and such well-known episcopal figures as Romero, Proaño, and Flores, to mention only a few. These were backed by priests, lay people, and the CLAR group. They were not too many, but neither were they too few. For in their favor was the fact that they shared a personal conviction about creatively exploring the thoughts of Medellín rather than acting timidly. They could count on the loyal service of a good number of theologians and of many people in the press corps whose professional and Christian commitment was admirable. And they could also point to representatives of the suffering people (e.g., some mothers of political prisoners and people who had disappeared) and representatives of the creative people (e.g., the thousand representatives of base-level communities who waited for them in Mexico City at the close of the Puebla Conference).

The city of Puebla itself symbolized the struggle to be found in the ecclesial reality of Latin America. On the one hand some businessmen and university students held demonstrations and press conferences denouncing the theology of liberation. They were backed up by an incredibly hostile and reactionary press. LIBERATION THEOLOGY ENTERPRISE HARMFUL! said one big headline. On the other hand the same city saw press conferences held with bishops who best represented the spirit of Medellín. At times these conferences turned into acts of homage. Such was the one given by Bishop Romero, which packed the hall of CENCOS as never before. And at the same time that manifestoes printing calumny against bishops and theologians were circulating through the streets of Puebla, so were lists telling the tragic truth about people who have disappeared in Argentina, El Salvador, and other countries.

Thus reality made its presence felt in Puebla in all these ways. And the same was true inside the Puebla Conference. The critical step came when the participants moved from small-group meetings to plenary sessions. In the beginning the participants were confined to small groups—"to write with pencil and paper," as one bishop put it. There was no opportunity for open-ended dialogue, and the atmosphere provided by public debate was missing. Many bishops felt ill at ease. For while it is true that bishops are and should be teachers of the truth, as John Paul II reminded them, it is equally true that they are pastors as well. In other words, they are teachers in concrete historical situations rather than in abstract, disembodied situations. The result was that the first two drafts were far more doctrinal—a fact which is quite apparent in the Final Document as well, and that almost all the drafts were dominated by the theological and social elaborations of the official experts sent by CELAM. There was a feeling of disgust among the bishops, and even fear of being ridiculed for the low caliber of the texts that they were producing. One bishop, alluding to the theologians left outside the conference, put the matter plainly: "We are facing a sick patient. We all want to cure the patient. But the doctor is outside."

The feeling that the ecclesial reality of Latin America was imprisoned, confined to previously imposed theoretical frameworks and limits, began to drain away in the plenary sessions. Everyone could have a say in them. Everyone could offer, not only needed ideas, but also living witness—or incarnate ideas, if you will. The Christian truth could better find expression precisely as Christian—i.e., as an incarnate truth. Thus a nun, who is working in a wretchedly poor neighborhood in Central America, was able to say that after reading the Gospels she found the life of Jesus to be very conflict-ridden because of his defense of the poor—a plain and simple truth that the commission dealing with Christology did not manage to come up with. Bishop Schmitz, a Peruvian, managed to evoke the only round of applause—despite the fact that such applause was forbidden by the rules of procedure—when the participants were discussing ideologies and the by now familiar fear of Marxist ideology. Pointing to those who were scandalized by the possible use of some aspects of Marxism, he said: "Let him who is without an ideology cast the first stone." And Bishop Flores was able to talk passionately about "meanness," when a draft was suppressed which somehow expressed gratitude for the services of a theology that explored liberation more deeply, in line with Medellín.

These are simply a few examples of what went on in the plenary sessions, and of how that particular environment allowed for not only the necessary doctrinal word but also the totality of the Christian message with all its challenging and questioning, its provocation and its creativity. The more total message of the plenary sessions and the open statements to the press restored a tone of greater ecclesial reality to the Puebla Conference, and gradually the documents began to improve. Reality struggled to get a hearing, and it succeeded in large measure despite many difficulties. This is the fact even though the conference could have come up with a better document, one that would have responded more directly to the expectations of those ecclesial groups and bishops who were more committed to Medellín.

The Documents of Puebla*

The Final Document of Puebla issued from this struggle between the ecclesial reality of Latin America and certain imposed channels and limits. Here it is impossible for me to provide a full and detailed analysis. Instead I shall simply proceed to point out certain things, starting with the lesser points and moving on to the more important ones. I shall consider in turn: some major lacunae in the Final Document; internal tensions in the document itself; recurring positive themes; and, finally, the core and principle of interpretation for the document as a whole.

Major Lacunae in the Final Document

By "lacunae" here I am not referring to certain concrete topics that might have been introduced but were not. To give two examples from the area of Christology, the Final Document might have discussed the conflict-ridden reality of Jesus or his activist dimension as the Servant of Yahweh seeking to establish justice. I am referring instead to more general contextual lacunae, whose absence is noticeable. I would mention the following:

Adequate space is not devoted to a sincere acknowledgement of the Church's own mistakes, errors, and sins. To be sure, such an admission is found at the start of the "Message to the Peoples of Latin America," but even there it is framed in a minor key. One notes excessive historical triumphalism in analyzing the past history of evangelization and the present overall activity of the Church. Also noticeable is what can be called doctrinal triumphalism. This is a mixture of justifiable pride in possessing the truth of Jesus and forgetfulness of the fact that we carry this truth in vessels of clay, as St. Paul pointed out. Those vessels have cracked repeatedly. The theological description of the Church suffers greatly from this doctrinal triumphalism. The real-life ecclesial situation did not manage to inject the needed quota of humility.

Another noticeable absence—though it might well be unrealistic to imagine that it would have been brought into the picture—is that of a sincere confession of the internal conflicts and divisions within the Church and within the hierarchy. There are vague allusions to such conflict, but no clear-sighted

*Translator's note: Various committees at the Puebla Conference drew up documents on various topics. These were ultimately incorporated into the single Final Document of the conference. But the author of this essay refers to them as originally individual *documents*, and I have retained his usage here.

admissions or analyses of its causes. I am not saying that the text should have indulged in ecclesial masochism, or made room for personal feelings of resentment. What I am suggesting here is that the unity and disunity in the Church should have been presented frankly and honestly so that a better solution might be worked out. For, as the document itself points out repeatedly, the witness of unity is very necessary and effective in terms of the Church's mission. The problem should have been analyzed because the bishops at Puebla were well aware of the internal tensions and were not reluctant to talk to the press about them. It is a regrettable situation, of course, but it is naive and idealistic to try to hide it, or to pretend that it can be solved by appealing directly and simply to unity. It would have been better to sincerely analyze the varying options at work and to uncover the mission that would unify the Church because it was both evangelical and Latin American.

There was also silence about that area of ecclesial reality that lies between the specifically evangelical and the concrete historical task that is necessarily bound up with political and ideological factors. The basic silence was due to the fact that these topics were broached in overly general and simplistic terms. As such, the remarks might be accepted or rejected, but they did not provide any authentic pastoral help. It is reality itself, not personal interests, that prevents us from drawing a clear-cut dividing line between the political and the ecclesial dimensions, between the activity of the laity and that of the clergy. The judgments and guidelines in the document are clear and represent a preliminary help; but they are too general and abstract. The area "in between" the political realm and the ecclesial realm is not illuminated; yet that is the area where pastoral work is carried out. In this case it would have been better to have followed the lead of Bishop Romero and Bishop Rivera y Damas in their last pastoral letter. For there we find a questing spirit and some general criteria that are a lot more concrete than those of the Puebla document. Those criteria offer real pastoral help.

Finally, there is another omission that is very difficult to explain. There were repeated petitions to correct it. I am talking about the concrete experience of martyrdom in the Latin American Church. It embraces the hierarchy, priests, religious men and women, and the people in general; and it has taken the form of threats, imprisonment, expulsions, and murders. Of course there are allusions to this experience. Joyous approval is accorded this experience of persecution for the faith and for justice; but it was not made one of the leading themes of the document. Perhaps there was fear of angering repressive governments. Perhaps the reason was that the hierarchy and clergy of some countries have not experienced this reality in person. Or perhaps there was some casuistic, canonical debate as to what technically constituted a person a martyr. What is certain is that the document did not give this experience the value it deserved. A great opportunity was lost. The Gospel tells us that in the last analysis "no one has greater love than he who lays down his life for his fellow human being." It is some consolation to recall that this experience of martyrdom was brought up in many press conferences, and that a good number of bishops did acknowledge it in explicit letters to Bishops Romero and Salazar.

Internal Tensions in the Final Document

The diversity of views and tendencies, combined with the very process that led to the elaboration of the Final Document, meant that the document would contain certain internal tensions. Here I am not talking about outright contradictions, but rather about inconsistencies and shifts of emphasis.

The final draft of the document is the result of four redactions. The basic outline and theoretical framework of each of the documents that went into the making of the Final Document were pretty well fixed in the very first redaction. In general, these preliminary documents were inadequate, except for the ones describing the Latin American situation, the consecrated life, and the option for the poor. So the story of the Final Document is the story of people's efforts to inject specific content-materials into the original outlines in order to improve the whole Final Document. And in fact they did improve it considerably. The content was greatly improved, and some obviously off-base items were eliminated. But the tension between inadequate theoretical frameworks and suitable content-materials remains in the Final Document.

We can also see tension between the more explicitly doctrinal documents —e.g., those on Christology and ecclesiology—and the other documents concerned more directly with pastoral activity. In general, the pastoral documents are better than the doctrinal ones. What should be noted is a certain parallelism between doctrine and pastoral reflection that might not be beneficial in the long run. The doctrinal statements are correct, but they do not seem to have any organic unity with the reflections to be found in the more pastoral documents, the ones on which ecclesial reality has had a greater impact. So we are faced with the irony that the Christology and, in particular, the ecclesiology underlying the pastoral documents are more inspiring than the doctrinal presentations of Christ and the Church in themselves. Undoubtedly this situation is due to the pope's urging that doctrine be properly safeguarded. That task continues to be necessary and important. But on the other hand the bishops lost an opportunity to clarify even doctrine itself in the light of a reality and a reflection-process that is more typically Latin American.

One can also notice a tension in the use of sources. The fonts used most are Paul VI's *Evangelii Nuntiandi* and the discourses of John Paul II. But the documents of Medellín and the working draft (*documento de trabajo*) for the Puebla Conference are also used, particularly in the section devoted to the relationship of evangelization to cultures, the people's religiosity, integral promotion, and ideologies. The tension is noticeable on two levels. First, there is a preponderance of papal citations over other sources that are more directly biblical or that would represent the magisterium of many Latin American bishops. Second, there is a subtle change in perspective in the use of *Evangelii Nuntiandi*, which is quoted repeatedly. This document itself begins with the figure of Jesus the evangelizer, the Kingdom of God, and the proclamation of the Good News to the poor. It then goes on to describe a Church that is supposed to continue this evangelizing work of Jesus and to find its innermost identity in this very mission. In the Puebla Final Document, however, we find a tendency to begin, at least logically, with the reality of Christ in himself and of the Church in itself—though this does not rule out the possibility of talking *later* about the relational and missionary aspect of Jesus and the Church. This is a methodological difference vis-à-vis *Evangelii Nuntiandi* of no small importance, even though its potential implications will only be noticeable when we see how Puebla is implemented in practice.

Another tension, partly resulting from what has been said above, is to be found in the general tone of the Final Document. It moves back and forth between a doctrinal tone and a pastoral tone. The overall result, it seems to me, is an excessively cold and dull tone, with pretensions of a systematic and logical bent rather than ones aimed at pastoral animation and inspiration. The three doctrinal documents—on Christ, the Church, and the human being—sound like dogma classes. By contrast, pastoral encouragement seems to mark many of the passages which describe the concrete situation of our continent and the preferential option for the poor. The same pastoral note is clearly evident in the introductory Message. I mention the tone of the Final Document for a preeminently practical reason, so that it can be read properly and utilized to the best advantage. Obviously the tone can help us to see whether the document does or does not correspond to the reality of Latin America. But it is also an important matter when it comes to communicating the Final Document to the grassroots level of the Church. Bishops and theologians can understand what the document is really trying to say, even if the language is predominantly logical in character. But Christians at the grassroots level, who are used to the tone of documents such as the pastoral letters of the Brazilian bishops, will have to be helped in trying to grasp the many positive things in the Final Document that are expressed in an excessively schematic, bland idiom.

Finally, there is another form of tension in the document. Unlike the kinds of tension noted above, this is in the area of content rather than of methodology. To put it in programmatic terms, it is the tension between "liberation" on the one hand and "communion and participation" on the other. Both phrases are used frequently. The terms are used as all-embracing realities to cover the reality, mission, and utopia of the Church. The point worth noting is that while "liberation" includes both the utopia that is to be realized *and* the process for bringing this about, "communion and participation" refer instead to the end result of the process. In the theoretical presentation, then, there is a clear danger of underestimating the element of process connected with liberation and the element of conflict involved in this process. These two realities are not sufficiently brought out in communion and participation. There is also a real danger of ideologizing these realities, or of simply declaring something to be a reality when in fact it is a utopia. A fair amount of this tack is evident in the systematic discussion of the Church. It is of the utmost importance that we clearly maintain the two poles in tension here: i.e., the process through which we are to arrive at a fuller reality, and the content of the fulfilled reality.

Recurring Positive Themes in the Final Document

Here I cannot spell out in detail the many positive items of content that appear in the Puebla Final Document in spite of all the lacunae and tensions noted above. I am going to concentrate on a few contextual themes that appear as positive elements in both the approaches and the content of the Final Document.

The first thing that must be said here is that the letter and spirit of the Medellín Conference is present in the Puebla Final Document. What we do not find in Puebla, and it is historically unlikely that we would, is the qualitative leap that Medellín signified. That is not due to subjective reasons having to do with the participants in the Puebla Conference; it is due to positive reasons of an objective, historical sort. It is hardly likely that there would be such a substantial change in the brief space of ten years. With good reason some have said that Medellín was a leap forward and that Puebla was a dainty step forward. But in any case Puebla does calmly reiterate what was fundamental in the Medellín Conference. It is no longer said with the surprising accents of something new, but rather with the calmness of something that continues to remain true and with a sense of urgency for it to start to become true where it is not yet a fact.

The presence of Medellín, and specifically of what we might call the "orthodoxy of Medellín," can be noted in many documents that came to be part of the Final Document of Puebla. Various basic outlooks on such matters as education, ministries, the religious life, and so forth are those that were hallowed by Medellín. Particularly noteworthy is the endorsement given to "liberation." The sense of that term is spelled out and dangers are warned against, to be sure, but in substance the reality is stoutly affirmed. There can be no evangelization without integral liberation, and the latter includes liberation from historical misery. The intuition that typifies Medellín and the theology of liberation remains in effect: there can be no history of salvation without salvation in history. And in at least two places the Final Document talks about Jesus Christ the Liberator.

Besides this basic reaffirmation of Medellín, we find certain themes that presuppose either a deeper exploration of Medellín or a novel formulation that was not evident in the Medellín documents. It is important to note that in various places the Puebla Final Document asserts that in terms of economic poverty, social marginalization, and political repression, the Latin American situation is worse now than it was ten years ago; that in general our continent has gone backwards; and that today there is more pauperization and repression. The fact that these points are well known does not diminish the importance of asserting them in the conference document. For that comes down to an objective endorsement of Medellín, even though the statements of Medellín are not cited explicitly. It thus rules out manipulation, such as that attempted by some people during the preparations for the Puebla Conference. Those people tried to suggest that today the situation is "different" from what it was when the Medellín Conference was held. The Puebla Final Document does indicate that there are now differences with respect to certain processes of industrialization, urban crowding, tendencies towards secularism, and so forth. But it makes it quite clear that "different" primarily means "worse" than at the time of the Medellín Conference. So Medellín remains valid, indeed even more valid than it was before.

There is also great stress on the theme of consumptionism. It is repeatedly called seriously harmful and a negation of Christian anthropology, which is based on being more and serving more rather than on possessing more. This spells out one of the consequences of dependence for Latin America, and it also provides positive guidance for the construction of a new society that will be more human and more Christian.

Also noteworthy is the frequency with which the Puebla Final Document talks about the "idols of our time" that enslave our continent. We already know what they are: the ambitious quest to accumulate wealth and power, sex, the growing eroticization, etc. The important element here is the recovery of the biblical term "idol" in trying to comprehend the tragedy of the Latin American situation. To be sure, in describing that situation the document warns against dangerous tendencies toward religious indifference, secularism, and atheism. But in mentioning idols, it zeroes in on the strongest and most typical form of atheism in Latin America. It is saying that the worship of idols dehumanizes human beings, causing them to sacrifice themselves and others to those idols. The vigorous and repeated condemnation of the worship of these false gods amounts to a denunciation of any attempt to justify poverty and oppression in the name of a God. It is true that the document could have more clearly drawn out the implications of such language for our understanding of doctrine. But there is no little merit in pointing out that the great problem of our continent is not, strictly speaking, agnosticism or abstract, passive atheism but rather the active atheism of idolatry and its sacrifice of human lives and human values. In this general context, it is equally important that the Puebla Final Document explicitly and repeatedly mentions regimes based on the principle of national security as new idols, which thereby seek to justify themselves and their atrocious crimes.

Moving to more positive levels, we must note that Puebla talks repeatedly of the option for the poor. A special document was devoted to this topic. This option was also made the theoretical backdrop for the mission of the whole Church and an integral part of all its various missions. The fact that the bishops are bringing up this theme "in season and out of season" proves that a focus on the poor and a preferential option for them can no longer be renounced today in the Latin American Church. The Puebla Final Document does point out that this option is preferential, not exclusive. But we can also note a big advance over the preliminary consultative document and the working draft. For the Puebla Final Document leaves no doubt as to who these poor people are: namely, indigenous peoples, peasants, laborers, shanty dwellers, the unemployed, the underemployed, and so forth.

Related to the theme of the poor is the insistent stress on taking seriously the problem of two other social groups: the indigenous peoples and women. Notice is taken of the oppression to which they are subjected, and also of the positive values that they can and should contribute to the continent and the Church. Also worth noting is the positive appreciation of base-level communities and their contribution to the Church. They are to be valued precisely because they are at the grassroots level, because they are exponents of the poor and exploited people who are the source of important, irreplaceable Christian values.

To these positive themes we must add the fact that there are no condemnations in the Final Document. There are warnings, admonitions, and specifications, but no condemnations. Given the general atmosphere and the expectations floating around prior to the Puebla Conference, one must say that this signifies a condemnation of condemnations. There was no condemnation of liberation theology, of base-level communities, of the initiatives of CLAR, or of the Church of the poor. Indeed, strictly speaking, there was not even a condemnation of Marxist analysis, though Puebla did criticize its overall ideology—along with that of capitalism and that of the national-security syndrome. This absence of condemnations signifies the positive presence of a pastoral spirit that, at bottom, is more interested in building up than tearing down. It is also an admission that there are many positive values in things that allegedly deserved condemnation.

The Core of Puebla and the Proper Principle of Interpretation

The outcome of the Puebla Conference is a bulky document that broaches a long list of topics. Because of this, and because of a certain encyclopedic approach in organizing the topics, it is important for us to determine what the core of Puebla is: i.e., the basic content of its message and the organizing principle that will enable us to comprehend the whole document.

To some extent, determining the core of Puebla already presupposes an interpretative decision. But the document itself offers us an objective criterion when it talks about a "preferential option" in the evangelization process. This option and the way it is to be put into practice are spelled out at the start of the "Message to the Peoples of Latin America." Reference is made to a reality that will be basic for evangelization: "the many who have little and the few who have much." Faced with this the Church must ask itself, not only who it is, but also what it ought to offer to the Latin American continent by way of contribution. The answer is clear. The Church offers a Christian liberation: "In the name of Jesus of Nazareth, get up and walk." The Church offers what is most characteristically its own: *the name* of Jesus. But it offers it in terms of the historical efficacy it possesses, in terms of what ought to happen *in the name* of Jesus.

Faced with a concrete historical situation and immersed in it, the Church addresses itself to human beings, denouncing the sinfulness that oppresses them and offering them a liberation. This is in germ the conception of a *theology of history* that follows the pattern of the prophets and Jesus. It is what we can call the core of the document. It is starting from that core that we can and should understand everything said in the Final Document about doctrine, evangelization, and the addressees and agents of evangelization.

This theology of history appears in the mutual relationship between the document that describes the reality of the continent and the one that describes the mission of the Church in terms of a preferential option for the poor. The former is of the utmost importance, not only historically but also theologically. We would be misinterpreting it if we saw it only as the first step in the familiar triad: analysis of reality, doctrinal reflection, and pastoral conclusions, or if we reduced it to a mere preamble, so that the *subsequent* theological reflection would have some minimum of realism.

What finds expression in the document describing the reality of the Latin American continent are "the successes and failures of recent years" (no. 16): i.e., the ultimate nature of history and the real world. We cannot go beyond those real events because in them God's history is literally being played out. It is in them that we must "discern the summonses of God in the signs of the times" (no. 15). Viewed as positive signs, signs through which God is pronouncing his yes and history is shaping up more as he would have it, are: the sharing and solidarity, particularly among the poor; the heightened cognizance of Latin Americans; the proliferation of community organizations, particularly among the common people; the growing interest in autochthonous values; and organized efforts to overcome injustices and win back one's just rights (nos. 17–20). These achievements are the historical version of a theological history in accordance with God's plan.

But alongside these signs, the document enumerates an even longer list of negative signs. The latter represent God's no to history, what will ultimately be labelled the mystery of sinfulness (no. 70). These negative signs center around such things as wretched poverty, the violation of human dignity, and the dehumanizing imposition of a culture upon the people. The growing gap between the rich and the poor is "a scandal and a contradiction to Christian existence" (no. 28). The bishops declare: "We brand the situation of inhuman poverty in which millions of Latin Americans live as the most devastating and humiliating kind of scourge. And this situation finds expression in such things as a high rate of infant mortality, lack of adequate housing, health problems, starvation wages, unemployment and underemployment, malnutrition, job uncertainty, compulsory mass migrations, etc." (no. 29). This poverty is clearly seen to be the product and consequence of economic, social, and political structures. So far from being a passing phase, it is deeply rooted in the very makeup of our history (no. 30).

Finally, this poverty "takes on very concrete faces in real life. In these faces we ought to recognize the suffering features of Christ the Lord, who questions and challenges us" (no. 31). Thus the much debated question as to who are the poor that the Church is talking about and addressing itself to gets a clear-cut answer, one of incalculable value for its mission. They are:

the faces of *young children*, struck down by poverty before they are born; . . . the faces of *young people*, who are disoriented because they cannot find their place in society, and who are frustrated . . . by the lack of opportunity to obtain training and work; . . . the faces of the *indigenous peoples*, and frequently of the *Afro-Americans* as well; living marginalized lives in inhuman situations, they can be considered the poorest of the poor; . . . the faces of the *peasants*, . . . in exile almost everywhere on our continent, deprived of land, caught in a situation of internal and external dependence, and subjected to systems of commercialization that exploit them; . . . the faces of *laborers*, who frequently are ill-paid and who have difficulty in organizing themselves and defending their rights; . . . the faces of *the underemployed and the unemployed*, . . . subject . . . to cold economic calculations; . . . the faces of *marginalized and overcrowded urban dwellers*, whose lack of material goods is matched by the ostentatious display of wealth by other segments of society; . . . the faces of *old people*, . . . frequently marginalized in a progress-oriented society that totally disregards people not engaged in production (nos. 32–39; emphasis added).

In addition to this wretched poverty, the bishops also focus on the ongoing violation of human dignity and of people's fundamental rights to life, health, education, housing, and work. Latin American men and women live in anxiety, due to abuses of power that are typical of regimes based on force, systematic or selective repression, and the accompanying evils of accusations, violations of privacy, improper pressures, tortures, and exiles. Citizens cannot participate in labor unions, particularly in countries where the government is based on force: "There they look askance at the organizing efforts of laborers, peasants, and the common people; and they adopt repressive measures to prevent such organizing. But this type of control over, or limitation on, activity is not applied to employer organizations, which can exercise their full power to protect their interests" (no. 44; see nos. 40–44).

Finally, on the cultural plane the bishops state that political, ideological, and economic power-groups are manipulating the information media. Through these media they penetrate the environment and the lifestyle of the people, creating false expectations and fictitious needs that often contradict the basic values of Latin American culture (no. 62).

I have dwelt on how the bishops view the concrete situation of the Latin American continent because it is important for grasping the theology of history that governs the Final Document. To understand history and operate satisfactorily with it, we must start with God's clear no to this type of world. The situation cries out to heaven and to God. On this point the Final Document is crystal-clear:

From the depths of the countries that make up Latin America a cry is rising to heaven, growing louder and more alarming all the time. It is the cry of a suffering people who demand justice, freedom, and respect for the basic rights of human beings and peoples. A little more than ten years ago, the Medellín Conference noted this fact. . . . The cry might well have seemed muted back then. Today it is loud and clear, increasing in volume and intensity, and at times full of menace (nos. 87–89).

This sinful situation is "the great challenge our pastoral work faces," and it entails "the task of fashioning a more fraternal society here" (no. 90). The response of the bishops to this challenge is given in their documents on the missionary Church in the service of evangelization, and it begins with a preferential option for the poor. There the bishops talk about the true substance of the Church, both in terms of its essence and its mission, which is to give life to all its structures, institutions, tools, and formulations: "The best service to our fellows is evangelization, which disposes them to fulfill themselves as children of God, liberates them from injustices, and fosters their integral advancement" (no. 1145). This service does not exclude any human being; but it finds its reason for being and its concrete direction when it is an option "expressing preference for, and solidarity with, the poor" (no. 1134).

Here again we hear echoes of the theology of history embraced by the prophets and Jesus. The point is brought out explicitly. Whatever may be the generic notions about God, Christ, and the Church, they find their Christian embodiment and opening out to the whole world in this option. The God of this history, the Father of Jesus, "takes on their [i.e., the poor's] defense and loves them" (no. 1142). The Son sent by the Father takes concrete embodiment in impoverishment and in solidarity with the poor. Jesus' mission is directed primarily to the poor, and that type of evangelization is "the supreme sign and proof of his mission (Luke 7:21–23)" (no. 1142).

It is on this basis that we are to grasp what I have called the substance of the Church: i.e., that which makes the Church what it is, without which it would not be the Church. With the pope the Final Document reiterates that "the evangelical commitment of the Church, like that of Christ, should be a commitment to those most in need (Luke 4:18–21)" (no. 1141). It is this commitment that makes the Church credible (no. 1145), and without such credibility the Church essentially would cease to be the Church. This commitment is the real gauge of charity, which can easily tend to be vitiated (no. 1146). It is the criterion for verifying the truth of the Church (nos. 1134–40), and it entails "persecution and oppression" (no. 1138). It is the historical wellspring of Christian spirituality, since the commitment to eradicate dehumanizing poverty takes the form of impoverishment in solidarity with the poor and is, as such, an openness to God (no. 1149).

So this preferential option for the poor is not just a highly laudable ethical option; it is also a theological option. It is the way to live history in accordance with God's reality. This option unveils the mystery of the Father, reveals the definitive exemplarity of Jesus' filiation, and unleashes the activity of the Spirit in prompting a life after the manner of Jesus. It is a historical option because it is incarnated in solidarity with real-life poverty and tries to eliminate that poverty as scandalous. And it is a theological option because in it there appears the very history of God; hence it is able to produce a spiritual experience that is Christian and transcendent.

Here, I think, we have the central core of the document. It is a theology of history that recovers and takes in all the Christian realities: God, Jesus, the Spirit, the Church, the praxis of charity, faith, and hope and, on the other side of the coin, sin and the mystery of iniquity. But it gives them a definite embodiment, beyond the generic truths correctly propounded in the more explicitly doctrinal sections. In the latter the talk is more *about* God, Christ, the Church, and so forth. In the former we see God, Christ, and the Church operating in terms of their own specific and proper reality. Hence I feel that here we have the proper hermeneutic or interpretative principles governing the whole Final Document. For on the basis of the incarnate idea we can more correctly understand the doctrinal idea, whereas the opposite is not necessarily true.

In the majority of the documents that would form part of the Final Document, the bishops spell out doctrinal criteria; they talk about such important pastoral problems as those of the family and young people; they discuss pastoral agents, including bishops, priests, religious, and laity; and they deal with the structural relationships between evangelization and such things as cultures, the common people's religiosity, ideologies, and human promotion. Each of these component documents possesses its own relative autonomy, and a more or less explicit link with the preferential option. But that option, as I noted above, runs like a thread through all the component documents. Sound logic and a more solid pastoral practice would dictate that all the component documents should be read and interpreted from the standpoint of the preferential option; for it provides the general framework that will enable us to do everything else in accordance with the "signs of the times," that is, in accordance with God's will.

The fact that the Final Document is careful to point out that this option is preferential but not excluding presents no problem in this connection. For the point of the assertion is that no one should feel excluded from a Church that has made such an option; but by the same token no one can presume to be included in that Church without such an option.

Nor is there any problem in the aforementioned tension between "liberation" as a process and "communion and participation" as the state of fulfillment. It is true that at times the Final Document seems to be upholding a theology of history based on an already realized eschatology more than what I have called a prophetic theology of history. But my feeling is that the emphasis on the final fulfillment and the element of fulfillment in present Christian existence can be understood *in Christian terms* only in terms of the *way* in which God offers this plenitude and the Church is to achieve it. And this concrete Christian way necessarily operates through the preferential option. All the component documents bear witness to this fact, even though they also and rightly spell out the historical moments in which ecclesial communion and participation are realized.

The Future after Puebla

It has been correctly pointed out that the best exegesis of the Puebla Conference will be the real life of the Church that follows it, just as the best exegesis of the Medellín documents was the ecclesial life that it triggered and that I summed up at the start of this paper. Obviously, too little time has passed since the Puebla Conference for us to be able to draw any conclusions about its historical repercussions. But there is no lack of positive signs that give us grounds for hope. A goodly number of cardinals, archbishops, and bishops wrote letters of solidarity to Archbishop Romero of San Salvador and Bishop Salazar, the President of the Nicaraguan episcopal conference. A few thousand representatives of Mexican base-level communities were waiting for the bishops and theologians when the Puebla Conference ended. And John Paul II, in his first general-audience talk dealing with Puebla, not only adopted the prophetic stance of denouncing sin and giving it concrete names but also had general words of praise for all theology that is liberating. All these things would indicate that the spirit of Puebla is in line with the spirit of Medellín, and that therefore there is reason to hope that it will trigger an ecclesial life along the lines of integral liberation.

In any case I would like to conclude with some reflections of both a theoretical and a practical nature on the future of Puebla. On the practical level of the Church's day-to-day life, Puebla represents the opportunity and the obligation to broaden the base of the Church in line with the spirit of Medellín. At bottom

Puebla has simply reminded us that the surprise of Medellín is really meant for the whole Church, even for those sectors of the Church that have been slow or reluctant to apply it for whatever reasons. Now there is no excuse for not knowing who the poor are, what "sinful situation" means, and what living in solidarity with the poor signifies. Amid other points brought out, these basic truths stand out as clear and compelling. Those ecclesial groups which still do not accept those truths, or which suffocate them under the weight of countless qualifications and distinctions, would not be faithful to the essential core of Puebla. So Puebla represents an opportunity to settle and solidify what was said at the Medellín Conference, and to truly implement it.

To those ecclesial groups that have already moved forward along the lines of Medellín, Puebla points up the necessity of developing and deepening all that they have already grasped to a large extent. This must be done both historically and spiritually. They must promote a Church of the poor along Jesus' lines, and they must explore more deeply the Jesus who instituted that Church. They must promote the Kingdom of God in history, and they must fully profess their allegiance to the God of that Kingdom. They must create an even greater unity between the historical experience of concrete praxis and their spiritual experience of the Lord's gift. The words of the pope on the necessity of the whole truth should not basically be understood as a warning, an admonition, or a restraint. Rather they should be viewed primarily as a spur to ever fuller expression of the whole Christian truth. And this expression should be based on the praxis of liberation and an ever-increasing commitment to the suffering faces of humanity. For that will enable us to spell out in ever-increasing depth and detail the whole Christian truth.

On a more theoretical level, the overall interpretation of the Final Document of Puebla and its sections will be a serious and important matter. To be specific, much is at stake in what comes to be viewed as its basic core. It is possible to offer a basically doctrinal interpretation of the truth, or to interpret it in terms of concrete history. It is possible to look for the core of Puebla in a correct, orthodox discourse *about* God, Christ, and the Church; or to look for it in the living, operative word *of* God, Christ, and the Church. Of course I am not suggesting that these two perspectives are opposed to one another. I am simply saying that one may prefer to start with the general idea or with the fleshed-out idea. Herein lies a major task for the theologians in their reflections and for the bishops in their pastoral declarations. From the very start the Church of the poor and the theology of liberation have opted for the fleshed-out idea, for truth realized in history, as their point of departure. No small contribution to Puebla will be made if we continue to explore more deeply into what is most specific and typical of the Christian truths: i.e., that God has assumed our history in the Incarnation of his Son and in the present-day workings of the Spirit. Immersing itself in the lowly depths of the Incarnation and human history, the Church will be able to be a sign of liberation, communion, and participation; and it will thus be able to bear witness to the full truth of God.

THE SIGNIFICANCE OF PUEBLA FOR THE CATHOLIC CHURCH IN NORTH AMERICA

Joseph Gremillion

The Puebla Conference of the Latin American bishops will have substantial influence upon the Roman Catholic Church in the United States and Canada. This impact may even be crucial in the coming generation and beyond. For Puebla shows decisively that the spirit of both Medellín and Vatican II is still very much alive within the Roman Catholic Church, regional and global. Its potential is by no means exhausted, as many had thought. The thrust of aggiornamento, in fact, has gathered fresh momentum from the creative initiatives of the Latin American bishop-pastors, with John Paul II supporting the efforts of his brother-bishops from the Chair of Peter.

We will examine Puebla's significance for the Roman Catholic Church in North America under four major headings: *confirmation* of Medellín and the aggiornamento, *channels* of influence, *topics* from the Latin American agenda, and *northern reality*.

Confirmation of Medellin and the Aggiornamento

The Medellín Conference has exercised notable influence on the Church of our region during the past decade. It sprang surprises of pastoral pioneering and theological originality upon our manual-trained clergy and canon-bound hierarchy, on our passive laity and tradition-tied religious.

This fresh tide of Medellín's regional influence came just as the Niagara force of Vatican II was sluicing into the ecclesial channels inherited from the Council of Trent four centuries before and supposedly hewn into immovable rock by the First Vatican Council. While currents swirled, minor dams cracked and a few levees collapsed, this regional Church of Latin America—belittled by Catholics of the northern colossus as a sluggish backwater begging for second collections and Yankee parochial know-how—this bumpkin rural cousin in the family of the faith produced Medellín.

Medellín truly surprised North Americans: the Church of some twenty "underdeveloped" nations, with four times the Catholics of the northern region, organized "its own Vatican II" less than three years after its seven hundred bishops returned from St. Peter's Basilica; theirs was an *episcopal*

310

assembly, in mode and mood, on matters that only a few bishops, major superiors, and pastors were gingerly broaching in the United States and Canada. This formal fifteen-day gathering, opened by Pope Paul himself the month after *Humanae Vitae,* with bishops thinking new thoughts and breaking new ground on a dozen subjects, was deemed doctrinally and politically daring by many.

Medellín contributed much to the Church Universal in the way of theological method and content. Specifically, the impact of liberation theology upon the Church of North America is already significant. Medellín's maturing methodology, Christology, and ecclesiology could have immense impact over the next decade and beyond. The affirmation and utilization by Puebla of this young Latin school of theology might well become the Conference's greatest contribution to the Church of our northern region.

Channels of Influence on the North American Church

Numerous channels for communication between the Roman Catholic Churches of Latin America and of North America have been created over the past twenty years. Relations were almost nil and mostly negative before 1959, the year in which Pope John solemnly declared that the Latin American Church was in a state of crisis. But by the mid-1960s a massive process of inter-communication and of "conscientizing" northern Catholics about the Latin American Church and people was in vigorous operation. And this was done under very *official* auspices: through bodies formed and financed by the U.S. bishops in close cooperation with the leaders of CELAM, under the urging of the Holy See.

In bare-bones summary, Puebla's influence in North America will be channelled through, at least, the following:

1. The several hundred *missionaries* who have returned to North American ministries are consciously marked by their years in Latin America. Forming nuclei within dioceses and religious houses, these "alumni" and "alumnae" readily articulate their experience and share concepts of Christ and Church, community and ministry that have transformed many of them.

2. Most U.S. and Canadian *religious orders,* women's groups in particular, are now deeply attuned to Latin American events—directly from their colleagues to the South, and indirectly via the effect of Medellín-Puebla upon generalates in Rome through international and provincial chapters to update constitutions and priorities. Notable among these is the Society of Jesus, whose 1974 congregation adopted for its apostolate on all continents the ministry of "faith at the service of justice."

Several U.S. provinces have had to deal directly with oppression of their members and ministry by Latin American governments. Examples are the Franciscans in Salvador and Brazil, Dominicans in Bolivia, and the Holy Cross confreres in Chile. Through their interregional experiences, northern religious orders are ready and willing conductors for Puebla's confirming message and for ecclesial creativity in our own region.

3. *Theologians* as a group form another channel through which Puebla's influence reaches North America. As professionals, northern theologians will

surely evaluate what their southern colleagues have wrought. Liberation theology, which—in the words of Bishop Thomas Kelly, USCC and NCCB general secretary—"provided the dynamics of the Puebla Conference," has aroused strong critics within the theological profession; at the same time it has won admirers, imitators, and adapters. In the coming decade, theological meetings, faculties and publications will be discussing the maturing role of the young school at Puebla and its future in Latin America and other regions.

4. *Journalists* will continue to report on Puebla's follow-up in northern media, secular and religious. Secular reporters were drawn to Mexico primarily by the new pope's presence. But a remarkable number stayed on for the bishops' assembly as well, including some representing papers not known for in-depth analysis and long-view features.

5. *Learned journals,* monthlies and quarterlies, secular as well as religious, have become increasingly aware of the new role of faith communities in developing regions. So have publishing houses. Puebla will draw new attention to the Latin experience, in tandem and comparison now with Islam's resurgence in the Middle East. Some Muslim scholars have acknowledged that the liberation motif of the Latin American Church exerts influence upon Islam's current interface with modernity and western power. A freshet of books and monographs now appears on both religio-cultural regions, Mideast and Latin America, with Puebla featured in the latter.

6. During the past decade dioceses, religious orders, and lay groups have set up over a hundred *justice and peace centers* in the United States, and a proportionate number in Canada. Their formation was stimulated by Vatican II and attendant events noted above and was directly promoted by the bishops' conferences. These centers have become major carriers of the Medellín message and have spurred its adaptation throughout the Church of North America, on local, national, and global issues. They now stand ready to become conductors of Puebla's surprising promise.

7. *The Hispanic community* of the United States has acquired since 1968 self-identity, structure, and voice, due in large measure to "liberation movements" comparable to those south of the Rio Grande. Medellín strengthened the vision and courage particularly of Mexican-American leaders such as César Chávez, Bishop Patricio Flores, and Father Virgil Elizondo.

8. *Other oppressed groups*—including the black community and other ethnic groups—have also felt the influence of Medellín. Black theology in the United States is partly nourished by Latin American liberation themes. The movement of women's liberation within the Church also draws from Medellín. Puebla promises to pump fresh currents through these circulatory networks.

9. The *Catholic bishops of North America,* individually and through their two national conferences, will also be major carriers of Puebla's influence. Many have worked with their Latin American brothers (as equals) during Vatican II and the Synods and on Vatican boards. Each year a score of U.S., Canadian, and Latin American bishops meet officially for several days. Trust, admiration, and friendship have flowered. During the 1970s over a hundred new bishops have been named in North America; the orientation of most is more pastoral, universal, and collegial, more open to Puebla's directions.

Topics from Puebla for a Northern Agenda

Nine clear channels exist for carrying Puebla's impact into the Catholic Church of North America. More could be found and traced. These living conduits will carry northward topics for an agenda that I choose to cluster under five headings. These are chosen from the richness of Puebla because in my judgment they bear special significance for our North American reality—as society, culture, and Church.

1. *Analysis of the societal reality* of the region is the starting point of the Medellín-Puebla method. Part One of the Puebla Final Document is entitled: "Pastoral Overview of the Reality That Is Latin America," and opens with a historical review of the continent's evangelization.

Puebla's first quote from John Paul II follows in this same context. Landing for the first time in the New World, the new pope gave recognition to "those religious who came to announce Christ the Savior, to defend the dignity of the native inhabitants, to proclaim their inviolable rights, to foster their integral betterment, to teach brotherhood as human beings and as children of the same Lord and Father God." However, the Puebla bishops add: "Unfortunately, the problem of the African slaves did not attract sufficient evangelizing and liberation-oriented attention from the Church" (no. 8n).

This historical review of four centuries concludes with the past decade: "Since Medellín in particular, the Church, clearly aware of its mission and loyally open to dialogue, has been scrutinizing the signs of the times and is generously disposed to evangelize in order to contribute to the construction of a new society that is more fraternal and just; such a society is a crying need of our peoples" (no. 12).

A chapter then follows on "Pastoral Overview of the Sociocultural Context." The overwhelming reality discerned is "the situation of inhuman poverty in which millions of Latin Americans live. . . . Analyzing this situation more deeply, we discover that this poverty is not a passing phase. Instead it is the product of economic, social, and political situations and structures . . ." (nos. 29, 30). Often this domestic dynamic has its origin and support in mechanisms that produce a situation "on the international level where the rich get richer at the expense of the poor, who get ever poorer" (no. 30, referring to OAP:III,3).

Cultural aspects are surveyed next, followed by demographic problems and the "underlying roots of these realities." Under "Human Dignity," there are reviewed visions that are deterministic, psychologistic, economicist, statist, and scientistic (nos. 304–15). A principal chapter on "Evangelization, Ideologies, and Politics" opens with these somber one-sentence paragraphs:

Recent years have seen a growing deterioration in the sociopolitical life of our countries.

They are experiencing the heavy burden of economic and institutional crisis and clear symptoms of corruption and violence.

The violence is generated and fostered by two factors: (1) what can be called institutionalized injustice in various social, political, and economic systems; and (2) ideologies that use violence as a means to win power.

The latter in turn causes the proliferation of governments based on force, which often derive their inspiration from the ideology of National Security (nos. 507–10).

This surface sampling of the lengthy Puebla document indicates the *range of societal reality* within which the Latin American bishops elaborate their pastoral vision and planning. Thus far, the episcopates of North America have not ranged as far, as deeply, or as daringly. A valuable beginning in this direction was made in the United States through the Bicentennial Program on "Liberty and Justice for All," 1975–76, especially through the grassroots hearings on societal and ecclesial issues in six of the nation's regions. The bicentennial format, however, allowed little space or time for study and analysis of U.S. economic, political, and cultural context and history, or for ecclesial follow-through. Few bishops became involved in the process, and theological reflection on the societal reality—so much a part of the Puebla event—was almost absent in the U.S. effort.

2. *Theological reflection as bishop-pastors* on the societal and ecclesial reality of the Latin American region is the hallmark of the Medellín-Puebla process. This Latin American model and method of theological reflection could exercise significant impact upon the Church of North America. I offer here some remarks with a view toward possibilities in this regard.

In line with Medellín, the Puebla bishops reflect upon societal reality within the context of their own pastoral experience, and vice-versa. This reflection takes place in the real-life, dialectical *tension of the ecclesial and the temporal communities,* as distinct but by no means absolutely separate or inimical. They accent salvation history, searching the signs of the times, past-present-future, for the ecclesial significance of God's liberating presence.

Latin American liberation theologians since Medellín have cultivated these vigorous sprouts from Vatican II's main theological stem in the context of their continent's state of domination-dependence. From this twofold *social sin* God's presence through Christ-and-his-people brings liberation, now as in the past.

Liberation theology as a coherent school does not yet exist, and probably never will in the classic scholarly sense because of this self-conscious "incarnation" within societal reality and the "revelation" it constantly discovers from pastoral ministry and the living Christian community. Consequently, the Puebla pastors do not, in the manner of academic professors, professedly embrace liberation theology. Rather, they jointly articulate and elevate to the regional ecclesial level their pastoral experiences of God's liberating experience within their respective national and local faith communities.

Christology pervades Puebla's theology much more deeply than Medellín's. Besides the chapters of theological reflection as such, the leitmotif of "liberation and total realization in Christ Jesus" returns throughout in constant refrain. The Puebla bishops profess a regional creed: "At the Medellín Conference we ended our message with these words: 'We have faith in God, in human beings, and in the values and future of Latin America.' Here in Puebla, taking up again that profession of divine and human faith, we proclaim: 'God is present and alive, in Jesus Christ the Liberator, in the heart of Latin America' " (MPLA:9).

This Christology of Puebla develops two thrusts beyond Medellín: *communion and participation*. These, together with the liberation theme of Medellín, take on complementary roles in Puebla's theological and pastoral dynamics. The liberating Christ shares with us his participation in the Trinity's life by communion with Father and Spirit (nos. 211–19); within the evangelizing Church the liberating mission is carried out through centers and agents of communion and participation.

Puebla's theology is more aptly described as a theology of liberation-communion-participation, and not of "liberation" alone. These newly-acquired attributes of "communion-participation" are extremely significant for the North American Church. The middle-class white males who now enjoy majority leadership status in the Catholic Church of Canada and the United States have no personal experience of the dependency, poverty, and oppression from which the Latin American majority demand liberation. So a theology symbolized by liberation alone has lacked direct appeal to the Church of the affluent powerful in North America. But now resource depletion, rampant pollution, and "the limits to growth" threaten northern consumerists and our American way of waste. And shifts in the world's power balance, as the industrial West becomes dependent upon the energy-rich countries, now accelerate economic and political *interdependence* on a transnational scale. Today no continent is an island, and "communion-participation" becomes an inescapable imperative.

But even if northern technological power and momentum counterbalance that shift, the need of communion and participation grows apace amid the alienation and violence and waste of North America's "me generation." U.S. and Canadian pastors and people might look to Puebla for ways to fashion an ecclesial response adapted to our own changing societal reality.

Liberation has its attractions, especially among blacks, Hispanics, and women. But it is also important for the powerful; liberation for the powerful involves the shedding and sharing of power and the establishment of a new world order. A theology of *kenosis*, of Christ emptying himself, of diminution and becoming small, could well converge with the liberation-communion-participation currents in North America. To this we must add the theology of fulfillment—in the eschatological All-in-All of the Omega Kingdom yet to come and already here amid God's People.

Marxist social analysis and dialectics have played a role in the development of liberation theology that is too complex for treatment here. To my mind, however, that role has been greatly exaggerated in media reports to North Americans. Our simplistic notions and fears so easily identify socialism with Marxism, without discrimination. Christian concern for the poor, powerless oppressed, with the concomitant criticism of the rich, powerful oppressors and the call for structural change, too readily draw the "Communist!" epithet in the United States.

But the Marxist reality in Latin America is much more substantial, and any ecclesial reflection upon the region's society as a whole must take seriously the Marxist philosophy and ideology to a degree unimagined here. In like manner serious theological reflection by the North American Church has to deal with the capitalist and individualist ideologies that permeate the U.S. and Canada, especially since these theories of the human person and society have seduced us so thoroughly.

Pope John Paul II warned liberation theologians against the danger of identifying themselves so closely with any ideology that the transcendent centrality of Christ and his message becomes obscured. The Church, he said, need have no recourse to any ideologies in order to love, to defend, and to collaborate in the liberation of human beings. The pope's insistence on Christ and *his* liberating truth, without further warnings, shows that the pope wants to accentuate the positive. Philosopher-theologian, professor-pastor that he is, we should expect John Paul to write frequently on these subjects in the future. Consequently this theological focus will become more prominent in the ecclesial mainstream for the coming decade or so. All the more reason for the North American Church to enter more seriously into this level of theological dialogue and societal analysis.

It is significant, in our present context, that the Puebla bishops issue their own warning, much more pointed than that given by the pope:

> We must also note the risk of ideologization run by theological reflection when it is based on a praxis that has recourse to Marxist analysis. The consequences are the total politicization of Christian existence, the disintegration of the language of faith into that of the social sciences, and the draining away of the transcendental dimension of Christian salvation.
>
> Both of the aforementioned ideologies—capitalist liberalism and Marxism—find their inspiration in brands of humanism that are closed to any transcendent perspective. One does because of its practical atheism; the other does because of its systematic profession of a militant atheism (nos. 545–46).

I believe that the Catholic Church of North America is awakening to the need for deep and perduring theological reflection upon the societal and ecclesial reality of our region. Many elements of the Latin American experience will influence this. And the commendation by Pope John Paul of the liberation approach will greatly encourage the northern effort, especially among bishops.

3. *Evangelization and pastoral praxis* is the third major topic from the Puebla document having special significance for the North American Church. This flows organically from the two topics already reviewed: analysis of the region's societal reality and theological reflection upon that reality.

The first mark of Medellín-Puebla to recall now is that pastoral ministry is not a mere consequence flowing from theology; it also generates theology. The act and place of evangelization are also the *locus* of theological reflection and provide in large measure the data and the prisms for reflecting *in* and *on* the light of Christ's Good News. God's People participate in this reflection as a faith community, in the concreteness of *these* believers and ministers at a particular place and date—and usually in the mud and dirt, flies and filth of that concreteness, as well as in the callous concrete of the jail cell.

This leads to the most talked about elements of Puebla's ministry: the base communities, and the pastoral option for the poor and powerless.

Comunidades de base will be rendered here as "base communities," because if the Latin American experience is to be adapted in significant degree to the North American reality, the name must be translated into our language until we find a fitting term of our own.

My remarks will stress the *ecclesiastical* significance of base communities in the Webster's dictionary sense of the term "ecclesiastical": of or relating to the Church "especially as a formal and established institution" (Collegiate Dictionary, 1973 edition). I foresee base communities entering into the "Canon Law" of the Latin American Church of the future. Will comparable bodies become part of the institutional Catholic Church of the United States and Canada?

The base community is accorded a prime role as a center of communion-participation, in the same category as the family, the parish, and the local Church or diocese. In the minds of Puebla's bishops the base community is not a transient gathering or occasional group. Rather, it partakes of the Church's own character and constitution. The bishops explain:

> As a community, the CEB [*Comunidad Eclesial de Base*] brings together families, adults and young people, in an intimate interpersonal relationship grounded in the faith. As an ecclesial reality, it is a community of faith, hope, and charity. It celebrates the Word of God and takes its nourishment from the Eucharist, the culmination of all the sacraments. It fleshes out the Word of God in life through solidarity and commitment to the new commandment of the Lord; and through the service of approved coordinators, it makes present and operative the mission of the Church and its visible communion with the legitimate pastors. It is a base-level community because it is composed of relatively few members as a permanent body, like a cell of the larger community. "When they deserve their ecclesial designation, they can take charge of their own spiritual and human existence in a spirit of fraternal solidarity" (no. 641, citing EN:58).

The document goes on to state that Christians united in the base communities attain a more evangelical life amid the people: They "work together to challenge the egotistical and consumeristic roots of society, and make explicit their vocation to communion with God and their fellow humans. Thus they offer a valid and worthwhile point of departure for building up a new society, 'the civilization of love' " (no. 642).

Furthermore, base communities are an expression of "the Church's preferential love for the common people," who express themselves and purify their religiosity through these communities. These also provide them "a concrete opportunity to share in the task of the Church and to work committedly for the transformation of the world" (no. 643).

North American Catholics, especially pastors and lay councils, ask quite naturally about the parish's relation with this new ecclesial structure. The parish is described in the document as the "center of coordination and guidance for communities, groups, and movements. In it the horizons of communion and participation are opened up even more." The limitations proper to small communities are overcome; the globality of the Church's mission is made present in a clearer way. The link with the diocesan community is assured through union with the bishop who confides pastoral care of the parish community to his representative, normally the pastor. Thus, the parish takes on services that are beyond the reach of the smaller communities, above all with regard to the missionary dimension, and the furthering of the dignity of the human person, "in general to the neediest" (no. 644). The Puebla bishops conclude that : "As pastors, we are determined to promote, guide, and accompany the CEBs" (no. 648).

North American Roman Catholics increasingly wonder what they might learn from the 150,000 base communities of Latin America. Some North American bishops and pastors and lay leaders are already experimenting with small groups. Charismatic prayer groups and family movements, social justice centers and neighborhood coalitions, testify to the yearning for communion-participation. Latin American pastoral creativity for liberation-communion-participation, now given the green light after a decade of yellow caution, could spur northern pastors to experiment more boldly.

A preferential option for the poor is affirmed by the Puebla pastors; this was the priority of Jesus Christ from the time he began his ministry in the synagogue of Nazareth (no. 1141; Luke 4:18–21). And who are these poor? That "vast majority of our fellow human beings [who] continue to live in a situation of poverty and even wretchedness that has grown more acute" during the decade since Medellín (no. 1135). "They lack the most elemental material goods in contrast to the accumulation of riches in the hands of a minority, often at the cost of the poverty of the many" (no. 1135n).

These poor lack not only material goods, but also miss, on the level of human dignity, full participation in sociopolitical life. Those in this situation are principally our indigenous peoples, peasants, manual laborers, marginalized urban dwellers and, in particular, the women of these social groups. The women are doubly oppressed and marginalized" (no. 1135n). To my mind "outcasts" would be a better translation of the Spanish "marginados," except that these oppressed have never been "in" and were consequently never cast out; their congenital lot is poverty and oppression, handed down generation unto generation since the conquistadors and Christ's Good News arrived in Mexico and Peru four hundred years ago.

This is the Latin American "vicious circle of poverty" that the Puebla pastors seek to break. This is the personal and social sin from which the region's people and structures must be liberated. Medellín had urged Catholic conversion into "the Church of the poor." Now Puebla calls for becoming "the poor Church."

From the start, U.S. Catholic clergy, faithful, and religious were mostly poor and powerless. Then together they ascended the American ladder of success, climbing as a group in social position, political power, and personal purse. As a rule the higher clergy's rate of climb outdistanced that of the laity. The faithful seemed to delight in the Renaissance pomp and privilege bestowed on their spiritual hierarchy by the Papal Court, transforming their lowborn cousins into eminent cardinal princes, lordly bishops, and empurpled monsignori, attendants all to the transatlantic Papal Throne. An ordinary Solemn Pontifical High Mass brought us together a dozen times a year, bowing and scraping, incensing and stumbling over each other amid the marble and magenta of Christ's sanctuary, all to celebrate his Holy Name and his Good News to the poor—in Latin, the imperial language of the thrice-crowned Head gloriously reigning from the lowly Fisherman's Chair.

By the mid-1900s the Catholic Church in North America was no longer poor; Catholics of European origin, over two-thirds of the U.S. Church, had "arrived," taking their place in the mainstream of national life, alongside white Protestants and Jews.

And yet, with perhaps 15 million Hispanics and 1.5 million black and native American Catholics, we must bear in mind that about a third of the U.S. Roman Catholic population is still poor in economic product and political know-how. Their barrios and reservations shunt them from the cultural mainstream. Worse yet they feel shut off from decision and policy roles, both as sparse clergy and numerous faithful, within the Church itself. They awaken now to the liberation evoked by Medellín and to the communion-participation promised by Puebla.

The majority of U.S. Roman Catholics can ill afford to be complacent about the poor *within* the Church, both in North and South America.

The U.S. and Latin American proportions of poverty and power are reversed. Here some 80 percent participate adequately, if not equitably, in U.S. economic product and political power; while about 20 percent do not as yet to an adequate degree. In the Latin American region some 20 percent receive goods and services sufficient for a life of human dignity; but 80 percent do not, and perhaps half of these live in misery as compared to northern standards. Over 200 million Latin Americans, a number approaching the population of the United States, live well below the poverty floor we have set for U.S. citizens. Worse still, only some 10 percent of the Latin American people (rich, poor, and miserable) have access to political participation and civil rights comparable to U.S. norms; the rest do not. So the poverty-power equation makes demands of the Puebla pastors that North American Church leaders find difficult to conceive.

Despite our hundred justice and peace centers, Catholic Relief Services, Network, the Committee for Urban Ministry, Campaign for Human Development, Call to Action, and similar fine programs, U.S. Roman Catholics have a long way to go before becoming the Church of the poor and oppressed of all God's human family. How much longer can the affluent People of God of our wealthy nation defer the "preferential option for the poor" made by Jesus in the synagogue of Nazareth—and the Latin American bishops at Puebla?

With regard to the *laity,* the Puebla document first offers recognition and further encouragement to "the many lay people who, through their witness of Christian commitment, help to carry out the task of evangelization and to present the face of a Church committed to the work of promoting justice among our peoples." It is clearly the laity's special concern to reshape the systems and structures of the continent, to redress the inequality of industrialization and the socioeconomic differences that increasingly oppress masses of people (nos. 777–78).

By Christian calling the layperson is placed both within the Church and within the world. The Puebla document treats both dimensions of the lay vocation, with emphases that respond to current Latin American reality: (1) in the world, *political* activity to promote human rights and just structures; (2) in the Church, the exercise of *diverse ministries* in collaboration with the pastors (nos. 786–826).

Building up a more just and peaceful world, at the service of God's Kingdom, remains the specific and primordial role of the laity. In today's situation it is political activity that must be given particular emphasis. This embraces the wide field from casting one's vote to "exercising party leadership" and public office at whatever level. "In every instance lay people should strive to seek and promote the common good: defending the dignity of human beings and their inalienable rights; protecting those who are weakest and most in need; fashioning peace, freedom, and justice; and creating more just and fraternal structures" (no. 792). To the workers at Guadalajara, Pope John Paul said, "It is not enough for Christians to denounce injustice; they are also required to be truly witnesses to, and agents of, justice."

More provocative, because more innovative, is Puebla's position on the diversity of ecclesial ministries to be exercised by laity within the Church itself. Side by side with the hierarchical ministries of bishops, priests, and deacons, the Church recognizes a position for *ministries without sacred orders:* "So the laity, too, can feel called or be called to collaborate with their pastors in service to the ecclesial community. For the life and growth of the community they may exercise various ministries, depending on the grace and charisms that the Lord gives them" (no. 804, and see no. 805).

Lay "animators" provide local leadership for the 150,000 base communities of Latin America. These groups provide, in the document's words, "a favorable atmosphere for the rise of new lay-sponsored services. They have done much to spread family catechesis and adult education in the faith, in forms more suitable for the common people" (no. 629). Many dioceses now have training centers expressly for the formation of animators for base communities.

The solid formation of laity becomes all the more urgent with their increased participation both in the Church's life and in its mission in the world. This formation, to which laity have a right, must be doctrinal, social, and apostolic. And it must include a profound spirituality appropriate to the lay state.

North American Roman Catholics will find here several points to ponder regarding the laity of our own region. We count many political and secular figures among our numbers, but concern for the poor and oppressed, locally and worldwide, is seldom an identifying mark, especially among our more affluent leaders. Little attention is given in ecclesial suburbia to the *formation* of lay leaders, to imparting our rich and exciting social teaching and to fostering a sense of vocation, with an apostolic spirituality, through organized and persevering groups.

Among the oppressed themselves, on the other hand, the United Farm Workers and the Mexican-American movement have emerged, and political awakening has become a ministry among the Latin parishes of Brooklyn. Also, hundreds of neighborhood coalitions, justice and peace centers, advocacy and pressure groups have cropped up almost everywhere. The great majority, however, are sponsored by religious orders and by dioceses with the support of their national ecclesiastical bodies; few are sponsored by the laity.

Women and their "margination" are treated in paragraphs 834 to 849 of the document. "In the Church itself there has sometimes been an undervaluation of women and minimal participation by them in pastoral initiatives." Nevertheless, we now see positive signs: the slow but growing appearance of women in the tasks of upbuilding society, and the upsurge of feminine organizations that work for the advancement and incorporation of women in all sectors of society (nos. 839–40).

In its doctrinal reflection, the document stresses the dignity and equality of women because they as well as men are made in the image of God. Women, as much as men, receive the task of ruling the world, of continuing the work of creation, of being co-creators with God. Women participate in the prophetic gift of Christ through baptism. Their role in the life of Christ, especially that of Mary, is well recorded in the Gospels. Consequently, "with her specific aptitudes, the woman should make a real contribution to the Church's mission, participating in organisms for pastoral planning, pastoral coordination, catechesis, etc. (MR:49–50). The possibility of entrusting *non-ordained ministries* to women will open up new ways for them to participate in the Church's life and mission" (no. 845, emphasis added).

Among the Puebla bishops the role of women, however, is not yet seen to be the pressing issue it has become among North American Roman Catholics, and in our society as a whole. In a Universal Church such as ours changes as profound as the full participation of women can come only through a certain consensus among a strong majority of the regional Churches. Puebla demonstrates that majority view is still not in sight; a consensus among the regions on optional celibacy, I believe, will come sooner because of pastoral imperatives and pressures from within the presbyterate.

These regional differences and pluralist positions within the Catholic Church fortify the tendency, loosed by Vatican II's collegiality and now reinforced by Puebla's conformation of Medellín, toward new macrostructures based on the ecclesial regions. Within such an authority system, the dozen or so ecclesial regions, under the presiding Chair of Peter, would each have much greater leeway than now obtains in Church discipline and pastoral ministry. Women's ordination, for example, could then be agreed upon by the regional Church of North America, with approval of the pope.

4. *Communal action for transforming the structures of society,* to promote justice, participation, and development for all, is the fourth Puebla topic of special significance to the North American Church. Puebla's approach to the transformation of economic and political structures proceeds along the regional trails blazed ten years before by Medellín, following the historic global guideposts of Vatican II in *Gaudium et Spes,* papal teaching in *Pacem in Terris, Populorum Progressio,* and *Octogesima Adveniens,* and "Justice in the World" of the Bishops' Synod of 1971.

The final two chapters in Part Four of the Puebla document (nos. 1206 –93) are especially noteworthy. They regionalize *Populorum Progressio* and the Synod's "Justice in the World," updating both them and Medellín with the sure touch of a decade's additional experience.

In both chapters, the historical and structural *situation* is first reviewed, then doctrinal *criteria* for ecclesial action are set forth. This is followed by directives for *pastoral action* and *services,* with meanings that are better translated for North Americans as "ministries." The scope and content of pastoral ministry are broadened enormously, but in constant conjunction with the Church's missionary nature.

North Americans, in studying these chapters, should note insistence upon a *pluralist* society and the "right to a new international order in accord with the human values of solidarity and justice" (no. 1279). This new world order will avoid "neo-Malthusian criteria. It will be grounded on legitimate human social needs. It will provide for a healthy pluralism, and for the adequate representation of minorities and intermediary groups so that it will not be a closed circle of nations. It will preserve the common patrimony of humanity, particularly the oceans" (no. 1280).

Puebla broke new ground in its concern for human rights and with regard to the political sphere in general. Since North Americans are familiar with Latin American initiatives in the human rights ministry, we will focus here on the section in the document that deals with "Evangelization, Ideologies, and Politics" (nos. 507–62).

This section opens with an acknowledgement of "the growing deterioration in the sociopolitical life of our countries" in recent years, which has brought with it corruption and violence (nos. 507–8). This violence is generated: (1) by injustice institutionalized in various social, political, and economic systems, and (2) by ideologies that use violence as a means to win power. "As a mother and teacher whose expertise is humanity, the Church must examine the conditions, systems, ideologies, and political life of our continent—shedding light on them from the standpoint of the Gospel and its own social teaching. And this must be done even though it knows that people will try to use its message as their own tool" (no. 511).

Points raised in the remaining paragraphs of this section are even more salient for North American Roman Catholics. They are *(a)* the reality of ideologies for society and the Church, *(b)* the risk of the Church's being manipulated by ideologies and parties for their own purposes, and *(c)* the role of Church, clergy, and religious in the political sphere.

a. The trilogy of *ideologies* treated at some length in this section, and adverted to repeatedly throughout the document, are (1) *capitalist liberalism,* the idolatry of wealth in its individualist form; (2) *Marxist collectivism,* which also leads by reason of its materialist presuppositions to an idolatry of wealth, but in its collective form; and (3) the Doctrine of *National Security,* an ideology linked with a predetermined economic-political model with elitist characteristics, which suppresses the broad participation of the people in political decisions (nos. 542–49).

Marxist collectivism and capitalist liberalism, the document warns, are both inspired by humanisms that are closed to every transcendent perspective: one due to its systematic and militant atheism, the other due to its practical atheism. This continues the Catholic social teaching begun by Leo XIII in 1891, on through Pius XI in the 1930s, John XXIII in *Mater et Magistra,* and Paul VI in *Populorum Progressio.*

Note must be taken of the term "capitalist liberalism." This means individualist *laissez-faire* free enterprise that absolutizes private property and profit without social obligations and without regulation by political authority on behalf of the poor and powerless and for the common good of all.

The document goes on to describe the other well-known marks of Marxism: class struggle, dictatorship of the proletariat and the party and the historical fact of totalitarian regimes closed to self-criticism and correction. The document does not speak here of socialism in its many forms, and presumes no equivalence between Marxism and socialism as is often found in the United States.

The Doctrine of National Security, the third ideology dealt with at Puebla, has come to the fore since Medellín. In the 1960s it was Marxism that shook the whole continent, Church as well as society. In the 1970s it is the National Security problem that more directly challenges the Church.

At times, the Doctrine of National Security is seen to express a clear intention of "geopolitical leadership" (no. 547). The document's politic phrase here refers, I believe, to Brazil's suspected intention of dominating South America, as their own "manifest destiny." Worse yet from the bishops' point of view, this ideology "justifies itself as the defender of the Christian civilization of the West" in some countries of Latin America (no. 547). In reality, however,

> The Doctrine of National Security, understood as an absolute ideology, would not be compatible with the Christian vision of the human being as responsible for carrying out a temporal project and to its vision of the State as the administrator of the common good. It puts the people under the tutelage of military and political elites, who exercise authority and power; and it leads to increased inequality in sharing the benefits of development (no. 549).

It is the suppression of human and civil rights under this ideology that has called forth the prophetic ministry of the Church in Brazil, Chile, and other countries, under pastors such as Cardinals Evaristo Arns and Raúl Silva. Their leadership, courage, and risk-taking will surely continue to have an impact on the pastors and people of Canada and the United States. American Roman Catholics should be doubly attentive because of support given some of these Latin American regimes by multinational corporations and by our own government.

The Puebla document does not condemn all ideologies. The innate problem is that every ideology is partial, in the double sense that it embraces only some fraction of human experience and society and life's meaning, and that it tends to absolutize its own partial aspirations to the detriment and often to the exclusion of others. An ideology can therefore be legitimate if the interests that it defends are legitimate, and if it respects the fundamental rights of the other national groups. To exercise critical judgment on ideologies, Catholics should rely on the social teaching of the Church (no. 538) and fortify their identities "in the original values of Christian anthropology" (no. 552).

b. The Puebla bishops and the pope perceive *the danger that the Church, and its ministers, may be manipulated* by ideologies and parties. The document cites four groups that try to make the Church and its ministers their own instruments:

First, "this manipulation of the Church, always a risk in political life, may derive from Christians themselves, and even from priests and religious, when they proclaim a *Gospel devoid of economic, social, cultural, and political implications.* In practice this mutilation [of the Gospel] comes down to a kind of *complicity with the established order,* however unwitting" (no. 558, emphasis added). In short, teaching and preaching deprived of their social justice dimension become ideologies through which the status quo uses the Church—including its teachers and preachers. This "purely spiritual" Gospel is ideology—in North America as well as in Latin America.

Second, "other groups are tempted in the opposite direction. They are tempted to consider a given political policy to be of primary urgency, a precondition for the Church's fulfillment of its mission. They are tempted to equate the Christian message with some ideology and subordinate the former to the latter, calling for a 're-reading' of the Gospel on the basis of a political option (OAP:I,4). But the fact is that we must try to read the political scene from the standpoint of the Gospel, not vice-versa" (no. 559).

The third form of manipulation of the Church is "traditional integrism," which "looks for the Kingdom to come principally through a stepping back in history and reconstructing a Christian culture of a medieval cast. This would be a new Christendom, in which there was an intimate alliance between civil authority and ecclesiastical authority" (no. 560). In pluralist North America, there is little to worry about in this regard though we do still see some yearning for the monarchical authority of the preconciliar Church, when everything was clear and simple.

Fourth, "the radical thrust of groups at the other extreme falls into the same trap. It looks for the Kingdom to come from a strategic alliance between the Church and Marxism, and it rules out all other alternatives. For these people it is not simply a matter of being Marxists, but of being Marxists in the name of the faith" (no. 561). In North America, such Marxist groups of Christians are uncommon.

c. In view of this complexus of ideologies and politics it is small wonder then that Puebla and the pope focus so intently upon *the role of the Church, clergy, and religious in the political sphere.* To my mind, however, this subject—much commented on in media reports on Puebla—does not receive a balanced treatment in the document (nos. 507–30).

It is marred by a collective timidity that ignores the direct courage shown by hundreds of bishops, clergy, and religious, and especially by thousands of leaders identified in some degree with the Church or inspired by its social teaching.

Its repeated warnings about risks and excesses seem to mute the "Call to Action" made by Pope Paul VI for "passing to the political dimension," for commitment by "Christian communities . . . in order to bring about the social, political, and economic changes seen in many cases to be urgently needed"(OA:4).

Its "Reflections on Political Violence," while properly condemning political torture and kidnappings, terrorism, and the inhuman structures often installed by violent revolutions, are not balanced with a treatment of the institutional violence of unjust structures stressed by Medellín, and of nonviolent social transformation practiced and preached by Helder Camara and others (nos. 531–34).

It tends to idealize political reality and the history of human liberty, dignity, and justice by ignoring conflict and violence, with all their ambiguities, as exemplified by our American War of Independence and by the Civil War to free our slaves.

Its elevated vision of "the Church's presence in the political field" and "for the evangelization of politics" seems to exclude many activities by Catholic bishops, clergy, and religious in Italy, and notably by the popes and Vatican Curia, in support of the Christian Democratic Party and the national government it has led for the past generation.

In short, the Puebla bishops have left many ambiguities about this subject. Perhaps they did this to leave national episcopal conferences and local Churches free to pursue their experiments in social ministry, making their own judgments according to the particular political situations. This local option by Christian communities was insisted upon by Pope Paul in his call to political action in 1971.

One very clear statement in the document concerns party politics. This is definitely a field proper to the laity, and not to bishops, clergy, and religious. Pastors, priests, and deacons are "ministers of unity," so they must especially avoid the partisanship of party politics, which by its nature fragments the community. In accord with their specific charisma, members of religious orders should cooperate in evangelizing the political sphere, without confusing the gospel values with a determined ideology. Pope John Paul is quoted in support of the position that "Christ's Gospel would not have had such an impact on history if he had not proclaimed it as a religious message: '. . . He does not accept the position of those who mixed the things of God with merely political attitudes' " (no. 526, citing OAP:I,4).

These Latin American views on the clergy and party politics correspond to those held by northern bishops. However, the Puebla document does leave a loophole: it can occur that "in concrete and exceptional circumstances . . . [it] is truly required by the good of the community" that a priest assume leadership in a political party, and then only with consent of the bishop and the national episcopal conference if circumstances so indicate (no. 527).

I have purposely dwelt upon the *political* elements of ecclesial action for transforming the structures of society because these still need development as compared with the document's position on economic power and justice. Also, while the economic elements are better known to North Americans, it is in the political field that Puebla breaks new ground.

5. *The regional Catholic Church,* with its own intra-Church dynamics, is the fifth Puebla topic having special significance for our North American reality.

Puebla advanced the awareness of Latin America as an ecclesial region with its own distinctive sociopolitical reality, one requiring theological reflection and pastoral action different from the Church in other regions. This calls for a *structural model* of the Church different from the homogeneous uniformity invoked and established before Vatican II took place and CELAM took shape. This orientation from Puebla has great long-range significance for the Church in North America, and in some ten other religio-cultural, sociopolitical regions of the world.

The concept of regional Churches dates back to the early centuries of the Church. Already in the Acts of the Apostles, Jerusalem and Antioch, with the territory around these hub cities, appear as regional communities of faith, each with distinguishing marks within the Christian Church. Rome and Alexandria were, respectively, the political-military and intellectual capitals of the empire. Their Churches became the other two patriarchates of the first century, both assuming supervisory roles over local Churches hundreds of miles outside these thriving imperial cities.

During the second century the regional Churches of Jerusalem, Antioch, and Alexandria gradually came to acknowledge the Roman bishop's ministry of unity and his supervisory role over the whole Christian *ecumene,* because he sat in the Chair of Peter. The early papacy took shape—and grew.

However, each regional Church—the term "patriarchate" came into use centuries later—retained enormous authority over the dioceses and Christian life of its own area, with regard to liturgy, theology, preaching, instruction, discipline, appointment of bishops, division of dioceses, relations with civil government, etc. The pope as successor of Peter exercised, de jure and de facto, only restricted responsibility over these eastern regions, as compared with his authority in the western ecclesial region at that time and in the whole Catholic world today.

Even in matters of grave *theological* substance, the eastern Churches were clearly in the lead for the first thousand years. They sought collegial responses to crisis. The eight Ecumenical Councils during that first half of the Christian era were all held in the East. Among the three hundred bishops present at the first of these, at Nicea in 325, only three came from Western Europe, one each from Spain, France, and Italy, "and since the great age of the Bishop of Rome forbade his making the journey he was represented by two of his priests" (Philip Hughes, *The Church in Crisis: A History of the General Councils 325–1870,* New York: Hanover House, 1961, p. 32).

Very significant for our present interest in ecclesial regions, the bishops at Nicea formally recognized the special status of Alexandria, Antioch, and Jerusalem: "The council confirms the ancient custom that gives the bishop of Alexandria jurisdiction over the bishops of the civil provinces of Egypt, Libya, and Pentapolis. And likewise the ancient privileges of the See of Antioch and of the other provinces. Jerusalem is a city apart, the Holy City par excellence" (ibid., pp. 34–35).

Within five years after Nicea, Constantinople was completed as the new imperial capital, the New Rome. Its bishopric took on patriarchical status with authority over the whole Byzantine Empire, the ecclesial region extending from the Adriatic to the Danube, from Russia to the Nile and the Persian Gulf. In 1054, after six centuries of intra-Church conflict between Rome and Constantinople, the Churches of West and East split into the Catholic and the Orthodox Churches. The spiritual leader of the latter remains the Ecumenical Patriarch of Constantinople (Istanbul).

This brief review of church history is intended to add historical perspective to our reading of the Puebla event. We have seen that God's People organize themselves in different ways in differing *ages,* as well as in function of societal reality in differing *places.* For a thousand years five ecclesial regions, presided over by the Chair of Peter, provided the macrostructure of the entire Christian Church. Since that time the institutional Church has been split into hundreds of divisions: along imperial-monarchical lines in the Roman Catholic Church, with every diocese answerable directly to Rome on all matters, without national or regional structure (prior to Vatican II); along national lines in most Orthodox and Reformation Churches; and along congregational lines in most Evangelical Churches and free sects.

I foresee the partial transfer of ecclesial authority from the papacy "outward and downward," and from dioceses and national bishops' conferences "upward," to gradually form regional church jurisdictions. These will assume roles comparable to those of the patriarchates during the first centuries. These regional Churches would correspond by and large to the dozen or so *multinational political* units now in formation as blocs and regions: Latin America and North America; Western Europe and Eastern Europe; Black Africa; Arabic-Orthodox-Jewish Middle East; South, Southwest, and Southeast Asia; China and East Asia; Pacifica.

I believe that the growing Latin American awareness and articulation of the regional Church could represent an immeasurable contribution to the ecumenical movement in North America and in other ecclesial regions. Its effect upon the Church's macrostructures and the papal role are especially significant in this regard. The scant attention that ecumenism receives in the document is thus especially disappointing.

The North American Church and Society

No simple transplant of Puebla's product from Latin American to northern soil is possible. North American societal reality differs from the Latin American in many primordial elements: racial and ethnic stocks, culture and history, population growth, social stratification, economic and political structures, industrialization levels, power and product distribution, global influence.

But if no facile transference of Puebla is possible, still it should be clear that the Puebla event does challenge us in the North American Roman Catholic Church to examine the "signs of the times" in our own social reality. For the sake of the Good News of Christ we also need a more penetrating grasp and integrating overview of our society and Church, including:

—liberal democracy and industrial capitalism
—mass education, elitist science, and "galloping technology"
—superpower status, war and peace, nuclear war, current shifts in power balance between blocs and regions
—participation and community, social justice, human rights and needs here and worldwide
—resource depletion, pollution, environment
—consumer society, the media, lifestyle, alienation, the "me" generation
—the family, sexuality, abortion, divorce
—women in society and Church

—continuing reforms within the Church, ecumenism, interfaith relations
—ideologies, value-systems, philosophies

Each of these must be examined in the light of the Gospel and elicit theological reflection by the North American Church, to guide our pastoral ministry preferentially for the poor and powerless, but reaching too the affluent and powerful.

These are elements of the agenda that Puebla and John Paul II help us North American Roman Catholics to perceive. But what are the chances that the Church in North America will move on these agenda items?

I said at the outset that the Puebla Conference will have substantial influence on the Roman Catholic Church in the United States and Canada. I offer the following in support of my contention that—inspired in part by Puebla and Medellín—the Church *will* move to take up this agenda.

1. In a major policy address to the *National Conference of Catholic Bishops* in May 1979, the body's president, Archbishop John Quinn of San Francisco, called Puebla, "An event of major significance to us." The archbishop, who headed the U.S. delegation to the conference, went on to say: "But now comes the question, pointed and obvious: What effect will Puebla have on us? And specifically: *(a)* Should Puebla serve as a model for a similar conference by the American bishops? *(b)* What can we do and what should we do in regard to the policies of our own government which affect and aggravate the scandalous conditions in Latin America? *(c)* What can we do and what should we do in regard to the policies of some American-based transnational companies which also aggravate the scandalous conditions in Latin America? *(d)* What can we do and what should we do to alleviate the problems of the un-documented aliens which are partially due to the failures of local Latin American governments to provide for their own citizens?"

Archbishop Quinn concluded by raising the question of the role of the U.S. Bishops' Conference. In seeking a response, he said, "Puebla's analysis of the Latin American reality is an invitation to us to assess with the key of revelation and the teaching of the Church the reality of the Church in our own situation."

Under leadership such as Archbishop Quinn's, there is solid reason to believe that the Bishops' Conference, the primary authority structure of the U.S. Catholic Church, will seriously examine the significance of Medellín-Puebla and the Latin American pastoral experience for our own ecclesial region.

2. *The major superiors of men and women religious,* the other principal authority structure and leadership channel of the U.S. Church, have already initiated programs into which Puebla follow-up will readily flow. These include the Convergence Assembly, co-sponsored by the Leadership Conference of Women Religious and the Conference of Major Superiors of Men (Cleveland, August 1978) and the Convivencia-Convergence-Solidarity program begun in April 1978.

What is significant about these programs is that for the first time in American Catholic history, women and men religious are meeting and cooperating as corporate bodies at the national level on an enduring basis. More important, we should note that it is the gospel challenge of the poor and oppressed and the imperative ministry of social justice that pull them together.

This awakening of the U.S. Church has been stimulated by the poverty-justice issues from Latin America and other ecclesial regions.

3. *The National Federation of Priests' Councils* forms another circulatory network into which Puebla and its social analysis model enter with growing force. NFPC is constituted by elected delegates from the priests' senates or councils of over a hundred dioceses. It forms among the 50,000 priests of the United States a communication and guidance system in many ways comparable to the Bishops' Conference and the two Conferences of women and men religious superiors. While NFPC does not exercise the formal jurisdictional authority enjoyed by the other ecclesial bodies, it does in fact carry considerable weight in the collegial reorganization of the Church that has been evolving since Vatican II.

The justice imperative has found prominence within this presbyterate structure since it began a decade ago, at national, area, and diocesan levels. It has provided during that period a major transmission belt for the method and message of Medellín into diocesan programs and chanceries, into deaneries, parishes and their lay and pastoral councils.

4. *The Canadian Bishops' Conference* has long welcomed the inspiration of other ecclesial regions. In January 1978, the Canadian Bishops' Conference issued a pastoral letter entitled "A Society to Be Transformed," which reads like Medellín-Puebla in Canadian dress. This major document calls for regional and diocesan meetings to take penetrating looks at Canadian societal and ecclesial reality.

In closing, we must again remember that no simple transplant of Puebla's product from Latin American to North American soil is possible. North American societal and ecclesial realities differ from the Latin American in many primordial elements: racial and ethnic stocks, culture and history, population growth, social stratification, economic and political structures, industrialization levels, power and product distribution, present global influence.

A socio-theological analysis of these elements would help us North American Catholics better understand who and what we are. For these elements are "signs of the times," which must be examined in the light of the Gospel by the North American Church, to guide its pastoral ministry preferentially for the poor and powerless, but reaching too the affluent and powerful, if God's People and Christ's visible Church are to be clearly seen as "a sign and safeguard of the human person."

These, then, form the agenda that Puebla and John Paul II help us North American Catholics to perceive—and, we hope, to act on—into the 1980s and beyond.

THE SIGNIFICANCE OF PUEBLA
FOR THE PROTESTANT CHURCHES
IN NORTH AMERICA

Robert McAfee Brown

Why should a conference of Roman Catholic bishops in Latin America concern Protestants in North America?

That's not a difficult question anymore. A couple of decades ago it would have been, when Catholics and Protestants were at loggerheads in Latin America and North American attention was directed toward Europe and the Far East but hardly toward the "subcontinent."

But things have changed. North American business interests in Latin America ensure that the destiny of the two continents will remain linked, for good or for ill—and what is presently good for the north is ill for the south. Many Catholics and Protestants in Latin America have discovered that they need to work together in the face of common enemies such as poverty, exploitation, and military dictators. And all Christians are learning that what happens to any part of the Christian family affects all the other parts as well. The ancient Pauline recognition that "if one member suffers, all the members suffer with it" (1 Cor. 12:26) attains new meaning when we reflect that the torture inflicted in a Chilean prison is of concern not only to Chileans but to North Americans as well. And if a family outside that prison is starving because North American interests have so supported the Pinochet regime that living wages are not paid, that must be a concern not only to the Chilean family but to North Americans, who must assume responsibility for changing North American practices so that the exploitation ceases.

There is another kind of linkage. It is exemplified by recent testimony to the Senate Foreign Relations Committee that President Carter has ordered the CIA to engage in surveillance of "activist" priests and nuns in Latin America, "lest he be confronted with another Iran-type situation." This is only an echo of Nelson Rockefeller's warning a decade ago that much of the agitation for change in Latin America was coming from the Latin American Church in ways that could be detrimental to U.S. business interests. This, in turn, shows that the tune remains constant; only the orchestration changes. To counter such ecclesiastical putdowns on the part of our elected officials is another reason why people must be well-informed about Puebla.

So there are a variety of reasons why North American Protestants followed the proceedings at Puebla with care and need to reflect on what happened there.

On Not Absolutizing Puebla: A Brief But Important Lesson for Protestants on How to Read Catholic Documents

An initial reading of the Puebla document is likely to be a letdown, particularly to Protestants unused to episcopal prose. The document is rambling, repetitious, and occasionally contradictory. Sometimes it rises to eloquent heights, on other pages it resembles an accumulation of trivia. One almost wishes there could have been a winnowing process so that the best could have emerged more clearly without being so hard to find. On the other hand, in such a situation everything depends on who is the winnower. The state of things being what it is, perhaps we are best served by a mammoth statement, so that we can emphasize what seems important to us, and let the rest fall by the wayside. (This has happened before: who now invokes the Vatican II document on "Communications" as a guideline to the Church's life?)

The length and frequent ambiguity need not, however, be cause for despair. For I learned something as a Protestant "observer" at Vatican II about reading Catholic documents that has held me in good stead ever since. I was complaining one night about the constant references to previous popes "of blessed memory" in order to show that the new statements were "what the Church has always taught." A bishop (whose name it would be madness to reveal) said to me: "Discount everything in the draft that simply repeats what was said by earlier popes or councils; that is Roman style and it appeases the conservatives. Look instead for the two sentences where something *new* is said, for that has a chance to emerge as the 'teaching' of the council, and it indicates the direction of the future of the Church. Concentrate on the two sentences. We often trade three paragraphs for two sentences. It's a good bargain."

The only difference between Vatican II and Puebla on this score is that with the teaching now in a state of flux it is interesting to note that the more *radical* parts of Puebla tend to rely most heavily on Medellín, or the best of Pope John Paul II's speeches while in Mexico. What all this means is that although the Puebla document has been written, we do not yet have a clear understanding of what it says. What it says will emerge by the way in which the document is used, and by which parts of it are highlighted in the subsequent discussion. Several will immediately sink into richly deserved oblivion. A few will be given critical attention. A few more will be strongly and enthusiastically embraced, and they will determine with what accents "the voice of Puebla" will speak. (One liberation theologian, who had been afraid his concerns would be scuttled, told a group of us excitedly, "There are fifty phrases we can use!")

This is not cheating. This is saying: "Truth is not made by a series of statements; truth is forged in the midst of human struggle. It can be corroborated by statements, and where we find corroboration we will employ it. But when the truth we have found in the midst of struggle is not corroborated by Puebla, that does not invalidate the truth; it only indicates the shortcoming of Puebla. We can find corroboration elsewhere—in Medellín or *Populorum Progressio* or *Gaudium et Spes* . . . even the New Testament."

Puebla is part of a process. It is not the end of the road. It is not understandable save in terms of what preceded it. Its teachings are not eternal, but are teachings for now. Events will validate some and invalidate others. Which statements will be validated? In the light of the realities of the Latin American situation, I propose the following as a criterion: *only those statements will have ongoing significance that can be read in the presence of the poorest of the poor and enable all who hear them to begin in a new way to see the world through the eyes of the poor and to make a preferential option to side with them.*

Let me give a brief example of some portions of the document that speak to this criterion, all found within the first dozen pages. This does not mean that the cutting edge is maintained throughout the next two hundred pages, but it does illustrate that those who seek occasionally find. There is frequent recognition of "the growing gap between rich and poor," often citing John Paul II as a source, along with a recognition that "the luxury of a few becomes an insult to the wretched poverty of the vast masses." This situation is not just the result of individual wrongdoing, but is the result of "social sinfulness" (no. 28). "The most devastating and humiliating kind of scourge" is "the situation of inhuman poverty in which millions of Latin Americans live" (no. 29). Furthermore, the bishops note that "this poverty is not a passing phase. Instead it is the product of economic, social, and political situations and structures." While this will, of course, demand "personal conversion," it will also demand "profound structural changes" (no. 30). The problem involves more than just economic analysis; it involves a recognition of "the abuses of power, which are typical of regimes based on force," with all of their "systematic or selective repression . . . accompanied by accusations, violations of privacy, improper pressures, tortures, and exiles" (no. 42). Lack of respect for human dignity is described by "the lack of social participation on various levels," a potentially innocuous phrase that is immediately redeemed by the words that follow: "We want to allude, in particular, to labor unionization." The bishops note a double standard: all kinds of repressive measures are directed against unions, but "this type of control over, or limitation on, activity is not applied to employer organizations, which can exercise their full power to protect their interests" (no. 44). There is specific scoring of "institutional injustice," noting that "the free-market economy . . . has increased the gap between the rich and the poor by giving priority to capital over labor, economics over the social realm" (no. 47). (Lest one be too euphoric that the bishops are about to espouse a socialist alternative, note that the next paragraph contains a parallel criticism of "Marxist ideologies," albeit less telling and much gentler).

No matter what evidence may be adduced that other statements from Puebla seem to move in reactionary directions that support the status quo with enthusiasm, the above themes are present, and have the chance of becoming the dominant themes in subsequent discussion.

First the Bad News: A Few Gaps

While there is value in Protestant reflection simply about what went on at Puebla, a more important consideration is the following: what did the bishops do in *their* situation that gives us help in coping with what we have to do in *our* situation? The task is not to impose Puebla's words on a situation (ours) for which they were not intended, but rather to observe Puebla speaking to its situation in ways that are suggestive of how we could speak and act in our situation. In attempting to spell out this scenario in more detail, it is necessary to indicate that with such a large amount of material, one can only sample randomly and therefore arbitrarily. After indicating briefly three lacks in the material that seem significant to North American Protestant eyes, the balance of the essay will be devoted to comments on four areas of the proceedings that are of positive importance to North American Protestants. Three disappointments:

1. A Protestant will look for evidences of *ecumenical concern.* There are almost none. There were only five non-Roman Catholic observers, a considerable retrogression in terms of the significant role played by Protestant, Anglican, and Orthodox observers at Vatican II. The document does not breathe an ecumenical spirit; there is almost no mention of non-Roman Catholics or the possibility of relationship with them, and some of the references to other faiths on the continent are demeaning. In a time when collaboration, particularly on social justice issues, is not only possible but mandatory, it is disheartening that Puebla saw no need, or even any apparent interest, in reaching out to closer relationship with Protestants of Latin America. Such overtures are important not only in terms of working to heal the divisions within the Christian family, but also as a way of working more effectively for social justice on a continent where injustice reigns and one of the few forces that could mount significant opposition remains the total body of Christians. Ecumenism in Latin America is going to have to proceed without much episcopal support.

The redeeming factor, of course, is that at the end of the day ecumenism is not dependent on episcopal support, though every kind of support helps. As Hugo Assmann has pointed out, true ecumenism is found in *praxis* rather than in documents. As the lines of oppression become even clearer in Latin America, Catholics and Protestants will perforce be drawn closer and closer to one another. The issue is not going to be Catholic coalitions versus Protestant coalitions, but open-minded Catholic and Protestant coalitions versus closed-minded Catholic and Protestant coalitions. Even so, an opportunity was lost, and Puebla is the poorer for it.

2. Much Protestant effort has been expended on the status and role of *women* in the Church and culture. While the Protestant track record is not yet very impressive, feminist concerns are at least in the center of discussion everywhere. So it was hoped that some new leads might come out of Puebla. There are few signs of encouragement. Of the 364 delegates, only 23 were women, mostly representing religious orders and not particularly involved in women's issues as such. Defenders of Puebla will point out that this is at least better than the 13 at Medellín, but the consolation afforded by this information is minimal. While there are some redeeming phrases and sections in the documents (Commission XVIII pointed out that women suffer under a "double oppression" [no. 1134n]) the tone of the documents as a whole suggests that the women's issue was far from the concerns of the bishops.

This may not be surprising, but it is surely disappointing. It is not surprising because the Latin culture is notoriously built on *machismo,* and even among the liberation theologians there has been little concentration on the liberation of women (Gustavo Gutiérrez has been conscienticized on this matter by his teaching stints in the United States, and Beatriz Couch has an obvious and profound concern about the issue, but they are exceptions). The Catholic Church is run not only on hierarchial lines but on exclusively male hierarchial lines, and it will be a long time before centuries of convictions and practices begin to be questioned within that hierarchy.

It is surely disappointing, however, that little attention was given to the concerns of women, who were present in great numbers in Puebla throughout the conference. There was a women's documentation center and a lobbying group, *Mujeres para el diálogo* (Women for Dialogue), that had daily meetings and conferences, but the dialogues were mostly with lay people and not very much with bishops. Wives and mothers of "disappeareds" were present, asking the bishops to speak strongly about the brutal treatment of political prisoners. But overall, the experience of the women seems to suggest, if we can improve on the Puebla document, that they are *triply* oppressed: first, as part of an oppressed people generally; second, as women who are the oppressed within the oppressed; and third, as members of a Church that has, in its own inner life, consistently enforced patterns of oppression and discrimination and refused to give women responsible positions of authority. The last-mentioned oppression is even worse than the other two, since upholders of the ecclesial oppression claim to be divinely mandated in their attitudes.

A story going the rounds of Puebla said that at Vatican III the bishops would bring their wives, while at Vatican IV they would bring their husbands. On that reckoning, any more Vatican Councils are a long way off.

Nonetheless, there are a few helpful passages. It is at least noted that "in the Church itself there has sometimes been an undervaluation of women" (no. 839). One might add that Puebla was one such instance. "In Mary," the bishops state, "the Gospel penetrated femininity, redeemed it, and exalted it. This is of capital importance for our cultural horizon, where the woman should be much more highly valued and where her social roles are now being defined more clearly and fully. Mary is the guarantee of women's grandeur . . ." (no. 299).

The chief treatment of women is in the report of the Commission on the Laity (nos. 834–49), and it surely provides materials on which to build. It is most appropriate to cite here the summary of this material by Rosemary Ruether, who was among the most active in the women's groups at Puebla:

The section speaks of the oppression and exploitation of women in many areas. It begins by mentioning the traditional marginalization of women by economic and cultural structures (machismo, unequal salaries), which results in their almost total exclusion from political, economic and cultural life. It goes on to note that new forms of marginalization arise in a consumer society that uses women as objects of commercialization, masking their exploitation under the cover of progress. It talks of the connection between increased female prostitution and oppressive economic conditions; of the ineffectiveness of laws intended to protect women; of the near absence of organizations to protect women's rights;

of the double burden of jobs and domestic labor that women bear, who often have to assume full economic support of the family alone. The section also mentions the exploitation of women as domestic servants.

The Puebla document then goes on to affirm the equality and dignity of women in the gospel perspective. Woman is man's co-equal in the image of God and co-creator with him in continuing the work of creation. Woman is in no way second in the order of creation, but equal partner. In the New Testament women share equally in the prophetic gifts. They are represented by the women who understood Christ's message, such as the Samaritan woman, the women who followed Christ, who remained faithful at the cross, and who were sent to the apostles by Jesus to announce his resurrection. They were also present in the women of the early Christian communities and especially in Mary, who announced the liberation of the children of God in the Magnificat.

The bishops affirm the need to use women's abilities more fully in the ministry and mission of the church, without, however, including ordination. Women are called to participate in pastoral planning and catechesis as lay persons and also in new nonordained ministries (*Christianity and Crisis,* 2 April 1979, pp. 78–79).

3. Protestants and Catholics can begin, even on official levels, to engage in some common worship together, and on unofficial levels there are virtually no barriers. From this point of view, as well as for the ongoing life of Catholicism itself, it is surprising that there is so little discussion of *liturgy.* There is not much more to say than to remark on the absence and lament it, since a good deal of exciting liturgical renewal has been going on in Latin America, particularly in the *comunidades de base* (to which we shall presently devote attention). A fresh recovery of Scripture has nourished some of this, as well as the situations of great stress under which many Christians live from day to day, in which not simply consolation but energizing power has been drawn from liturgical and particularly eucharistic celebrations. Puebla could have provided an opportunity to capitalize on this fact and call renewed attention to the possibility of liturgical creativity. There are important connections between liturgy and liberation, and Latin America is an obvious place in which to spell them out. It must be hoped that lay groups and priests with these concerns will fill the lacuna left by the bishops.

A Sampling of Issues That Concern Protestants

As indicated above, it is not possible to touch more than a few of the many items treated by the bishops. For the purpose of this essay, four have been selected that have not only inherent worth but relate in special ways to concerns of Protestants in North America.

Comunidades de Base

We will use the Spanish term *Comunidades de base* not to be academically coy, but so that the distinctiveness of the concept will not be lost by translation ("grassroots communities" is probably the closest English equivalent). But we should remember in the ensuing discussion that *comunidades eclesiales de base,* or grassroots communities that are *part of the church,* is the full term, and the one employed in the document itself. One of the most exciting results of Medellín was a structural breakthrough it energized, so that in the following decade perhaps as many as 100 thousand *comunidades de base* emerged as the vital centers of church life for renewal and revolution. Brazil alone claims 80 thousand. No longer was the old hierarchical pattern sacrosanct, e.g., that ideas had to be generated from the top and work their way down—from pope to bishops to priests to laity, with an occasional assist from the religious orders. Instead, local groups, perhaps fifteen to twenty in size, have been gathering since Medellín to begin to deal with a great variety of local problems, usually with a priest involved, but not always. In the midst of their action to bring about change, nurtured by Scripture study and liturgy, a new way of doing theology has emerged, usually called "liberation theology." (It is important to remember that liberation theology was not spawned in the academies by well-paid experts, but in the *barrios* and the *campos* by the struggling poor. It has been, in Gustavo Gutiérrez's helpful definition, "critical reflection on praxis in the light of the Word of God." Commitment came first, theology second, theology as a way of thinking about commitment. So the destinies of the *comunidades de base* and liberation theology are intertwined.)

Not only because of their connection with liberation theology, but because of their challenge to orderly procedures for doing things in the tried and true Roman way, the *comunidades de base* became one of the chief targets of the conservative forces that attempted to "manipulate" Puebla. A non-Latin American Curia conservative, Cardinal Baggio, was put in charge of the commission dealing with the subject. But even his efforts, along with those of others, were unable to curb this new expression of the vitality of the Church. And while the Puebla document does not everywhere give the ringing endorsement one might hope for in the best of all possible worlds, it does give a strong affirmation of the reality of the *comunidades de base* and offers a clear go-ahead for the future.

Let us briefly summarize some of the points Puebla emphasized. On the one hand, there are words of high praise: whereas at Medellín, *comunidades de base* were just beginning, "they now are one of the causes for joy and hope in the Church" (no. 96). Their vitality "is now beginning to bear fruit" (no. 97) as a source of lay leadership. So "the validity of the experiences" of the *comunidades de base* "will be recognized, and their further growth in communion with their pastors will be fostered" (no. 156). In the crucial report on the laity, the bishops write, "We are happy to single out the multiplication of small communities as an important ecclesial event that is peculiarly ours, and as the 'hope of the church' " (no. 629). Most important, perhaps, is the clear acknowledgment that the *comunidad de base* is an expression of the Church's "preferential love for the common people" (no. 643).

But the bishops are also uneasy. Some *comunidades de base* have become "purely lay institutions or have been turned into ideological radicals" (no. 630). While good things have happened in them, "on the other hand," as the document reports clumsily and a little archly, "the impact of the secularized milieu has sometimes produced centrifugal tendencies in the community and the loss of an authentic ecclesial sense" (no. 627). In certain places, "it is regrettable that . . . clearly political interests try to manipulate them" (no. 98). Horizontalism . . . radicalism . . . socialism . . . One can practically hear the case being mounted for more rigid control.

What kind of control? The answer is clear: episcopal and clerical control. Again and again this insistence is mounted. The *comunidades de base* can, indeed, be "centers of evangelization," but only "in communion with their bishops" (no. 96). Two paragraphs later the same phrase recurs, with adjectival strength added: the *comunidades de base* must not be separated "from *authentic* communion with their bishops" (no. 98). Development of *comunidades de base* is to proceed "in communion with their pastors" (no. 156). Number 648 also stresses the need for pastors to be centrally involved.

So the laity are not finally trusted to act on their own. The document calls for priestly and episcopal control. It is quite unlikely that such a call will be universally heeded. More and more leadership will come from below. The vitality of Latin American Catholicism will be increasingly nurtured by these groups; while hierarchical structures will remain, the impulses are more likely to come from the bottom up rather than from the top down. Perhaps the bishops will even learn to follow their leaders. Their leaders are the people. . . .

What might this model of *comunidades de base* mean for North American Protestants? I believe we could learn from the Latin American experience in ways that would enrich whatever counterparts might be created on the North American continent. The image I have used has been that of "the remnant within the remnant," i.e., a recognition that Christians are not only a remnant of society, but that even within that remnant there is need for another remnant, those (however few or many) who are committed to the Gospel's expression in the field of social justice. *Comunidades de base* strike me as "the remnant within the remnant." In our North American situation, we, too, are often inhibited by church hierarchies and structures that are timid at best and reactionary at worst. They will not significantly move; particularly they will not significantly move against the dominant forms of power in our society. While we need to stay within our Churches rather than simply jumping ship, we need coexisting communal forms as well, not only to shore us up but to provide networks that in time may be able to exert some modest clout on the ecclesiastical and civic scene. So we might well explore adaptations of the *comunidades de base* model. In local situations, groups of people would find themselves united around (perhaps initially) local issues that need attention in the light of the Gospel. Such groups would be ecumenical, crossing not only Protestant denominational lines but Protestant-Catholic lines as well; they would have some kind of inner sustaining liturgical life of their own, very informal but very central; they would concentrate on issues around which to focus their energies so that they would not be mere inward-directed or privatized groups, but could be enlisted in the struggle for change; and they would, as time went by, create networks with one another.

There are surely other characteristics needed, but the above will do for starters. The more that could be learned about Latin American experiences in such matters the better, both to profit by their successes and to learn from their failures. What we need, of course, are new models relevant to our own situation, rather than mere copies of models created for other situations, and it would be important, in our context, to see that the control remained lay rather than clerical. But at one point we must be particularly careful not to be indulgent or exotic: the *comunidades de base* are not just groups, they are groups with a special intent. Recall Puebla once again: the *comunidades de base* are an expression of the Church's preferential love for the "common people" (no. 643).

Seguridad Nacional

One of the most crucial problems in the last decade in Latin America has been the rise of the philosophy of *seguridad nacional,* or national security. (Once again we will retain the Spanish term so that the impact will not be lost by the over-familiarity of the English equivalent.) *Seguridad nacional* assumes that we are in the midst of ongoing war, war between the forces of the West (the Christian forces of goodness, in case that's not immediately clear) and the evil forces of communism. Church and State must enter into alliance to see that communism does not prevail. So widespread and pervasive and subtle is the latter's influence that anything that goes against the status quo, i.e., anything that proposes change, can, by definition, be called "communist." It must be opposed by whatever means are necessary. And the "means" that are deemed "necessary" have become devastatingly clear: they can run the gamut from banning the works of Paulo Freire to torturing political opponents, not only to silence them but to extract information from them and use terror to teach a lesson to others so that they will neither speak nor act. The worst aspect of the technique is not simply the torturing and killing, but the thousands of "disappearances." One day individuals are on the scene; the next day they are not on the scene. No accounting is given of their disappearances, save that mutilated bodies sometimes turn up months later in a river or swamp. The lesson is clear: don't rock the boat, don't speak up, and (especially) don't act, in ways that challenge the authority of the authorities, who, needless to say, are "good Christians," go to Mass regularly, are prominently photographed with the cardinal, and are clearly dedicated to the survival of the values of "Christian civilization."

One of the most telling criticisms of the preliminary consultative document and the working document that preceded Puebla was their paucity of critical reference to *seguridad nacional.* This meant that more attention had to be focussed on the issue at Puebla, and a few (not many) paragraphs got into the Final Document that do strongly challenge the position. Given the dynamics of the conference and the pre-conference "preparation," the achievement is not a slight one.

The matter was of concern to several of the commissions, and brief excerpts from the reports of three of them are worth citing, to indicate the convergence of concern from various sources. Commission I stated:

> In many instances the ideologies of National Security have helped to intensify the totalitarian or authoritarian character of governments based on the use of force, leading to the abuse of power and the violation of human rights. In some instances, they presume to justify their positions with a subjective profession of Christian faith (no. 49).

Commission IV, in its section on "The View of Statism," had perhaps the strongest critique: *Seguridad Nacional*

> . . . enrolls the individual in unlimited service to the alleged total war against cultural, social, political, and economic strife—and thereby against the threat of communism. In the face of this permanent danger, be it real or merely possible, individual freedoms are restricted as they are in any emergency situation; and the will of the State is confused with the will of the nation. Economic development and the potential to wage war are given priority over the dire needs of the neglected masses. Now National Security is certainly necessary for any political organization. But when framed in these terms, it presents itself as an Absolute holding sway over persons; *in its name the insecurity of the individual becomes institutionalized* (no. 314; emphasis added).

The italicized portion above is surely one of the most important and memorable insights emerging from Puebla.

The longest treatment is the report of Commission VIII. After condemning both "capitalistic liberalism" and "collectivistic Marxism" for leading to an "idolatry of riches," the report continues:

> In recent years the so-called Doctrine of National Security has taken a firm hold on our continent. In reality it is more an ideology than a doctrine. It is bound up with a specific politico-economic model with elitist and verticalist features, which suppresses the broad-based participation of the people in political decisions. In some countries of Latin America this doctrine justifies itself as the defender of the Christian civilization of the West. It elaborates a repressive system, which is in line with its concept of "permanent war." . . .
>
> The Doctrine of National Security, understood as an absolute ideology, would not be compatible with the Christian vision of the human being as responsible for carrying out a temporal project, and to its vision of the State as the administrator of the common good. It puts the people under the tutelage of military and political elites, who exercise authority and power; and it leads to increased inequality in sharing the benefits of development (nos. 547, 549).

What does this concern about *seguridad nacional* mean for North American Protestants? At least two things are important here:

1. We need to be conscienticized about the degree to which North Americans are complicit in the maintenance of brutal regimes in Latin America. Many of them could not survive a week without our financial and military aid. Many of the sophisticated torture techniques used to maintain *seguridad nacional* are taught to Latin American military in U.S. police academies in Panama and Washington. The degree of success of *seguridad nacional* in Latin America is determined in no small part by the degree of support we give to the maintenance in power of regimes that not only work against social justice but affirm terror, torture, and economic exploitation as appropriate modes of intimidating those who oppose them.

2. But the discussion of *seguridad nacional* says a second thing to us as well, serving to remind us that what is now true in South America could well become true in North America, and may already be on the way to becoming true. The description of *seguridad nacional* given above evokes recollections of the United States during the McCarthy era of the fifties and the Nixon era of the sixties and early seventies. While torture of political prisoners has not been widespread in the United States, though blacks by the thousands could testify to its reality for them, the philosophy behind it—that dissenters are guilty of something akin to treason and can therefore have the boom lowered on them—has been an ugly reality within living memory, and remains such. United States citizens, especially the young, can attest by the hundreds of thousands to what it meant for them to oppose the United States presence in Vietnam: scorn, detention, trial, prison, exile. The story is a sorry and scary one.

As our power in the world is increasingly threatened, as we discover that we can no longer be "the policeman of the world" (Vietnam and Iran are only initial lessons), as we learn that our presence overseas is often more feared and hated than appreciated, we will be tempted to stonewall it, to go it alone (buttressed by our nuclear overkill capacity), and those who find such a policy not only distasteful but immoral (not to mention unrealistic) will more and more find themselves the targets of official attack. The danger is that in the eighties the United States will mount its own version of *seguridad nacional*, which, while more subtle than its Latin American counterpart, will be just as devastating. If that is so, it is not too early to mount offenses against it. We had better make use of every good insight and phrase from Puebla, and come up with some of our own, as well as seek to absorb some of the courage of those in Latin America who have paid such heavy prices for their words, and even more for their deeds.

The above discussion suggests that church members will need to be involved in the political struggle, not only to avert the further spread of *seguridad nacional* but also to work positively for social justice. While the issue is too large to explore in detail in the present essay, we must look briefly at what Puebla had to say on this matter.

The record is ambiguous. Commission VIII dealt with it most fully—but not very well. The report begins strongly, asserting that "far from despising political activity, the Christian faith values it and holds it in high esteem" (no. 514). Indeed, politics, in the broad sense of the term, "is a way of paying worship to the one and only God" (no. 521).

But when it comes to politics in the narrower sense of party politics, those to whom this option is open are limited. Party politics, the bishops remind their readers, "is properly the realm of lay people" (no. 524), who can use the long experience of the Church, its social doctrines, and the papal encyclicals for guidance. The strong emphasis on lay involvement serves a double function. It is not only to affirm the appropriateness of lay participation in politics but to affirm the inappropriateness of pastoral, priestly, episcopal, or religious participation in politics.

"Pastors . . . must be concerned with unity. So they will divest themselves of every partisan political ideology that might condition their criteria and attitudes. . . . Christ's Gospel would not have had such an impact on history if he had not proclaimed it as a religous message. . . . 'He does not accept the position of those who mixed the things of God with merely political attitudes' " (no. 526, quoting OAP:I,4). And since priests are "ministers of unity," they ought to practice the same personal detachment: "If they are active in party politics, they will run the risk of absolutizing and radicalizing such activity; for their vocation is to be 'men dedicated to the Absolute.' . . . Leadership or active militancy on behalf of any political party is to be excluded by every priest unless, in concrete and exceptional circumstances, this is truly required by the good of the community." But the exception would demand "the consent of the bishop after consultation with the priests' council and, if circumstances call for it, with the episcopal conference. Certainly the present thrust of the Church is not in that direction" (no. 527). Religious also "will have to resist the temptation to get involved in party politics, so that they do not create confusion between the values of the Gospel and some specific ideology" (no. 528).

All this is pretty depressing stuff. One wonders how priests and religious can retreat to the rectories and monasteries and become aloof spectators the minute sides are drawn. The clerical track record of those who have had political engagement thus far in Latin America leads one to believe that withdrawal is not likely to occur to anything like the degree that the bishops would desire. Ernesto Cardenal probably speaks for many of these when he says, "No ecclesiastical document will stop us from doing what the Gospel tells us to do."

The good side of this particular bad news, however, is that at least the bishops had to come down very strongly on the side of lay engagement. Indeed, some beginnings of an "ideological" perspective can be discerned. "Let him who is without ideology," one of the bishops said at Puebla "cast the first stone."

"The Preferential Option for the Poor"

The most challenging of all the Puebla statements is surely the report of Commission XVIII, dealing with "the preferential option for the poor." Showing traces of the fine hand of Gustavo Gutiérrez, this statement points in new directions, at the same time that it emphasizes that what is says is consistent with, and builds upon, not only the Gospel, but also the Medellín documents and the speeches John Paul II gave during his visit to Mexico. It points out that in the ten years since Medellín the situation of the poor, far from improving, has actually gotten worse, and includes a recognition (one of the few in the whole Puebla document) that not only are *campesinos* and workers marginalized, but that women "are doubly oppressed and marginalized" (no. 1134n). In the decade concluded, some within the Church have made a deeper commitment to the poor, but what is probably more important, the poor "have begun to organize themselves to live their faith in an integral way, and hence to reclaim their rights" (no. 1137). This has frequently been done with the encouragement of the Church, although many within the Church have not encouraged or supported these trends: "Not all of us in the Latin American Church have committed ourselves sufficiently to the poor. We are not always concerned about them, or in solidarity with them." (no. 1140).

The paragraphs on doctrinal reflection deal with the Jesus of the Gospel and the poor, pointing out that Jesus' commitment to the poor in becoming one of them and giving them preferential attention should also be the commitment of the Church that professes to minister in his name. Pope John Paul II is effectively quoted in this connection and reference is also made to the Magnificat. This means "service to our fellows," in an evangelization which "liberates them from injustices" (no. 1145). This means, in a statement from Vatican II the bishops quote, "the demands of justice should first be satisfied, lest the giving of what is due in justice be represented as the offering of a charitable gift. Not only the effects but also the causes of various ills must be removed. Help should be given in such a way that the recipients may gradually be freed from dependence on others and become self-sufficient" (no. 1146, quoting AA:8).

As for how this is to be done, the document states that new attitudes must be engendered: the Church must "re-examine its structures and the life of its members" (no. 1157), affirm an "austere lifestyle," and be able to present "the image of being authentically poor" (no. 1158). It must take into itself the tension and conflicts arising from conversion toward the poor, and it must support the pastoral agents in their commitment to the poor (nos. 1139, 1157).

In terms of concrete actions, the conference "condemns as anti-evangelical the extreme poverty . . . on our continent" (no. 1159) and, more than that, endeavors "to understand and denounce the mechanisms that generate this poverty" (no. 1160). This means going beyond a view that the poor are poor due to indolence, and suggests clearly that there are structures and systemic causes of ongoing poverty. Pope John Paul II is invoked as authority for a posture that must invite both workers and *campesinos* to share in making decisions concerning their lives and their futures, as well as supporting the right of the poor "to freely create organizations to defend and promote their interests, and to make a responsible contribution to the common good" (no. 1163).

Behind these words is a stern call; it is a call that has been repeated from as far back as Medellín: rather than simply being "the Church of the poor," the Catholic Church in Latin America must become "the poor Church." This would mean a radical break with the Church's historical role in the culture of Latin America, as well as forfeiting certain kinds of access to those with power. Such a commitment, however, might be the salvation of the Church, since far too often those who have had "access to those in power" have been co-opted by that power rather than issuing prophetic challenges to it.

So the implications of the document are far-reaching. That such a message got into the final draft at all is a tribute to the tenaciousness of its espousers and their willingness to work very patiently throughout the conference. (As one of them said later, reflecting on what had happened, "It is not clear whether this document got through because we were strong or because the enemy was weak.")

What does this mean for North American Protestants? It probably means much more than we are ready to take on. The Latin American Church is *already* "the Church of the poor," and it does not have to go out and find them; they are already in the Church. North American churches, by and large, are the Churches not of the poor but of the middle and upper classes. It is Pentecostals, most black Churches, and some small sect groups who minister to the poor. Mainline Churches do not. So it will be a long jump to begin to describe them as "the Church of the poor," let alone "the poor Church." Nevertheless, the clear "preferential option" *in the Gospel* for the poor, to which Puebla calls attention, is a reality that we North Americans cannot be allowed to ignore, and Puebla should force us to confront the privileged status of those who also make a preferential option, but make it for the middle class. This is not to say that God does not love anybody but the poor, and even Puebla says that the preferential option is not "exclusive." But if, indeed, God loves the poor first, and sees the poor as the way through whom the Good News can finally be heard by the rich as well, then some re-ordering and new priorities are mandatory for North American Churches.

This will not be easy. It will mean confronting whether or not we even have the capacity to embrace the notion, let alone act on it. It will mean challenging the economic system by which the Church gains its financial support and which provides the means of livelihood for most of its members, including its pastors. It will mean a radical solidarity with segments of the society that have seldom if ever been within the walls of the Church. It will mean, in all likelihood, a vocation that will appeal only to those few North American counterparts of the *comunidades de base.* But that would at least be a start.

At a post-Puebla conference of the Christian Peace Conference in Matanzas, Cuba, it was stated that evangelization in our day will go "from the periphery to the center," originating with the marginalized in society and going from them toward those with the power. A century ago it was the other way around. The nineteenth century was the "great advance" of missions from the center to the periphery. Perhaps Puebla can be one of the first visible signs of the need to reverse the momentum, signaling that those in North America who are the non-poor will have to confront what it means to be non-poor in the light of the hard and uncompromising nature of the Gospel.

A New View of the Church; or, Demystifying Popes and Bishops

> *Question:* What is the Latin American Church's greatest problem?
> *Answer (by José Comblin):* Antibiotics.
> *Question (an arched eyebrow):*?
> *Comblin (by way of elaboration):* They keep bishops alive long after they stop functioning.

Before Puebla there was tremendous discussion about the potential of the pope's visit. Would he "repudiate" liberation theology? Would he give the bishops the go-ahead for change, or would he urge restraint? Similar questions whirled around the bishops themselves. Would they move in forward-looking or reactionary directions?

Perhaps the fact that nobody repudiated liberation theology, or turned the clock back (however gingerly the hands of the clock were moved forward), makes one more tranquil about what conclusion to draw than would be the case had things gone otherwise. But the conclusion I draw is that the pope and the bishops may not be quite as important as the pre-Puebla furor assumed. The real power in the Church, the real catalyst for change, the real source of renewal and deepening of the spiritual life, is in the people rather than in the hierarchy. It is "the People of God" who truly are the Church, as Vatican II said so well. If one is a Roman Catholic, it is still helpful to have popes and bishops on your side, but that is no longer essential. If the *comunidades de base* had been condemned, they would not have ceased to be; they would simply have functioned without episcopal approbation. That they got even qualified episcopal approbation is good news; had they failed to get it, however, that would not have been irredeemably bad news. Had liberation theology been condemned, that would not have been the end of liberation theology; it would simply have meant that those with liberation concerns would have had to struggle a little harder to legitimate their claims. They would not have given up the struggle. In a struggle between the hierarchy and the Gospel it is clear that the Gospel will finally win, no matter how many setbacks there are along the way.

The pope learned a number of things during his trip. His first speeches had little reference to the poor. But by the end of his trip, having mingled with the poor, he was speaking in ringing tones about the need for basic social change and the need for the Church to work with the poor and not only on behalf of them. Who taught him? The people themselves.

If the voice of the people was not massively supported by the bishops, neither was it massively repudiated. By any measure of institutional performance, that is clear gain. As Enrique Dussel commented, it was the kind of contest in which even a tie symbolizes victory.

Concerns "from below" have emerged, and nobody on top will finally be able to stop them. If necessary, the Church will move ahead in spite of the bishops rather than because of them. It didn't come to that at Puebla, but an emerging new model of the Church began to be visible, which will be part of the pattern of the future: impulses from below surface, are clarified and acted upon, and receive (in due time) the approbation of those in authority. The "use" that is made of Puebla, then, can capitalize on this fact: things are going to happen in the Latin American Church regardless of what bishops do or do not do. We can hope that the conference at *Puebla* (the conference of the bishops) will finally turn out to have been the conference of the *pueblo* (the conference of the people), who, though not directly listened to, and not directly represented, nevertheless represent the Church's future.

Medellín let loose an impetus in the Church that is not going to be stopped. The "manipulations" at Puebla were not able to stop it. The military dictators have not been able to stop it. Torturing of priests and sisters and laity has not been able to stop it. Economic pressures from the United States have not been able to stop it. Least of all will bishops be able to stop it.

"From the depths of the countries that make up Latin America," the bishops report, "a cry is rising to heaven, growing louder and more alarming all the time. It is the cry of a suffering people who demand justice, freedom, and respect for the basic rights of human beings and peoples" (no. 87).

It is this cry, this shout, indeed, this scream (*el grito*) that must continue to be heard by the bishops. In certain portions of the document they did hear it. In others they did not. In neither event can they control or stifle it. But they can amplify it. Their task is not only to speak, but first of all to listen, and then to speak only after having listened very carefully.

Conclusion

The lessons from Puebla for North American Protestants are pretty clear:

1. We, like the Latin Americans, will make use of those portions of the document that look ahead rather than back, and we will claim for them the authority that they represent Christian voices with whom, whenever possible, we must seek to join in chorus. It is always better to act with the reality of a global community surrounding one than simply to act from a narrow and parochial stance. In this exercise I couldn't care less about being a "North American Protestant"; I merely want to claim membership in the same community of Christians.

2. We can be instructed by the documents about the basic issues with which our sisters and brothers in Latin America are struggling and gather insight not only from the documents, but from the whole process that surrounded their creation. We can learn from statements by liberation theologians made "outside the walls" as well as from episcopal statements made within. Sometimes we will learn more from what was not said than from what was said. In this way we can share in the ecclesial struggle all of them are waging, and perhaps even begin to learn a little bit about what it means to view the world "from the underside of history."

3. We can learn more clearly how what we do "up here" affects what happens "down there." We will always need to be reminded that there is a connection between North American affluence and South American poverty, between low wages to workers in Chile and high profits to stockholders in Chicago, and that the poor are getting poorer *because* the rich are getting richer (a conclusion, incidentally, that the Puebla documents themselves emphasize).

4. We can glean help for our own situation even more directly. As was suggested above, if Puebla argues for a radical option on behalf of the poor in Latin America, that suggests something about missing elements in the life of affluent Churches in North America. If Puebla affirms the significance of *comunidades de base*, that suggests something about the formation of such groups in our own situation. Puebla, in other words, can be part of a charter to us for our own future.

But something even more direct than that is possible. For some paragraphs from Puebla speak so directly to us that we cannot avoid their immediate message. Take only the following paragraph from the concluding "Message" of the Puebla assembly:

> The civilization of love rejects subjection and any dependence prejudicial to the dignity of Latin America. We do not accept the status of satellite to any country in the world, or to any country's ideology. We wish to live fraternally with all nations, because we repudiate any sort of narrow, irreducible nationalism. It is time that Latin America advised the

developed nations not to immobilize us, not to put obstacles in the way of our progress, and not to exploit us. Instead they would do well to help us magnanimously to overcome the barriers of our underdevelopment while respecting our culture, our principles, our sovereignty, our identity, and our natural resources. It is in that spirit that we will grow together as fellow members of the same universal family (MPLA:8).

5. Finally, to expand point 2 above in a different direction, we can learn, from the overall process of Puebla, some lessons that are useful in our own processes of ecclesiastical life. We discover that those in power in the Latin American Church are not immune from abusing that power and trying to manipulate it to silence the concerns of the poor; that should help us to remain alert to the fact that those with power in the North American Churches can likewise respond not to the Gospel but to the pressures for conformity. We discover from Puebla that if voices are excluded from official meetings, they can organize unofficially and perhaps gain an even greater hearing than would otherwise have been possible. Certainly the press conferences of CENCOS, the speeches of the liberation theologians outside the walls, and liturgical events on behalf of the "disappeared" in the public squares, spoke more thunderously than the bishops ensconced behind high seminary walls and out of touch with the people. That some of the bishops *were* open to the voices outside meant that there was, through them, at least some access from outside to inside. (Some journalists estimate that at least 25 percent of the Final Document was written not by bishops inside but by theologians outside who had friendly bishops to take the drafts inside. My own guess would be that most of what is good in the Final Document is the fruit of this intramural-extramural journey).

It is a putdown when the best thing that can be said about a conference is that "it could have been a lot worse." Puebla deserves, and will increasingly get, a better assessment than that. But in the light of realistic expectations, nurtured by the disastrous consultative document and the manipulative efforts to exclude bishops and theologians who would rock the boat, it is no small victory to be able to claim that it could have been a lot worse. It could have been. And it wasn't. That it wasn't is due in no small part to a lot of human sweat and struggle on the part of those who were deliberately being excluded, and to the help they got from some friendly bishops. But there was some providence mixed in with it too. We Protestants (at least we Presbyterians) put a lot of stock in providence. The outcome of Puebla tells me that the value of the stock has been increased.

INDEX

This index is based on the index of the original Spanish volume of the Puebla documents. It has been expanded to include the material found in this English edition that is not included in the original Spanish. It was also edited to conform more closely to English-language style. The index was prepared by Sr. Mary Eucharista Coupe, M.M.

Light face numbers refer to pages;
bold face numbers refer to paragraphs of the Final Document.

Light face numbers refer to pages;
bold face numbers refer to paragraphs of the Final Document.

Light face numbers refer to pages;
bold face numbers refer to paragraphs of the Final Document.

Light face numbers refer to pages;
bold face numbers refer to paragraphs of the Final Document.

Light face numbers refer to pages;
bold face numbers refer to paragraphs of the Final Document.

Light face numbers refer to pages;
bold face numbers refer to paragraphs of the Final Document.

Light face numbers refer to pages;
bold face numbers refer to paragraphs of the Final Document.

professionals and merchants in, 277 **(1249)**

public functionaries in, 277 **(1248)**

religious and ideological, 259 **(1099)**

thinkers in, 276 **(1240)**

those holding power of decision in, 275 **(1237)**

those responsible for media communication in, 276 **(1241)**

Political asylum, 279-80 **(1266)**

Politicians, noble function of, 275 **(1238)**

Politicization, excess of, 129 **(45)**, 232 **(824)**

Politics, 101-2, 324, 339-40

  abuses of, 193-94 **(500)**

  all-embracing aspect of, 195 **(513)**

  and bishops, 102, 196 **(526)**, 325

  and Christian faith, 195 **(514)**

  deterioration of in LA, 130 **(54)**, 194 **(507)**

  distinguishing between segments of Church in, 195 **(520)**

  and laity, 196 **(524)**

  and lay pastoral action, 102, 197 **(530)**

  legitimate autonomy of, 195 **(519)**

  of party, 102, 196 **(523)**, 325, 340-41

  presence of Church in, 100, 195 **(515-18)**

  and priests, 102, 196-97 **(527)**, 325

  and religious, 102, 197 **(528)**, 325

  social teachings of Church regarding, 196 **(525)**

  wide range of, 229 **(791)**

Pollution, environmental, 140 **(139)**, 193 **(496)**

  see also Ecology

Poor, 47, 49, 51, 53, 60, 332

  cry of, 90, 134 **(89)**, 344-45

  and evangelization, 263 **(1130)**, 265 **(1141, 1142, 1145)**

  evangelizing power of, 265-66 **(1147)**

  likeness to God of, 265 **(1142)**

  and Medellín, 264 **(1134)**

  need of commitment to, 264 **(1134, 1140)**, 267 **(1157-58)**

  need of justice to, 265 **(1146)**

  number of, 128 **(28)**, 134-35 **(87-90)**

  objective of option for, 266 **(1153)**

  organization among, 267 **(1163)**, 342

  and persecution for commitment to, 90, 267 **(1163)**, 299

  predilection of God for, 265 **(1143)**

  preferential option of Church for, 108, 176 **(382)**, 220 **(707, 711)**, 222 **(733)**, 226 **(769)**, 264 **(1134, 1136, 1140)**, 265 **(1144, 1145)**, 267 **(1165)**, 274 **(1217)**, 303, 304, 307, 308, 318-19, 332, 341-43

  spirit of Christ and, 149 **(205)**

tensions regarding, 264 **(1139)**

types of, 264 **(1134n.)**

and U.S. Church, 319

Pope

  as interpreter of faith, 176 **(374)**

  in popular piety, 186 **(454)**

Popular Church, *see* People's Church

Popular piety, 19, 98

  challenges of, 187-88 **(461-68)**

  defined, 184 **(444)**

  deprivation of, 245 **(961)**

  and faith, 241 **(911)**, 245 **(960)**

  forms of, 188 **(466)**, 241 **(910, 912)**

  and gospel values, 243 **(935)**, 245 **(959)**

  and liturgy, 188 **(464)**

  native cultural elements in, 243 **(936)**

  need of constant purification of, 243-44 **(937)**

  need of gospel renewal of, 187 **(457)**

  negative aspects of, 186 **(456)**, 241 **(914)**

  positive elements of, 185 **(448)**, 186 **(454)**, 241 **(913)**

  repression of, 241 **(915)**

  as strength of people, 240 **(895)**

  see also Popular religiosity

Popular religiosity, 100, 291

  as challenge to evangelization, 187-88 **(460-68)**

  characteristics of, 185 **(448)**, 186 **(455)**

  defined, 184 **(444)**

  diverse constituents of, 185 **(447)**

  and life of poor and simple, 185 **(447)**

  and liturgy, 188 **(465)**

  need for constant re-evangelization in, 187 **(457, 462)**

  negative aspects of, 137 **(109)**, 186 **(456)**, 187 **(460)**

  and obligation of Church to reinterpret, 188 **(469)**

  positive elements of, 186 **(454)**

  and power to bring together multitudes, 185 **(449)**

  and transcendence of God, 180 **(413)**

  as way for self-evangelization of people, 178 **(396)**, 185 **(450)**

  see also Popular piety

Population growth, 132 **(71)**, 133 **(78)**

Populism, 8

Populorum Progressio, 9, 103, 321, 322

Pornography, 205 **(577)**, 233 **(834)**

Porres, Martin de, 124 **(7)**

Poverty, 305

  causes of, 128 **(30)**

  and education process, 250 **(1014)**

  and generating mechanisms of, 67, 267 **(1160)**, 279 **(1264)**

Light face numbers refer to pages;
bold face numbers refer to paragraphs of the Final Document.

Light face numbers refer to pages;
bold face numbers refer to paragraphs of the Final Document.

Terrorism, 101, 129 **(42)**, 198 **(532)**, 279 **(1269)**
TFP (Tradition, Family, Property), 9, 16, 26 n.43
Theologians
functions of, 176 **(375)**
and "parallel Magisteria," 218 **(687)**
at Puebla Conference, 14-15, 22,35ff., 346, 297, 311-12
Theological ambiguities, 172 **(342)**
Theology
and catechesis, 248 **(990)**
risks in, 200 **(545)**
as a specific methodology, 218 **(687)**
"Theology of conspiracy," 33
Theology of history, 304, 306-7
Theology of kenosis, 315
Theology of liberation, 10, 13, 21, 33, 34, 36, 291, 297, 304, 312, 314, 315, 336, 343
and Marxism, 315-16
and Vatican Commission, 22
"Third Way," 13, 23, 24
Toribio de Mogrovejo, St., 72, 124 **(7)**
Torres, Camilo, 9, 18, 25n.19
Torture, 101, 129 **(42)**
extent of, 279 **(1262)**
kinds of, 197-98 **(531)**
Touraine, Alan, 26n.38
Tradition, as containing word of God, 175 **(372)**
Tradition, Family, Property, see TFP
Transculturation, necessity of participation in, 256 **(1072)**
Trent, Council of, 4
Triumphalism, 298
Trujillo Arch. Alfonso López, 14, 21, 23-25, 28-30, 34-37, 39-42
Truth, 47, 48, 49-52, 59, 61-64, 92-93, 293, 341-42

U Thant, 8
Unemployment, 128 **(29)**, 128-29 **(37)**, 205 **(576)**
Union of Fathers of Families, 38
United Farm Workers, 320
Universities
and culture, 255 **(1060)**
and demand for higher education, 254 **(1051)**
as example of operative Christianity, 255 **(1061)**
needed to train leaders, 254 **(1054)**
need for evangelization in, 254-55 **(1055, 1057)**
need to combat dangerous ideologies in, 254 **(1053)**

and scholarship in, 255 **(1059)**
and service to Church and society, 255 **(1058)**
Unwed mothers, 205 **(577)**
Urbanization, alarming proportions of, 193 **(496)**

Valdivieso, Antonio, 125 **(8)**
Valle, Juan del, 125 **(8)**
Valle, Luis del, 21
Values, subversion of, 130-131 **(54-58)**
Vatican II, see Second Vatican Council
Vekemans, Roger, S.J., 13, 14
and Christian Democrats, 126
and Frei, 126
and theology of liberation, 21, 22, 24, 126
Venality, 132 **(69)**
Verticalism, 170 **(329)**
Vidales, Raúl, 27n.2, 28n.25
Violence, 5ff., 53-54, 68, 83, 103, 194 **(508, 509)**, 197-98 **(521)**
as engendering new forms of bondage, 198 **(532)**, 294
institutionalization of, 11-12, 14, 41, 278-79 **(1259)**, 322
as neither Christian nor evangelical, 198 **(534)**
as prohibited by Gospel, 191 **(486)**
Virginity, as gift from JC, 163 **(294)**
Vocation, 55, 70
diversity of, 236 **(853-54)**
initiation of, 236 **(860)**
necessity of prayer for, 239 **(882)**
privileged time for option of, 237 **(865)**
resurgence of in some countries, 138 **(116)**, 216 **(674)**, 235 **(850)**, 236 **(859)**
scarcity of, 133 **(78)**
see also Pastoral programs for vocations
Vorgrimler, Herbert, 22

Wealth, see Riches
Wisdom, 276 **(1240)**
of common people, 68, 180 **(413)**, 185 **(448)**
Witness
and ecumenism, 262 **(1121)**
and evangelization, 246 **(971)**
constituents of, 246 **(968-70)**
danger in lack of, 274 **(1221)**
manifestation of, 245 **(965)**, 296
presence of in LA Church, 245 **(964-65)**
Women
absence of in political, economic, social life, 233 **(834)**, 234-35 **(849)**
crisis among, 268 **(1174)**
dignity of as image of God, 234 **(847)**, 233-34 **(841)**

Light face numbers refer to pages;
bold face numbers refer to paragraphs of the Final Document.

CONTRIBUTORS

ROBERT McAFEE BROWN is Professor of Theology and Ethics, Pacific School of Religion, Berkeley, Calif. He has taught at Union Theological Seminary (New York), Macalester College (Minnesota), and Stanford University (California). His books include *Is Faith Obsolete?*, *Religion and Violence: A Primer for White Americans*, *The Pseudonyms of God*, and *The Bible Speaks to You*. His latest book, *Theology in a New Key: Responding to Liberation Themes*, is an overview of Latin American liberation theology for North Americans.

VIRGILIO ELIZONDO is a Mexican American diocesan priest in San Antonio, Texas, where he is president of the Mexican American Cultural Center. With a doctorate in theology from the Catholic Institute in Paris, he is author of *Christianity and Culture* and *The Human Quest: A Search for Meaning Through Life and Death*. He has long been active in inter-American affairs, participating in the Inter-American Conference of Religious Symposium in Bogota (1974). He attended the Puebla Conference as a journalist and, at the request of Bishop Thomas Kelly, assisted the English-speaking press.

MSGR. JOSEPH GREMILLION served from 1967 to 1974 as Secretary of the Pontifical Commission for Justice and Peace. He is coordinator of the Interreligious Peace Colloquium (Washington, D.C.) and spends part of every year in social and interfaith ministry in his own diocese of Shreveport. His previous books include *The Gospel of Peace and Justice: Catholic Social Teaching Since Pope John* and *Food/Energy and the Major Faiths*. He has been working with and writing about the Latin American Church for twenty-five years.

PENNY LERNOUX is an American journalist who has worked in Latin America since 1962. Among the many awards she has received for her articles are two citations from the Overseas Press Club of America, the Latin American Studies Association annual award, and an Alicia Patterson Foundation grant to study the changing role of the Catholic Church in Latin America. She is the author of *Cry of the People* (Doubleday, 1980). She writes for *Newsweek*, the *National Catholic Reporter*, and *Maryknoll* Magazine and is the Latin American correspondent for *The Nation*. She was in Puebla for the bishops' conference.

MARCOS McGRATH, C.S.C., is archbishop of Panama. A native of the Canal Zone, he was educated in Latin America, Europe, and the United States. At the

Second Vatican Council he was a member of the steering committee for *Gaudium et Spes*. He was a vice-president of CELAM from 1966 to 1972 and a member of the organizing committee of the Medellín Conference. He was one of the four bishops invited by Cardinal Lorscheider to draft the working document of the Puebla Conference. At Puebla he was elected to the influential Coordinating Committee.

MOISES SANDOVAL is editor of *Maryknoll* magazine and has travelled extensively throughout Latin America. He has a Bachelor of Science degree in Journalism from Marquette University and a certificate in International Reporting from Columbia Graduate School of Journalism. The winner of an Alicia Patterson Fellowship, he made a study in 1977–78 of the Latinization of the United States. He was in Puebla during the bishops' conference and has written on Puebla for *Maryknoll, St. Anthony Messenger,* and *Columbia Journalism Review*.

JON SOBRINO, S.J., is Professor of Theology at the Universidad José Simeón Cañas of El Salvador. Born in Barcelona into a Basque family during the Spanish Civil War, he has lived in El Salvador since 1957. His books include *Christology at the Crossroads* and *El celibato cristiano en el tercer mundo*. He is a regular contributor to *Estudios Centroamericanos* (San Salvador) and *Christus* (Mexico). He was one of the theologians "outside the walls" at Puebla, where he collaborated with Archbishop Oscar Romero of San Salvador.

ABBREVIATIONS

AA	*Apostolicam Actuositatem*. Vatican II. Decree on the Apostolate of the Laity.
AAS	*Acta Apostolicae Sedis*.
AG	*Ad Gentes*. Vatican II. Decree on the Church's Missionary Activity.
AID	Agency for International Development.
ALP	Address to Lay People, 29 January 1979, Mexico City. John Paul II.
AO	Address to the Indians of Oaxaca and Chiapas, 29 January 1979, Oaxaca. John Paul II.
AP	Address to Priests, 27 January 1979, Basilica of Guadalupe. John Paul II.
AR	Address to Religious, 27 January 1979, College of San Miguel, Mexico City. John Paul II.
ARG	Address to Religious in Guadalajara. John Paul II.
AU	Address to University Students, 31 January 1979. John Paul II.
AWG	Address to Workers in Guadalajara, 30 January 1979. John Paul II.
AWM	Address to Workers in Monterrey, 31 January 1979. John Paul II.
AY	Address to Youth, 30 January 1979, Mexico City. John Paul II.
CAL	Pontifical Commission for Latin America.
CD	*Christus Dominus*. Vatican II. Decree on the Bishops' Pastoral Office in the Church.
CEB	*Comunidades Eclesiales de Base*, Base-level Ecclesial Communities.
CEDIAL	Center for Development and Integration of Latin America (Bogotá).
CELAM	Latin American Episcopal Council.
CENCOS	National Center of Social Communications.
CLAR	Latin American Confederation of Religious.
CNBB	National Conference of Brazilian Bishops
CP	*Communio et Progressio*. Exhortation of Paul VI.
DC	*Documento de consulta*, preliminary consultative document of Puebla Conference.
DH	*Dignitatis Humanae*. Vatican II. Declaration on Religious Freedom.
DIM	*Divini Illius Magistri*. Encyclical of Pius XI.
DT	*Documento de trabajo*, working document of Puebla Conference.
DV	*Dei Verbum*. Vatican II. Dogmatic Constitution on Divine Revelation.
EC	Sacred Congregation for Catholic Education. Document on the Catholic School.
EN	*Evangelii Nuntiandi*. Exhortation of Paul VI.
ES	*Ecclesiam Suam*. Encyclical of Paul VI.
ET	*Evangelica Testificatio*. Exhortation of Paul VI.
FD	Final Document of the Puebla Conference.
GE	*Gravissimum Educationis*. Vatican II. Declaration on Christian Education.
GS	*Gaudium et Spes*. Vatican II. Pastoral Constitution on the Church in the Modern World.
HG	Homily at the Basilica of Guadalupe, 27 January 1979. John Paul II.
HM	Homily at the Cathedral in Mexico City, 26 January 1979. John Paul II.
HP	Homily at the Seminary in Puebla, 28 January 1979. John Paul II.
HSD	Homily in the Cathedral of Santo Domingo, 25 January 1979. John Paul II.
HZ	Homily in Zapopán, 30 January 1979. John Paul II.
LG	*Lumen Gentium*. Vatican II. Dogmatic Constitution on the Church.
MC	*Marialis Cultus*. Exhortation of Paul VI.

MCG	Media of Group Communication.
MCS	Media of Social Communication.
Med	Second General Conference of Latin American Bishops (Medellín, Colombia, 1968). Official English edition edited by Louis Michael Colonnese, Latin American Division of United States Catholic Conference, Washington, D.C.: *The Church in the Present-Day Transformation of Latin America in the Light of the Council;* Vol. I, Position Papers; Vol. II, Conclusions.
Med-ED	Medellín document on Education.
Med-Intro	Medellín documents, Introduction.
Med-JPP	Medellín document on Joint Pastoral Planning.
Med-JU	Medellín document on Justice.
Med-OA	Medellín documents, Opening Address.
Med-P	Medellín document on Peace.
Med-PC	Medellín document on Poverty of the Church.
Med-PE	Medellín document on Pastoral Concern for the Elites.
Med-PM	Medellín document on Pastoral Care of the Masses.
Med-PR	Medellín document on Priests.
Med-Pres	Medellín documents, Presentation.
Med-Y	Medellín document on Youth.
MM	*Mater et Magistra.* Encyclical of John XXIII.
MR	*Mutuae Relationes.* Criteria governing the relationship between bishops and religious in the Church.
MPLA	Message to People of Latin America. Puebla Conference.
NA	*Nostra Aetate.* Vatican II. Declaration on the Relationship of the Church to Non-Christian Religions.
NCCB	National Conference of Catholic Bishops.
NFPC	National Federation of Priests' Councils.
OA	*Octogesima Adveniens.* Apostolic Letter of Paul VI to Cardinal Maurice Roy. Eng. trans., *The Pope Speaks,* 1971, 16:137–64.
OAP	Opening Address at Puebla. John Paul II.
OCIC	International Catholic Film Organization.
OT	*Optatam Totius.* Vatican II. Decree on Priestly Formation.
PC	*Perfectae Caritatis.* Vatican II. Decree on the Appropriate Renewal of the Religious Life.
PO	*Presbyterorum Ordinis.* Vatican II. Decree on the Ministry and Life of Priests.
PP	*Populorum Progressio.* Encyclical of Paul VI. Eng. trans., *The Pope Speaks,* 1967, 12:144–72.
PT	*Pacem in Terris.* Encyclical of John XXIII.
RH	*Redemptor Hominis.* Encyclical of John Paul II.
RMS	Address to Religious Major Superiors, 24 November 1978. John Paul II.
SC	*Sacrosanctum Concilium.* Vatican II. Constitution on the Sacred Liturgy.
SUDENE	Superintendency for Development of the North East (Brazil).
UCLAP	Latin American Catholic Press Union.
UNDA	International Catholic Association for Radio and Television (UNDA is the Latin name for wave).
UR	*Unitatis Redintegratio.* Vatican II. Decree on Ecumenism.
USCC	United States Catholic Conference.